ENTRÉE TO

CATALUNYA

ENTRÉE TO
CATALUNYA

Catherine Clancy

Quiller Press

ACKNOWLEDGEMENTS

There is nothing quite as sound as personal recommendation, especially when it comes to food and hotels. Without the help and advice of a large number of people – connoisseurs and enthusiasts of Catalunya – I wouldn't have found many of the places in the following pages.

I'd like to thank Josefina and Alfredo, Silvia Mari and Josep, Alfredo and Mónica, Ignacio and Tere, Josep Fusté, Carmen Noguera, Manel Vidal, Motse Bofill, Carmen del Río and Diego Domene for their suggestions and help; Carles and Mercé Pintos, and Xavier for their shepherding in the Vall d'Aran; Josep Costa, Agustí and Rafa for their profound knowledge of the country; Joaquim Amat, Julio Alegre and Miguel Angel Sánchez for their professional guidance; and Lluís for his great patience.

Catherine Clancy

First published 1995 by Quiller Press Ltd
46 Lillie Road, London SW6 1TN

Cover Illustration: Tim Jaques
Inside Illustrations: Emma Mcleod-Johnstone

Town Maps: Pete Welford
Area Maps: Helen Humphreys

ISBN 1 899163 04 2

Design and production in association with
Book Production Consultants plc, Cambridge
Photoset by Cambridge Photosetting Services

Printed and bound by Cox and Wyman Ltd, Reading, Berks

CONTENTS

FOREWORD

The culture of a people may be viewed in different ways: through its history, its architecture, its traditions, its language or even its cooking. Catalunya possesses an ancient culture that has developed through the ages, and a cuisine that has always been open to worthwhile influences from abroad. As the gastronomy of a country is connected with its culture, its way of thinking and its way of life, it is rightly said that the how and what of cooking are determined by the spirit of the land that has created it. We Catalans have always been open to the outside world. We love to welcome foreigners and show them our homeland. And we like them to feel as comfortable here as if they were at home. Perhaps it is for this reason that we are a people with an innate flair for tourism and everything that relates to it, such as gastronomy.

When we speak of gastronomy today, however, two factors of recent origin must also be considered: the leisure component in all that concerns food, and the importance of cuisine as a feature of travel.

Every year millions of tourists congregate on the Catalan coast without realising that away from the beaches, yet still close to our splendid Mediterranean, there are many places of artistic interest, historic sites and scenery which are well worth visiting, as well as an excellent cuisine to be explored and savoured. The information in this book may help to broaden your visit to Catalunya and make it all the more rewarding.

We hope you will find it helpful and we wish you an enjoyable stay.

Lluís Alegre i Selga
Minister of Trade, Consumer Affairs & Tourism of the Generalitat, the Autonomous Government of Catalunya

ENTRÉE TO CATALUNYA

As in the French Entrée guides, the hotels and restaurants have been graded in three categories: L for Luxury, M for Medium and S for Simple. There are some lovely hotels in the L category, usually above 12,000 ptas per night, but I've included relatively few as many top quality hotels here verge on the very large and thereby lose the personality that I've looked for. Family-run hotels are mostly in the M category, and there are a handful in the S group which usually cost less than 7,000 ptas. 'Agrotourism', the B & Bs and farm lodgings, are a growing category of simple accomodation, but I've left this group untouched – ask for the booklet on **Residències-Casa de Pagès** for a list. Amongst the restaurants, the L and M categories sometimes cross boundaries in terms of cost from 4,000 ptas upwards, but the L usually denotes a degree of formality that you won't encounter in the M group. Fish is clearly an expensive ingredient, so nearly all restaurants specialising in fish are in the M category. You'll generally find the *degustació* menús don't include wine, so take care when judging prices. The S restaurants signal good food at below 2,500 ptas for a full meal, always good value, and are usually rustic and out of town. Costs may have varied by the time you read this book, and remember to add the seven per cent tax to your estimate of any hotel or restaurant costs.

My arrows are very personal – not necessarily the places where you eat the best food, but rather the places I enjoyed being in most – be it for the cuisine, the ambience, the welcome or the setting. Yes, there are a lot of arrows, and the book is over-flowing with recommendations – but I've found myself overwhelmed not only by the beauty of the countryside, but by the quality of the cooking and hospitality. Catalunya is not famed for its cuisine (although there are a remarkable number of Michelin stars), but I am now completely convinced that this is nothing more than ignorance.

SPECIAL RECOMMENDATIONS (ARROWS)

Outstanding Hotel-Restaurant

Arties, in the Vall d'Aran. Valarties (HR)M-L. Outstanding for the excellent cooking (exceptionally good value for guests at the hotel), the lovely garden, the mountain scenery and the friendly hosts.

Chapter 1 **Barcelona**

Agut d'Avignon (R)L. Good cooking in pretty setting.
Cal Pep (R)S-M. Excellent tapas.
Cangrejo Loco, el (R)M. Good value fish menú.
Can Ramonet (R)M. Very good fish, up-market tapas.
Florian (R)L. Excellent modern Catalan cooking.
Fonda, la (R)S. Very good value, comfortable.
Gaig (R)L. Excellent cooking.
Tragaluz (R)L. Good cooking in striking designer setting.
Racó d'en Freixa (R)L. Welcoming with original creative cuisine.
Roig Robí (R)L. Excellent cooking.

Chapter 2

Arenys de Mar. *Hispania* (R)L. Finest traditional cooking.
Cabrils. *Hostal de la Plaça* (HR)M. Tranquil, welcoming hotel.
Sant Celoni. *El Racó de Can Fabes* (R)L. Superlative culinary art.
Sant Cristòfol. *Cal Jepet* (R)M. Simple country ambience with good cooking.
Sant Martí Sarroca. *Ca L'Anna* (R)M. Creative cooking.
Sant Pol de Mar. *Sant Pau* (R)L. Imaginative, excellent cooking with welcoming ambience.
Vilanova i la Geltrú. *Peixerot* (R)M. Superb traditional fish dishes.

Chapter 3

Figueres. *Ampurdán* (RH)L. Excellent cooking.
Girona. *El Celler de Can Roca* (R)M-L. Creative Catalan cuisine.
Llagostera. *Els Tinars* (R)M. Excellent traditional Catalan cooking, good value.
Llança. *Gri Mar* (HR)M. Good setting.
Monells. *L'Hort del Rector* (R)S-M. Delightful setting.
Palamós. *La Gamba* (R)M. Good seafood, welcoming.
Palol de Revardit. *Can Mià* (R)S. Country restaurant serving home-grown produce.
Platja de Pals. *Sa Punta* (RH)L. Culinary excellence.
Ripoll. *El Racó del Francès* (R)SM. Eccentricity and frogs' legs.
Rocabruna. *Can 'Po'* (R)S. Great country cooking.
Roses. *El Bulli* (R)L. Wonderful setting and culinary excellence.
S'Agaró. *Hostal de la Gavina* (HR)L. Luxury.

Santa Pau. *Cal Sastre* (HR)M. Old-world charm, interesting country cooking, peacefulness.
Torrent. *Mas de Torrent* (HR)L. Beautifully restored masia.

Chapter 4

Andorra la Vella. *Andorra Park Hotel* (HR)L. Elegant luxury and delightful garden.
Arties. *Valarties* (HR)M-L. Outstanding hotel-restaurant (see above).
Arties. *Casa Irène* (R)M-L. Elegant informality, wonderful cooking.
Berga. *Sala* (R)M. Good cooking, speciality wild fungi.
Betren. *La Bòrda de Betren* (R)M. Good country cooking.
Bolvir. *Torre del Remei* (RH)L. Wonderful setting for beautiful château, height of luxury.
Escunhau. *Hostal Casa Estampa* (HR)M. Welcoming, in lovely country setting.
Martinet de Cerdanya. *Boix* (HR)M-L. Superb Catalan cooking.
Peramola. *Can Boix* (HR)M-L. Beautiful setting, comfort.
Puigcerdà. *La Vila* (R)M-L. Creative cooking and pretty room.
Sant Julià de Lòria. *Coma-Bella* (HR)M. Exceptional surroundings.
Seu d'Urgell, la. *El Castell* (HR)L. All-round excellence and comfort.
Torà. *Hostal Jaumet* (HR)S-M. Great traditional Catalan fare.
Vielha. *Era Mola* (R)M. Charming restaurant with good cooking.

Chapter 5

Lleida. *El Petit Català* (R)M. Inventive excellence and personality, good value.
Solivella. *Cal Travé* (R)M. Extrovert home production, good value.

Chapter 6

Arbolí. *El Pigot d'Arbolí* (R)S-M. Enthusiasm and country cooking.
Cambrils. *Joan Gatell-Casa Gatell* (R)M-L. Superb fish, lovely views.
Cambrils. *Can Bosch* (R)M-L. Excellent cooking.
Cubelles. *Llicorella* (HR)L. Lovely gardens, fine interior decoration and furniture, good cooking.
Les Masies de Poblet. *Masia del Cadet* (HR)M. Welcoming, peaceful country setting.

A BRIEF NOTE ON HISTORY

Catalunya, an autonomous region of Spain, is historically and geographically close to France, and treasures an immensely strong sense of its own national identity. This national pride springs from Catalunya's long history as an independent county, kingdom and great Mediterranean power.

Early connections were formed in the Mediterranean by the Greeks who set up the coastal town of Empúries as a trading post in 550 BC – today an impressive archaeological site (see L'Escala). The Carthaginians followed, only to be ousted in the third century AD by the Romans, from whom Catalunya has some impressive ruins. Constantine introduced Christianity to the peninsular, which then took a battering by various peoples from the north of Europe, (from Franks to Visigoths), and was finally taken over by waves of Arabs (711 onwards). Their rule in the centre and south lasted for upwards of 500 years, but most of Catalunya escaped with less than one hundred years of occupation thanks to the might of the ruling dynasty in France. As a result, the stamp of Arab culture barely exists here.

Independence was first granted to the county of Barcelona in 878, under the rule of the Bishop of La Seu d'Urgell. The first Count was Wilfred the Hairy (Guifré el Pelós), who started a dynastic line which didn't run out of heirs until some 400 years later. He founded some of today's most prominent landmarks, including the powerful monastery of Ripoll (in which he himself rests), and the sanctuary of Montserrat, whose virgin is patroness of Catalunya. Things developed fast and before the end of the century Barcelona already had a codified system of feudal law.

The county linked up with the crown of Aragón by dynastic marriage in the twelfth century, and the ruler became known as the Count-King of Aragón and Catalunya. During the thirteenth century the Catalan parliament was set up: the *corts,* which included representatives of church, nobility and people. (It weakened in the early eighteenth century, and only regained its energy and verve after 1979.) The Catalan kings, starting with Jaume I the Conqueror, built up a great Mediterranean empire, stretching from Rousillon and Cerdanya in southern France to as far away as Greece, including Sicily, Malta, Corsica, Sardinia and Naples on the way. At its high point there were fifty-two consulates under the commercial sway of Barcelona.

The Count-Kings ruled until 1410 when the lack of an heir made it necessary to decide whom to appoint, and to the Catalan people's everlasting chagrin, an appointee from Aragón was selected at the conference of Casp. It has never been forgotten or forgiven. Thus in time the title of Count passed to Ferdinand of Aragón, and by his marriage to Isabella of Castile, Catalunya was joined to the rest of Spain under the dominance of Castile.

The independence which had lasted for six hundred years has never been recovered. Under the later Habsburgs, Catalunya plunged into a serious economic and social depression, top-heavy with nobility and with a diminishing maritime power. The Catalans attempted at various times to loosen the strong Castilian hold, particularly in the wars of succession which sprang up after the death of the Bourbon Charles II in 1700, when England and Catalunya fought together to support the Archduke Charles of Austria, while the rest of Spain and France supported Philip of Anjou, the eventual winner. Stubborn to the last, Catalunya persisted in her stand against the monarch, and suffered uncomfortably repressive results – the end of regional government (the Generalitat), the banning of her language, and the loss of her universities.

From the mid-eighteenth century onwards things got better. The Chamber of Commerce was established, wine and textile production multiplied, and commerce with the rich Americas bumped up the wealth. Within another century came the benefits of industrialisation and city expansion, while intellectual and literary movements boosted Catalan culture.

After hosting the 1888 International Exhibition in Barcelona, Catalunya entered the twentieth century in much better shape than the central government, which was weakened by a century of political difficulties – the Carlist wars, the dissolution of the monasteries, and then the loss of the royal dynasty. But Catalunya's attempt to set up an independent republic in the early 1930s enjoyed only partial and short-lived success, and by the end of the civil war she was once again without administrative power or autonomy.

Subservience has always rankled. While suppression of the indigenous language has been used as a means of central control at various times in Catalunya's history, it has never worked.

The latest attempt, by General Franco, drove the language off the streets, but it survived strongly in the homes and villages. Catalunya's national identity has flourished since she was granted autonomy in 1979 by King Juan Carlos I, and the Generalitat, her regional government, was re-established. Released from oppression, her language – the voice of her culture – is in full flower.

Catalunya today

Modern Spain is divided into sixteen autonomous regions, of which Catalunya is certainly one of the most important. It is a triangular-shaped region of 12,000 square miles which occupies the north-eastern corner of Spain, and sweeps down from the Pyrenees bordered by the Mediterranean sea to the east, Aragón to the west and Valencia to the south. Statistics, those horrors of modern life, tell us that Catalunya has roughly six per cent of the land mass of Spain, sixteen per cent of the population and twenty-six per cent of the wealth. All the sixes, you might say.

Catalunya has its own language, Catalan, which is spoken here, in the Balearic Islands, in Andorra and also just across the border in France, where Perpignan and the surrounding area were once a part of Catalunya. A similar language is spoken in Valencia, and there is even a pocket of Catalan-speaking villages in Sardinia. It is said that Catalan is closer to Latin than are either Spanish or French, and the Languedoc language has also had an impact.

The four provinces – Barcelona, Girona, Lleida and Tarragona – have principal cities which bear the same names.

Barcelona province. This is the central and dominating section, lying on the Mediterranean coast with Girona to the north, Tarragona to the south, and Lleida inland to the west. Outside the city, the countryside varies from wooded hills and green pastures to dry expanses of olive and nut groves. Outstanding areas are the spectacular abrupt pinnacles of Montserrat, the thickly-wooded mountain of Montseny, the wine-growing area of the Penedès, the wild Garraf hills, and of course the miles and miles of beaches.

Girona province. The gateway to or from France. There is every kind of landscape here, from the high rugged peaks of the Pyrenees, to soft pastureland below, from the red-blue volcanic hills of the Garrotxa to the rocky coves and beaches of the Costa Brava. More excellent wine comes from the plains of the Empordà, and there are wonderful vegetables, remarkable veal and lamb, and special cheeses. Historic sites are scattered throughout the region: sites of dolmens, the Greek settlement in Empúries, great Roman roads like the Via Domitia, and an abundance of medieval walled villages.

Lleida province. Inland, away from the sea, with its southern region like one vast fruit garden. Here are grown cherries, plums, peaches and apricots in profusion. This province has the largest storage chambers for fresh fruit in Europe. Misty in the winter and baking in the summer, the province of Lleida extends north to the Pyrenees, where the mountains cradle the huge Aigües Tortes and Lake Sant Maurici National Park. The surrounding lush green valleys are awash with rivers and sprinkled with little villages and wonderful romanesque churches, and the best Spanish skiing is to be had in the northernmost Vall d'Aran.

Tarragona province. The southernmost section of Catalunya, a land of wine and nuts. Almonds, filberts, hazelnuts, and quantities of olives. Catalan oil is superb, and the best of it comes from the little grey-green Arbequino olives. Fabulous beaches again, and through this province the great river Ebro runs, to reach the sea at its delta near Tortosa. Nearby Sant Carles de la Ràpita is home to the fishing industry, and the delta itself is a vast expanse of rice paddies. High hills behind the coastal strip separate the interior rather dramatically from the beachline. The city of Tarragona is bursting with Roman ruins, and amongst the inland groves of olives are the two great monasteries of Poblet and Santes Creus.

CATALAN FOOD AND WINE

FOOD

Mar i muntanya, sea and mountain, is the keynote of eating in Catalunya. The two are often combined in dishes of chicken with lobster, lamb with prawns, and of course the varied paella-type dishes which contain pretty well everything.

From the mountains and foothills in the north with their wonderful pastures comes the best meat: lamb from Ripoll is famous, so is the veal from Girona. There's a duck foie gras industry in Girona, too, so this is a delicacy you can enjoy fairly easily, and as a corollary there are excellent ducks. The pig, and pork products, are another tremendous feature. Every district has its own particular *embotits* or kinds of sausage, everything from black puddings to salami-types, by way of liver sausage, mortadella-types, white puddings, dry pure pork sausage and so on. Ham is eaten in enormous quantities, mostly dried or semi-dried, and eaten uncooked, cut in the thinnest possible slices. Pigs' trotters are often on the menú.

All down the coast you can find superb fish, especially where there are fishing fleets. At the southern end of Tarragona province, the town of Sant Carles de la Ràpita on the Ebro delta, has a very large fishing industry which supplies much of Catalunya. It's really pointless to eat anything else in in most coastal towns. Special anchovies in salt come from L'Escala on the Costa Brava. Sardines abound, and the most typical fish are the hake (*lluç*) and monkfish (*rap*). Shellfish is consumed with tremendous enthusiasm, from oysters to clams, several different kinds of prawns, lobsters and crawfish, and of course squid and inkfish, not to mention octopus. There is no need to be worried about quality or safety, the standard is very high and inspections are rigorous. There is no-one more finicky than the Catalan about the freshness of his seafood, so you can enjoy these good things as much as you wish.

Fruit and vegetables are superb, from the orchards of Lleida and the market gardens throughout the area. In the spring there is the *calçot* or young onion, looking something like a leek through being grown earthed up, which is grilled over vine prunings in enormous quantities and eaten with a special sauce (of which more later). Dried haricot beans are popular, as are lentils.

As to typical dishes, the greatest of them all, and the one that any Catalan will mention first, is the *escudella i carn d'olla*. This is in the great tradition of the pot-au-feu in France and the bollito misto of Italy. We have nothing like it in Britain – boiled beef and carrots simply doesn't compare. A variety of meats, which should include chicken, beef, veal, marrowbone, a piece of bacon, several different sausages and a *pilota* (a kind of monumental meatball), are cooked for hours with leeks, carrots, etc., and chickpeas. The broth is strained off and served as a starter with pasta cooked in it, this being followed by all the meats and vegetables and chickpeas. At Christmas this is the traditional feast and is then followed by the roast turkey!

There are five basic preparations which are used throughout the cooking style. These are: *sofregit*, which is a mixture of onion and tomato cooked in olive oil until almost dry and then used as a basis for sauces, stews, etc.; *picada*, a mixture of nuts, garlic and parsley all pounded together with toasted or fried bread, sometimes with saffron or dried spicy peppers added; *samfaina*, a mixture of onion, tomato, aubergine, courgette and peppers, all cut up and cooked in olive oil – very like a ratatouille; *allioli* a sauce made from a pounded mixture of garlic and olive oil, often made as a garlic mayonnaise; *romescu*, a pounded mixture of toasted almonds, garlic, red pimentoes, dried peppers called *nyoras*, fried bread and tomato, with olive oil added to make a smooth pinkish sauce about as thick as mayonnaise. The romescu is what goes with the *calçots* and is also often served with grilled or fried fish. It's delicious.

You will see from this that Catalan cooks spend hours over their pestle and mortar, indeed there is no utensil so essential to them, and in every block of flats in the cities you can hear the tap, tap, tap of the pounding every single mealtime.

Chocolate is used too to thicken and darken game dishes and casseroles. Fish is very often cooked quite plainly, grilled or fried, so that there can be no doubt about its freshness. Poultry and meat are often cooked with fruits, and anything *a la catalana* is likely to contain pine nuts and raisins.

Typical desserts are *crema catalana*, something in the style of a crème brulée, *flam* which is caramel custard and heavily commercialised, and, best of all, *mel i mató* which is freshly made unsalted curd cheese served with honey. Heaven.

WINE

Talking about wine is another whole subject, since Catalunya is one of the major wine regions of Spain. Most of the restaurants in this book use wines from Catalunya as their house wines and they are always reliable. Sometimes you might find a Catalan white and a red from Rioja – either way don't hesitate. I'm not a wine buff, but I know what is good and honest. When the experts write of 'a delicate reminiscence of roses... toast... apples, etc.', I give up – perhaps it's due to lack of practice. Anyway, here is a brief outline of the regional wines.

First of all, wine has been made in Catalunya for at least 2,000 years, and naturally it now plays a big part in the agricultural sector. Over the last forty years modern viticulture and experiments with French grape varieties have advanced the quality of the wines to top level in international competitions.

As I can only advise from my own experience, I will just set down a few words of wines from specific areas which I recommend and one or two well-established labels. I'll look at the areas as they are located broadly from north to south. Most have *denominació d'origen* status, rigorously controlled.

The **Empordà**, north of Girona. To give you an idea of Catalan originality, the oldest European oenology manual was written here in the twelfth century. Its wines are young and fresh. I recommend the Blanc Pescador, a dry white, slightly pétillant, which goes well with all fish. Some *cava* is made here too (see Penedès, below).

Just north of Barcelona is **Alella**. Again its first wine in my view is its white. Straw-coloured, it is sold under the Marfil (ivory) label.

Near Lleida is **Raïmat**, where you find the Raïmat winery. Under this label you have truly dependable reds and whites. There are also single-grape variety wines – such as Chardonnay and Cabernet, described as 'notable' and which win prizes at international competitions – but these are not cheap.

Finally, the huge area of the **Penedès**, south of Barcelona, is for me the most important. This is where the famous *cava* is produced, where one single company, Freixenet, exports more *cava* every year than champagne is made in France. The big names are Freixenet, of course, and Codorniu, Juvé i Camps, Mascaro, Segura Viudas. Codorniu and Freixenet offer good tours of their cellars. *Cava* is sparkling wine produced in exactly the same way (second fermentation in bottle) as that other famous sparkling wine from France – champagne. Indeed, it is often spoken of as *xampany* in Catalunya, but it's not. It's different. Much less acid, as a rule, while remaining perfectly dry. Of course it's different: made from different grapes and in a different climate, how could it be otherwise? The nature of the wine is very strictly controlled and there is a vast production.

The *brut nature* is the driest (and most expensive) of the styles made. I might add that some craftsman-made *cavas* rival in price the most expensive champagnes, but don't be alarmed – you will never see these in a restaurant as there is simply not enough of it!

My two favourites are from Segura Viudas and Agus: the first a large concern and the second a small one (craftsman-made wine) – both excellent and based in Sant Sadurní d'Anoia, the *cava* centre, some forty-five kilometres south of Barcelona, on the motorway.

But much, much more is produced in the Penedès than *cava*: it is a huge area of multi-level micro-climates where quality red, white and rosé wines are made with many different characteristics.

I am just going to talk about one house: Torres of Vilafranca del Penedès. Suffice it to say that in the 1979 Wine Olympics their Gran Coronas was top of its class, taking all the prizes and defeating, among other famous wines, Château Latour! The Torres wines and the history of the winery are legendary: I like two particularly – the young white Viña Sol and the full red Viña Magdalà.

In **Tarragona** there are sweet wines, luscious muscatels, just the thing to take home for Gran. The table wines are not as fine as from the other districts.

I've left out wines from other districts and even from other *denominacions d'origen*, not through their lack of quality or appeal, but from my own lack of knowledge of them.

CATALUNYA

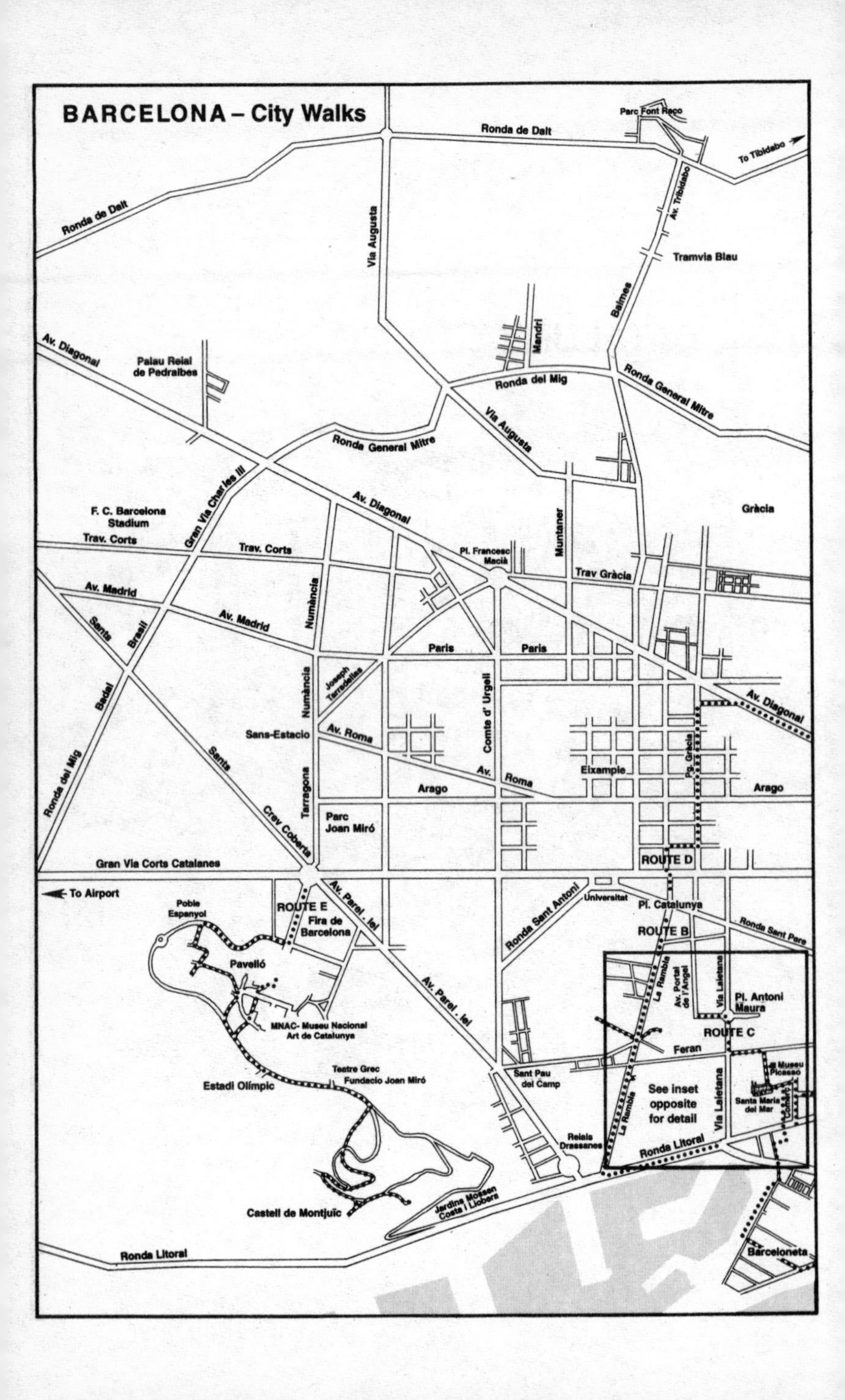
BARCELONA – City Walks
Parc Font Reco
Ronda de Dalt
To Tibidabo
Ronda de Dalt
Via Augusta
Av. Tribidabo
Tramvia Blau
Balmes
Mandri
Av. Diagonal
Palau Reial de Pedralbes
Ronda del Mig
Ronda General Mitre
Via Augusta
Ronda General Mitre
Gran Via Charles III
Av. Diagonal
F. C. Barcelona Stadium
Gràcia
Trav. Corts
Trav. Corts
Pl. Francesc Macià
Muntaner
Trav Gràcia
Av. Madrid
Av. Madrid
Numància
Sants
Brasil
Paris
Paris
Joseph Terradelles
Numància
Comte d' Urgell
Av. Diagonal
Badal
Sans-Estacio
Av. Roma
Pg. Gràcia
Sants
Av. Roma
Eixample
Ronda del Mig
Arago
Arago
Tarragona
Parc Joan Miró
Crev Coberta
Gran Via Corts Catalanes
ROUTE D
To Airport
Av. Parel . lel
Ronda Sant Antoni
Universitat
Pl. Catalunya
Poble Espanyol
ROUTE E
Fira de Barcelona
ROUTE B
Ronda Sant Pere
Pavelló
La Rambla
Av. Portal de l'Angel
Via Laietana
Pl. Antoni Maura
Av. Parel . lel
MNAC- Museu Nacional Art de Catalunya
ROUTE C
Feran
Museu Picasso
Teatre Grec
Fundacio Joan Miró
Estadi Olímpic
Sant Pau del Camp
See inset opposite for detail
Santa Maria del Mar
La Rambla
Via Laietana
Reials Drassanes
Ronda Litoral
Jardins Mossen Costa i Llobera
Castell de Montjuïc
Barceloneta
Ronda Litoral

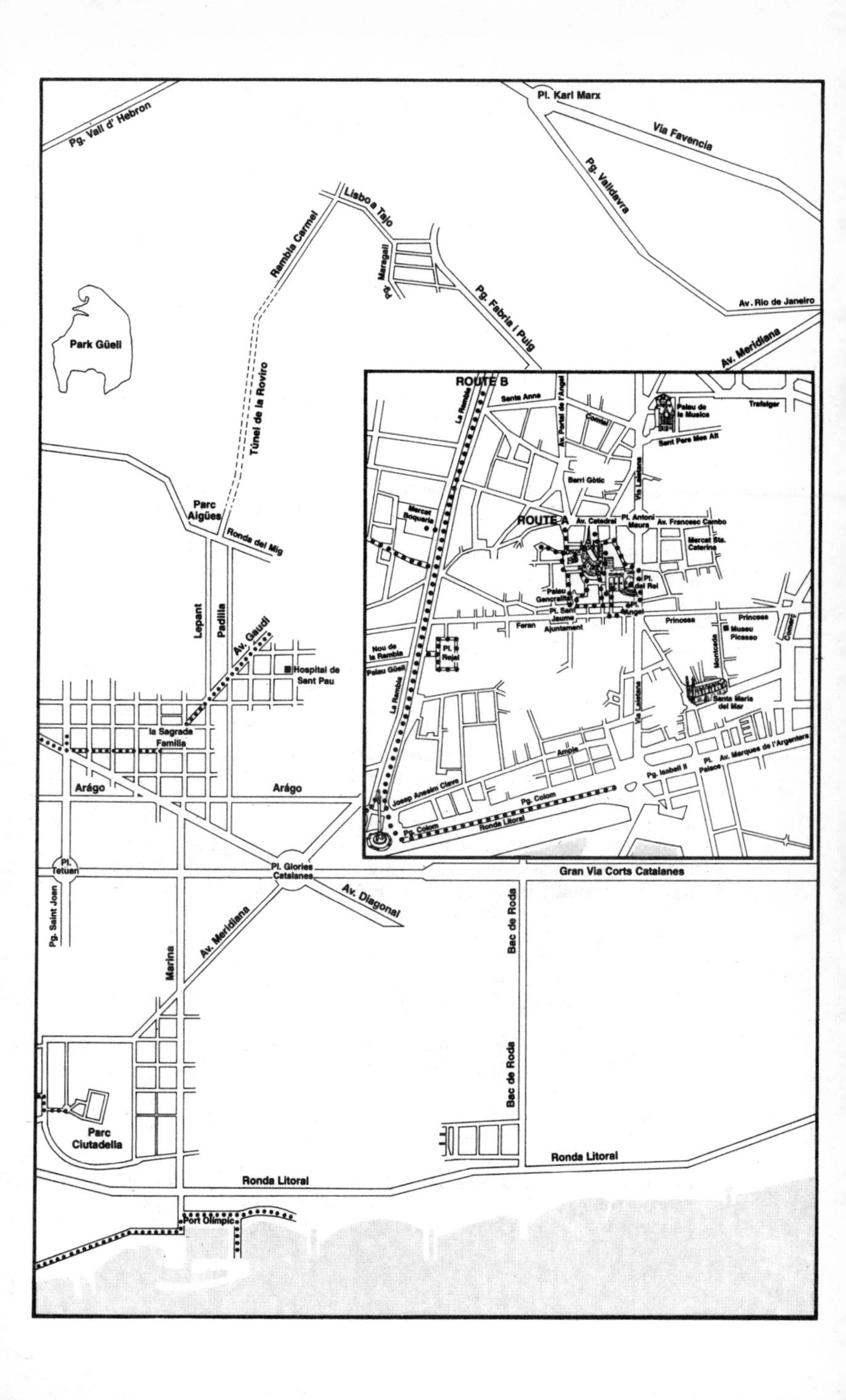

Pg. Vall d' Hebron
Pl. Karl Marx
Via Favencia
Pg. Validavra
Lisbo a Tajo
Rambla Carmel
Pg. Maragall
Pg. Fabria i Puig
Av. Rio de Janeiro
Av. Meridiana
Park Güell
Túnel de la Roviro
Parc Aigües
Ronda del Mig
Lepant
Padilla
Av. Gaudi
Hospital de Sant Pau
la Sagrada Familia
Arágo
Arágo
Pl. Tetuan
Pl. Glories Catalanes
Gran Via Corts Catalanes
Av. Diagonal
Pg. Saint Joen
Av. Meridiana
Marina
Bac de Roda
Bac de Roda
Parc Ciutadella
Ronda Litoral
Ronda Litoral
Port Olimpic
ROUTE B
ROUTE A
La Rambla
Santa Anna
Av. Portal de l'Angel
Comtal
Palau de la Musica
Trafalgar
Sant Pere Mes Alt
Barri Gòtic
Via Laietana
Mercat Boqueria
Av. Catedral
Pl. Antoni Maura
Av. Francesc Cambo
Mercat Sta. Caterina
Pl. del Rei
Palau Generalitat
Pl. Sant Jaume
Pl. Angel
Feran
Ajuntament
Princesa
Princesa
Museu Picasso
Montcada
Nou de la Rambla
Pl. Rejal
Palau Güell
La Rambla
Via Laietana
Santa Maria del Mar
Ampla
Josep Anselm Clave
Pg. Isabell II
Pl. Palace
Av. Marques de l'Argentera
Pg. Colom
Pg. Colom
Ronda Litoral

1 THE CITY OF BARCELONA

Barcelona is the capital of Catalunya, a cosmopolitan and European city, full of trees, flowers, sunshine, art, architecture and music. It sits stately on the sea, surrounded by hills, bordered by rivers, criss-crossed by boulevards, respiring age and youth and beauty. Above all, it is teeming with life, with people.

To enjoy it to the full you need to appreciate its history and know your way about. It has everything – museums, theatres, attractive architecture, a medieval quarter, monumental churches, a port and a marina, restaurants, shops, hotels – you name it! And the best climate.

You could spend your entire holiday here and still not see the whole of it. I live in Barcelona and so can introduce you to the parts I love the best. I've worked out some walks, to include some of the most important streets and vistas, a boat ride, a bus ride and some individual visits.

Under the Romans Barcelona was a small city – not their capital by any means (this was Tarragona, further south) – but important enough to be walled and garrisoned. The governing centre of today's city still remains in the Roman part, and some of the Roman wall can be seen. Barcelona became a visigothic capital before succumbing to Moorish rule, which lasted for a mere hundred years and left behind few signs of influence. In the middle ages Barcelona's strength began to surge, establishing parliamentary government and controlling maritime commercial law. The medieval city, today's **Barri Gòtic**, expanded to a second and then third ring of walls, with great gothic churches, civic buildings and mansions. It wasn't until the 1860s that the walls were demolished and the city began to sweep north of Plaça de Catalunya, with the construction of the **Eixample**, which linked the outlying villages to the main city. Here, in the gridded part of the city, are Barcelona's famous Modernist monuments. This century the city's commercial power has multiplied and there is now a thick covering of neoclassical and contemporary buildings. The Olympic Games were held on the hill of Montjuïc in 1992.

The people of Barcelona are immensely proud of their city, and investment in renovation and new development is huge – the city becomes more attractive every day.

Route A *The Barri Gòtic.* The cathedral, Plaça de Sant Jaume, Saló del Tinell, Santa Agata, Museu Frederic Marès, antique shops.

Route B *La Rambla.* The Bird market, La Boqueria market, Santa Maria del Pi, Museu Marítim, the port.

Route C *From the Museu Picasso to the Port Olímpic.* Museu Picasso, Museu Tèxtil, Santa Maria del Mar, La Barceloneta, the Museu d'Art Modern and the Zoo in Parc de la Ciutadella, Port Olímpic.

Route D *A 'Modernist' stroll in the Eixample.* Passeig de Gràcia (Gaudí's Casa Batlló and Casa Milà), Temple Expiatori de la Sagrada Família, Hospital de Sant Pau.

Route E *Montjuïc.* Museu Nacional d'Art de Catalunya (MNAC), Fundació Joan Miró, the Olympic Ring, the castle.

Route F *Bus no. 100 and sites further afield.* Parc Güell, Tibidabo, Monestir de Pedralbes, the Thyssen-Bornemisza Collection.

Route A – *The Barri Gòtic.* The cathedral, Plaça de Sant Jaume, Saló del Tinell, Santa Agata, Museu Frederic Marès, antique shops.

You can spend a pleasurable few hours strolling through the medieval part of Barcelona, with the fine cathedral and the narrow streets around it full of life and bustle.

Plaça Nova is a good place to start, with a view of the cathedral and the **Portal del Bisbe** ahead of you. In passing through this gateway you have just entered what was the Roman city of Barcino, the city of Augustus. As with all Roman cities this was surrounded by walls, and crossed by two main streets which intersected in the middle of the city where the forum stood. On your right is the **Episcopal palace**, built at the end of the twelfth century, and on the left, opposite the cathedral, the **Casa de l'Ardiaca** which has a pretty cloistered patio. Hidden down a passageway beyond the Episcopal palace to the right is the delightful little square, **Plaça Sant Felip Neri**. Back on the main C/ del Bisbe, you come to the the doorway of the **cathedral cloisters** on your left. Go in and see the palm trees and evergreen magnolias, feel the coolness from the fountains and see the white geese. They say this flock has been here generation by generation for 900 years – it may even be true. You'll be surprised by the tranquillity of the cloisters even though they are filled with people and animation. The romanesque chapel of Santa Llúcia opens off the cloisters.

This is a lovely way to enter the **cathedral**, a magnificent but intimate early gothic building with a high ceiling and slender columns. The fourteenth-century alabaster sarcophagus of one of the city's patron saints, Santa Eulàlia, is in the crypt. The fine choir stalls contain a European curiosity: a gathering of the Order of the Golden Fleece was held here in 1519 and for the occasion the coats of arms of the invited monarchs were painted above the choir stalls reserved for them. You can see the arms of Henry VIII here, although by the time the meeting took place he had fallen out with the church of Rome and did not attend. The chapel of Sant Oleguer guards the much-venerated Christ of Lepanto. It is said that at the battle of Lepanto, the event which ended the Muslim threat to Christianity in the sixteenth century, this effigy was raised on the deck of the flagship and it miraculously twisted to avoid a missile fired by the Turks.

Returning to C/ del Bisbe, you can walk down to Plaça de Sant Jaume passing under the gothic-style bridge which connects the **Casa dels Canonges**, official residence of the President of Catalunya, with the government palace. Better still, leave the cathedral by going back into the cloister, and go out through the gate immediately on your left, the Gate of Piety, which brings you into a very narrow old street, C/ Paradís. At the corner ahead there is a millstone set into the paving which marks the highest point of the Roman city. Wander into the patio of the building on the left, home of the **Centre Excursionista de Catalunya**, and you will see the Roman columns which belonged to the temple dedicated to Augustus rather incongruously preserved within.

Following the street and its turns, you finally come out into the **Plaça de Sant Jaume**, the heart of Barcelona since Roman times. The two seats of power face one another across the square: the city hall opposite you as you emerge and on your right the seat of regional government, the Generalitat. The former is open to the public on 11 February, the feast of Santa Eulàlia, and has a magnificent salon with a tiled floor which represents one hundred guilds of Barcelona dating from the middle ages, extensive murals and a breathtaking ceiling. The gothic palace of the Generalitat is always open to the public on St George's Day (Sant Jordi), 23 April. If you can, queue up with the Barcelonese to see its fine arcaded patio, its court of orange trees, the silver-filled chapel, the muralled council chamber, the splendid ceiling of Saló de Sant Jordi, and the delightful statues of the saint, patron of both Catalunya and England.

Exit Plaça de Sant Jaume by C/ Llibreteria, and turn into another old street, C/ de Veguer. On your right is the **Museu d'Història de la Ciutat**, where you can go down into the Roman city of Barcino concealed beneath the present day streets, and ahead of you is the stately **Plaça del Rei**. Here came Columbus on his return from the New World with his collection of strange animals, treasures and even people, to be received by Ferdinand and Isabella on the steps in the far corner. If you go up these steps and enter the royal palace, you'll find on your right the chapel of **Santa Agata**, very beautiful, small and intimate, with a fine fifteenth-century retablo by Jaume Huguet. Nowadays it's used for exhibitions. On your left is the famous **Saló del Tinell**, a vast hall of the fourteenth century with huge semicircular arches which are among the largest spans of unreinforced masonry ever built in Europe. This hall has had a chequered history: it's been used as a convent, divided into two floors, had walls added to make it smaller, and only comparatively recently it was cleared out to reveal the astonishing hall beneath the clutter. It has a great sense of tranquillity and repose, when you think of its turbulent past.

Leaving by the other street, Baixada de Santa Clara, you come back to the cathedral. As you walk down beside it towards the main façade, you pass the Museum of the Archives of the Crown of Aragón, then the **Museu Frederic Marès**. This is an extraordinary personal collection of just about everything. There are pre-Roman sculptures, primitive and medieval religious statuary and paintings, and in contrast, a huge collection of everyday objects from the fifteenth century to the early twentieth.

The street continues on to the front of the cathedral in **Pla de la Seu**, with some attractive medieval façades on both sides.

If you feel like continuing on a little further, turn sharp right here, almost doubling back on your tracks as you walk along C/ Tapineria. This will take you along a pleasant gardened stroll along the attractive rebuilt old walls of the city, bringing you to the second of the two main Roman roads which leads to the centre of the old city – C/ Jaume I.

Antique-lovers should head for the triangle between the cathedral, Plaça de Sant Jaume and La Rambla which is full of antique shops.

If you are dying for a drink, either dive into the sunken gothic patio of the Museu Frederic Marès where there's a quiet bar tucked into the corner, or go to C/ Jaume I where you'll find the Dos Pacos, a tiny, typical, friendly bar where you can revive your spirits.

Route B – *La Rambla* The bird market, La Boqueria market, Santa Maria del Pi, Museu Marítim, the port.

This is where you start to understand Barcelona. All the world passes here, up and down this walk which stretches from the Plaça de Catalunya to the seafront. It could lay claim to be the most famous street in Europe and is certainly the soul of Barcelona. I recommend that you start at the top.

The **Plaça de Catalunya** itself has not a great deal to recommend it except that it is the centre-point of Barcelona, and all roads lead to it. It lies just outside the old city, and La Rambla begins at the southwest corner. The word *rambla* is nothing to do with rambling, but is an Arabic word for a culvert or watercourse, and in fact the water still flows beneath your feet. Walking down the central mall as people have done for hundreds of years, you have to your left the Roman and medieval city – this culvert was still outside the city when the thirteenth-century walls were built.

There are five ramblas here, one running into the next. The first of the five is the **Rambla de Canaletes**, named after some towers which stood here in the middle ages. Legend has it that if you drink from the iron fountain that stands on the right of the mall you will always return to Barcelona. Where the first side streets join, C/ Santa Ana on the left and C/ Tallers on the right, begins the **Rambla dels Estudis**, named from the days when it filled with students from the university which once occupied part of the Rambla de Canaletes. Nowadays it would be more appropriate to call it the Rambla of the birds – the home of the biggest cage-bird market in Europe. They have been selling birds here for centuries; finches, parrots, ornamental fowl, ducklings, and all sorts, and now goldfish and tortoises, mice and hamsters, gerbils, rabbits and even kittens. George Orwell, in his *Homage to Catalunya* tells of a shoot-out just here in La Rambla, between various factions of Republicans, a local civil war within the great one, but one from which Barcelona suffered greatly.

Next comes the cheerful, flower-filled **Rambla de Sant Josep**, which starts from the big church of Betlem which juts out into the roadway on the right. The flower vendors can trace their history to the thirteenth century when flowers were grown here for sale, and fruit and fish were sold, until the covered market was built in 1836 and the foodstuffs transferred to it. Now only the flowers are left, but what brilliance they display. As you walk you can enjoy the wonderful colours and the flower perfumes. Opposite the church of Betlem is the Palau Moja, an early eighteenth century palace with a grand façade. This palace opens onto a street called Portaferrissa, the Iron Gate, one of the entries to the medieval city, and today one of the main trendy clothes avenues of the city. On the right, a little set back from the roadway, is a late eighteenth-century palace. It was built by the Viceroy of Peru for his young bride in the 1770s; he died soon after it was completed but she lived there for many years and it is named after her, the **Palau de la Virreina**. Seasonal exhibitions are held here. one hundred metres more, and you come to **La Boqueria**, (Mercat de Sant Josep) perhaps the most famous food market in Europe. Here you can buy absolutely anything. Go in through the principal entrance and enjoy the display of fruits and vegetables, go further and you'll come to the circular fish market. Here the art of display reaches its height, all the fish you can imagine are laid out in their pink, silver, brown, striped and freckled, finned and scaly variety. (Remember that on Mondays there's little fish.) Around the outside of the ring are shellfish and salt-fish stalls, all busy doing a tremendous trade. People in Spain eat more fish than any other nation except for the Japanese, and you really can appreciate it here. All around the fish market are fruit and vegetable stalls, pork butchers, poulterers and stalls selling beef and lamb, veal and kid. At the back of La Boqueria is a special stall selling wild fungi, sometimes as many as twelve different kinds. Here, and in the fish market, you may see the top restaurateurs of the city making their daily selection of fresh produce, doing their shopping like you or I. There is a sprinkling of bars too – even market folk get thirsty. Kiosko Pinocho, just to the right in one of the first alleys on the way in from La Rambla, is reputed to serve the best coffee in Barcelona. Ask for a *tallat*, coffee with just a little milk, and enjoy the creamy texture, served to you in a little tumbler. There's nowhere to sit, so stand and watch the world go by.

There are forty-two of these markets in Barcelona – part of the way of life. This is the biggest, but they are all just as active and just as vital to the city's inhabitants.

Continuing down La Rambla you come to the **Pla de la Boqueria**, a meeting point, marked by a mosaic disc designed by Miró. Next is the Gran Teatre del Liceu, so tragically destroyed by fire in an hour and a half on 31 January, 1994.

On the opposite side is another old gateway, Santa Eulàlia, and the street Cardenal Casañas which was once a river flowing into the stream of La Rambla. On the building to your left are the decorative dragons and parasols which used to advertise an umbrella shop below. If you stroll up C/ Cardenal Casañas, you'll come to a lovely string of squares set round the gothic church **Santa Maria del Pi**, where a painters' market is held on Sundays often to the accompaniment of operatic buskers. This is a delightful place for a quiet drink, and only a few minutes on you come to the cathedral square.

On the right of La Rambla is C/ Hospital, along which stands the **Hospital de la Santa Creu** – a fine gothic complex of church, cloisters and halls.

Back on the mall, you are now in the **Rambla dels Caputxins**, and opposite the Liceu is the Cafè de l'Òpera, where all kinds of people meet and pass the time, or sit out on La Rambla, enjoying a drink or ice-cream. A bit further on we pass C/ Ferran, leading up to **Plaça de Sant Jaume** (see Route A), and then come to the entrance to the lively **Plaça Reial**, a graceful paved square of arcaded façades, with tall slender palm trees, an iron fountain in the centre and lamp standards which are early Gaudí works. On Sunday mornings it's teeming with stamp collectors, mineral and fossil sellers and stalls of coins and trinkets.

To the right of La Rambla here is C/ Nou de la Rambla, and just into this street is one of the most interesting buildings of the Gaudí's early career, the **Palau Güell**, now a museum of the dramatic arts. Spare a few minutes to visit it – it is full of astonishing architectural and decorative detail. Next we arrive at Plaça del Teatre, with the monument to Frederic Soler, considered the founder of Catalan theatre. On the left here opens the C/ Escudellers, another interesting old street.

The final stage of La Rambla, the **Rambla de Santa Mònica** leads to the Gateway of Peace, the Portal de la Pau, the opening to the port. On the right here is the **Museu Marítim**, in the **Reials Drassanes**. This is where Don Juan of Austria's flagship for the battle of Lepanto was built, and there is a full-size replica in the museum. It is one of the most fascinating museums in the city, there's lots to see, and the building itself is one of the oldest surviving industrial buildings in Europe. Once it opened to the sea, but the silt and sand changed the shoreline long ago. The Columbus monument stands in the middle (everyone says he's pointing in the wrong direction), and it is well worth going up to the viewing gallery to enjoy the view across the city.

You could extend the walk along the palm-treed waterfront to look at the boats and finish at the foot of Via Laietana or at the bars of **Pla del Palau**. Or you could go on a *golondrina* for a half-hour boat ride around the big port or out to the end of the breakwater (where there's a good simple fish restaurant), or take a two-hour ride to the Port Olímpic. It all depends on where you want to eat.

Route C – *From the Museu Picasso to the Port Olímpic.* Museu Picasso, Museu Tèxtil, Santa Maria del Mar, Museu d'Art Modern and the Zoo in Parc de la Cuitadella, La Barceloneta and the Port Olímpic.

This walk starts with the old and finishes with the very new. A couple of museums, a church, a village, a promenade and a port.

We start in **Avinguda de la Catedral** and go to the left of the cathedral, on the lower level, through C/ Tapineria to the **Plaça Ramon Berenguer el Gran**, and on to **Plaça del Angel**. Here on the right we have the old Roman walls and the outer side of Santa Agata's chapel – built so high up, you begin to understand the contours of the Roman city. On your left is the Via Laietana which was cut through in the late nineteenth century to link the port to the new urban development of the Eixample. A lot of old medieval streets were destroyed during the construction of this straight road, which explains how the side streets

Picasso Museum

meet the main line at odd angles and sometimes even continue across it. The palace that houses the Museu d'Història de la Ciutat comes from these works – it was taken down, stone by stone, to make room for Via Laietana, and eventually reconstructed up the hill in the Barri Gòtic.

Cross the busy street and go down C/ Princesa as far as the right turn to the **Museu Picasso**, in C/ Montcada. This museum you must visit. It houses a great deal of the artist's very early work, and a substantial amount of late work which he donated to it. The middle years are not so well represented, but the whole is fascinating. This street, Montcada, is what you might call 'new and old'. It is later than the area around the cathedral, and it is here that the nobility of the time built palaces in the thirteenth and fourteenth centuries. From the windows on the far side they could watch the tourneys that took place on the open ground beyond. These palaces are particularly graceful, with their courtyards and exterior stairs to the principal floor. Some of the rooms have been preserved with their magnificent ceilings, and there is always a feeling of space and serenity. The Museu Picasso occupies two of these palaces, but there are many more. On the opposite side of the street is another, the Palau del Marqués de Llió i Nadal, which now houses the

Museu Tèxtil i d'Indumentària – well worth a visit. Barcelona has always been deeply involved in textiles and here you find an exquisitely chosen and beautifully displayed collection of hispano-egyptian weaving, early and later vestments, court dress of the time of Louis XV and XVI, finest lace – quite wonderful – and so through to the present day. Both these museums have very pleasant cafés.

C/ Montcada itself continues on towards the sea – there are entrances to more palaces all along it, some of them still privately owned – and finally it widens out and meets the **Passeig del Born**. If you look left you will see the Mercat del Born, a soaring wrought-iron structure which used to be the wholesale market for the whole of Barcelona. Not so now, since it was replaced, just as Covent Garden was, in the mid-twentieth century. It is now used for exhibitions and suchlike, but still is an impressively large span.

On the right is the bulk of the church of **Santa Maria del Mar**, which you can enter by the main door at the far end. This church is, to me, the most beautiful in Barcelona and one of the most inspiring that I have ever seen. High Catalan gothic, stark and plain, those uplifting columns soar towards the distant roof. It was built in the thirteenth century in thanks for deliverance from the angry high seas. Royal permission was granted, and the stevedores carried the stone on their backs from Montjuïc so that it could be built. They took no pay for this, and are commemorated on the main doors where you can see on each side, high up, a figure bent over under his heavy burden. The church was burnt out in the civil war – you can still see the blackness up in the highest parts – and the restoration has brought out the sublime poetry of the architecture. This is now one of the most fashionable churches to be married in and, if you're lucky, all the lights will be on and there'll be a lovely girl in white and a small crowd of family and friends to wish her and her bridegroom well.

The Born is a fashionable social area too, where fringe theatres, small bars and little restaurants abound.

From here it is a short step to the gardens of the **Parc de la Ciutadella** and the **Museu d'Art Modern**, or you could stroll seawards to enjoy **La Barceloneta**.

The **Ciutadella Park** is a lovely green expanse, romantically landscaped with a monumental fountain and lake. At the back is a baroque palace which serves today as the Catalan parliament, and the Modern Art museum, hung with a wide range of works mostly from the eighteenth and nineteenth centuries. The main entrance to the park is heralded by a splendid brick **Arc del Triomf** which heads a wide promenade, and just inside is the curious **Castell dels Tres Dragons**, a brick-escutcheoned building designed by the modernist architect Domènech i Montaner to be the restaurant for the 1888 Universal Exhibition. It is today the **Museu de Zoologia**. Barcelona also has a well looked-after **Zoo** here, carefully landscaped and very pretty.

Leaving the Born, you can go right towards the **Pla del Palau**. The building looming on the right is the gothic **Llotja**, the home of the Chamber of Commerce of the city, founded in the fourteenth century. Crossing the square, we come to the Passeig de Joan de Borbó, and the new marina. These huge open spaces are the delight of the roller-blade skaters, who dash and swoop among the staid walkers, but there is plenty of room. Set into the ground are the names of all the prevailing winds in huge iron letters: the Tramontana, Xaloc, Garbi, Llevant, Ponent, Mistral, Gregal. This is **La Barceloneta**, which is full of places to eat. All along the *passeig* are bars and restaurants, and on the other side the boats. I'm an addict when it comes to harbours and boats, and I always want to walk round to look at the yachts – perhaps it's envy! When you've had enough of the boats, take any street to the left to go through the Barceloneta and come to the Passeig Marítim. There are some four kilometres of beaches, all in good condition and very well-kept, extremely popular in the summer. Walking along the promenade you can enjoy the sea air, watch the regattas offshore, admire the bathing belles and boys, and eventually you will come to the Port Olímpic. From far off you'll have seen the glimmering sculpture of a huge golden fish which fronts the hotel Arts, the newest and most spectacular in Barcelona, and beyond it the Mapfre tower – the twin towers that you can see from all over the city. This is a popular place for the traditional Sunday stroll. The Port Olímpic itself is modern and efficient, and you can walk right round it to the far breakwater to watch the races. There is a multitude of bars and restaurants here – on the upper level and the lower you can find anything you have a fancy for. My own favourite is El Cangrejo Loco (the Mad Crab), which was the first to open and is still one of the most popular.

To get back to the centre of the city, the buses no. 45 and no. 59 go along the Passeig Marítim, the no. 45 will take you to Plaça Urquinaona and the no. 59 goes by Plaça de Catalunya.

Route D – *A 'Modernist' stroll in the Eixample.* Passeig de Gràcia, (Gaudí's Casa Batlló and Casa Milà) Temple Expiatori de la Sagrada Família, Hospital de Sant Pau.

This is a walk up through the most splendid of the **Eixample** avenues, lined with smart shops and fine buildings. This extensive area was planned in grid form by the engineer Ildefons Cerdà in the mid-nineteenth century, with plenty of gardens within the blocks (*ma çanas*) and throughout the city although most of these didn't survive the demand for housing. Some say that the regular pattern of his design helped strengthen the reaction of the Modernist architects against classic designs. The general European phenomenon of Art Nouveau was inspired by a renewed interest in craft techniques of building, and the availability of new materials like brick, iron and glass, which was helped by the increasing use of railways for transport of materials. In Catalunya this took on a fervent energy, backed by the strong political and intellectual forces of the nationalist Catalan movement known as the *Renaixença*, and the rising economic vitality of the city.

The walk starts in Plaça de Catalunya, the point where the old city gives way to the new, and passes some splendid buildings by three of the master architects of the time, Lluís Domènech i Montaner (1850–1923), Josep Puig i Cadafalch (1867–1957), and Antoni Gaudí (1852–1926).

To get the feel of the dignified, noble air of Barcelona, walk up **Rambla de Catalunya**, one of the most gentle *paseos* of the city. Look up, to ease your eye into the style of the buildings, and turn into **Passeig de Gràcia** via C/ Diputació. The wrought-iron street lanterns in this street are splendid examples of Modernist design. From the far side of the Passeig you get a fine view of the eccentric decorated cupola of **Casa Lleó Morera** (just above the leather shop Loewe on the left-hand side) designed by Lluís Domènech i Montaner between 1902 and 1906. Quite recently the cupola was restored to its original state using photographs for guidance after having been removed years ago when it became unstable. The splendid main entrance is open on weekdays, and you can go up and be shown one of the finest Modernist interiors of the city. This is the first of the three famous buildings of the **Mançana de la Discordia**, completed by Puig i Cadafalch's **Casa Ametller** and Gaudí's **Casa Batlló**. The former has a Flemish-style façade with fine stencilling and lovely arched galleries. Casa Batlló, fashioned from an existing building, is extraordinary – with a sculptural roof resembling a scaly dragon and cross (St George, perhaps), and bone-shaped columns separating the windows with strange balconies and a dappled mosaic front. You really need to get close to look at the undulating surface in detail.

Just down C/ Aragó towards Rambla de Catalunya, you can take a look at the **Fundació Antoni Tàpies** (a gallery of his work), one of the earliest industrial brick buildings of the city, topped today with one of his extrovert wire sculptures, *Cloud and Chair.*

Walking further up Passeig de Gràcia you come to the big apartment block **Casa Milà**, famous for its stepped-roof terrace of chimneys, its amazing wrought-iron balconies, and its extraordinary eroded-stone exterior (hence the popular name *La Pedrera* – stone quarry). Gaudí had his masons finish sculpting the stone in place to achieve the final harmony. There are almost no straight lines anywhere in the building – to appreciate it fully, book early in the office below to be included in the select groups taken up hourly each morning to explore the marvelous figured shapes of the chimneys (seven floors up without a lift).

Just round the corner, on Av. Diagonal, 373, is the **Museu de la Música**, with a lovely mock-gothic façade and a marvellous interior with the added attraction of the fine old instruments housed within. A little further down is the elegant, six-sided **Casa Terrades**, known as 'house of the needles' for its silhouette of turrets and tall, iron spikes.

A good few strides from here will take you to **Casa Macaya**, in Passeig de Sant Joan, 108, just as it crosses Av. Diagonal. Another building by Puig i Cadafalch, this has a lovely stencilled façade, with a fine staircase within – it's used for seasonal exhibitions, and should be open.

A few minutes further along C/ Mallorca brings you to the awesome masterpiece of Antoni Gaudí: his **Temple Expiatori de la Sagrada Família**. It's an incredible work, as yet with only the main apse and half of the sixteen spires built. Another cluster of four towers and the two giant steeples, planned to be 170 metres high, remain on the drawing-board, but little by little the building progresses, financed only by

Sagrada Família

donations. The two portals are strikingly different – the ***Naixement***, an exuberant façade finished in Gaudí's lifetime (with a notable lack of fine sculpture), and the remarkable ***Passió***, built after his death following his designs but influenced by modern fashions, with monumental strident figures by the contemporary Catalan sculptor, Josep Maria Subirachs. You should go in to appreciate the detail of the building, and climb the spiral stairs inside the towers to appreciate their monumental size. Drawings here illustrate Gaudí's plans, steeped in religious symbolism, and the museum downstairs gives you a further insight into Gaudí's philosophy of building – the graphic depiction of the root and trunk of a tree demonstrates his argument that curves were the natural bearers of weight rather than straight lines and right-angles.

A diagonal avenue leads uphill from here to the **Hospital de Sant Pau**, designed by Domènech i Montaner. This you really should visit. It is a complex of nine small, beautifully decorated, domed buildings, (originally planned to be forty-six until the money ran out), all linked together by underground passageways, with some bigger blocks added in later years. Gardens surround the buildings, and birdsong fills the air. This still operates as a hospital, although more at odds every day with the demands of hygiene and modernisation. Wander round, look up and relax. It is a special place.

You are now quite a way from your starting point – worth a tube, bus or taxi ride back to save the feet.

There are three other important places which aren't included in the walk, but are well worth visiting: Gaudí's **Parc Güell** (see Route F), his marvellous crypt in the **Colònia Güell**, just outside the city (see Chapter 2, Route C) and the **Palau de la Música Catalana**, where you could drop by on your wanders around the Barri Gòtic. The latter was designed by Domènech i Montaner, and is spectacularly decorated both on the main façade and inside, where the ceramic half-protruding busts of eighteen muses surround the stage, and the walls and ceiling are covered with fine mosaic and tiling, and crowned with a monumental stained-glass lantern. The best way to appreciate it is at a concert, but be sure not to sit far back in the upper gallery, as the acoustics there are less than ideal.

Route E – *Montjuïc.* Museu Nacional d'Art de Catalunya (MNAC), Fundació Joan Miró, the Olympic Ring, the castle.

Montjuïc is planted with an abundance of beautiful gardens amongst which some of the city's great monuments stand, and there are spectacular ever-changing views over the city and port from the winding paths. You can get here from Plaça d'Espanya (metro and bus), or via the funicular from Av. del Paral·lel, or from the telecabins which run from the port. The mountain was originally the site of a Jewish cemetery, hence the name, and its castle was strategically important from the seventeenth century. The rest of it was only seriously developed as the grounds for the International Exhibition of 1929. Most of the buildings date from this event. Plaça d'Espanya is at the foot of Montjuïc, very splendid when the cascades of fountains are working (Friday and Saturday evenings, and Sunday mornings). The trade fair buildings on either side are dominated by the monumental domed palace of the **Museu Nacional d'Art de Catalunya (MNAC)** which is just above, reached via open-air escalators. This has one of the most important collections of romanesque art in the world, containing a myriad of religious imagery and mural work from the eleventh and twelfth centuries. The marvellous *Christ in Majesty* from Sant Climent de Taüll, and the apse paintings of most of the Vall de Boí (Lleida) churches are here, each displayed and carefully lit in its own vaulted room. Very special. Gothic religious art is also very well represented, and the collection goes on through to the classic Spanish painters like El Greco, Zurbarán and Velázquez, and is planned to absorb many works from the Museu d'Art Modern.

If you follow the road up the hill instead of taking the escalators, you come to the **Pavelló Mies van der Rohe**, designed for the 1929 Exhibition. It's small and serene – stark walls of green onyx, straight lines, water, and space. Further up is the famous **Poble Espanyol**, also built for the Exhibition to illustrate the varied character and many different styles of architecture which exist in Spain. It's very well laid-out, pretty and worth a visit. There are plenty of restaurants and bars here, again offering a taste of different regions of Spain, and the traditional crafts of glass blowing, pottery, etc. are still practiced here, with inviting shops selling their work.

Uphill again, and curving round, you join the path that leads up from the **MNAC**. The road now brings you to part of the Olympic Ring – the Palau Sant Jordi, built to a Japanese design especially for the Olympics, and the stadium, originally used in 1929 Exhibition. Round the back you can visit a small exhibition celebrating the 1992 Olympic Games in the Galeria Olímpica. The **Fundació Joan Miró** is just a little further on, purpose-built and spacious with light pouring in from the skylights, showing his work extremely well. This is a pleasure to visit, colourful, thoughtfully displayed, with a corner reserved for small works by other important sculptors of the time – Henry Moore, Eduardo Chillida, etc. The whole is completed with a well-stocked art library, a café and a good print shop.

At the top is the **castle**, built in the seventeenth century, and now housing a fine **Museu Militar**. From its battlements the views of the huge port and the city's seafront are superb.

You'll also find the **Museu Arqueològic**, with Greek and Roman finds, and the **Museu Etnològic**, strong in artefacts from African, South America, the Philippines and Japan. In the summer, a music festival holds performances in the charming ivy-hung amphitheatre nearby – the **Teatre Grec**.

The gardens of Montjuïc are beautifully kept – greener and more varied than anywhere else in Barcelona. Round the back, on the steep side rising above the commercial port, you can stroll amongst a fascinating range of different types of cacti. A steep walk down from here will bring you to the quayside of the port.

Route F – ***Bus no. 100 and sites further afield.*** Parc Güell, Tibidabo, Monestir de Pedralbes, the Thyssen-Bornemisza Collection.

In the summer months the tourist bus no. 100 travels round the city, linking most of the central and far-flung sites. One bus pass is valid throughout the day. You can leap off and on at will – it passes every fifteen minutes, and starts from the main railway station, Sants-Estació.

Parc Güell is beyond the lively narrow streets and old squares of the **Barri de Gràcia.** This lovely park was planned by Gaudí to consist of some sixty houses with gardens. Little was built: an excentric entrance with turreted gatehouses, and a fine stairway (where the splendid dragon sits) leading up to a magnificent ceramic-roofed hall. The hall was to be the market place of the area, supporting on its eighty-six doric columns a roof-plaza surrounded by wavy ceramic-decorated seats. One of the two houses, in which Gaudí lived from 1902–1906 before moving to the site of the Sagrada Família, is kept today as a museum with examples of his furniture designs and those of his contemporaries. The gardens are beautiful, with an amusing network of

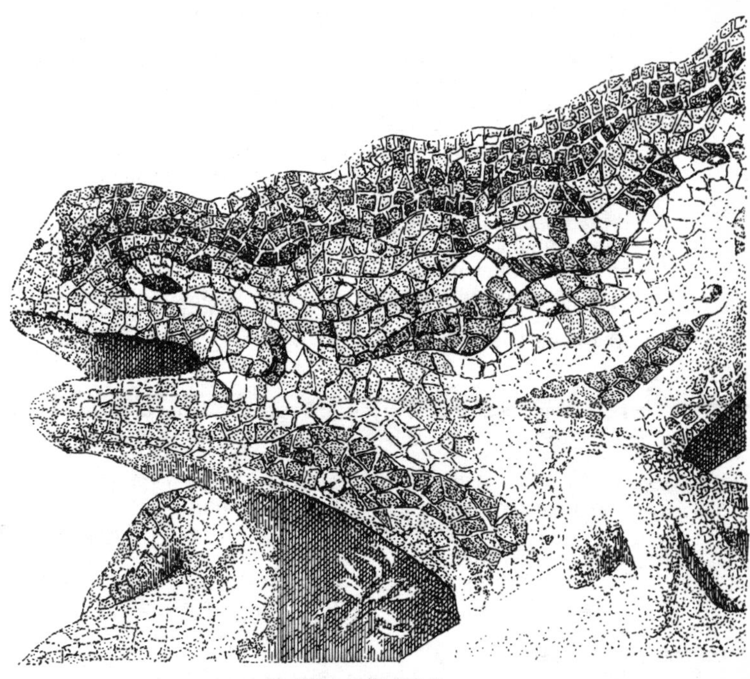

Gaudí Lizard – Parc Güell

paths and strange viaducts, and sensational views of the city. (Metro Lesseps, Buses no. 24 and no. 25.)

Beyond, at the end of the metro green line (Montbau), you'll find the romantic gardens of **El Laberint d'Horta**, complete with a hedged maze, neo-classical follies, woodland, statues and fountains.

Further round to the west rise the wooded hills of **Serra de Collserola** which form the inland boundary of the city. A footpath runs the length of the hills, not far below the crest. Stroll along here of a clear, bright morning and you get the most uplifting view of the city and the deep blue Mediterranean beyond. The peak is **Tibidabo**, crowned with the neo-gothic Byzantine-style basilica which you see silhouetted from the city below, and an old-fashioned amusement park. Getting here can be fun: taking the traditional *Tramvia Blau* (blue tram) from the top of C/ Balmes, followed by a funicular ride straigt up.

The **Monestir de Pedralbes** is a rather beautiful fourteenth-century Catalan-gothic building in the upper part of the city, now one of the most select residential areas. Apart from the church, with its fine stained glass, you should visit the museum, where you can see the splendid three-tiered cloisters and the chapter-house. This is the new home of a important part of the magnificent **Thyssen-Bornemisza** art collection – which you simply must see – most of which is housed in

Madrid. The distinguished collection is beautifully hung, and fills several rooms with works ranging from the early Italian masters to the eighteenth-century baroque. You will see Fra Angelico's *Virgin of Humility*, as well as works by Tintoreto, Titian, Veronese, Rubens, Velázquez, Canaletto, Zurbarán, etc. (Bus nos. include 22, 64, 75 and 114. Metro Maria Cristina).

Walking down Av. Pedralbes, you'll pass a pair of splendid gates at the entrance to the Palau de Pedralbes estate. The wonderful wrought-iron dragon is one of Gaudí's finer monsters. You can enter the Palau de Pedralbes from Av. Diagonal, where you can see the great range of pottery (thirteenth-century onwards) in the **Museu de Ceràmica** and stroll in the pretty gardens.

Crossing the Av. Diagonal here, you get to **Camp Nou**, the colossal stadium of *Barça*, the famous Catalan football club. You enter the Museu del Fútbol Club Barcelona by gate no. 9.

OPENING TIMES

Museums are shut on Sunday afternoons and Mondays, unless stated otherwise.

CHURCHES:

Cathedral 8.00 a.m.–1.30 p.m. & 4.00 p.m.–7.30 p.m.
Santa Maria del Mar, Passeig del Born, 1 8.45 a.m.–12.30 p.m. & 4.30 p.m.–6.15 p.m.
Temple Expiatori de la Sagrada Família Oct.–Apr. 9.00 a.m.–6.00 p.m. every day, May–Sept. 9.00 a.m.–8.00 p.m. every day.

MUSEUMS AND GALLERIES

Fundació Joan Miró, Montjuïc 11.00 a.m.–7.00 p.m.
Fundació Antoni Tàpies, C/ Aragó, 255 11.00 a.m.–8.00 p.m.
Galeria Olímpica (south door) Apr.–Sept. 10.00 a.m.–2.00 p.m. & 4.00 p.m.–8.00 p.m., Oct.–Mar. 10.00 a.m.–1.00 p.m. & 4.00 p.m.–6.00 p.m.
Monestir de Pedralbes, Thyssen-Bornemisza Collection, C/ Baixada del Monestir, 9 10.00 a.m.–2.00 p.m., Sat. 10.00 a.m.–5.00 p.m.
Museu Arquelògic, Passeig de Santa Madrona 39, Monjuïc. Open Tues.–Sat. 9.30 a.m.–1.30 p.m., 3.30 p.m.–7.00 p.m.; Sun. 9.00 a.m.–2.00 p.m.
Museu d'Art Modern, Parc de la Ciutadella Wed.–Mon. 9.00 a.m.–9.00 p.m.; cl. Tues.
Museu de Ceràmica, Av. Diagonal 686, Palau de Pedralbes. Open Tues.–Sun. 9.00 a.m.–2.00 p.m.
Museu de la Ciencia, Teodor Roviralta, 55 10.00 a.m.–10.00 p.m. incl. Sun. p.m.
Museu de la Música, Av. Diagonal, 373 10.00 a.m.–2.00 p.m.
Museu del Fútbol Club Barcelona, Av. Arístides Maillol, 12–18 Apr.–Oct. 10.00 a.m.–1.00 p.m. & 3.00 p.m.–6.00 p.m. incl. Mon.; Nov.–Mar. 10.00 a.m.–1.00 p.m. & 4.00 p.m.–6.00 p.m. cl. Sat. p.m., Sun. p.m., Mon.
Museu de Zoologia, Parc de la Ciutadella 10.00 a.m.–2.00 p.m.
Museu d'Història de la Ciutat, Pl. de Verguer, 2 10.00 a.m.–2.00 p.m. & 4.00 p.m.–8.00 p.m., summer 10.00 a.m.–8.00 p.m.

Museu Etnològic, Passeig de Santa Madrona, Montjuïc. Open Tues.–Sat. 10.00 a.m.–5.00 p.m.; Sun. 9.00 a.m.–2.00 p.m.
Museu Frederic Marès, Pl. St Iu, 5 10.00 a.m.–5.00 p.m.
Museu Marítim, Av. Drassanes, 1. Open Tues.–Sat. 9.30 a.m.–1.00 p.m., 4.00 p.m.–7.00 p.m.; Sun. 10.00 a.m.–2.00 p.m.
Museu Militar, Castell Montjuïc. Open Tues.–Sun. 9.30 a.m.–2.00 p.m., 3.30 p.m.–8.00 p.m.
Museu Nacional d'Art de Catalunya (MNAC), Palau Nacional, Montjuïc Wed.–Mon. 9.00 a.m.–9.00 p.m.; cl. Tues.
Museu Picasso, C/ Montcada, 15–19 10.00 a.m.–8.00 p.m.
Museu Tèxtil, C/Montcada 12. Open Tues.–Sat. 10.00 a.m.–5.00 p.m.; Sun. 10.00 a.m.–2.00 p.m.
Theatre museum, Palau Güell, Nou de la Rambla, 3 Mon.–Sat. 10.00 a.m.–1.30 p.m. & 4.00 p.m.–7.30 p.m.

Other sites

Casa Batlló, Passeig de Gràcia, 43. Entrance open during office hours.
Casa Macaya, Passeig de Sant Joan, 106. Exhibition centre. Open Tues.–Sat. 11.00 a.m.–8.00 p.m.; Sun. 11.00 a.m.–3.00 p.m.
Casa Milà, Passeig de Gràcia, 92 (93) 487 36 13 Hourly visits 10.00 a.m.–1.00 p.m.; cl. Sun., Mon.
El Laberint d'Horta, Horta 10.00 a.m.–5.00 p.m., Sun. 10.00 a.m.–2.00 p.m.
Hospital de Sant Pau – An active hospital, best visited in daylight.
Palau de la Música Catalana, Sant Francesc de Paula, 2 (93) 268 10 00 Visits Sat. 10.00 a.m. & 11.00 a.m. (reserve); cl. Aug.
Parc Güell, C/ Olot Nov.–Feb. 10.00 a.m.–6.00 p.m., Mar. & Oct. 10.00 a.m.–7.00 p.m., May–Aug. 10.00 a.m.–9.00 p.m.
Poble Espanyol, Montjuïc Mon., 9.00 a.m.–8.00 p.m., Tues.–Sat. 9.00 a.m.–3.00 p.m., Sun. 9.00 a.m.–10.00 p.m.
Zoo, Parc de la Ciutadella Summer 9.30 a.m.–7.30 p.m., winter 10.00 a.m.–5.00 p.m.

HOTELS

Most of the hotels I've chosen are in and around La Rambla. Barcelona's full of hotels but it seems a shame to stay far from the ***Barri Gòtic*** if you've only a short time to explore the city.

Around La Rambla and Barri Gòtic

Colon
(H)L *Avinguda de la Catedral, 7 (93) 301 14 04 Open all year*

One of Barcelona's classic hotels, in the very heart of the city looking straight on to the cathedral square. A hotel with poise, dignity, and all comforts. Garage.
Double room 20,500 ptas

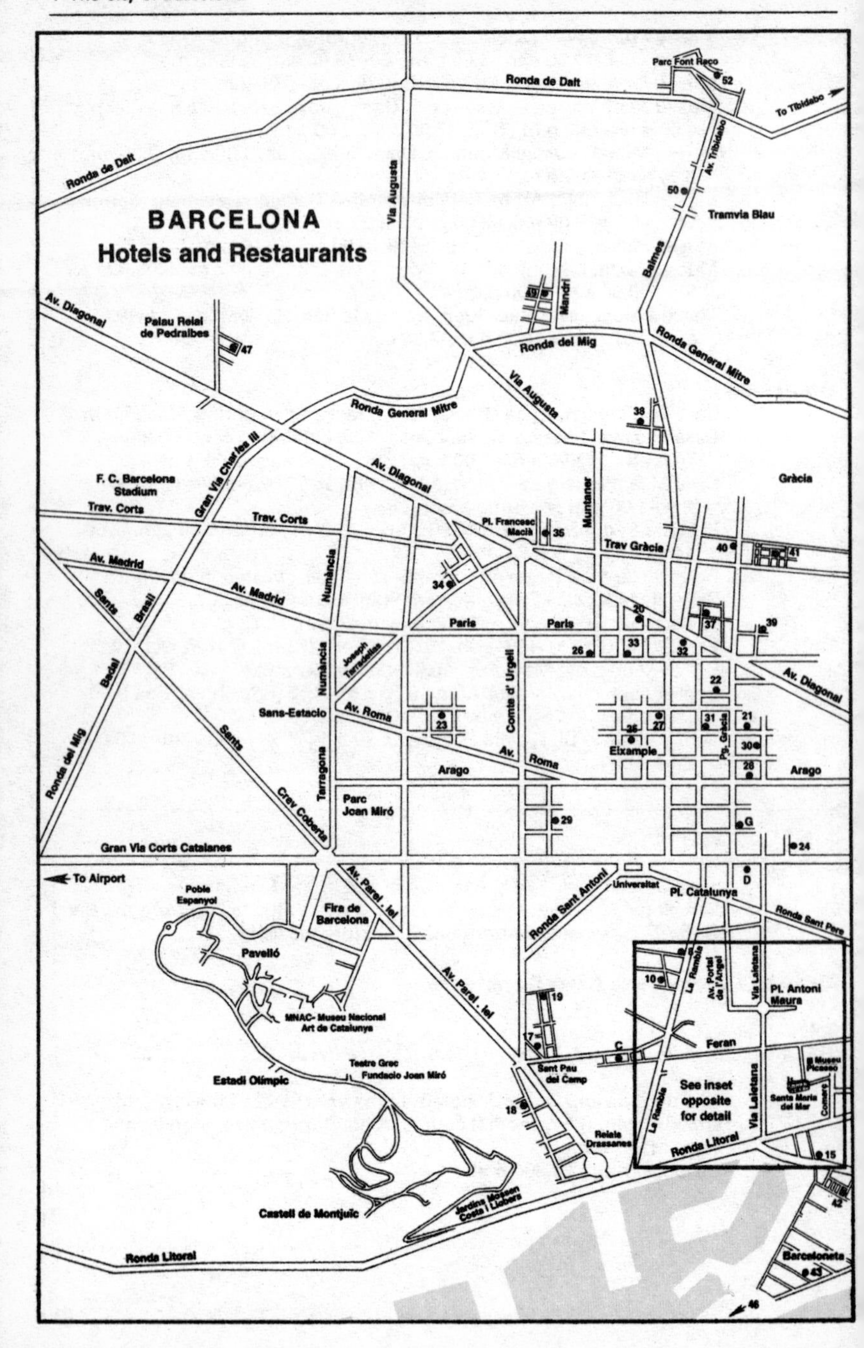
BARCELONA
Hotels and Restaurants
Ronda de Dalt
Parc Font Reco
To Tibidabo
Av. Tibidabo
Via Augusta
Tramvia Blau
Balmes
Mandri
Ronda del Mig
Ronda General Mitre
Av. Diagonal
Palau Reial de Pedralbes
Via Augusta
Ronda General Mitre
F. C. Barcelona Stadium
Trav. Corts
Gran Via Charles III
Muntaner
Gràcia
Pl. Francesc Macià
Trav Gràcia
Av. Madrid
Sants
Brasil
Numància
Paris
Joseph Terradellas
Comte d' Urgell
Badal
Sans-Estacio
Av. Roma
Eixample
Ps. Gràcia
Arago
Ronda del Mig
Tarragona
Crev Coberta
Parc Joan Miró
Gran Via Corts Catalanes
To Airport
Av. Parel . lel
Ronda Sant Antoni
Universitat
Pl. Catalunya
Ronda Sant Pere
Poble Espanyol
Fira de Barcelona
Pavelló
La Rambla
Av. Portal de l'Angel
Via Laietana
Pl. Antoni Maura
MNAC- Museu Nacional Art de Catalunya
Feran
Teatre Grec
Fundacio Joan Miró
Sant Pau del Camp
Museu Picasso
Estadi Olímpic
See inset opposite for detail
Santa Maria del Mar
Comerç
Reials Drassanes
Ronda Litoral
Castell de Montjuïc
Jardins Mossen Costa i Llobera
Ronda Litoral
Barceloneta

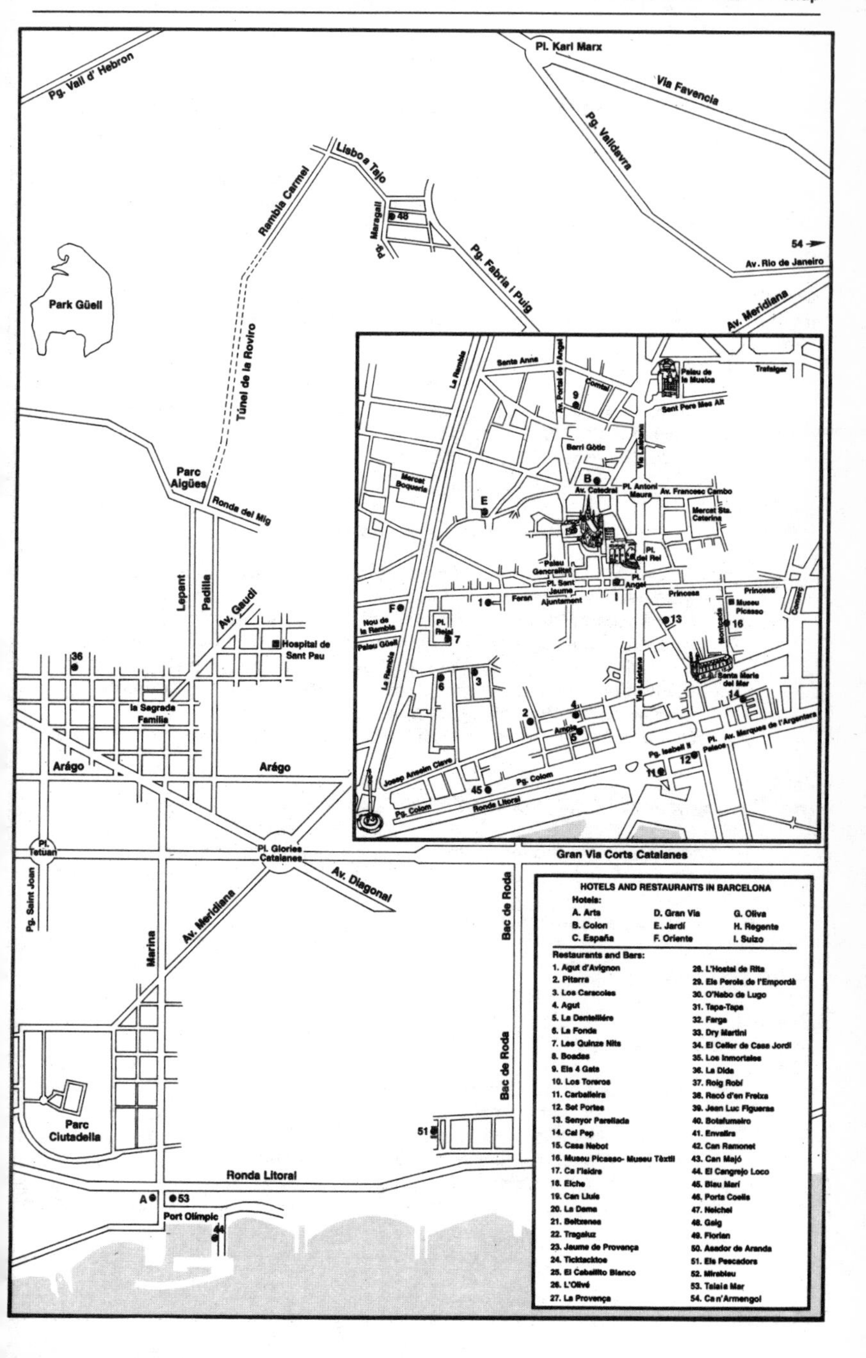
Pg. Vall d' Hebron
Pl. Karl Marx
Via Favencia
Pg. Valldavra
Lisboa Tajo
Rambla Carmel
Pg. Maragall
48
Pg. Fabria i Puig
54
Av. Rio de Janeiro
Av. Meridiana
Park Güell
Túnel de la Roviro
Parc Aigües
Ronda del Mig
Lepant
Padilla
Av. Gaudi
Hospital de Sant Pau
36
la Segrada Familia
Arágo
Arágo
Pl. Tetuan
Pl. Glories Catalanes
Av. Diagonal
Gran Via Corts Catalanes
Pg. Saint Joan
Marina
Av. Meridiana
Bac de Roda
Bac de Roda
Parc Ciutadella
51
Ronda Litoral
A
53
Port Olímpic
44
Santa Anna
Av. Portal de l'Angel
La Rambla
Comtal
9
Palau de la Musica
Trafalgar
Sant Pere Mes Alt
Barri Gòtic
Via Laietana
B
Av. Catedral
Pl. Antoni Maura
Av. Francesc Cambo
Mercat Boqueria
E
Mercat Sta. Caterina
Pl. del Rei
Palau Generalitat
Pl. Sant Jaume
Pl. Angel
Ajuntament
Ferran
1
Princesa
Princesa
Museu Picasso
Montcada
F
Nou de la Rambla
Palau Güell
Pl. Reial
7
13
16
6
3
Santa Maria del Mar
14
2
4
Ample
5
Pl. Palaos
Av. Marques de l'Argentera
Pg. Isabell II
12
11
Josep Anselm Clave
45
Pg. Colom
Pg. Colom
Ronda Litoral
HOTELS AND RESTAURANTS IN BARCELONA
Hotels:
A. Arts
B. Colon
C. España
D. Gran Via
E. Jardí
F. Oriente
G. Oliva
H. Regente
I. Suizo
Restaurants and Bars:
1. Agut d'Avignon
2. Pitarra
3. Los Caracoles
4. Agut
5. La Dentellière
6. La Fonda
7. Les Quinze Nits
8. Boadas
9. Els 4 Gats
10. Los Toreros
11. Carballeira
12. Set Portes
13. Senyor Parellada
14. Cal Pep
15. Casa Nebot
16. Museu Picasso- Museu Tèxtil
17. Ca l'Isidre
18. Elche
19. Can Lluís
20. La Dama
21. Beltxenea
22. Tragaluz
23. Jaume de Provença
24. Ticktacktoe
25. El Caballito Blanco
26. L'Olivé
27. La Provença
28. L'Hostal de Rita
29. Els Perols de l'Empordà
30. O'Nabo de Lugo
31. Tapa-Tapa
32. Farga
33. Dry Martini
34. El Celler de Casa Jordi
35. Los Inmortales
36. La Dida
37. Roig Robí
38. Racó d'en Freixa
39. Jean Luc Figueras
40. Botafumeiro
41. Envalira
42. Can Ramonet
43. Can Majó
44. El Cangrejo Loco
45. Blau Marí
46. Porta Coelis
47. Neichel
48. Gaig
49. Florian
50. Asador de Aranda
51. Els Pescadors
52. Mirablau
53. Talaia Mar
54. Ca n'Armengol

Suizo
(H)M *Plaça de l'Angel, 12 (93) 315 28 57 Open all year*

This is a comfortable hotel with some fifty bedrooms which has been going for over sixty years. It's only a minute's walk from Plaça de Sant Jaume or the cathedral, and as it's on the opposite side of the square to the La Rambla, it's quieter even though a lot of traffic passes. Convenient and close to everything. You get a good buffet spread for breakfast. Garage.

Double room 13,500 ptas

Oriente
(H)M *Rambla dels Caputxins, 45-47 (93) 302 25 58 Open all year*

A big hotel in a rather splendid building which first opened its doors in 1842. The rooms are completely modern, but there are a couple of grand chandelier-hung salons which retain some of the history of the place. On the lower, rougher end of La Rambla.

Double room 6,000–12,000 ptas

España
(HR)M *C/ Sant Pau, 9–11 (93) 318 17 58 Open all year*

An old, faded favourite. The building is a good example of the Modernist architecture of Barcelona. It was designed by Lluís Domènech i Montaner, with walls filled with an amazing array of ceramic decoration and tile work, and ceilings finished in carved and painted wood. If you don't stay here, at least visit it – the splendour of the two diningrooms makes a memorable frame for an ordinary Catalan lunch. Just off La Rambla.
Menu 950 ptas incl. eves., 1,500 ptas weekends; double room 9,710 ptas

Jardí
(H)S *Plaça Sant Josep Oriol, 1 (93) 301 59 00 Open all year*

A no-frills hotel overlooking two of the pretty, tranquil squares by the church Santa Maria del Pi. Be sure to ask for an outward-facing room. No lift.

Double room 6,500 ptas

In the Eixample

Regente
(H)M *Rambla de Catalunya, 76 (93) 487 59 89 Open all year*

This is a rather executive hotel with eighty rooms in a fine modernist building. Its trump card is that it opens onto the Rambla de Catalunya, the most elegant Rambla in the city. The Barri Gòtic is a very pleasurable ten-minute stroll down the boulevard.

Double room 8,500–12,000 ptas

Gran Via
(H)M *Gran Via, 642 (93) 318 19 00 Open all year*

Very close to Plaça de Catalunya, this is an old nobleman's palace converted into a hotel. The entrance and staircase are old-fashionedly grand, as are some of the main rooms. It's comfortable, well-appointed and convenient, with an attractive roof terrace. Garage.
Double room 12,000 ptas

Hostal Oliva
(H)S *Passeig de Gràcia, 32 (93) 488 01 62 Open all year*

I add this because it is one of the prettiest hostels here. It's very simple, with only a few private bathrooms. The rooms are small, but most are light with views out over Passeig de Gràcia. You enter through a stairwell, take an old wooden lift up and at the top the passageway is full of flowers. Welcoming.
Double room 5,500 ptas

At the Port Olímpic

Arts
(H)L *C/ de la Marina, 19–21 (93) 221 10 00 Open all year*

This latest and brightest of the galaxy of hotels in Barcelona belongs to the Ritz-Carlton group. The tower building is forty-four storeys high and very spacious, since all the supporting structure for the construction is external. This makes it unlovely to look at but fantastic to be in. The decor is in welcoming tones of peach, pink and pale brown, with smooth modern lines softened by fine carpets, careful lighting, flowers, and paintings. The bedrooms are flooded by light from the huge windows, and are deliciously spacious, with fabulous marble-lined bathrooms and plenty of modern gadgetry which you can control without actually getting out of bed. There is an elegant Californian restaurant (evenings only), a light-hearted tapas bar and a good international restaurant where you can enjoy an extensive and excellent buffet. You are only a step away from the Port Olímpic and the beaches, and the views are truly astonishing. Garage.
Double room 30,000 ptas, 18,000 ptas weekends (all year)

RESTAURANTS AND BARS

Barcelona is full of good restaurants – far too many for the confines of this book. At lunchtime you can eat a good honest meal for around 1,000 ptas almost anywhere, so your possibilities are infinite. In the evening these good-value menus usually don't apply (although they often do in the country) so eating out is more of an event. If you don't feel like a full-blown meal, all bars have dishes of salads, *embotits,* fish and shellfish on the counter which can do the trick nicely. In general, the rule is: if it's full of Catalans, it's good.

Around Barri Gòtic

An area charged with places to eat – as it's the key area for tourism, some are excellent and some aren't.

→ Agut d'Avignon
(R)L *C/ Trinitat, 3 (just off Avinyó) (93) 302 60 34 Cl. Easter week*

Hidden in a tiny alley on the right as you walk into C/ Avinyó from C/ Ferran, but well worth finding. This is yet another old Catalan city house, with compartmented spaces and an intimate feeling. The cooking is impeccable, in the time-honoured Catalan style, but lightened to modern tastes. Their *advocat a la tropical* is a delicious purée of avocado with anchovies that I have tried to copy many times, lamb is excellent, so is *ànec amb figues* – duck with figs. The service is good and the wine list impressive.

Allow 4,500–5,500 ptas

Arrowed for its fine cooking and Catalan country house atmosphere in the middle of the city.

Pitarra
(R)M *C/ d'Avinyó, 56 (93) 301 16 47 Cl. Sun*

One of the old-timers, with a century of history behind it. It's small, prettily tiled and typical, with professional service and good food. When I was there they had wicker trays displaying the day's varieties of mushroom, and their list of game was extensive. I had a rather good wild duck with mandarin, though the pheasant with blackberries sounded tempting too. The Catalan classics are on offer here, and from spring onwards the fish is plentiful and excellent.

Allow 3,500–4,000 ptas

Los Caracoles
(R)M *C/ Escudellers, 14 (93) 302 31 85 Open all year*

Deep in the Barri Gòtic, a very old restaurant, typical, offering traditional fare. You can see the chickens spit-roasting on the corner of the street. A lot of little rooms upstairs and downstairs, tiled walls, plain furniture, and an atmosphere of old-fashioned friendliness. Excellent *serrà* ham and first courses. To follow, try the roast kid, or *suquet* of fish. Puddings are basic – *crema catalana*, ices and sorbets, and fruit.

Allow 3,000 ptas

Agut
(R)S-M *C/ Gignàs, 16 (93) 315 17 09 Open every day*

Another old favourite, just behind the splendid **Correus** (main post office). You dine to classical music in old-fashioned elegance where the

walls are lined with dark wood and hung above with rows of pictures. The kitchen is highly professional, and the carte is stylish. The starters are particularly good here – a warm salad of peas with *botifarra*, a terrine of aubergine with cured goat's cheese, or a dish of *gambes al-all*. The presentation is well up-to-date too, they served a fine beef carpaccio with mushroom and truffle vinagrette which tasted as good as it looked. Good value, with a short carte and lots of "del dia" choice.
Lunch menu 1,600 ptas; carte approx. 3,000 ptas

La Dentelliére
(R)S-M *C/Ample, 26 (93) 319 68 21 Cl. Sun. eve., Mon.*

This is a tiny place, a French restaurant tucked in amongst the doorways near the **Correus**. It's decorated in a romantic, almost over-intimate style, and serves a range of lovingly produced dishes from cassoulet to crêpes of wild mushrooms or fricassé of *rap* with saffron. If you order in advance, you can eat the most delicious goat's cheese fondue – or any other kind that takes your fancy.
Lunch menu 1,000 ptas, dinner 1,590 ptas; carte approx. 3,000 ptas.

➔ **La Fonda**
(R)S *C/Escudellers, 10 (93) 301 75 15 Open all year*

La Fonda does a roaring trade. So much so that the queues start forming before it opens and continue until the kitchen stops. The secret is twofold: a pleasant, comfortable decor – cane furniture, plenty of potted palms, a hint of the old-fashioned cosiness mixed with the clean lines of modern fashion; and a carte of appetising dishes that barely goes over 700 ptas even on main courses, served with the panache of a high-quality restaurant. The food is good – carpaccios, good rice dishes, chicken with *samfaina* and rice, duck with prunes, and delicious puds. When it opened in 1993, success was overnight, and the quality is still holding fast. So successful, in fact, that Barcelona now has two more of these restaurants, astutely run by the same team. I've cited them all, and would give an arrow to any of them. The best value in town. No reservations taken. Service starts at 1.30 p.m. and 8.30 p.m.
Allow 1,500–2,500 ptas

Les Quinze Nits
(R)S *Plaça Reial, 6 (93) 317 30 75 Open all year*

At last there is a really worthwhile, refreshing place to come to in this beautiful but little-cherished square. The same management as La Fonda – the carte is different, but the philosophy is the same – and success has followed. Allow 1,500-2,000 ptas

Boadas
(B)M *C/Tallers, 1 (93) 318 95 92 Cl. Sun.*

This is the most individual place to come to for cocktails. Presided over by the immaculately elegant Sra. Boada, this tiny bar was opened by her father in 1936. The decor has been carefully preserved, full of cartoons and sketches from the thirties, and Sra. Boada mixes the cocktails with the same dexterity as ever. Dry martinis take some beating, there are elegant little bits to eat, it's a great place to start an evening – or to finish one after dinner, come to that. It will still be open around 1 a.m.

Els 4 Gats
(BR)M *C/ Montsió, 3 bis (93) 302 41 40 Cl. Sun. midday*

Best as a bar, for a coffee or beer. This is where the artists gathered in the early years of the century; Ramon Casas, Santiago Rusiñol and, of course, Picasso. There are some originals and many reproductions of their works here and the rooms have been restored. The building itself is interesting and the big dining room is just as it was. The menu and carte are fairly standard, but people like it and it's often full.
Allow 3,000 ptas

Los Toreros
(BR)S *C/ Xucla, 3–5 (93) 318 28 25 Cl. Sat.*

Round the corner from La Boqueria, in a dingy back street, you'll find this animated bar. The walls are covered with bullfight posters, action photographs and portraits of famous matadors. If you are an aficionado, this a must. There is a selection of bar tapas all along the bar, the standard is high although the atmosphere is unsophisticated. They also serve a *menú del dia* and do a good Sunday lunch. It is always full of local people, and they certainly know good value for money.
Allow 2,500 ptas

Kiosko Pinocho
(B)S *Mercat de la Boqueria*

Enter by the main entrance, and take the first aisle to the right. A busy market bar, coffee, snacks, drinks, and an unwritten menu at midday. It's the best coffee in town and a good place to pause for breath in the middle of your shopping morning. A specially buzzing atmosphere and a queue for the few barstools.

Around Via Laietana, Pla del Palau

Carballeira
(R)M *C/ Reina Cristina, 3 (93) 310 10 06 Cl Sun. eve.*

Specialising in fish, of which you can see today's selection in the glass-fronted cold cabinets. A series of little rooms, all inter-connecting, which seem to go through two or three old houses. Select a number of first courses and share them all, that way you get to taste everything. Grilled razor-shells, for example, clams, *gambes a la planxa, truita de pernil serrà* (a revelation, that one), salads, etc. Main course dishes are well-prepared. For a light dessert, there are *teules gegants*, enormous

almond tuiles. You order one for the table and break it up. Order it early as they only make a few each day, and they can't be kept.
Allow 4,000 ptas

Set Portes
(R)M *Passeig Isabel II, 14 (93) 319 30 33 Open all year*

This restaurant claims to be the oldest in Barcelona. It occupies a large area and has several rooms. Traditional decor, the walls crowded with modern art posters – you'll wish you could be there when it was empty to go round and look. The menu is long, all the typical dishes are there. Its *paellas* are famous, all the seafood is good. If you go at the weekend, don't be late: the doors open at 1 and by half-past there is a queue for the second sitting. Immensely popular with the Barcelonese, and good value.
Allow 4,000 ptas

Senyor Parellada
(R)M *C/Argenteria, 37 (93) 315 40 10 Cl. Sun., feast days*

Big, spacious, bustling. Usually full, even on a Monday. The cooking is typical, portions are generous, but they do serve half-portions of quite a number of the dishes. Try the *galets farcits* (giant stuffed pasta), or the carpaccio of tongue, fish is good and the old-fashioned casseroles are excellent. They do a wonderful chocolate mousse.
Allow 3,500 ptas

➜ Cal Pep
(R)S-M *Plaça de les Olles, 8 (93) 315 49 37 Cl. Sun., Mon., Aug.*

In a tiny old square near Santa Maria del Mar, a busy and fashionable bar for eating freshly cooked seafood. Get there early to secure a barstool, there are not that many. Choose your fish or shellfish from the cabinets and displays in front of you and it will be cooked for you on the spot. There are a few tables in a little room beyond, seating about thirty at a maximum. Reserve if you want one of these – sitting at a bar doesn't work too well for more than two or three people. There's no menu, the waiter tells you what there is and you say what you want. Or you can leave it to him to bring you a selection of things to share to start with and follow with a portion of the freshest fish you've ever had. The day I was there this is just what we did, and he brought us – for three – little squid rings done with onion and sherry (no batter!), grilled green peppers, clams cooked with port, *xanguets*, grilled razor shells, deep fried *calamarsons*, and fried prawns so crisp you could eat the lot, all of which was followed by a piece of seabass beautifully cooked in the oven with potatoes; one of us had shoulder of kid which was also marvellously sweet and tender.
Desserts are their own, mostly ices and creams and some fruit.
Allow 2,000–2,500 ptas at the bar; 5,000 ptas at the table
Arrowed for the wide selection of excellent fish tapas, and the bustling ambience.

Casa Nebot
(R)S-M *Plaça Palau, 16 (93) 319 11 23 Cl. Sun. eve., Mon.*

Run by Sr. Nebot whose father founded the business in 1940, this bar/restaurant is well-placed and welcoming, unfussy and cool. The tapas are good and it's a great place to take a breather between the port and la Barceloneta. Specialties are meat: *entrecot al orujo* (an eau de vie from Galicia) and *entrecot a la pedra*, when the steak is sealed only and brought to you on a hot stone for you cook as you like it. The house wine is strong and very fruity. One of my favourite stopping places.

Menú del dia 925 ptas midday and evening; menú especial 1,300 ptas (not Sat. or Sun.); carte approx. 3,000 ptas

Museu Picasso
(R)S *C/ Montcada, 15–19 (93) 315 47 61 Open Tues.–Sun.*

A good little restaurant, hung with photographs of the painter, in which there is a short but good selection of daily dishes, alongside the buffet of pâtés, cheeses, and salads.

Allow 2,500 ptas

Museu Tèxtil i d'Indumentària
(R)S *C/ Montcada, 12 (93) 310 45 16 Open Tues.–Sun.*

In the gothic patio of the museum, with refreshing salads and simple, wholesome food. A delightful Sunday morning stop.

Allow 1,500–2,000 ptas

Around Av. del Paral·lel

There are plenty of popular restaurants in the streets climbing up towards Montjuïc, mostly of the rustic *pa amb tomàquet* variety.

Ca l'Isidre
(R)L *Les Flors, 12 (93) 441 11 39 Cl. Sun. May–Sept. weekends*

Ca l'Isidre is quite out of the ordinary for this area. An elegant, top-class restaurant which attracts the real gastronomes. It's been here for some twenty-five years, building itself the highest reputation for the culinary mastery of the chef. It's a small place (only forty tables) but well-lit so that the ambience is not over-intimate. The carte is creative but based on the traditional Catalan cooking – turbot with tomato accompanied by a cream of turnips, wild mushrooms tossed with *botifarra*, a salad of *llagostins* perfumed with a light orange vinagrette. Delicately worked, and beautifully presented. Enjoy the wine list – the cellar is impressive.

Menú del dia 2,500 ptas, menú *degustació* 6,000 ptas incl. wine.

Elche
(R)S *C/ Vila Vilá, 71 (93) 441 30 89 Cl. Sun. eve.*

A simple, unsophisticated place close to Montjuïc near the metro

Paral·lel. Above all, you come here to eat rice Alicante style. The portions are big, and pâté comes with warm bread before you start, so go easy on the first courses. I had the most delicious *escalivada* with a lovely tang of charcoal (half-portion), and could hardly finish the rich black rice with *sípia*. The *perol de arròs amb costre* – a mighty rice dish cooked with rabbit, chicken, chickpeas, sausage and egg – is an excellent choice at lunchtime, but not to be considered at night. The *paella* is very popular, or you might try the rather lighter variety with *bacallà* and vegetables. There's no pud to speak of, just that last sip of fresh wine from Alicante.

Allow 2,500 ptas

Can Lluís

(R)S *C/ Cera, 49 (93) 441 11 87 Cl. Sun. eve.*

A simple, old-fashioned place on the far end of C/ Hospital, as it goes into Ronda de Sant Pau. It has a couple of small dining rooms (the second is through the back) decorated with the odd singing-hall poster on the wall, lots of light and a pleasant informal friendliness. Come here to eat the *bacallà al pil-pil*, the monkfish salad, or whatever's special today. The old Catalan favourites are all here, the cooking is good, and the prices are even better. A popular place, and very convenient if you've been hunting for books in the Sunday morning fair round the market of Sant Antoni.

Allow 2,500 ptas

Around the Eixample

This is a vast area, mostly rather off the tourist trails unless you have the time to explore.

La Dama

(R)L *Av. Diagonal, 423 (93) 202 06 86 Open all year*

In a setting of great style and elegance, with superb Modernist decor, it is quite an experience to dine in rooms like these. This is a place with exquisite cooking, one of the finest chefs in Barcelona, and everything else to match, including the prices. The menu changes every three months and offers some dishes of great sophistication and inventiveness among others more conventional. I had a marvellous *daurada* baked in salt here, following one of the spectacular house specialities, the *patata rostida i farçida de llagostins*. The desserts are as spectacular as the house.

Allow 6,000 ptas

Beltxenea

(R)L *C/ Mallorca, 275 (93) 215 30 24 Cl. Sat. midday, Sun.*

There's nothing to show you where the entrance is, just a brass plate on the side of the door and two bay trees. Ring the bell and they'll let you in. This is one of the grander settings for a restaurant, the principal floor of a very grand city house. The furnishings are opulent and very comfortable. The main dining room looks onto a garden, and in the summer you can eat there under a parasol – quite sublime. The cooking is Basque, very refined, the *menú degustació* brings you a number of small dishes, all excellently done. I've had stuffed clams and oysters, salad of baby vegetables with lobster, *filet* with foie gras, wild mushrooms, to name but a few. Two desserts, and you will have enjoyed every mouthful. It's expensive.

Allow 6,500–7,000 ptas

➜ Tragaluz
(R)L *Passeig de la Concepció, 5 (93) 487 01 96 Cl. Sun.*

Just off the Passeig de Gràcia. First-class modern design here in an old house completely revamped to produce a roomy restaurant. The roof is entirely of glass so that the main floor, upstairs, seems to be a vast and airy terrace. It's most inventive and at the same time comfortable. The cooking is based on traditional Catalan dishes, brought up-to-date, and with the addition of the chef's own creations. He prepares the best foie gras in Barcelona. I have had some beautiful dishes here: a 'tatin' of quails, *calamar farçit i rap amb ceba*, magret of duck, and a stunning chocolate dessert. Downstairs there's a bar for quicker and less formal meals, called Tragaràpid.

Allow 5,000 ptas

Arrowed for its sophisticated cooking and striking designer setting.

Jaume de Provença
(R)M-L *C/ Provença, 88 (93) 430 00 29 Cl. Sun. eve., Mon., Easter, Aug.*

This is an elegant restaurant, with smooth modern lines and wood-panelled walls. The cooking is Catalan and French, with creative ideas presented artistically. For a very good starter, try the rich aubergine rings stuffed with pigs trotters and topped with a soft allioli; or the delicate *panellets de foie gras*. Delicious. The *romescada de bacallà i llagosta* makes a sophisticated and most unusual main course. The fish here is superb, and it is also renowned for wild fungi and game in autumn. The haute cuisine skill continues through to some fine desserts. An ambience of business during the week, and family parties at the weekend. It's a busy restuarant – you should book.

Menú degustació 4,750 ptas; carte approx. 6,000 ptas

Ticktacktoe
(R)M *C/ Roger de Llúria, 40 (93) 318 99 47 Cl. Sun.*

Modern decor and good cooking make this a pleasant place to eat. At midday it's full of business people and fairly smart. Service is slick and professional. Fish dishes are very good and the roast lamb and kid excellent. An amusing place in the evenings, when the second bar is open and you can play snooker.

Allow 4,000 ptas

El Caballito Blanco
(R)M *C/ Mallorca, 196 (93) 453.10 33 Cl Sun. eve., Mon.*

I'm very fond of this restaurant. It's an old-fashioned place, with a decor which should have been changed years ago. This was *the* restaurant some thirty years back, and is now rather forgotten except by the old-faithfuls. The ambience may not have the swing of the fashionable places, but its staff and kitchen have all the personality you could wish for. As you go through to the back, you pass the narrow open kitchen where the chefs are as old as the restaurant, and delightfully good-natured. The food is excellent, – it's refreshing to eat so well without modern fashion-dictated restaurant trappings. I ate a very good *esqueixada de bacallà* and followed it with a wonderful *lluç estil Santurce,* with onions and a light white sauce. When I could eat no more, the waiter came over, boned the rest most deftly, and passed it ceremoniously across the table with a great beaming smile. He was quite right – you can't waste a fish like that. Fine traditional cooking, by people who've been experts for years.
Allow 3,500–4,500 ptas

L'Olivé
(R)M *C/ Muntaner, 171 (93) 430 90 27 Cl. Sun. eve.*

On the corner C/ Còrsega, this may be a bit off the beaten track. It's a good informal Catalan restaurant, decorated in a simple, elegant style. They've taken olive green as their colour, tiled the floors and walls, hung large plain mirrors and created a modern but attractive ambience. The dishes are up-to-date too, ranging from a variety of omeletes to monkfish with burnt garlic, magret of duck, partridge with stuffed cabbage, or baked salmon with spinach. Good cooking and pleasant presentation. If you haven't reserved, go early or you won't get a table.
Allow 3,000–4,000 ptas

La Provença
(R)M *C/ Provença, 242 (93) 323 23 67 Open all year*

A quiet, pretty restaurant, done in primrose and a light blue-green, with tables round the side of the dining room with banquettes and chairs, and big round tables in the centre of the room. It looks welcoming and cool. The menu varies seasonally, there are dishes of the day, and the service is excellent. The cooking is interesting, different, and very good. When I tried it they were offering a warm camembert salad, a salad of prawns, flaky pastry with ratatouille among the first courses, then hake in a cream sauce, venison, monk fish, duck. The puddings are prepared in their own kitchen: excellent profiteroles, chocolate mousse, sorbets, all simple but good. Reserve well in advance – it is very good value and always booked out.
Allow 3,000 ptas

L'Hostal de Rita
(R)S *C/ Aragó, 279 (93) 487 23 76 Cl. Sun.*

The second of the La Fonda trio (see Barri Gòtic above), popular with businessmen by day, and with everyone by night. Between Passeig de Gràcia and C/ Pau Claris. A more elegant decor and perhaps more adventurous carte, but again along the same lines. It's worth queueing – the efficiency achieves quite a turnover. A tip on the puds – I've tried four so far, and I've never missed, although my best strike was the "Tim Baon" – a luxurious iced mixture of coffee and *torró* creaminess.
Allow 1,500–2,000 ptas

Els Perols de l'Empordà
(R)S *C/ Villarroel, 88 (93) 323 10 33 Cl. Sun. eve., Mon., Easter, Aug.*

Just opposite the theatre, at the junction with C/ Diputació. A small but pretty restaurant, narrow and finished in wood, with a second room at the back. A good place to come with several of you; order a load of the starters and have a tapa supper. Simple dishes of mussels, clams, baby octopus, squid, *gambes*, etc., along with toasts with anchovy, *botifarra, escalivada* and more. Informal, quiet and very good value.
Allow 1,500–2,000 ptas

O'Nabo de Lugo
(BR)M *C/ Pau Claris, 169 (93) 215 30 47 Cl. Sun.*

Cooking from Galicia here in a pleasant, smart bar with an upstairs diningroom. A good place for a *tapa* lunch on your Modernist walk. Excellent salads and shellfish, polite and helpful service.
Lunchtime menu 2,500 ptas

Tapa-Tapa
(BR)M *Passeig de Gràcia, 44 (93) 488 33 69 Open every day*

Easy to find, in a useful place almost opposite the famous *Maçana de la Discordia* where Casa Batlló and two other splendid Modernist houses stand. Best in the summer, when you can sit outside in one of Europe's most beautiful streets and watch the world go by. A large selection of *tapas* and beers, good but hurried service. There are plenty of tables inside for a more formal meal.

Farga
(BR)M *Av. Diagonal, 391 (93) 416 10 12 Cl. Sun.*

This is actually my favourite place in the whole of Barcelona for breakfast. Particularly on a Sunday, when at any time from 9 a.m. up to going on 1 p.m., you can have the most elegant little bits of sandwiches, quiches, croissants with *serrà* ham, prune and bacon rolls, etc., which you select from a big rack and pay for as you leave.
To drink, anything from orange juice to *cava*, in the form of Buck's fizz if you like, or chocolate, coffee, etc. It's wonderful, and you feel tip-

top for the rest of the day. There's a pleasant restaurant upstairs with roomy tables, excellent linen and china, and a short menu of well-prepared dishes for lunch or dinner.
Breakfast approx. 1,500 ptas; lunch allow 4,000 ptas

Dry Martini
(B)L *C/ Aribau, 162 (93) 217 5072 Cl. Sun., feast days*

The name of this bar tells you what it does best. It's a very elegant place offering all kinds of cocktails and little things to eat. Watching the barman prepare the dry martini from your chosen gin is a real pleasure – he's an artist. This is a great place to start your evening, perhaps going on to La Dama which is just a couple of blocks away.

Around Plaça de Francesc Macià

El Celler de Casa Jordi
(R)S-M *C/ Rita Bonnat, 3 (93) 430 10 45 Cl. Sun.*

Just off Plaça de Francesc Macià, down Av. Josep Tarradellas and second on the right. This is a small place with a very unassuming entrance. The dining rooms are on past the quiet bar, with pretty wall and floor tiling, and a splendid cellar tucked in below. Here you eat good country soups, *bacallà*, casseroles or grilled meat and there's always a good list of seasonal dishes – wild mushrooms, asparagus, today's fish. A wholesome place, a little off the beaten track.
Allow 2,500–3,000 ptas

Los Inmortales
(R)M *C/ Sagués, 25 (93) 202 35 79 Cl. Sun.*

One street up from Av. Diagonal, close to Plaça de Francesc Macià. Just the place if you feel like a variation from Catalan cuisine. This is an excellent Italian restaurant, where the pasta is something special, and the carte of main courses makes your mouth water. The restaurant decor has a fashionable air to it – clean brickwork, pale warm tones and hung with plenty of colourful modern-style prints. Be prepared to choose between the wonderful risotto with Italian mushrooms or white truffles, and the luxurious raviolis. For seconds, one of their fine carpaccios will just leave you room for the gorgeous desserts.
Allow 3,000 ptas

Around Sagrada Família

La Dida
(R)M *Roger de Flor, 230 (93) 207 23 91 Open all year*

An attractive restaurant installed in what was an old milking parlour and house, decorated in typical Catalan style. The main room is built with wide brick arches, and is lit by a pair of huge wrought-iron lanterns. At the far end, the chef can be seen toiling away to produce your fillets of hake with a subtle sea-urchin sauce, or *bacallà* with a mousse of *allioli*. He makes some fine desserts too – a *sabaglione* of summer fruits, or strawberries flambéed with pepper. Unless it's occupied, see if you can visit the private diningroom – a small room for some ten people. It's a most beautiful, original modernist room, complete with full decoration and authentic furniture.

Allow 6,000 ptas

Around Gràcia

Gràcia is full of places to eat, most of them not at all expensive, and many offering either typical Catalan food, or a particular style of cooking – Mexican, vegetarian, Italian, etc. You only need to wander around to appreciate the variety.

➜ Roig Robí

(R)L *C/ Seneca, 20 (93) 218 92 22 Cl. Sun.*

Seneca is a tiny street to the left, up at the top of the Passeig de Gràcia, just at the beginning of the area of Gràcia itself. The restaurant hides its virtues from passers-by, but do go in. The welcome is first-rate and the rooms are elegant and comfortable, and there's a garden for the summer. Cool and green, cane chairs, no traffic noise – it's delightful. Sra. Navarro modestly describes her cooking as 'traditional Catalan brought up-to-date' without adding that it is elevated to a refinement of execution rarely found. The dishes are beautifully presented and served by smiling waitresses, and include, for example, *terrina de cap de vedella a la planxa amb oli de tòfones* and a sauté of *calamarsons i cigrons*. If you have lacked the courage to try some of the stranger-looking foods so far, you can do so here in complete confidence that all will be utterly delicious. There is always a dish of poultry of some kind, guinea-fowl or chicken, perhaps, usually brought from France. The roast meats are also excellent. For afters, wonderful ices and lots of chocolate. There's a *menú del dia* at 3,100 ptas, but don't expect to eat cheaply here. Much depends on which wine you choose – the house wines are very good and there's really no need to have anything smarter.

Allow 5,000–6,000 ptas

Arrowed for its refined presentation of classic Catalan dishes for modern tastes.

➜ Racó d'en Freixa

(R)L *C/ Sant Elies, 22 (93) 209 75 59 Cl. Sun. eve., Mon., Easter, Aug.*

This restaurant is in a little street quite far from the centre, but it's worth the effort to find it. There is parking opposite. The room is welcoming, half-tiled, and the atmosphere is warm and intimate. Again, it's a family business. In the kitchen are Josèp Maria Freixa and his son Ramon while the dining room is run by his wife Dorita. The cooking is based upon classic Catalan cuisine, but with an original interpretation. Here the carte is changed with the seasons, and there is also a special menu from time to time: in February the menu is inspired by truffles; in May it's composed entirely of flowers, ranging from broom through to roses (rather romantic); and in the autumn there is a menu of game and wild mushrooms. Dedicated people with a professional approach – not cheap, but then this kind of cooking never is.

Allow 6,000 ptas incl. wine; menú degustació 4,850 ptas plus wine.

Arrowed for the warm welcome and the refreshing originality of its menus.

Jean Luc Figueres
(R)L *C/ Santa Teresa, 10 (93) 415 28 77 Cl. Sat. midday, Sun. eve.*

This is a graceful restaurant, recently opened in a small house in the barri Gràcia, very close to Av. Diagonal. There are only ten tables here, lit by glittering chandeliers, and dressed with fine linen and pretty glass. The food is very refined and delicately presented. Light canelones of *escamarlans* with tomato and black olives, moistened with hollandaise; delicate caviar toasts with lobster, garnished with quince and fresh cheese; roast pigeon with a rich soya sauce; or rack of lamb with mandarin sabayon. The desserts are just as tempting – a glorious coconut cream pastry with cinnamon, or a chocolate souflé with star anis and candied fennel. If you prefer to finish on a savory note, the cheeseboard is superb. This is the preserve of businessmen at lunchtime, and for elegant dining at night.

Menú del dia 3,500 ptas; Menú degustació 6,500 ptas

Botafumeiro
(R)M-L *Major de Gràcia, 81 (93) 218 42 30 Cl. Aug.*

The chef-proprietor here is from Galicia and has named his restaurant after the huge incense burner that hangs in the cathedral at Santiago de Compostela. There are several rooms, decorated in polished wood and well-furnished. There's also a small bar with stools if you want a quick informal tapa-style meal, but you'll have to get there early. Galicia produces great cooks, and Moncho Neira is a great specialist in fish and shellfish. Don't eat meat here, except for possibly some *serrà* ham while you think about what to have. The *marisqueria* is a succession of shellfish and crustaceans, there is also a good selection of excellent fish, all of the freshest of course. You could try the *gambes de Palamós al all fresc* or the *nero a la planxa amb escalivada,* or *espardenyes* which are a type of mollusc only found in Catalunya.

Allow 5,000 ptas

Envalira
(R)S-M *C/ Planeta, 35 Plaça del Sol (93) 218 58 13 Cl. Sun. eve., Mon., Easter, Aug., Christmas*

This is an traditional place, family run, on the upper side of one of Gràcia's squares. The restaurant itself doesn't have a terrace, but it's pleasant to sit in the square of a late afternoon and enjoy its quaint array of mis-matched buildings. (Late at night, when things get a bit rowdy, the square loses its magic.) The restaurant is barely announced, and is very plain and old-fashioned inside. The carte is rather confusingly categorised, with omelettes and fish together, and the rice dishes insignificantly hidden here and there. The latter are the renowned house specialities – a quite superb *paella*, and very good black rice, which you should take as a second course after perhaps a tapa-style selection of starters. They do *paellas* for one here, so you don't necessarily have to share. At the weekends, it's a-buzz with Catalan families, so go early to get a table.

Allow 2,500–3,000 ptas

From Barceloneta to the Port Olímpic

➜ Can Ramonet
(R)M *C/ Maquinista, 17 (La Barceloneta) (93) 319 30 64 Cl. Mon., Aug–15 Sept.*

One of the best fish restaurants in Barcelona, in the seafront district of La Barceloneta. It also claims great age, 1735 or thereabouts. In the front bar area you can stand around barrels and have your tapa-style meal served on their tops. This is what I always do. Go over to the display of fish and seafood and choose what you would like or ask the maítre, Pepe, for the list. I love the *dàtils de mar a la planxa*, the *gambes*, the *cloïsses*. There are oysters, and excellent ham. The atmosphere is great, everyone relaxed and enjoying themselves. I've seen people come here just for a glass of wine and a plate of mussels. Beyond, there are cosy old-fashioned dining rooms where you can sit down to a meal in comfort, especially welcome if you've been overdoing the walking. You have an excellent carte to choose from, and good house wines.

Allow 4,000 ptas; if you're at the barrels, it all depends on what you order

Can Majó
(R)M *C/ Almirall Aixada, 23 (93) 221 54 55 Cl. Mon., Sun. eve., Aug.*

At the head of Barceloneta triangle, you'll find this long, thin restaurant with the dining rooms hung with pictures. It's famous here for its *paellas*, and its excellent *suquet*, and you can eat a fine selection of the freshest shellfish. It's only been going some ten years, but it has become a favourite of the area, appreciated for the quality of the cooking, the personality of the family who run the restaurant, and for the good value they offer. They do a good sole stuffed with *marisc*, but this is not really the place to come for new ideas or modern cooking – its art is steeped in Catalan culinary tradition. Normal puds.

Menu 3,500 ptas; Carte approx. 3,500 ptas

Talaia Mar
(R)M–L *C/ Marina, 16 Torre Map Fre, (93) 221 90 90 Cl. Sun. eve., Mon. from Nov.–May.*

This restaurant has one of the prize positions in the Port Olímpic – just a couple of floors up in the tower which twins the Hotel Arts. The round tables are carefully arranged to take full advantage of the panoramic view from the huge windows, and the elegant wood-paneled décor heighten the sensation of privilege.

It has a first-rate pedigree, working under the aegis of El Bulli – that pinnacle of culinary excellence near Roses in Girona (see chapter 3).

Whether you take the sophisticated lobster *gazpacho*, or the rich *suquet de peix de roca*, or maybe a platter of delicious grilled vegetables, the elaboration is artful and the presentation most delicate. This is a place to enjoy true haute cuisine. Above all, don't miss the marvellous dessert trolley – the work of a very fine patissière.

Allow 5,500–6,500 ptas

➔ El Cangrejo Loco
(R)M *Moll de Llevant, 29–30 (Port Olímpic) (93) 221 05 33 Open all year*

The first restaurant to open here in the new port, and still one of the most popular. The owners are Catalan and the chef is French. They offer a terrific *menú degustació* which changes every day, composed of some ten dishes, about eight of which are fish or shellfish, with a minimal nod to the meat-eaters just before the dessert. Tremendous value and fun. If you want just a *paella* or plain dish, these are excellent too. You can sit upstairs, air-conditioned, with a good view out over the sea, or downstairs – indoors when it's too hot or very cold and windy, and outside at other times. For tapas, sit at the little terrace tables upstairs. The place is always full, so it's wise to book.

Menú degustació 3,000 ptas

Arrowed for value, good cooking and sheer fun.

Blau Marí
(R)M *Moll de la Fusta, 2 (93) 221 96 11 Cl. Mon., Jan.*

This is the best of the restaurants along the Moll de la Fusta, in the port. A great view, comfortable room, air-conditioned indoors, or outdoors under a big awning. Rice dishes are recommended, fish done in the oven is always good. Ask what they have today as it depends on the market. There is a good selection of tapas to start with. To finish with there are home-made ice-creams. Reserve at weekends.

Allow 3,000 ptas

Porta Coelis
(R)S *Moll de Llevant (93) 221 50 41 Open all year*

Right at the far end of the breakwater is a simple self-service restaurant. You will need your car to get here, or you can come on the boat trip round the port in one of the *golondrinas*. Choose what kind of fish you want and collect from the counter. No frills, but the fish is fresh and good and highly recommended.

Allow 2,500 ptas

OTHERS AREAS:

Neichel
(R)L *Av. de Pedralbes, 16 bis (93) 203 84 08 Cl. Sat. midday, Sun., Christmas, Easter, Aug.*

This is one of the very top restaurants of Barcelona. Jean-Louis Neichel is from Alsace and produces impeccable cuisine, French with a Spanish accent. The room is elegant, formal, modern, comfortable. Anything you choose here will be wonderful – from the salads to the puds, which are of course all made here. The wine list is extensive and there is every possible variety of liqueur and cigar. Don't expect bargains, this is a Michelin two-star and figures in the Relais Gourmet list.

Allow 6,000 ptas

➜ Gaig
(R)L *Passeig Maragall, 402 (93) 429 10 17 Cl. Sun. eve., Mon., Christmas, Easter, Aug.*

A bit off the general route, but in fact it's near the big exit road from Barcelona, the Meridiana, and worth a detour, as they say. The restaurant was founded in 1869 by the great-grandfather of the present chef-patron. It seats seventy with a few more in the summer season in the garden. It is well-appointed, with pretty china, cutlery and glass, and comfortable basketwork chairs.

This is very much an up-market restaurant. Sr. Gaig keeps an extensive cellar of Spanish and French wines, liqueurs and brandies, and Havana cigars in prefect condition. His very modern and immaculate kitchen also produces all the bread, and the desserts are all made here. Menus change with the seasons, and the traditional Catalan cooking has his personal touch to lighten the dishes for modern tastes. Specialities are a dish of rice with ceps and Bordeaux pigeon, a special boned pig's trotter stuffed with confit of duck and a *suquet* of *gambes*. Excellent. You should book.

Allow 6,000 ptas; *menú gastronòmic* 5,000 ptas; grand menú 8,000 ptas includes six dishes, two desserts and wine to match.

Arrowed as a classic house of Catalan cuisine, the epitome of fine tradition.

➜ Florian
(R)L *C/ Bertran i Serra, 20 (93) 212 46 27 Cl. Sun.*

Although it's way above Av. Diagonal, so not in the tourist part of the city and will take a bit of finding, it's well worth trying. The chef, Rosa Grau, is considered to be one of the best cooks in Catalunya and the restaurant which she runs with her husband has the highest reputation. It's a small place, in which you feel very much like a guest. Sra. Grau is a specialist in wild mushrooms, pastas and good beef (*toro*), within a context of modern Catalan cuisine. Inventive and traditional, with a distinctive personal touch – try the salad of smoked *bacallà*, the sea anemonies, or the *cua de bou al Cabernet*. The desserts are fabulous.

The wine list merits attention too, Catalan, Riojan and French, – and the short list of recommendations changes every couple of weeks. Very pleasant.
Allow 5,000 ptas
Arrowed for Rosa Grau's superb cooking.

Asador de Aranda
(R)M *Av. Tibidabo, 31 (93) 417 01 15 Cl. Sun. eve.*

There's no menu here and the food is not Catalan. What is Catalan is the house, a fantastic Modernist brick-built mansion which was actually a private family home up to about fifteen years ago. I met someone who actually used to go to dine with the family that lived there. If building skills interest you, you'll love it. The brick- and tile-work is virtuoso and quite stunning. There's a terrace with fountain and flowers in the summer where you can dine under the tall trees. The cooking comes from Burgos, from where some of the finest lamb comes. The waiter will ask you if you'd like to have the standard meal. Yes, you would. They will bring you a series of little dishes to start with, dried ham, roasted little red peppers, various kinds of sausages, a few little bits of kidney. Then comes a bowl of salad and a dish of roast milk-lamb, brought from Burgos and roasted Castillian-style to a succulent tenderness in a wood-fired oven – the 'asador'. Plenty of good Burgos bread, and a jug of wine to go with it – you can't go wrong. There are icecreams and pastries if you're still hungry, to be followed by coffee and a little dry doughnut which you dip in a glass of eau de vie. Service is excellent.
Allow 3,500 ptas

Els Pescadors
(R)M *Plaça Prim, 1 (93) 309 20 18 Cl. Easter, Christmas, New Year*

This restaurant started building its reputation in the 80's, several years before the building of the Olympic village, when the Barri Poble Nou was still very much apart from the centre of the city. Now it's just a matter of minutes from the new marina. The restaurant is on a quiet square, just off the Rambla de Poble Nou. One of the three dining rooms still carries the old fishermen's café decoration, while the other two are more up-to-date. You shouldn't think of eating anything but fish here – the seabass baked with fennel is wonderful, and the *rossejat de fideus* with clams is renowned. You'll come across contemporary Catalan cuisine superbly worked, as well as the great traditional dishes.
Allow 3,500 – 5,500 ptas

Ca n'Armengol
(R)M *Prat de la Riba, 1 Santa Coloma de Gramenet (93) 391 05 54 Cl. Sun. eve., Mon., Aug., Easter*

This is really miles away from the centre, an unlikely destination for dinner unless you are in Barcelona for some length of time. Check well on the map before you set out. It'll be worth it when you get here – the cooking is superb. Ca n'Armengol has been here since 1923, when it started as a simple café – part of it is still a local bar – and it has since grown into one of the finer restaurants of the province. The room is quite modern, with wood-lined ceiling and floor, and a simply-presented carte. The star dish is the *bacallà Colomenc*, which is accompanied by a quince allioli, a dish they created a generation ago. The carte is an extensive mixture of traditional Catalan dishes and contemporary creations: starters ranging from scrambled egg with mushrooms to *marisc*; then *rap* with burnt garlic, brochettes of *gambes* with bacon; *châteaubriand* and *entrecot*. The dishes sound misleadingly simple – you have to come here to appreciate the skill and technique of the chef. Very good desserts – particularly the aromatic apple ice-cream.

Allow 4,000–5,000 ptas

Mirablau
(B)M *Plaça del Funicular del Tibidabo*

This is a smart bar at the foot of the funicular railway which connects Tibidabo with the old Tramvia Blau, the blue tram which runs up from the top of C/ Balmes. It has a crystal wall overlooking the whole city and the sea beyond – stunning by day and very beautiful at night when all of Barcelona is glittering with lights. There's a pleasant terrace beside the bar.

2 DAY EXCURSIONS FROM BARCELONA

Route 1 The coast south of Barcelona – Sitges, Vilanova i la Geltrú
Route 2 The coast north of Barcelona – the Maresme
Route 3 The wine and cava region of the Penedès – Sant Sadurní d'Anoia, Vilafranca del Penedès
Route 4 The Cistercian monasteries – Santes Creus, Poblet
Route 5 Muntanya de Montserrat Natural Park
Route 6 Sant Llorenç de Munt Natural Park
Route 7 Montseny Natural Park

Catalunya is not very big, and most places except the far north-east are accessible within a day: France is but two hours by motorway from Barcelona, Tortosa takes about two hours, and the most northern reaches of Lleida are only about five hours away. For this chapter, I've taken the areas closest to the city which make comfortable round trips with little time in the car.

Route 1 The coast south of Barcelona – Sitges, Vilanova i la Geltrú

For a quick dash to the beach, and the opportunity to eat very good seafood, the small coastal towns to the south are easy to get to. The long beaches of **Gavà** and **Castelldefels** are only twenty minutes away. From here until **Sitges** the spectacular road hugs the coast, winding round the steep rocky curves of the **Garraf** mountains, high above the sea. If you are happier on straight roads, a short but very useful motorway tunnels through the mountain to Sitges and **Vilanova i la Geltrú** in a matter of minutes.

Map 6F CASTELLDEFELS

There are two parts of Castelldefels: the seaside area with long, wide beaches, and the older inland village, near which they built the Olympic Canal in 1992 for the flat-water canoeing races. Needless to say, the holiday spirit is on the coast.

Nàutic
(R)M *Passeig Marítim, 374 (93) 665 01 74 Open all year*

This is a short stroll from the centre along the sea front, with a clear view across the sand. It's decorated in nautical style, with splendid old brass lanterns and fishermen's bric-à-brac hanging from the ceiling, and has a pleasantly informal feel. Fish is, of course, what you eat here, and it's superb: sea bass *a la sal*, or fish baked, en papillotte, or as a *suquet*. Their gently grantinéed spinach and shellfish crêpes make a delicious starter, and for afters try the almond mousse with raspberry coulis. Lovely food – great for a Sunday lunch. You must reserve at weekends.

Menú degustació 3,500 ptas. Carte approx. 4,500 ptas.

La Canasta
(R)M *Passeig Marítim, 197 (93) 665 68 57 Cl. Tues.*

In the centre of the seaside village on the highstreet with a shaded terrace at the back. When they started here as a small, local restaurant the fish was served in baskets, hence the name. It's gone up-market since then, although tables are still furnished with tomatoes for you to rub on your toast. It enjoys a high reputation for the excellent rice and *fideuà* dishes, especially the *caldereta d'arròs* (a small cauldron of rice with a thick fish stock) and the good *entremesos* of the house – a selection of shellfish. For a complete meal, try the *brou amb peix de roca* which is a two-course dish of poached fish and shellfish accompanied by potatoes, followed by rice cooked in the rich fish bouillon and served with *allioli*. You must reserve at weekends.

Menú del dia 2,500 ptas; carte approx. 4,500 ptas

Map 6F **GAVÀ**

Gaudí Garraf
(R)M *Ctra. Barcelona-Sitges C246, Km 25 (93) 664 55 59 Cl. Sun., Mon., Tues., Wed. eves.*

If you're taking the coast road to Sitges, this is a curious building which will certainly catch your eye. It's one of Gaudí's smaller works, built as a home and now partly used as a restaurant (in a small vault-like room in the house) and as a backdrop for communion or wedding parties. It's difficult to turn into from the Barcelona direction, but there's plenty of parking once inside. Notice the ironwork on the gate, and if you're eating here (traditional Catalan cooking), ask to see the gallery upstairs.

Allow 3,000–4,000 ptas

Map 5F **SITGES**

This is one of the favourite destinations for those who need a breath of refreshing sea air away from the city. The heart of Sitges is the old fishing village around the parish church, now a pedestrian area of pretty streets lined with white houses which spreads down to the sea. There are two beaches, one small and the other never-ending, separated by the outcrop of rock on which the parish church stands.

Two interesting museums are installed in the old houses overlooking the sea near the church. The **Museu Cau Ferrat** *(C/ Fonollar (93) 894 03 64 Open 10.00 a.m.–2.00 p.m., 4.00 p.m.–6.00 p.m.; cl Sun. p.m., Mon.),* the house and studio of the artist-writer Santiago Rusiñol, exhibits his collections of wrought iron, ceramics, furniture and paintings by himself, Ramon Casas, Picasso and many Catalan artists of the epoch. The house is a delightful building of various small rooms. The **Museu Maricel** is next door, another attractive building with huge windows looking out over the sea. Here you can browse through a wide collection of gothic religious art. Behind, close to the quarter of modernist houses, is the **Museu Romàntic** *(C/ Sant Gaudencio 10.00 a.m.–1.30 p.m., 4.00 p.m.–6.00 p.m.; closed Sun. p.m., Mon.)* with a collection of toys, music boxes, dolls, etc. From here to the station, Sitges has an area of fine nineteenth-century villas. Three of them make up the hotel *Romàntic,* C/ Sant Isidre, 33 ((93) 894 83 75 – Open Apr.–Oct. – giving its ground floor a chain of delightful interconnecting rooms each with its own tiled decoration – a pretty place to take an aperitif.

From spring onwards, Sitges fills at the weekends with people from the city, and in the summer you can't move for the tourists. Its seafront is almost exclusively restaurants – most fairly up-market. Behind are the cheaper places and multitudes of bars. Festivals here are a treat: on the Saturday of Corpus Christi, Sitges decks its streets with flowers – a spectacular array of patterns sculpted with flower heads of all colours – ready for the afternoon processions. This is also a favourite spot to enjoy *Carnaval,* not so much for the civic processions as for the general party atmosphere, brought alive by the wild and wonderful transvestite costumes.

Subur Marítim
(H)M-L *Passeig Marítim, s/n (93) 894 15 50 Open all year*

This is a peaceful, spacious hotel, a comfortable stroll along the sea front from the centre of town. It's a modern building with forty-two rooms which all have balconies overlooking the sea. In front there's a grassy garden surrounding a large pool for those who prefer a more tranquil swim. The restaurant in the adjoining old town house has dark wooden ceilings, paintings and an old-fashioned dignity.

Double room 9,000–10,000 ptas

Maricel
(R)M *Passeig de la Ribera, 6 (93) 894 20 54 Open all year*

This is an excellent young restaurant on the seafront with an original creative menu, set in an elegant room hung with pictures. The cuisine is Catalan-French, worked with sophistication and presented with pride. New dishes are constantly appearing. When I was there, the offering included stuffed sole 'en papillotte' perfumed with a purée of rose and beetroot, and a salad of baby monkfish and *llagosta* with a saffron vinaigrette, as well as a refined fish soup and *fideuà* with clams.

Menú gastronòmic 5,500 ptas; carte 4,500–5,000 ptas

Cal Pinxo
(R)S-M *Passeig de la Ribera, 5 (93) 894 74 64 Cl. Sun. eve.,Mon.*

A hive of activity right next door to Maricel. Very popular, always busy, and decorated with designer-blue walls and a vaulted ceiling crossed with pale wooden beams. Fresh grilled fish, *marisc*, and the favourite rice dishes. Good value and good fun.
Allow 3,000 ptas

El Velero
(R)M *Passeig de la Ribera, 38 (93) 894 20 51 Cl. Sun. eve.*

This is rather like two rooms in a cottage – walls crowded with pictures and fishermen's kit, plants here and there, small tables and a cosy ambience. The cooking is both traditional and contemporary: fish and shellfish *a la planxa, sarsuela*, rice dishes, etc., speckled with a number of more modern dishes like sole with a sauce of crabs, clams with cava or monkfish with grapes and almonds. There are *gambes* to munch while you choose.
Allow 4,500 ptas

La Masia
(R)M *Passeig de Vilanova, 164 (93) 894 10 76 Open all year*

If you feel like traditional country food rather than fish, try this restaurant on the main road out towards Vilanova. It has several rooms, attractively decorated with ceiling beams, ceramics and old bottles. *Bacallà*, roast or charcoal-grilled meats, *escudella* and stews, finishing with *crema catalana*. The menu is rather misleadingly translated in the English version, but what you get is good.
Allow 3,500 ptas

La Estrella
(B) *C/ Major, 52 (93) 894 00 79*

This is a particularly attractive patisserie and charcuterie which also has a few small round tables for taking breakfast or a snack. I just mention it because it's such an old establishment (running for 150 years so far, they say) and its decoration is pleasingly dated.

Map 5F VILANOVA I LA GELTRÚ

This is a big town with a fishing port and a long seafront. It is just up the road from Sitges, but has a completely different character. While the latter is pretty, and almost coquettish in its village pride and restaurant sophistication, Vilanova has the seaside character of a Catalan provincial town – not the material for a weekender's camera. For this reason it makes a very good alternative to Sitges if you want to feel a real Catalan ambience. The restaurants here are unpretentious and excellent, and in the summer the beaches are uncrowded and happy.

Hotel César
(H)M *Isaac Peral, 4–8 (93) 815 11 25 Open all year*

For a tranquil stay close to the beach, this is an attractive place with rooms overlooking the garden of pine trees and shrubs, where you can take a quiet aperitif or an afternoon nap. The entrance is covered with bougainvillea and inside there are spacious rooms with welcoming floral upholstry. The family have been looking after travellers for over a century.

Double room 6,500–9,500 ptas

Resaurante La Fitorra
(R)M *Isaac Peral, 4–8 (93) 815 11 25 Cl. Jan, Sun. eve. and Mon. except in summer*

The restaurant of hotel César is highly-regarded, with small elegant dining rooms and a terrace, where good Catalan seasonal dishes are served.

Allow 3,500–4,000 ptas

➔ **Peixerot**
(R)M *Passeig Marítim, 56 (93) 815 06 25 Cl. Sun. eve. except 15 Jul.–15 Sept.*

For rice dishes you couldn't be in a better place. This is a great traditional seaside restaurant now in its third generation. Big glass windows look across to the port, simple green or blue straw-bottomed seats colour the rooms, and there's a relaxed ambience of contented Catalans who know a fine *arròs negre* with lobster when they taste one. Here you can eat excellent fish cooked in the oven or in salt, braised *sípia* with potatoes and *allioli*, succulent shellfish, or rich delicious rice and *fideus* dishes. For starters, I thoroughly recommend the *pica-pica* selection of tapas, particularly the fried baby squid and the croquettes, which you simply mustn't miss. Highly professional.

There is a second restaurant in Barcelona, serving the same excellent quality but in a more executive ambience: Peixerot C/ Tarragona, 177 (93) 424 69 69.

Allow 4,500–5,000 ptas

Arrowed for the excellent fish and happy ambience.

Bernard et Marguerite
(R)M *C/ Ramon Llull, 4 (93) 815 56 04 Open all year*

A restaurant that's been cooking good food for the last 27 years, one street back from the beach just by hotel César. There's a small terrace outside and the room itself holds just eight tables. The cuisine is modern, Catalan touched with French sophistication, and the carte is short and appetising. Apart from Saturday evenings, there's a tempting

Vilanova i la Geltrù – Peixerot

menú especial which includes a wide choice of dishes, a good french table wine and a fine selection of French cheeses or pâtisserie. There might be an Alsatian onion tart, an *escalivada* mousse with a coriander-scented tomato coulis, duck with fresh peaches (a lovely dish), or salmon with a sorrel sauce; and in winter there's always game. You must reserve on Friday and Saturday evenings.

Menú especial 2,600 ptas; carte approx. 3,700 ptas

Bar El Giraldillo
(B)M *C/ Pelegrí Ballester, 19–21 (93) 815 62 02*

This is the top spot for a snack in Vilanova i La Geltrú –a great place for *gambes a la planxa* or a plateful of mussels. It's a smart and very popular bar where the tapas are excellent, and it tends to get very crowded around mealtimes at the weekend. If hunger overtakes you it's worth waiting for a table or squeezing round the bar.

La Cucanya
(R)M *Racó de Santa Llúcia (93) 815 19 34 Cl. 1–15 Nov., Mon. lunch*

Just beyond **Vilanova i la Geltrú** this is a lovely sea-hugging restaurant out on its own.

Watch out for the signs on the C-246 between Vilanova and Cubelles which take you off to Santa Llúcia. Carry on across the bridge and you'll reach the villa sitting on the edge of the sea. In the daytime or on a moonlit evening this is an exceptionally pretty setting, with an open terrace in summer and a garden that goes right down to the rocks. Here you eat Italian food of distinction: starters of wonderful paper-thin raviolis of nettles and fresh cheese (*tortelli d'Erbette*) or stuffed with gorgonzola; slivers of *porchetta* (a herby, well-seasoned cold roast-pork – best taken as a half portion), crêpes of *marisc*, and all sorts of superb fresh pasta with baby octopus, hot peppers etc. There is plenty of choice of meat and fish – from filet steak *al vinagre de Modena* to sole with a delicate leek sauce, and the set menu offers a wide selection of fish and shellfish dishes. If you're still able, try the house speciality – *nonna Julia* – a creamy bitter-sweet almond treat.

Menú degustació 3,500 ptas; Carte approx. 4,500 ptas

Route 2 The coast north of Barcelona – the Maresme

A straight road runs up the coast, separating the small towns from the beach. Just behind there's a roll of hills spotted all along with villas, and greenhouses which produce early summer fruits. Traditionally, these were villages of summer residences for Barcelona families.

Map E7 **ALELLA**

This is an important village for the wine trade – a worthy place to linger and sample the local produce.

El Niu
(R)S-L *Rambla Àngel Guimerà, 16. (93) 555 17 00 Cl. Sun. eve., Mon., 15 Aug.–30 Aug.*

This is up a narrow passageway leading off the main street of the town. Maria Salvans has earned the highest reputation for her cuisine. Her daughter is the pâtissière, while her husband and other daughter look after the dining room. The room itself is quietly elegant, finished in wood, and the tables set with fine china. The starters are attractively presented – perhaps a pâté de foie, a salad of lobster with wild mushrooms. Then a sole with a subtle hint of cider vinegar or seabass served with *llardons*. My favourite dish here is the *cabrit al forn*, kid gently braised with pears and bathed in a deliciously rich sauce. The desserts should not be missed (created from the seasonal fruits), nor should the cheeseboard which has, in winter, an exceptional selection of French and Spanish cheeses.

On the tree-shaded terrace and in the room above the restaurant you can dine at red-check tables on typical country stews or grills for around 2,000 ptas, served from the same kitchen.

Carte approx. 5,000 ptas; menú degustació (surprise) 6,800 ptas

Map E7 **CABRILS**

This is a pretty village up in the hills, flower-filled with white houses and little streets.

→ **Hostal de la Plaça**
(HR)M *Plaça de l'Església, 32 (93) 753 19 02 Cl. 15 Sept.–15 Oct.; rest. cl. Sun. eve., Mon.*

A delightful hotel which has been around as a *hostal* for over fifty years, just beside the church. You enter through the various levels of the *masia*-style diningrooms to reach the stairs which lead to the nine bedrooms. Each room is named after a wild flower, and is decorated individually in a welcoming country style. Rooms to the front look out across the green woods to the sea, while those at the back have views of village houses and beyond to woods. Breakfast is a delight, taken on the ivy-covered terrace, enjoying the lovely vistas with an accompaniment of bird-song. The restaurant is informal, spacious and attractive, serving good traditional food.

Carte approx. 3,000 ptas; double room 8,000 ptas

Arrowed for the family welcome, and the attractive tranquility.

Map E7 **CABRERA DE MAR**

Santa Marta
(R)M *C/ Josep Domènech, 35 (93) 759 01 98 Cl. Sun. eve., Mon., Nov., Easter*

There are signs up to Santa Marta from the main road. Follow them or you'll never find it. One of the attractions of this restaurant is its location – in the midst of the splendid traditional summer residences that typify the hills behind the seafront towns. The restaurant itself has a view stretching over the pine woods to the sea. On weekdays it serves mostly as a businessman's retreat, so the best time to enjoy its fine Catalan cuisine is at the weekend or during the summer, when the evenings are delightful. An interesting speciality here is the *tronc de peix*, a succulent fishcake of monkfish, *daurada*, seabass, *gambes* and mussels.

Menu (midday) 1,450 ptas; carte approx. 4,000–5,000 ptas

Map E7 ARGENTONA

This is a pretty town, several kilometres inland with a refreshing, lively ambience, and some fine mansions.

Racó d'en Binu
(R)M *C/ Puig i Cadafalch, 14 (93) 797 04 64 Cl. Sun. eve., Mon.*

This is a good restaurant just off the main square of the town, run by the brothers Francesc and Albi Forti. The decoration inside is elegant country style, with trophies of deer on the walls and a great round fireplace in the middle. The cooking is classic and sophisticated, much governed by fish – oysters with *cava*, seabass 'en papillotte', or millefeuille of turbot – and by game in winter – civet of venison with chestnut purée, or pheasant with grapes and apple. If you come here in the right season, try the delicious green asparagus puffs. For dessert there are the lightest soufflés of mint, pinenuts or citrus fruits.
Allow 6,000 ptas

El Celler d'Argentona
(R)S-M *C/ Bernat de Riudemeya, 6 (93) 797 02 69 Cl. Mon.*

A happy place full of tables, set in the big hall-like basement of an eighteenth-century house with a gallery upstairs. Quarry-tiled floors, straw-seated chairs, and good traditional food. Lamb, kid and steak *a la brasa*, pig's trotters, *escudella*, and a small selection of fish of the day.
Menu 2,500 ptas; carte approx. 3,500–4,000 ptas

Map E7 SANT ANDREU DE LLAVANERES

This is a summer village surrounded by pine trees in the hills overlooking the coast. As with the other Maresme towns, it's patronised mainly by Catalan families.

La Bodega
(R)M *Av. Sant Andreu, 6 (93) 792 67 79 Cl. Sun. eve., Mon.*

At the top of the main road leading from the coast you come to a nineteenth-century mansion set back from the road. Most of the building is used for receptions and parties, while the restaurant proper is in the beamed house at the back, with terracotta floor-tiles, pretty curtains and old wooden chairs and tables. The rustic elegance is matched by the food – traditional but fashionable, with a personal and frequently changing carte. Carpaccios, glazed baby onions with *cava*, sea urchins, rice and *fideus*, lots of interesting salads and plenty of meat and fish dishes. The fruit tartlets are a good way to finish.
Allow 5,000 ptas

Map E7 ARENYS DE MAR

This is a small town built round a busy central rambla which leads down to the sea. The famous Hispania restaurant is on the main road about one kilometre before you reach the town.

➜ **Hispania**
(R)L *C/ Real, 54. Km 655 de-la N-11 (93) 791 04 57 Cl. Tues., Sun. eve., 1–15 Oct.; Easter*

This is one of the great restaurants of Catalunya, much loved and highly respected throughout all Spain, in which the celebrated sisters Paquita and Dolores Rexach work with a seemingly magic touch. Theirs is Catalan cuisine at its very, very best, with an immensely varied carte which modestly presents dishes such as *amanida provençal, rap a l'all, suquet,* lentils with pigs' trotters, braised rabbit, *sípia* with potatoes, barely hinting at the exemplary art of the kitchen. The *plats de les mestresses* announce the day's special dishes – excellent advice if you are unable to make a choice. For dessert, probably the finest *crema catalana* you will ever taste. The wine list is fabulous.

Menu 4,500–6,000 ptas

Arrowed for the mythical perfection reached by the sisters in the most traditional of Catalan cuisine.

Can Martínez
(R)M *Passeig Marítim, Platja (93) 792 12 78 Cl. Mon., 15 Dec.–7 Jan.*

Decorated inside with nautical polished wood, this is a refreshing restaurant on the seafront close to the marina, with a tree-shaded terrace that reaches out to the sand. Lovely in the spring. As you'd expect, it is almost exclusively dedicated to fish, with a simple carte listing a lengthy selection of the *marisc* and fish that is available today in the local marketplace. Much careful cooking *a la planxa,* and some good classic rice dishes – particularly the *paella* with *llagosta.*

Allow 3,500–4,000 ptas

Map E7 CANET DE MAR

This was a fashionable village at the end of the last century, and as a result has a most attractive main street, lined with a number of splendid late nineteenth-century houses.

El Sant Jordi de Canet
(R)M *Riera St Domènec, 1 (93) 795 46 96 Cl. Sun. eve., Mon.*

In keeping with the street, this building is a glorious example of Modernist architecture, designed by Lluís Domènech i Montaner

Canet – El Sant Jordi

between 1889 and 1892. As you enter, two little rooms lead off at each side. One fills a turret – a charming circular room with a startling ceiling – and the other is a small square room decorated with stencilling and mosaics, with the walls crowded with photographs of the famous Catalan soprano, Montserrat Caballé. Operatic music fills the air. The main dining room is quite stunning – a hall with with a decorated wooden ceiling the height of a church, galleried and frescoed, with a magnificent baronial fireplace on the side wall. Throughout, the ceilings and floors are examples of the finest craftmanship, as are the stained-glass windows and even the light fittings. The chef is from the Empordà, and you will find the peas with fresh mint and the croquetes (granny Flora's recipe) rather delicious. For a little of everything take the *pica-pica*. The second courses cover a wide range of classic Catalan dishes, with a good *suquet*, meatballs with *sípia* and plenty of roasts, grills and braises. A friendly, splendid place.

Allow 4,000 ptas

Map E8 SANT POL DE MAR

This is a pretty seaside town with a long beach, a marina, the romanesque hilltop chapel of Sant Pau, and a marvellous restaurant.

→ **Sant Pau**
(R)L *C/ Nou, 10 (93) 760 06 62 Cl. Sun. eve., Mon., fortnight after Easter, fortnight in Nov.*

Sant Pau is graceful little restaurant, elegantly decorated with magnolia walls and ruby floors, which looks out across the garden to the sea. Carme Ruscalleda has only ever worked in her own kitchen, and as a result her cooking is highly individual and very imaginative. The carte is short and select, inspired by the seasonal changes in the market and the creative whim of the chef. The ingredients are traditional but the dishes are not – a soup of chickpea and sea bass, a light curry sauce accompanying a hake and *gambe* brochette, a sweet-sour purée of figs with duckling, – and the desserts are absolutely unmissable; perhaps a baked pear with fragrant pear ice-cream, or the lightest sablée with summer fruit. Wonderful.

Menú tradició e inspiració 5,600 ptas; menú degustació 7,200 ptas; carte approx. 6,000–10,000 ptas

Arrowed for the culinary imagination, and the delightful experience of eating here.

Gran Sol
(H)M *Ctra N-11, Km 670 (93) 760 00 51 Open all year*

A comfortable hotel with forty-four rooms at the top of the town beside the old chapel, with splendid sea views.

Double room 8,000–11,000 ptas

Route 3 The wine and cava region of the Penedès – Sant Sadurní d'Anoia, Vilafranca del Penedès

Although this excursion is completely based around the great wine region of the Penedès, there's a very interesting detour you can make on the way to the *cava* area of **Sant Sadurní d'Anoia**.

Map F6 SANTA COLOMA DE CERVELLÒ

Having crossed the Llobregat on the main route out of Barcelona, continue along the N340 through the Ordal mountains. In Cervelló you can visit Gaudí's extroadinary crypt in the **Colònia Güell**, part of the textile estate planned for his patron Eusebi Güell. The crypt (1908–1916) is all that was built of the church, but it is a fascinating piece of engineering which shows Gaudí's philosophy of design most dramatically. The ground plan is an irregular oval shape, with four inclined main columns supporting the rough brick ribs, with curious idiosyncratic vaulting above. The building material is mostly rough basalt stone and brick. Notice the benches too – designed by Gaudí and worked from iron and wood. The Cooperative and some other buildings here were designed by disciples of Gaudí. Information *(93) 640 29 36.*

Map E5 SANT SADURNÍ D'ANOIA

This is the heart of the cava-producing region, as you will see as you potter through the town. It holds the prestige here that Rheims enjoys in France. Production is huge, and there are cellars everywhere, many of which you can visit – the modernist architecture of the Codorniu buildings, designed by Josep Puig i Cadafalch, is the most splendid. The making of *cava* is also a craft here, which is a very different matter where the wine is produced in small quantities with great personal care and individuality – this traditional method produces another fine quality of wine. *Cava* is often drunk *semi-sec* (a little sweet) but the finest is the *brut nature,* also the driest.

Mirador de les Caves
(R)M *Ctra. Ordal–San Sadurní, Km 4 Els Casots (93) 899 31 78 Cl. Sun. eve., Mon. eve., fortnight in Aug.*

This is a lovely place – an elegant restaurant nestling in the hills above Sant Sadurní with huge windows from which you can contemplate wonderful views stretching from the vineyards across to the peaks of Montserrat. The views make the restaurant. The little garden with its trickling stream makes a refreshing entrance, and the cooking is a pleasure. *Cava,* of course, is an important ingredient – the lobster touched with a *cava* vinaigrette is delicious, and the paupiettes of sole are light and delicate. You will find a varied carte to choose from, with plenty of *marisc* and fish, and duck from the Penedès farms. Almost any *cava* you wish for is in stock.
Menú degustació 5,000 ptas; carte approx. 6,000 ptas

Map F5 VILAFRANCA DEL PENEDÈS

Since the end of the eighteenth-century they've been cultivating vines here, and Vilafranca is the central town of the rich Penedès vineyards from which the excellent *cavas* and huge quantities of wine are made. (See Catalan food and wine). The museum dedicated to winemaking is just opposite the large church of Santa Maria, with its vaults full of old presses and other wine paraphernalia. A great wine festival takes place here in April. The Penedès is also renowned for its poultry, including ducks and turkeys, and a traditional poultry fair is held on the last

Saturday before Christmas where the centre is crammed with Catalan cooks and crowing cockerels – quite an occasion, though not for the squeamish.

Cal Ton
(R)M *C/ Casal, 8 (93) 890 37 41 Cl. Sun. eve., Mon. lunch*

Just off the *rambla*, on the seaward side, this is a small but light-filled restaurant with a glass-roofed room set in the patio of the house. There are green plants everywhere. It has an interesting carte, with imaginative dishes created by the chef who works with pasta, fish, and the Penedès poultry, perfumed with herbs and wild mushrooms. The cooking is sophisticated and artistic – and the desserts superb.
Allow 3,500–4,500 ptas

Casa Joan
(R)M *Plaça de l'Estació, 8 (93) 890 31 71 Open lunch only except for Sat. Cl. Sun., Easter, Christmas, end Aug.–early Sept.,*

Right opposite the railway station – a traditional restaurant with old-fashioned Modernist tiles decorating the rooms, which tends to be busy particuarly during the week. It serves classic Catalan food.
Menú del dia 1,750 ptas; carte approx. 3,500 ptas

Map F5 **OLÈRDOLA**

Olèrdola is on the road from Vilafranca del Penedès to Sitges. Just up the hill beyond the hamlet, you come to the ruins of a medieval castle with walls two metres thick in parts, within which is the early romanesque chapel of Sant Miquel.

Celler del Penedès
(R)M *C/ Anselm Clavé, 13 (93) 890 20 01 Open all year*

The history of this huge *masia* is well-preserved in the many dining rooms – each named after its original use and hung with old farming tools and twisted pieces of vine. The main room is the old cart hall, with the cellar (complete with barrels) next door. It is a tremendous family place – thoroughly rustic and packed with Catalan weekend parties. It started years ago serving bread and sandwiches to the farming folk, and soon progressed to its 'pièce de résistance', rabbit with garlic. Today you still come here for the rabbit, and for grilled meat and traditional catalan food. They are delighted to show you round the old kitchen with its coal-fired range (no longer used) and explain the various rooms of the building.
Allow 3,000–4,000 ptas

Map F5 **SANT MARTÍ SARROCA**

On towards the monastery of Santes Creus from Vilafranca del Penedès, you come to the little town of Sant Martí Sarroca. A ruined castle with a pretty romanesque chapel dominates this village from the promontory behind. A small museum now occupies the remains of the castle, and if you drop by on a Saturday or a Sunday you may come across a wedding in the chapel. The views from up here are spectacular.

➔ **Ca L'Anna**
(R)M *C/ La Roca, 4 (93) 899 14 08 Cl. Sun. eve., Mon.; last orders 3.30 p.m. and 10.30 p.m.*

As you come down from the castle, there's a turning off to Ca L'Anna. Follow the track for some fifty metres, and you'll arrive at the the last house, covered with ivy with a white front door. Inside is the elegant restaurant with magnolia walls, which extends into a light glass-walled terrace, with a polished wood roof supported on classical pillars. Although there's no view, it's a very pleasant, spacious place where the food is creative, beautifully presented and delicious.

Either you can leave everything up to Paco, the chef, and take the *menú sorpresa* which brings you four courses and dessert, or opt for the carte. Between us we had a fragrant cool soup of tomato with fresh basil and a pressed terrine of sardines with sweet tomatoes, baby broad beans and goat's cheese, followed by sole stuffed with crab and fresh tomato accompanied by a sweet turnip purée, and a saddle of rabbit stuffed with raisins and nuts with a hint of ginger. The dessert (no room for two) was a crunchy apple tart with a light whipped cream of banana. If your appetite is not ample, you can always ask for half-portions. You must book at weekends.

Menú del dia 3,750 ptas; menú sorpresa 4,500 ptas; carte 4,000–5,000 ptas

Arrowed for the excellent service and the enjoyment the chef gets from his cooking.

Sant Jordi "Ca la Katy"
(R)S *Ctra Vilafranca-Pontons, Km 8 (93) 899 13 26 Cl. Sun. eve., Mon.*

This simple restaurant, just outside the village, has made its reputation with one key dish – *l'ànec mut del Penedès* (the regional duck) roasted with prunes and pinenuts. It's a delicious dish, rich and sweet, which allows you to appreciate the great flavour of the local speciality.

Allow 2,500 ptas

Map E4 PONTONS

El Papa
(R)M *Ctra de Santes Creus (93) 897 11 26 Open lunchtimes, Fri. and Sat. eves. Cl. Aug., Mon.*

This is on the southern side of town, a restaurant which serves a tremendous *mariscada*. You arrive, take your seat at a table, and relax. Without a murmur of a menu, the table begins filling first with dried ham, salad, smoked salmon and good country bread, and then the dishes of crab, all kinds of shellfish, prawns, lobster, etc. start coming up. Don't expect sauces – it's all left completely plain. Unless you specifically ask for one, there is no carte here, and you need a healthy appetite to enjoy the feast of the best 'fruits de mer' in this unpretentious dining room. It's run by a small family team, whose cooking has earned them a fine reputation. Very popular, and very good.

Allow 6,000 ptas

Route 4 The Cistercian monasteries – Santes Creus, Poblet

The great monasteries are barely an hour away from the city by motorway, or you could reach Santes Creus via the vineyards of the Penedès, and then go on to Poblet.

Map F4 SANTES CREUS

The abbey of Santes Creus is less dominating than Poblet, but nonetheless impressive. It has a very peaceful approach through hilly countryside, with the monastery tucked into a fold. You enter through the walls which encircle it, and walk up to the splendid romanesque church façade through a short wide street lined with quiet pottery shops and a bar or two. The church has a huge rose window and hefty piers supporting the high vaults. Like Poblet, it is a royal pantheon for Aragonese kings, although to a lesser extent, and several men of fourteenth-century military fame also lie here.

You can wander about without a guide here, and stroll around the early gothic cloister lined with tombs, the chapter house, the refectory, the ruins of the old kitchen, and the remains of the royal palace. The oldest part of the abbey is the small romanesque chapel of the Trinity, the only part which remains from when the abbey was founded in 1158.

Visiting hours are 10.00 a.m.–1.00 p.m., 3.30 p.m.–6.00 p.m. (5.30 p.m. in autumn and winter). Tel. (977) 63 83 29.

Map 3F POBLET

The monastery of Santa Maria de Poblet is a colossal walled complex which still dominates the olive and fruit groves of the surrounding wide plain with an awesome majesty. It was founded in 1149 by Ramon Berenguer IV and you can appreciate its erstwhile power just from the rings of walls – no less than three surround the buildings. The first gate, **la Porta Daurada**, leads into the complex past a couple of chapels, and the hospices; the second, **la Porta Reial** is between the two vast hexagonal towers; and the third, built later, opens onto the church, which you can visit without a ticket if you are pressed for time.

The church is a fine Cistercian building of pale stone with high early gothic vaults, and guards the tombs of Catalan-Aragonese monarchs – Jaume I, Pedro IV the Ceremonious, Martí I, Alfonso II and others. The

Poblet Monastery

retablo is one of the key works of the Catalan renaissance, by Damià Forment.

You are guided round the monastery and the fifteenth-century royal quarters of King Martí by monks who are adept linguists (there is a permanent community of some thirty monks). As you walk round the beautiful romanesque/gothic cloisters and the square chapter house with its fine capitals, notice the sepulchres of past abbots amongst the flagstones. You are shown the huge wine cellars, a splendid kitchen, the refectory, the library, and upstairs the huge lofty dormitory. The collections of the museum are displayed in the *Palau del Rei Martí* (King Martí's palace).

This is one of the major cultural sights of Catalunya, so be prepared for lots of people in the summer season. *Visits run from 10.00 a.m.–12.30 p.m. and from 3.00 p.m.–6.00 p.m. (5.30 p.m. in autumn and winter). Tel. (977) 87 02 54.*

For restaurants you have lots of choice. From Santes Creus there are good restaurants closer to Barcelona, which you will find in the Penedès section of Chapter 2 (Pontons, Sant Martí Sarroca, etc.). I've talked about the restaurants near Poblet in Chapter 6 (Les Masies de Poblet, l'Espluga de Francolí, Valls, etc.).

Route 5 Muntanya de Montserrat Natural Park

Montserrat, religious and patriotic symbol of Catalunya, is an extraordinary and wonderful mountain quite unlike any other. It's strangely well-defined – a colossal ridge of knuckles that bursts out of the surrounding plain, only ten kilometres long and five kilometres wide, with quantities of finger-shaped peaks some of which reach up to nearly 1,240 m. The best views are from the north (around Manresa) or from the south (around the Penedès wine region), from where you can really appreciate the suddenness of the mountain and its uncanny incongruence with the surrounding countryside. Since 888 there has been a sanctuary here dedicated to the Mare de Déu de Montserrat, the patroness of Catalunya. (Many Catalan women are called 'Montse' for short.) The small black-faced Madonna is a gilded wooden figure dating from the twelfth century, known here as **la Moreneta**. Her shrine today is a monumental early twentieth century temple with a highly decorated neo-plateresque façade, which replaces the church ravaged by the Napoleonic forces in the early nineteenth century. Inside, she sits in a splendid silver niche up behind the altar, where a steady flow of people file through to pay her their respects. You need to get here for the 1.00 p.m. Salve Regina or the 6.45 p.m. vespers to enjoy the singing of the **Escolania** – the renowned boys' choir.

The monastery next door is an unlovely building – a great monotonous block housing a thriving community of some seventy monks. There are also a number of museums here: one dedicated to the study of the bible, another displaying archaeological finds from the mountain, and a couple of art galleries.

You need a whole day to enjoy Montserrat if you want to walk in the mountain as well. You can drive up to the sanctuary, or else park down by the railway station (trains come every two hours from Barcelona,

Plaça d'Espanya) and take the spectacular cable car up. The highest peak, Sant Jeroni, is some two hours' walk from the monastery through the pretty holm oak woods of the mountain. The first and last legs are hard going uphill with lots of steps, but it's well worth it – the excursion is a delight and the views marvellous. Most of the other peaks, with names like the Mummy, the Bishop's Belly, the Pregnant Woman, or the Enchanted Friars, are for the privileged few who know about rock-climbing, but as you walk you can certainly put a few names to the shapes – especially the Camel and the Elephant's trunk.

Make sure you take provisions and something to drink with you, as the restaurant, shops and cafés are all down by the monastery. You can get hold of a good walking map from the tourist office, Plaça de la Creu *Tel. (93) 835 02 51.*

Abat Cisneros
(HR)M *Plaça del Monestir (93) 835 02 01 Open all year*

A hotel without luxuries installed in a fifteenth-century building in the main square of the monastery complex – it's well worth staying here if you are attracted by the evening tranquility and early morning beauty of the surrounding rocky peaks.

Menú del dia 2,500 ptas; double room 7,700 ptas

There are a handful of good restaurants around the mountain – northwards to the tiny Cal Jepet, and southwards to the excellent Tall de Conill and the straightforward Nou Racó de la Queixalada.

Map E5 **SANT CRISTÒFOL DE CASTELLBELL**

➔ **Cal Jepet**
(R)M *Sant Cristòfol, Castellbell i Vilar (93) 835 72 72 Only open Sat. midday & eve., Sun. midday; cl. mid-Jul.–Sept.*

This is in the middle of nowhere – several km along the country road between Castellbell and the road leading from Manresa to Montserrat. The simple restaurant is housed in the upstairs and vaults of a small cottage set on the brow of a hill overlooking the mountain, which is spectacularly close (although there are no views from within the house). The ambience is rustic, with beamed ceilings, check tablecloths and decorative wild flowers on each table. It offers a short but explicit range of dishes: on the one hand the simplest country fare of grilled meats and sausages, and on the other, dishes of great sophistication. Its fame is local – the chef, Jaume Pastallé, is a charismatic television personality whose promotion of Catalan cuisine (*la Bona Cuina*) is much applauded. Here he maintains a humble profile, cooking very much 'en famille'. The finer line of cuisine here changes from weekend to weekend, dictated by the market and the fashion. Classic and creative Catalan cooking, stamped with the pedigree of an investigative enthusiast.

Allow 4,000 ptas

Arrowed for its simple country ambience and good cooking.

Map E5 CAPELLADES

Capellades is just to the south of the mountain, an important producer of paper in the eighteenth and nineteenth centuries. It preserves an interesting museum, the **Museu Molí Paperer**, in the old mill over the river where you can appreciate the developing process of paper-making from ancient times to today, with museum pieces from the East and Latin America. Downstairs they use the river to power the mill and you can watch the craft of making paper by hand. It makes quite an unusual present to take back home.

Tall de Conill
(RH)M *Plaça Àngel Guimerà, 11 (93) 801 01 30 Cl. 1–15 Jul., Sun. eve., Mon.*

On the other side of the river from the museum, down the next street, you come to a little square in which the restaurant stands. It is also a small hotel, modern and comfortable like the restaurant, which means that after a superb dinner you needn't rush off if you don't feel like it.

This is a classic of Catalan cuisine, where the chef Jaume Saumell works the great traditional dishes of the region with the art of a passionate chef. Strangely for a restaurant named after rabbits, his menu is based on a daily delivery of the freshest fish, although there is a good selection of meat dishes too. His creations range from onions stuffed with *bacallà*, little *piquillo* peppers filled with *marisc*, to an exquisite dish of sea bass or a splendid *paella*. His *bollabessa* is extraordinary. For meat-lovers, try the rabbit *en salsa*. The menu reads simply – the sophistication is not in the ingredients but in the skill of the chef.

Allow 4,000 ptas

Map E5 MASQUEFA

A few kilometres from Capellades heading towards Barcelona.

Nou Racó de la Queixalada
(R)S *Ctra Capellades-Martorell, Km 17 (93) 772 51 33 Cl. Tues., last week Sept.–first week Oct.*

This is a simple place – a restaurant to come to for a straightforward country meal. The rooms are large and light, with check tablecloths and an open, unpretentious ambience. In *calçot* season it's packed every weekend, and out of season there is roast kid, shoulder of lamb, grilled rabbit with *allioli*, and *bacallà* in abundance. *Pa amb tomàquet* is done by you at the table. Peppers, aubergines and artichokes are delicious, grilled over charcoal. *Crema catalana* for pud.

Allow 2,500–3,000 ptas

Route 6 Sant Llorenç de Munt Natural Park

This splendid mountain rises just beyond **Terrassa**, and is crossed by the winding road which leads on to Talamanca and Santpedor. A good forty-minute walk from Can Pobla will bring you to the magnificent romanesque monastery of Sant Llorenç de Munt, commanding a marvellous view from the highest peak (La Mola, 1,095 m). There's a restaurant here. The grey rock juts out abruptly, in rounded forms caused by heavy erosion, and the mountain is clothed with pine, oak and holm oak, and thickly covered with bramble. There are lovely footpaths here, easily taken from any of the plentiful stopping places on the road through, and on your way you'll surely come across ruins of a castle or church that used to guard the medieval route from Barcelona to Manresa. If you return via Manresa, you can enjoy stunning views of the mountain of Montserrat as you curve south towards Barcelona.

Information office: Coll d'Estenalles (93) 831 73 00 Open 10.00 a.m.–3.00 p.m.

Map E6 **MATADEPERA**

El Celler
(R)M *Gaudí, 2 (93) 787 08 57 Cl. Sun. eve., Tues., 1–15 Aug., 15–30 Nov.*

This is a fine restaurant on the corner of the road leading towards Caldes de Montbui, with a very high local reputation for the skillful cooking of its chef, Lluís Bernils. His dishes are creative and thoughtful, based firmly in the Catalan tradition but with up-to-date sophistication and culinary technique. *Bacallà* with baby broad beans, *rogers en escabet*, saddle of rabbit with wild mushrooms – and delicate desserts to finish. His dishes are beautifully presented, to be accompanied by a choice from an impressive cellar.

Carte approx. 3,500–4,500 ptas; menú degustació 5,400 ptas

Map 6E **TERRASSA**

This is a commercial and industrial town, not very attractive for a tourist visit, but it has an ancient centre dating from pre-Roman times. Here it preserves a number of fine buildings – the visigothic-romanesque churches of Santa Maria, Sant Pere and Sant Miquel, and an ancient castle and monastery. There is also a textile museum with an interesting collection of fabrics, carpets, religious pieces and weaving tools.

Museu Tèxtil, C/ Salmerón, 25 Open 9.30 a.m.–1.00 p.m & 4.00 p.m.–7.00 p.m., Sun 10.00 p.m.–2.00 a.m.

Map E6 SANT CUGAT DEL VALLÈS

A small residential town just over the hill from Barcelona, which treasures a splendid romanesque Benedictine abbey, dating originally from the ninth century. The church is magnificent, tall with a fine gothic eight-sided dome and eleventh-century bell tower. The romanesque cloisters have spectacular carved capitals.

Route 7 Montseny Natural Park

This is a beautiful wooded mountain just an hour north of Barcelona, soaring above the two main roads which run south from **Girona** and **Vic**. At its highest it reaches some 1,700 metres, and at its lowest only a few metres above sea level, so the trees range from oak, cork and beech to conifer and juniper. There are two routes which explore it – one goes through **Sant Esteve de Palautordera**, via the village of **Montseny** to **Tona** and the other, more spectacularly, goes from **Sant Celoni** via the hermitage of **Santa Fe** and **Viladrau**. This is great walking and mushroom-hunting country, full of red squirrels and birds.

To reach the most striking viewpoint (if the weather is not playing havoc) turn off at **Fontmartina**, about nineteen kilometres from Sant Celoni, where a track will take you up towards the **Turó de l'Home** (1,712 m), the highest peak here. The other peak, Matagalls, is an hour's uphill hike from the Montseny road, leaving from the Coll Formic, several kilometres beyond the village. The castle hamlet of **El Brull** is a popular starting point for walks.

Information office: Fontmartina (93) 847 51 02 Open 10.00 a.m.–2.00 p.m.; Santa Fe (93) 847 51 13 Open 10.00 a.m.–5.00 p.m.

In Sant Celoni one of the greatest chefs of Catalunya has his kitchen, and there are a couple of inviting hotels and a welcoming restaurant up in the Montseny park, where the herbs, wild mushrooms, honey and fresh cheese can be savoured.

Map D7 SANT CELONI

This has always been a departure point for a reconnaissance of the forests of Montseny, but of late its gastronomic fame has spread far beyond the country borders.

➔ El Racó de Can Fabes
(R)L *C/ Sant Joan, 6 (93) 867.28.51 Cl. Sun. eve., Mon.*

A wonderful restaurant housed in a small seventeenth-century cottage in a back corner of the town, beneath the herb-filled mountain of Montseny. Santi Santamaria has the unusual distinction of having never worked outside his own kitchen – his art and creation is therefore highly individual, being bred exclusively from his own personal experience and that handed down from his family. The restaurant is cosy and intimate – several small rooms with stone walls and polished wooden floors, furnished with linen-clothed tables and antique furniture. The glass front of the kitchen gives you a glimpse of the meticulous care with which the dishes are prepared. An exquisite carte, a marvellous wine and an experience of the finest cuisine that you will never forget.

Garlanded with three Michelin stars, and a Relais Châteaux member.
Menú gastronòmic 9,000 ptas; carte 10,000 ptas
Arrowed for excellence.

Map D7 **SANTA FE**

Sant Marçal
(R)S *Sanctuario de Sant Marçal (93) 847 30 43 Cl. weekday eves.*

High up in the mountain, some six kilometres beyond Santa Fe, this is an old place, tucked in beside a tiny romanesque chapel. When I first ate here there was no electricity, and the dark room was lit by candles. Today it is only a little more modern, with a additional gallery room looking out over the forest. The food is the same though – pâtés, warming stews of wild boar or beef, roasts of lamb or kid, jugs of strong wine and good mountain cheeses. If you haven't booked, be prepared to wait.

Allow 2,500–3,000 ptas

Map D7 **VILADRAU**

Hostal de la Gloria
(HR)M *C/ Torreventosa, 12 (93) 884 90 34 Cl 22 Dec.–7 Jan.*

This is a pretty and thoroughly welcoming hotel close to the centre of the village, set on the northern edge of the massif with views which stretch across to the Matagalls peak. The house is bright and refreshing, with a big terrace onto the garden, and lots of space for lawns, flowers and a swimming pool. It's a family place, unpretentious and comfortable, with a good country restaurant.

Double room 6,500 ptas

Map D7 MONTSENY

This little old village merits a short wander, and there are shops selling the local honey and herbs, as well as a couple of restaurants and bars. The two hotels are outside the village, one on either side.

Can Barrina
(HR)M *Ctra Palautordera-Montseny, Km 12,6 (93) 847 30 65 Open all year*

An abrupt, downhill turning off the main road brings you to this peaceful spot, with views which sweep down to the foot of the Montseny. The house dates from 1620, and its age shows in the narrow stone stairways (no lifts), the small windows and the successive chain of thick-walled rooms downstairs. The food is home style, pâtés, rabbit cooked with the local herbs, *botifarra amb escalivada*, stuffed cabbage, *bacallà*. The simple rooms overlook the pool and garden, which continues into the surrounding woodland.

Double room 9,500 ptas

Sant Bernat
(HR)M *Sant Bernat, Montseny (93) 847 30 11 Open all year*

About 10 minutes beyond the village of Montseny, a turning uphill takes you winding up to this ivy-covered house, which has the romanesque chapel to Sant Bernat in its garden. The views from the terrace and balconied bedrooms are superb. This is a comfortable place, with walks which lead off into the woods in all directions. At weekends the dining room is popular – a place for local cooking, with good salads, chicken and prune casserole, herby roast lamb, beef and mushroom stews and rabbit.

Menu 2,700 ptas; double room 11,725 ptas

There are several towns between Barcelona and Montseny. Sabadell and Granollers are perhaps better by-passed, although each has a good restaurant, but the quiet old centre of Caldes de Montbui makes a nice stop.

Map 6E CALDES DE MONTBUI

This is a tranquil town, mostly pedestrianised, with the ruins of the old Roman baths in its centre. Here the water from the **Font del Lleó** comes out at over 70°C. Several spa hotels are dotted around either treasuring their late nineteenth-century decoration, or flaunting their up-to-date installations.

One of Barcelona's most traditional excursions can be reached just beyond the town, turning off at **Sant Feliu de Codines** towards **Sant Miquel del Fai.** For centuries, this has been a small paradise of woodland, surrounding the clear pool of water formed by the Rossinyol river which brims over into a spectacular waterfall. Beneath there is a cave-shelter, the chapel to Sant Miquel, and beyond that you can reach a second waterfall. Today, the beauty of the area is radically altered after a terrible forest fire in 1994 destroyed the shrubs and forest, but the rocks and water still hold their own as beautiful landscape.

Balneario Broquetas
(HR)M *Plaça Font del Lleó, 1 (93) 865 01 00 Open all year*

This spa hotel opens onto the central square, with a generous expanse of landscaped garden behind, and some very fine Modernist tile-work within. The garden, full of trees and shrubs, also contains a swimming pool and sports facilities, and the hotel is generally equipped for stays of several days. If you come for the treatments, it offers all you could wish. The restaurant serves good Catalan food.

Carte approx. 3,000 ptas; double room 10,000–12,000 ptas

Map 7E GRANOLLERS

This is not a good destination for a traveller, being a small but concentrated commercial town with frustrating parking problems.

In the centre there is a splendid sixteenth-century covered grain-market with fifteen Tuscan columns, which bustles with life on Thursdays when there is a huge street market.

Fonda Europa
(RH)M *C/Anselm Clavé, 1 (93) 870 03 12 Open all year*

Dating from 1714, this is hailed as the first *hostal* of Catalunya with a history of seven generations, and it basks in its air of old-world tradition. The café and diningrooms, which are always packed, are lined with old pictures and furniture, and upstairs the few bedrooms have been refurbished to maintain the same look of distinction. You'll be offered the great Catalan country dishes – *cap i pota*, duck with figs, civet of wild boar or venison, and good wholesome desserts of the house. Be prepared for slow service. It's on the old main road, now a one-way street, crossing the centre of the town. Parking is no problem –it has its own car park.

Carte approx. 3,500–4,000 ptas; double room 10,000 ptas

Map 6E SABADELL

An industrial town of some size, known years back as the Manchester of Catalunya, where the textile, metal and chemical industries are important. The **Amics de l'Òpera** of Sabadell put on operas annually, and travel to the capital and on to provincial towns. Check where and when they are performing – the quality is first-rate and the ambience delightfully refreshing.

Marcel
(R)M-L *C/ Advocat Cira, 38–40 (93) 725 23 00 Cl. Sat. lunch, Sun., Aug., Easter*

This is a small but highly distinguished restaurant, in the centre of the town, serving French haute cuisine. It's cosy and welcoming, finished in polished wood and upholstery, with Fausto Terradó in the kitchens while his wife runs the dining room. You might try the truffled foie gras, gigot of duck or the fricassée of scallops with a leek confit. In season, there are superb creations of game. The dishes are original, elaborate, and produced with the culinary skill of a superb chef. The cellar list makes interesting reading.

Allow 5,000–6,000 ptas.

MAPS

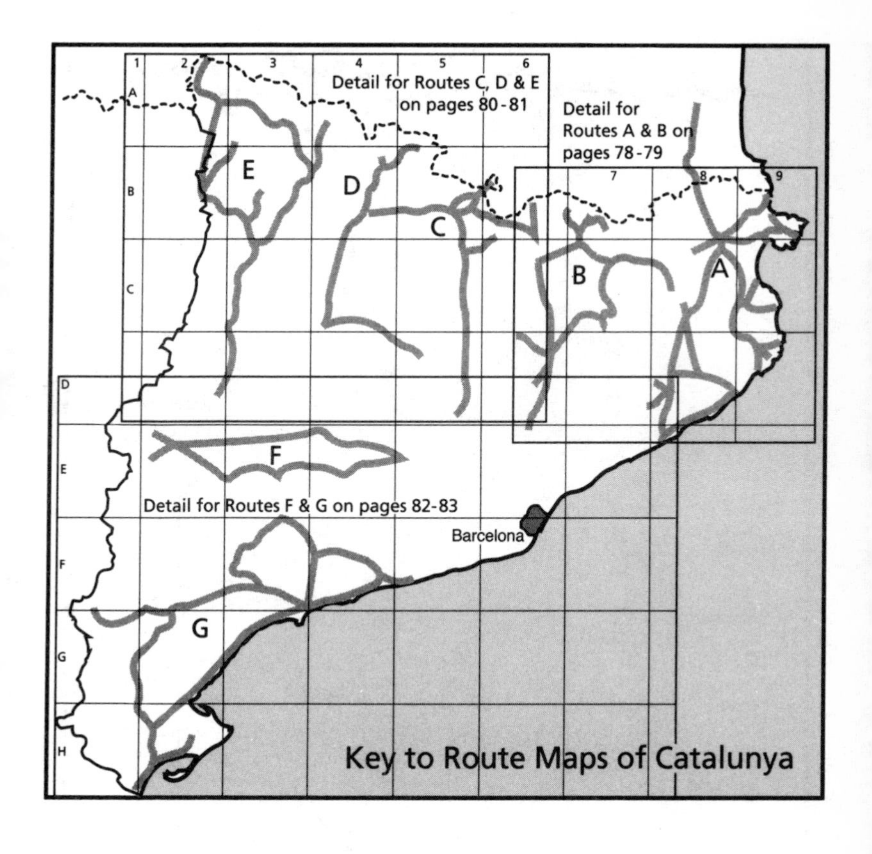

1
2
3
4
5
6
7
8
9
A
B
C
D
E
F
G
H
Detail for Routes C, D & E on pages 80 - 81
Detail for Routes A & B on pages 78 - 79
Detail for Routes F & G on pages 82-83
Barcelona
Key to Route Maps of Catalunya

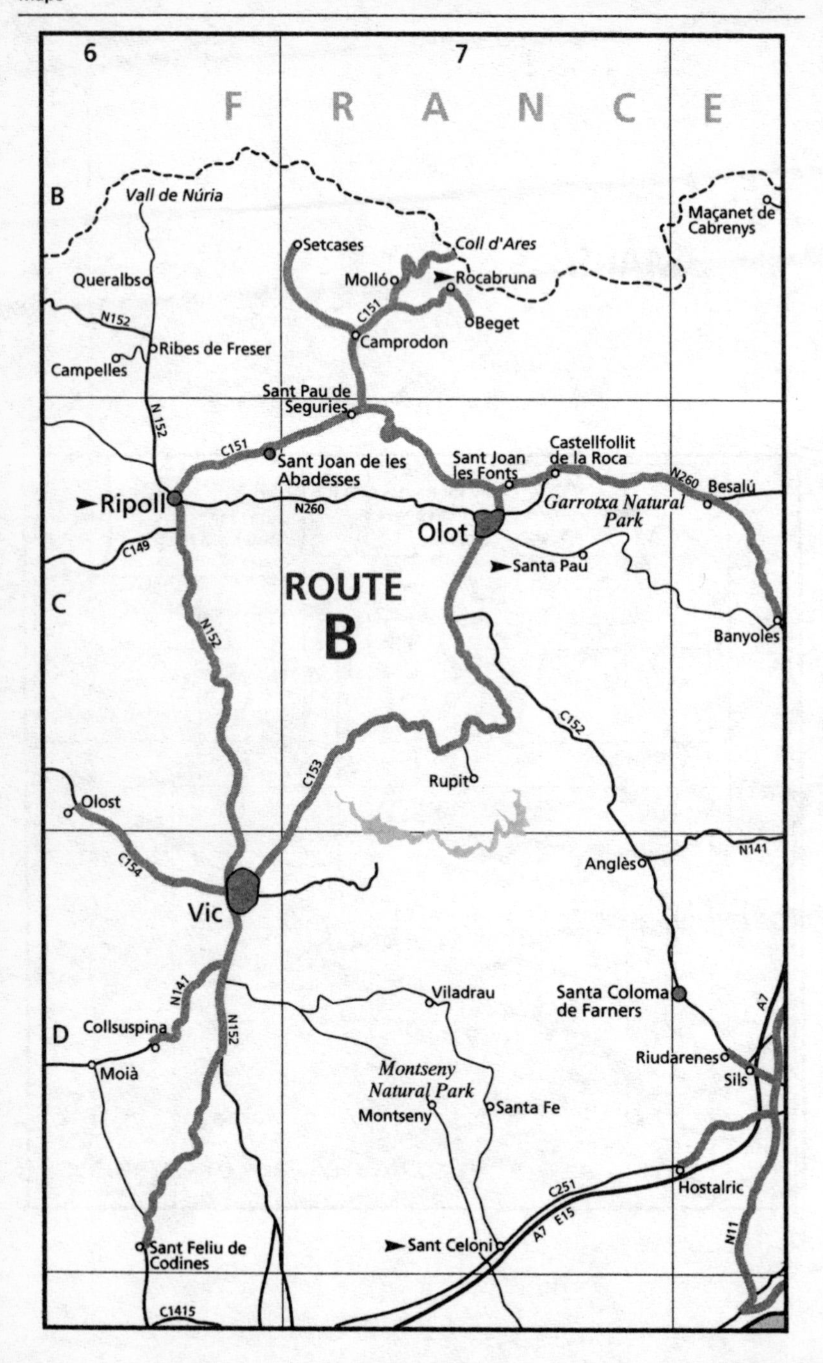

6
7
FRANCE
B
C
D
Vall de Núria
Maçanet de Cabrenys
Setcases
Coll d'Ares
Queralbs
Molló
Rocabruna
N152
C151
Beget
Ribes de Freser
Camprodon
Campelles
Sant Pau de Seguries
N 152
C151
Sant Joan de les Abadesses
Sant Joan les Fonts
Castellfollit de la Roca
N260
Besalú
Ripoll
N260
Garrotxa Natural Park
Olot
C149
Santa Pau
ROUTE B
Banyoles
N152
C152
C153
Rupit
Olost
N141
Anglès
C154
Vic
N141
Santa Coloma de Farners
A7
Viladrau
N152
Collsuspina
Riudarenes
Moià
Sils
Montseny Natural Park
Montseny
Santa Fe
C251
Hostalric
A7 E15
N11
Sant Celoni
Sant Feliu de Codines
C1415

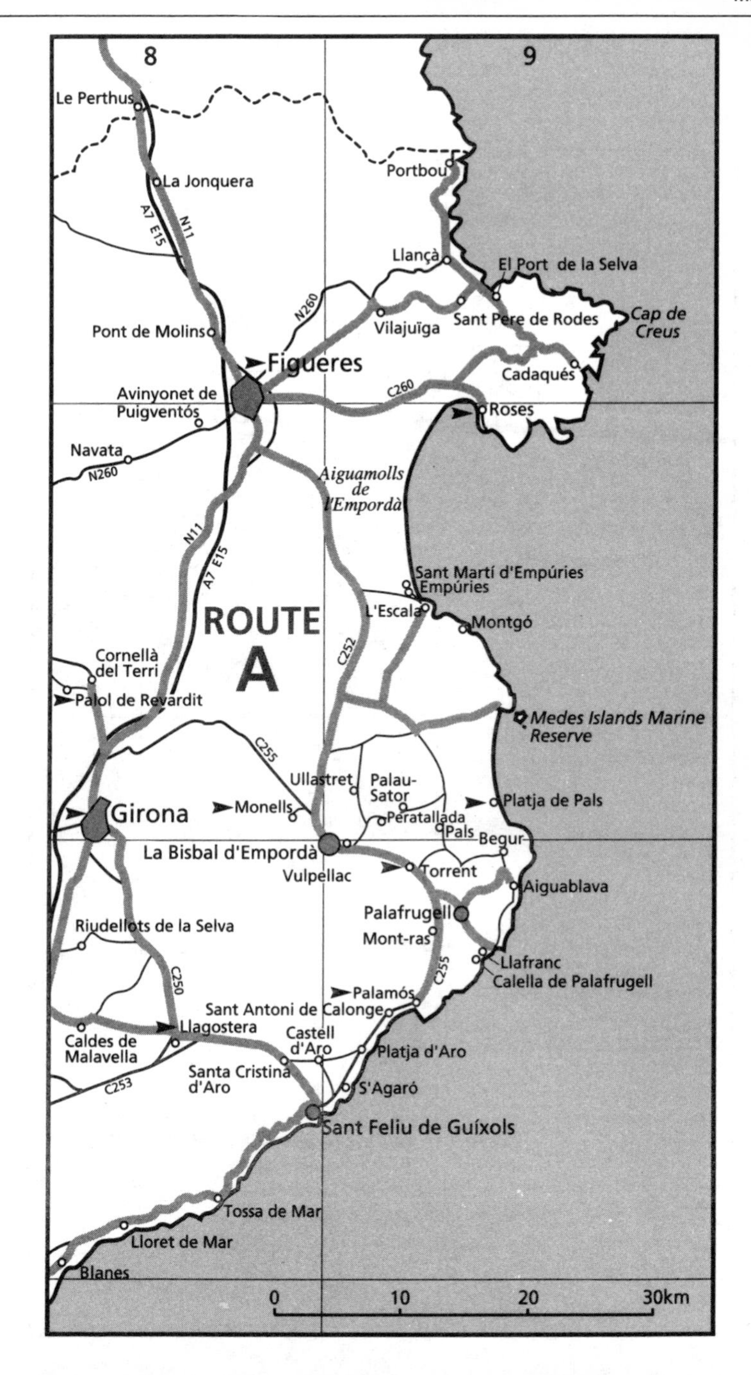

8
9
Le Perthus
La Jonquera
A7 E15
N11
Portbou
Llançà
El Port de la Selva
N260
Pont de Molins
Vilajuïga
Sant Pere de Rodes
Cap de Creus
Figueres
Cadaqués
Avinyonet de Puigventós
C260
Roses
Navata
N260
Aiguamolls de l'Empordà
N11
A7 E15
Sant Martí d'Empúries
Empúries
L'Escala
Montgó
ROUTE A
C252
Cornellà del Terri
Palol de Revardit
Medes Islands Marine Reserve
C255
Ullastret
Palau-Sator
Platja de Pals
Girona
Monells
Peratallada
Pals
La Bisbal d'Empordà
Begur
Vulpellac
Torrent
Aiguablava
Palafrugell
Riudellots de la Selva
Mont-ras
Llafranc
Calella de Palafrugell
C250
C255
Palamós
Sant Antoni de Calonge
Llagostera
Castell d'Aro
Caldes de Malavella
Platja d'Aro
Santa Cristina d'Aro
C253
S'Agaró
Sant Feliu de Guíxols
Tossa de Mar
Lloret de Mar
Blanes
0
10
20
30km

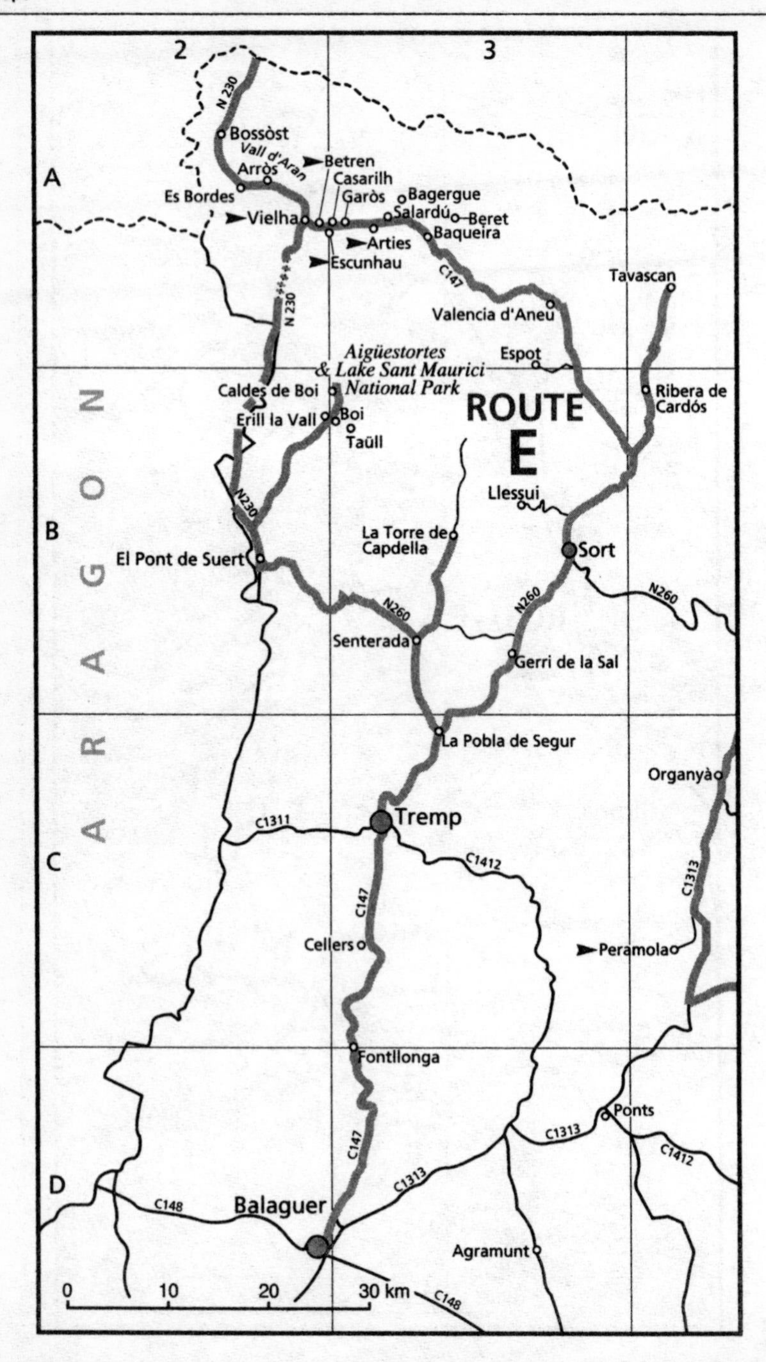

2
3
A
B
C
D
ARAGON
ROUTE E
N 230
Bossòst
Vall d'Aran
Betren
Arròs
Casarilh
Es Bordes
Garòs
Bagergue
Vielha
Salardú
Beret
Arties
Baqueira
Escunhau
C147
Tavascan
Valencia d'Aneu
Aigüestortes & Lake Sant Maurici National Park
Espot
Caldes de Boi
Ribera de Cardós
Erill la Vall
Boi
Taüll
N230
Llessui
La Torre de Capdella
Sort
El Pont de Suert
N260
Senterada
Gerri de la Sal
La Pobla de Segur
Organyà
Tremp
C1311
C1412
C1313
Cellers
Peramola
Fontllonga
Ponts
C148
Balaguer
Agramunt
0
10
20
30 km

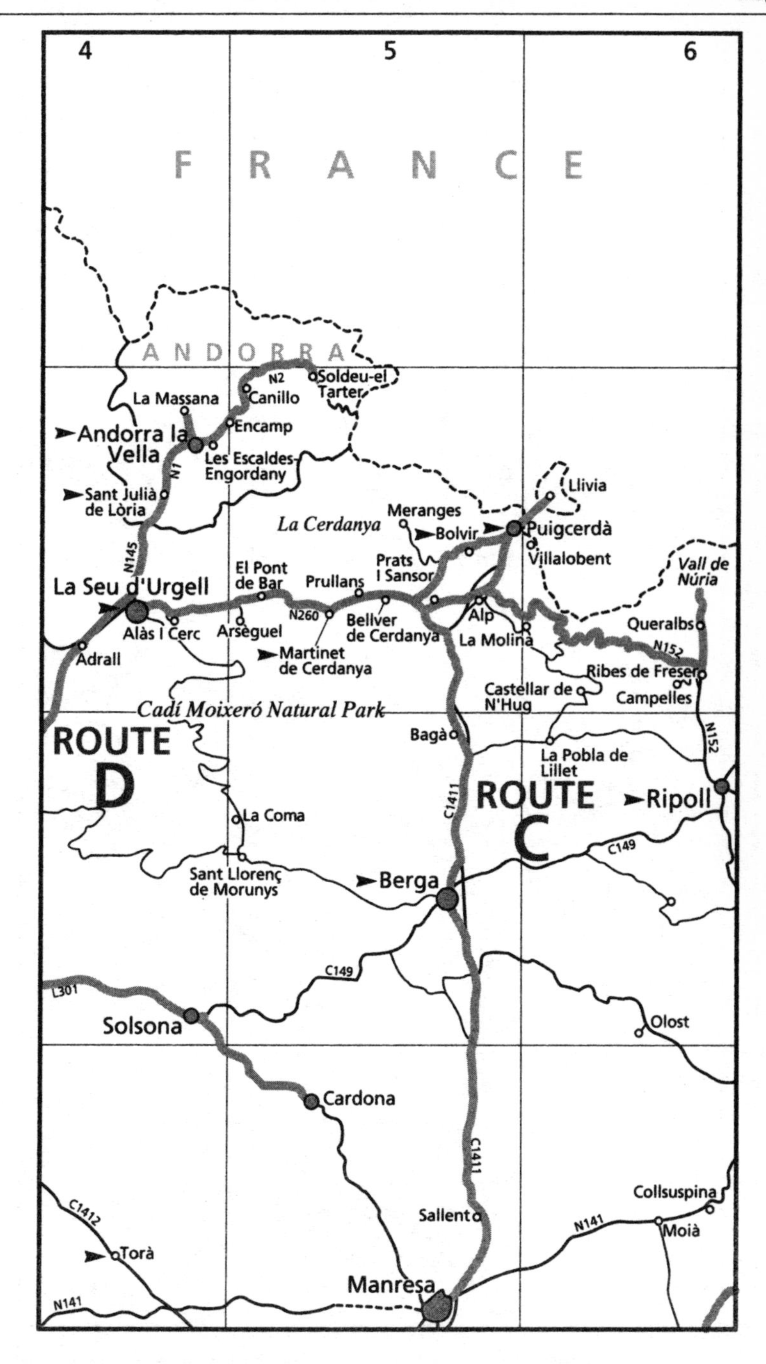

4
5
6
FRANCE
ANDORRA
N2
Soldeu-el Tarter
La Massana
Canillo
Encamp
Andorra la Vella
Les Escaldes-Engordany
N1
Sant Julià de Lòria
Llivia
Meranges
La Cerdanya
Bolvir
Puigcerdà
Villalobent
N145
El Pont de Bar
Prats i Sansor
Vall de Núria
La Seu d'Urgell
Prullans
Alp
Queralbs
Alàs i Cerc
Arsèguel
N260
Bellver de Cerdanya
La Molina
N152
Adrall
Martinet de Cerdanya
Ribes de Freser
Castellar de N'Hug
Campelles
Cadí Moixeró Natural Park
ROUTE D
Bagà
La Pobla de Lillet
N152
C1411
ROUTE C
Ripoll
La Coma
C149
Sant Llorenç de Morunys
Berga
C149
L301
Solsona
Olost
Cardona
C1411
Collsuspina
C1412
Sallent
N141
Moià
Torà
Manresa
N141

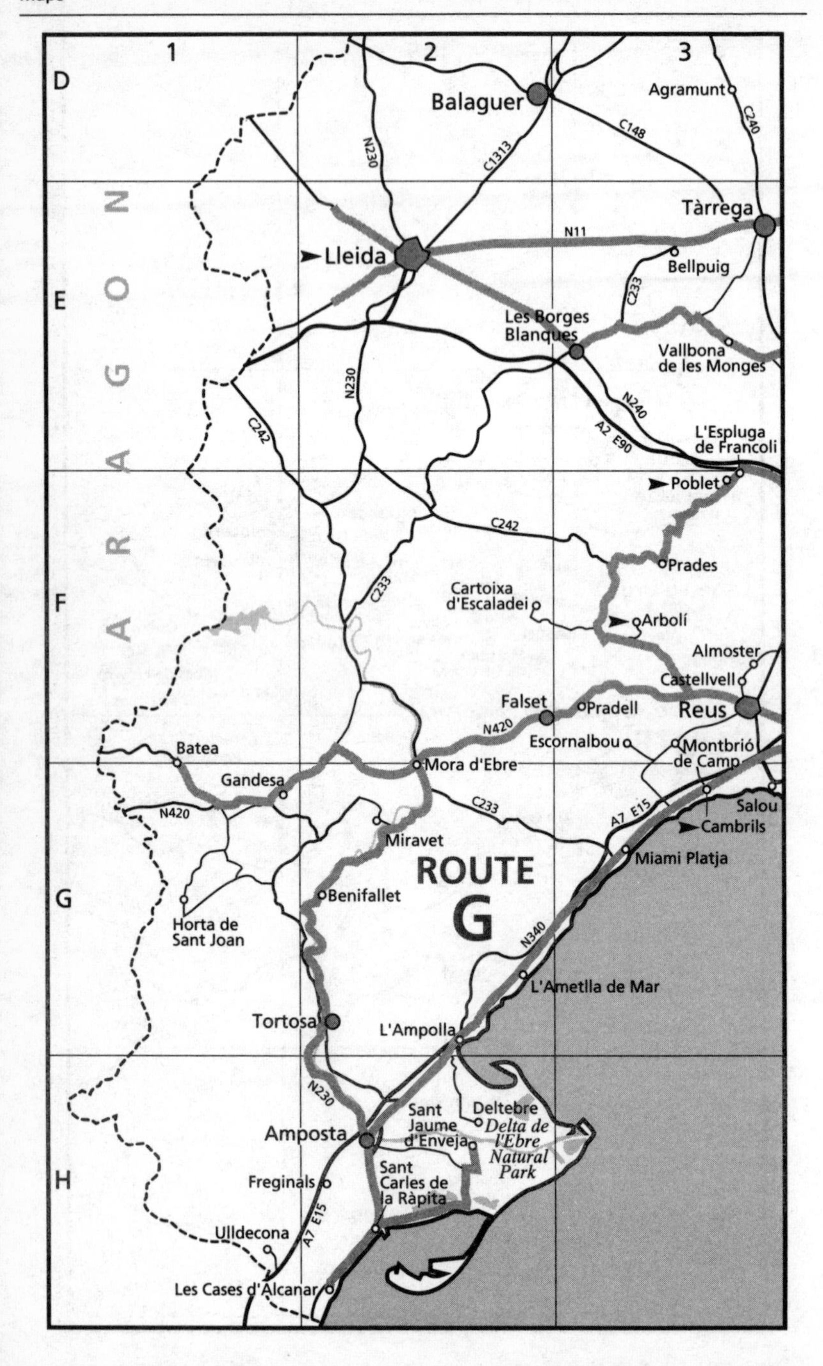
1
2
3
D
E
F
G
H
A R A G O N
Balaguer
Agramunt
C148
C240
N230
C1313
Tàrrega
N11
Lleida
Bellpuig
C233
Les Borges Blanques
Vallbona de les Monges
N230
C242
N240
A2 E90
L'Espluga de Francoli
Poblet
C242
Prades
C233
Cartoixa d'Escaladei
Arbolí
Almoster
Castellvell
Falset
Pradell
Reus
N420
Escornalbou
Montbrió de Camp
Batea
Mora d'Ebre
Gandesa
N420
C233
Salou
A7 E15
Cambrils
Miravet
Miami Platja
ROUTE G
Benifallet
Horta de Sant Joan
N340
L'Ametlla de Mar
Tortosa
L'Ampolla
N230
Sant Jaume d'Enveja
Deltebre
Delta de l'Ebre Natural Park
Amposta
Freginals
Sant Carles de la Ràpita
Ulldecona
A7 E15
Les Cases d'Alcanar

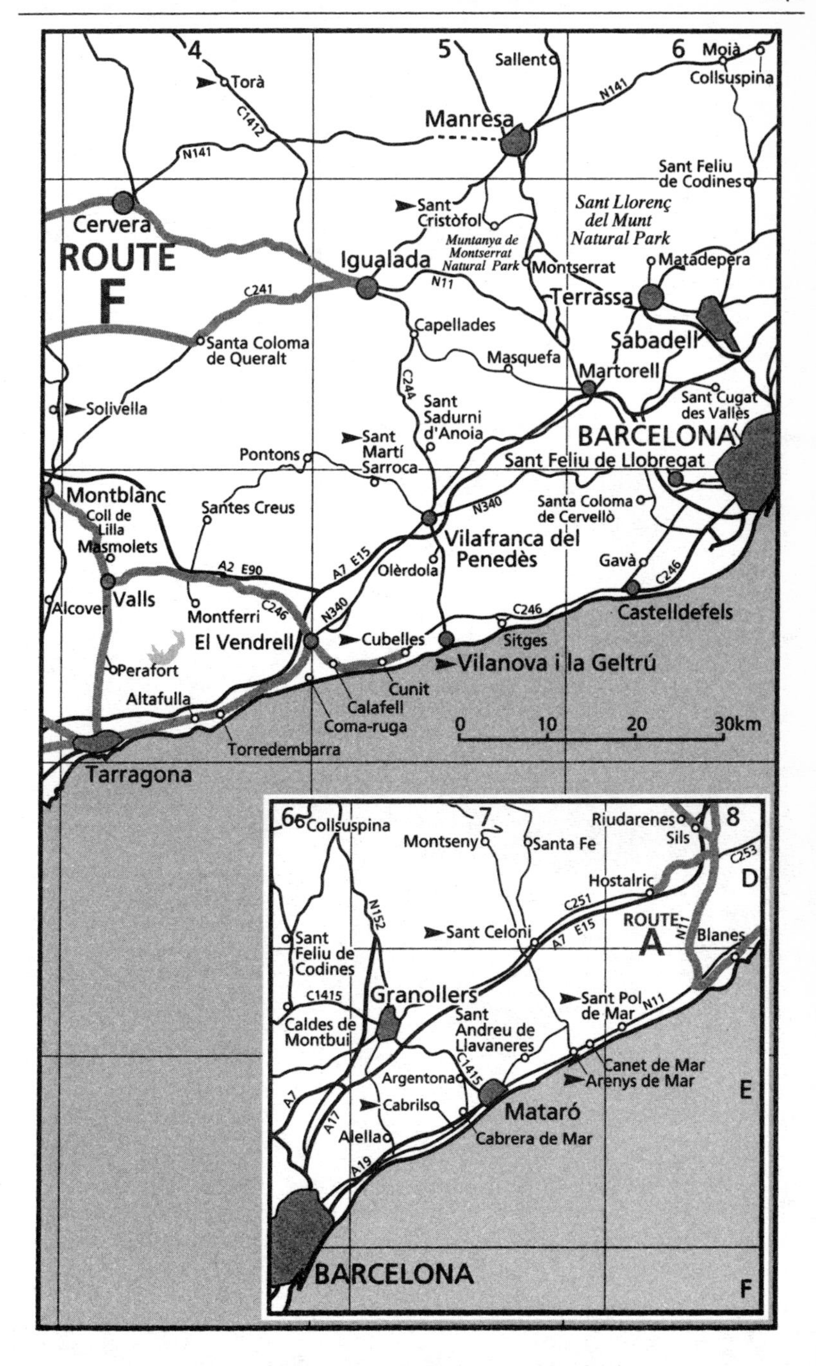

4
5
6
Torà
Sallent
Moià
Collsuspina
N141
C1412
Manresa
N141
Sant Feliu
de Codines
Sant Cristòfol
Sant Llorenç
del Munt
Natural Park
Cervera
ROUTE
F
Muntanya de
Montserrat
Natural Park
Igualada
Montserrat
Matadepera
C241
N11
Terrassa
Capellades
Santa Coloma
de Queralt
Sabadell
Masquefa
Martorell
C244
Sant Cugat
des Vallès
Solivella
Sant
Sadurni
d'Anoia
Sant
Martí
Sarroca
BARCELONA
Pontons
Sant Feliu de Llobregat
Montblanc
Santes Creus
N340
Santa Coloma
de Cervellò
Coll de
Lilla
Vilafranca del
Penedès
Masmolets
A7 E15
A2 E90
Olèrdola
Gavà
C246
Alcover
Valls
C246
Montferri
N340
C246
Castelldefels
El Vendrell
Cubelles
Sitges
Perafort
Vilanova i la Geltrú
Cunit
Altafulla
Calafell
Coma-ruga
0
10
20
30km
Torredembarra
Tarragona
6
Collsuspina
7
Riudarenes
8
Montseny
Santa Fe
Sils
C253
Hostalric
D
N152
C251
ROUTE
A
Sant Celoni
A7 E15
N11
Blanes
Sant
Feliu de
Codines
C1415
Granollers
Sant Pol
de Mar
N11
Caldes de
Montbui
Sant
Andreu de
Llavaneres
Canet de Mar
Argentona
C1415
Arenys de Mar
E
A7
Cabrils
Mataró
A17
Alella
Cabrera de Mar
A19
BARCELONA
F

3 THE COSTA BRAVA AND INLAND GIRONA

ROUTE A FROM PERPIGNAN (COASTAL)

* Figueres and east to Cap de Creus, Aiguamolls de l'Empordà Natural Park
* Girona and east to L'Escala, Medes Islands Marine Reserve, Palafrugell, Palamós, Sant Feliu de Guíxols
* Girona south-east to Tossa de Mar, Blanes, Hostalric

Figueres and east to Cap de Creus, Aiguamolls de l'Empordà Natural Park

The old way into Spain from France, before the motorway was built, was by **Le Perthus** and over the mountain to **La Jonquera.** The motorway runs parallel with this route, which has itself been enormously improved and is now a very fine road. If you're not in a tearing hurry, it's much nicer to take the old road and you can stop when you feel like it.

The French town of Le Perthus is not much fun, and neither is La Jonquera. This is the principal Spanish customs post and is always full of big container lorries, but you pass through it quickly and the countryside itself is stunning. The first real stop is the market town of **Figueres,** and after that you have choices. Left to the **Cap de Creus** with its pretty coastal villages, right to the beautiful wooded volcanic riches of La **Garrotxa,** or straight on to the historic splendours of **Girona.** The area which swells outwards to the coast from the city is dotted with medieval villages, and the rocky coastline is a jigsaw of dozens of small coves. Down towards Barcelona, the countryside is lush and green practically all the way.

There are two other Entrées that might attract you, but both are hard work: the tortuous coastal road leading to **Portbou** and on to the pretty village of **El Port de la Selva** (see below); or the tiny mountain pass beyond Amélie-les-bains which crosses from Coustouges to the mountain village of **Maçanet de Cabrenys.**

Map 8B MAÇANET DE CABRENYS

This is a refreshing summer retreat for those who know it, and is favoured by a surprising warmth in the winter months. Surrounded by woodland of cork trees, holm oak, ash and ferns, its old centre is now thinly extended by small new holiday villas.

Els Caçadors
(HR)M *Urbanització Casa Nova (972) 54 41 36 Open all year*

The hotel has been here for thirty years, mainly patronised by Catalans who go yearly for a breath of mountain air. The main part of the hotel is a old stone-walled building, with pretty arched ground-floor rooms which house the restaurant. The food is regional fare: wild mushrooms, *bacallà*, grilled meats, lots of game, the typical pork dishes, and braised duck. The desserts are healthy, made with whatever fruit is in season.

Beside the hotel there's a mountain stream, and the mature garden with its huge trees crosses to the other side where there is a pool and tennis court. The eighteen rooms are likely to be taken by regulars in August, but in other months you might get one. Only full- or half-board.

Rest. allow 3,000 ptas; half-board 6,000 ptas

Map 8B **PONT DE MOLINS**

Just before you get to Figueres, there's a turning inland towards this riverside village. Continue through and keep going along the river for a couple of kilometres towards Les Escaules and you'll reach an old *masia*.

El Molí
(RH)M *Ctra Pont de Molins – Les Escaules (972) 52 80 11 Hotel Cl. Nov.–Easter; rest. open all year, Cl. Tues. eve., Wed.*

This is an eighteenth century stone watermill which was still working thirty years ago. The restaurant is attractive, in a long stone-vaulted gallery with beamed ceiling and huge windows. The bedrooms above are charming, with small windows overlooking the river and woods, and period furniture collected by the family Lladó. If you're lucky your wooden bed will be a splendid Isabelline antique (with modern mattress, of course) the chest of drawers will be a fine old piece decorated with marquetry, and the table will be topped with marble. The restaurant is very popular with French visitors, and serves good local produce – particuarly the fine selection of *embotits* which arrive at your table hanging from a rack so that you can cut as much as you wish. The carte also includes traditional dishes of snails, magret of duck, and roast lamb.

Menú del dia 1,450 ptas, 2,400 ptas; carte approx. 3,000 ptas

Map 8B **FIGUERES**

This is the central market town of the surrounding fertile plain, with ghastly traffic to match. It's pleasant to visit on shopping days, when you can feel the true Catalan character in the smart pedestrian zones or in the small vegetable shops in the side streets. The modernist buildings and the *rambla* are evidence of the eighteenth-century prosperity of the town, which it still enjoys. On Sundays it is almost completely closed and there is liveliness only around the **Teatre-Museu Dalí** – one of the most visited of Catalunya's tourist attractions. Here you can see some wonderful paintings and sketches, sculptures and curious decorative objects by Salvador Dalí. It is interesting and great fun, though often terribly crowded.

Teatre-Museu Dalí (972) 51 19 76 Oct.–Jun. open 10.30 a.m.–6.00 p.m., Cl. Mon.; Jul.–Sept. open every day 9.00 a.m.–9.00 p.m.

Durán
(HR)M *C/ Lasauca, 5 (972) 50 12 50 Open all year*

A traditional hotel in the centre of town, comfortable and well-arranged, which has been in the Durán family for generations. There is a garage for your car, which is a great advantage as parking in Figueres is difficult. The restaurant is famous all over Catalunya – it's big, fashionable, and traditional in the best possible way. The dining room is arched with those typical wide Catalan arches, all outlined with old attractive ceramic plates and bowls. The chairs are upright, painted in a Catalan style, and the whole effect is elegant and comfortable. The staff are very welcoming and the food is, of course, excellent. *Cuina catalana* (traditional Catalan cooking), with some inventions of their own, such as *guatlla farcit amb foie gras i passes* (stuffed quail), meatballs with *sípia*. Fish is good, and the locally-produced meats are well-known, served here grilled or *a la brasa*.

Menú del dia 1,600 ptas; carte approx. 3,000–4,000 ptas; double room 5,800 ptas

Casa Jeroni
(R)S *C/ Castelló, 36 (972) 50 09 83 Cl. Sun., 1–15 Nov.*

A very simple restaurant in the centre of Figueres, beside the open marketplace. Although it looks dark and sombre, it's a lively place to eat with homely food which includes all the local favourites: *rossejat de fideus*, rabbit with little peppers and tomato, braised beef with wild mushrooms, and good puds – *crema catalana* and preserved figs with walnuts.

Menú del dia 950 ptas

➔ **Ampurdán**
(RH)L *Antiga carretera a Franca (972) 50 05 62 Open all year*

Just a few minutes outside the town. This is a famous hotel and restaurant which enjoys a very high reputation, and so it should. The rooms and amenities are all that you could expect of a high-class hotel and the restaurant is outstanding. It's another family business, and the executive chef, Sr Jaume Subirós, son-in-law of the founder, is supremely talented and inventive. I've eaten here several times, and his *menú del dia* is always attractive and always changing. Special dishes included in the spring carte were: a salad of skate with a sherry vinaigrette, a warm mousse of asparagus with watercress sauce among the starters; tunny with fresh fennel and wild mushrooms, *suquet de nero amb patatas*, for fish; rack of lamb with rosemary, aubergine and anchovies, and other excellent meat dishes; followed by an exquisite *pastís de formatge fresc* (bilberries) or wonderful sorbets of mint and of bitter almonds.

Menú del dia 3,650 ptas (four courses); carte approx. 5,000–6,000 ptas; Double room 9,500–11,000 ptas

Arrowed for its longstanding creative cuisine.

Map 8C AVINYONET DE PUIGVENTÓS

Mas Pau

(RH)M *Ctra Figueres – Besalú (972) 54 61 54 Cl. 15 Jan.–15 Mar., Sun. eve., Mon.; Open every day Jul., Aug., Sept.*

Not in the village itself, but on the main road.

Principally a restaurant, but there are six rooms and one suite, all excellently appointed, a swimming pool, and the gardens are quite lovely. The restaurant is installed in a splendid ivy-covered seventeenth-century mansion and has a roofed terrace for outdoor eating in the summer. It's impressively decorated inside both downstairs and up with a mixture of antique furniture which gives each room its own particular character. There are several small dining rooms, each high-ceilinged with its own style of period chairs, heraldic paintings, old chests, and fireplaces. Chef Xavier Sagristá varies his carte according to what he finds in the market. It's both original and classical, with a definite touch of sophistication. A super place to stop.

Menú del dia 3,000 ptas; carte approx. 4,000 ptas; double room 8,000 ptas

If you choose to visit the volcanic natural park of La **Garrotxa**, you can get there very easily from here, driving via the charming medieval town of **Besalú** (see Route B) which is only some twenty minutes from Figueres. On the way, there's a simple restaurant tucked into the woods.

Map 8C NAVATA

Mas Cucut

(R)S *Ctra Besalú – Roses, N260, Km 9,5 (972) 56 52 05 Cl. 1–15 Feb., 1–15 Jun., Mon. eve., Tues.*

On the road towards Besalú, a few kilometres after **Navata**, you come upon this family place, a sudden turn-off after a big bend. If you feel like

a straightforward meal of grilled rabbit with *allioli*, lamb chops, or a plateful of sauce-covered snails, this is it. *Crema catalana* for afters. In summer the terrace is open and, as it is above the road, the views are just pine woods, with grassy fields round the back.
Allow 2,000–3,000 ptas

If you drive seawards from Figueres, you can enjoy the coast of the Alt Empordà. It's really very beautiful with only a handful of towns to interrupt the difficult mountainous terrain that juts like a fist out to sea. There are many little coves, but they're mostly inaccessable, unless you have a boat, a four-wheel drive vehicle or a stout pair of legs clad with walking boots. The two coastal towns, **Cadaqués** and **El Port de la Selva** started as simple fishing villages, and the nature of the landscape has prevented them from growing much. The exception is **Roses**, which has expanded to the extent of being one of the largest resorts of the Costa Brava. Similarly bred of the harsh landscape is the great monastery of **Sant Pere de Rodes**, one of the mightiest romanesque ruins of Catalunya.

Driving towards Vilajuïga, you pass through the medieval enclave of **Peralada** with its famous palace-castle set in fine gardens, and which serves today as a splendid casino.

Map 9B **VILAJUÏGA**

Right in the middle of the cape this is the first town you come to where you can stop for a good meal on your way to the sea or the monastery.

Can Maricanes
(R)S *Ctra de Roses, s/n (972) 53 00 37 Cl. Sun. eve., Tues. (except in summer) 15–31 Oct.*

You can't miss it, at the edge of town on the road which runs directly to Roses, with a big car park marked by a cartwheel. You can eat a great regional lunch here, with excellent grilled meats and braises like duck with pears, or rabbit with snails. They also serve a good *arròs negre*. The room is a simple as could be, with white walls and odd ceramic plates as decoration.
Allow 2,000–3,000 ptas

There are several lovely excursions near Vilajuïga. If you drive on beyond **Vilamaniscle**, park and then climb on foot, you will come to the romanesque sanctuary of San Quirze, a magnificent tenth-century basilica with the ruins of the weed-ridden cloisters still standing. Further to the west is the lovely mountain area of the **Serra de l'Albera**, which you can approach along a trackway from **Espolla** or, better still, by the minor road up from **La Jonquera** via **Cantallops** to the ruined castle of Requesens. This is a most beautiful but little frequented area to walk, with woods, streams and views. The local tourist offices have a good map of the paths.

Map 9B SANT PERE DE RODES

This is a splendid romanesque abbey founded by the Benedictines, with wonderful views looking over the Cap de Creus to the sea. It is some ten minutes' walk away from the pre-romanesque chapel of Santa Creu de Rodes, which you first come to on the steep road up from Vilajuïga. Within you can see the solid eleventh-century church, pre-romanesque in style with three apses and heavy-based columns with decorated capitals. The tower is three storeys high, decorated with classic Lombard motifs, and stands tall over the ruins of the cloister, the cellars, the abbot's palace and the mighty fortifications. An inspiring visit. Sadly the forests surrounding the abbey were swept by fires a couple of summers ago, so the mountainside is now rather harsher than it used to be.

Map 9B LLANÇA

Only fifteen kilometres from the French border, this is a quiet inland town which has stretched down to the sea. Its coastal village has a wide beach and marina, which kick into life during the summer months, and although it has grown in recent years, the skyline and the density have remained low.

Berna
(H)M *Passeig Marítim, 13 (972) 38 01 50 Cl. Oct.–15 May*

A popular summer hotel on the sea front, which spills out onto the beach promenade. The rooms have big square balconies and, of course, uninterrupted views over the bay.
Double room 6,000–7,500 ptas

➔ Gri Mar
(HR)M *Ctra de Portbou, s/n (972) 38 01 67 Cl. 15 Oct.–Easter*

This is a lovely place, a hotel a couple of kilometres from the beach of Llançà surrounded by extensive grounds full of plants, with a huge pool, tennis courts, groves of trees, and lots of space. The rooms are big, all with wide balconies looking over the mountains or across to the sea. This is a place for families who can spend the mornings soaking in the seaside sun, and the afternoons splashing about and or relaxing at home. Aperitifs can be taken on the terrace by the pool. Good Catalan food, and a very happy atmosphere. The sort of place you come back to.
Double room 6,000–8,500 ptas

La Vela
(R)M *C/ Pintor Martínez Lozano, 3 (972) 38 04 75 Cl. 15 Oct.–15 Nov.*

This is an elegant restaurant in the town behind the seafront, easy to find with the clear signposting. They serve an interesting selection of fish dishes ranging from baby octopus with *samfaina*, a mousse of asparagus and anemonies with a sauce of sweet peppers, to monkfish with *rossinyols*, and hake with sea urchins. They will also prepare a splendid *bollabessa* (a great fish stew).

Menú *especial* 2,000 ptas; carte approx. 4,000–5,000 ptas

Map 9B EL PORT DE LA SELVA

This is a tranquil place, a fishing village curving round the big bay which fills in the summer with moored yachts. It's a pleasant spot mainly enjoyed by Catalan holiday-makers, and practically closes down from October until Easter.

Porto Cristo
(HR)M *C/ Major, 59 (972) 38 70 62 Open all year*

A comfortable hotel in a fine old town building, close to the front, with fifty-four simple, spacious rooms. You get lovely views from the higher floors. There is a good restaurant downstairs which specialises in shellfish.

Double room 8,000 ptas

Ca L'Herminda
(R)M *C/ Lilla, 7 (972) 38 70 75 Cl. Sun. eve., Mon., Oct.–May*

A pretty restaurant on the port front, with a dining room divided between two floors. From upstairs you have wonderful views across the bay. Straw-seated chairs, wooden tables, plants hanging from the ceiling and sardine lights illuminating the room. The rough stone walls add to the rustic sense of informality. The fish is good here – particularly the *suquet* and *sarsuela*. A jolly place.

Allow 3,000–4,000 ptas

Map 9B CADAQUES

Cadaques is exceptionally pretty, with a small bay with fishing boats pulled up on the coarse sand, and a promenade lined with nineteenth-century houses. An old white village of steep narrow cobbled streets is wrapped round the parish church. As it is isolated and difficult to get to, it has been a fashionable village for artists and writers for years – the house of Salvador Dalí stands in the neighbouring bay (Portlligat). Today it still retains a rather special ambience particularly out of season when an air of utter peace hangs over the bay. Galleries of modern art abound, and there is an important museum, the **Museu Perrot-Moore d'Art Gràfic Europeu** which treasures works by Brueghel, Zurbarán, Dürer, Van Dyck, Rubens, etc. as well as by Dalí, Picasso and Goya. The **Museu Municipal d'Art** exhibits works of art connected with the village. Cadaqués attracts large numbers of visitors throughout the summer and at weekends, so parking is not easy in the village itself. Much better to park at the back.

Museu Perrot-Moore, C/ Vigilant Open daily 11.00 a.m.–1.00 p.m., 5.00 p.m.–9.00 p.m.

Rocamar
(H)M *C/ Verge del Carme, s/n (972) 25 81 50 Open all year*

A lovely place, on the outer limb of the village, set over a tip of rock with sea on both sides. The garden has been cultivated over the rocky surface, and there are steps which take you down to the little coves below where you can bathe, perhaps after having played a quick game of tennis. There are two pools, one with sea water from where you can look out to sea while you swim, and the other indoors with warm water beside which you can spoil yourself with saunas and hydromassage (a winter treat). The hotel is thoroughly traditional in style – big hallways and plenty of spacious downstairs rooms with old wood furniture, decorative tiles and wooden beams. Of the 70 rooms, there are 40 which overlook the sea. Check when you reserve.

Double room 8,000–9,900 ptas (low season), 12,000–16,000 ptas, (high season)

Playa Sol
(HR)L *C/ Platja Pianc, 3 (972) 25 81 00 Open all year*

At the other extreme of the bay, right on the sea with a small patch of beach in front (although it's mostly taken up with the hulls of little boats). From here you get a pretty view of the white village and the bay speckled with boats. The hotel is modern with excellent rooms all with wide balconies, and there's a big pool and expanse of carefully-planted garden behind. The restaurant is good.

Double room 10,900–15,900 ptas (low season), 12,900–15,900 ptas (high season)

S'Aguarda
(H)M *Passeig S'Aguarda, Ctra Portlligat, 28 (972) 25 80 82 Hotel Cl. 1–15 Nov.; rest. Cl. Oct.–June*

This is a more economical hotel up in the hills behind the village amongst a small group of villas and apartments, on the road that leads to the cove where Dalí's house stands. The hotel is modern and straightforward, designed so that all the twenty-eight rooms and the

restaurant get fine views over the bay. It has a terrace, a small swimming pool and a garden.
Double room 6,000–8,000 ptas

Es Baulard
(R)M *C/ Riba Nemesio Llorens, 2 (972) 25 81 83 Cl. Thurs., 15 Oct.–1 Dec.*

Over towards the right side of the bay, set on the road which hugs the rocky coast, amongst a small group of restaurants. You go up an outside flight of stairs to the room, which is in an old, barrel-ceilinged building, without views over the port. In the summer it is very busy, with a party atmosphere, and serves almost nothing but fish. I couldn't get a table when I went, so I can only pass on the recommendation that here you can eat one of the finest *suquets* in the neighbourhood.
Allow 3,000–4,500 ptas

La Galiota
(R)M *C/ Monturiol, 9 (972) 25 81 87 Open 1 Jul.–30 Sept., Sat. & Sun. in winter*

Amongst the streets behind the church, there is one which curves steeply down to the more open area at the back of the village. La Galiota is here, close to the local museum, subtly announced as if it were just another of the little white houses. It's been going for thirty years, and inside it is bright and homely, with comfortable big wooden chairs, and a touch of Modernist decoration. The two sisters serve a sophisticated modern Catalan cuisine. The first courses make tempting reading and you might find it difficult to choose, but remember, you can always order a selection and share them all. If it's on, the *pastissos de peix* is very good, and I had an excellent oven-baked seabass with fennel.
Allow 3,500–5,000 ptas

You can continue round the cape from Cadaqués and visit the rocky, harsh, and almost treeless area of **Cap de Creus**, where bird watchers can find a great variety of birds including manx shearwaters, blue rock thrushes, pallid swifts, Bonelli's eagles and peregrines, gannets, razorbills, and even red-rumped swallows.

Map 9C **ROSES**

Roses is a place you either love or hate. This is not a picturesque, romantic bay, but a thoroughly lively coastal resort which has grown carefully over the last decades. The bay is wide and splendid, and the high, ugly blocks of apartments have only been built around the area you first drive past. The town itself is attractive – a big maze of streets bursting with bars, restaurants and boutiques. In August it's packed with Catalan fun-lovers, while the rest of the season attracts European tour groups. The hill above and beyond the centre sparkles at night with the lights of up-market summer villas.

Roses is blessed with one of the finest restaurants in Catalunya, and a couple more that are very much in the running. It caters for all sorts of holiday-makers, but even for the most selective there is a splendid range of choice.

Hotels here are typical resort hotels – not much character, efficient, and on the beach. I've recommended one fabulous hotel, and a couple of general places.

Almadraba Park
(HR)L *Platja de l'Almadraba (972) 25 65 50 Cl. 15 Oct.–Easter*

Go right through Roses and follow the signs round the curve of the cape for a couple of kilometres. This hotel is splendid, occupying an entire knuckle of rock, with a swimming pool almost hanging over the edge. The garden has been landscaped around the rockline, with lots of shade and space for aperitifs, and there is a beach just down to the left. There are exceptional views all round. Here you come to get away from it all, although there are, of course, sixty-four rooms of you doing the same. The food is wonderful too – the freshest fish, and excellent salads worked by a very professional kitchen.

Double room 8,500–13,500 ptas

Coral Platja
(HR)M *Av. de Rhode, 28 (972) 25 62 50 Cl. Nov.–Easter*

This is on the coastline as you come into Roses, so if you've reached the main village, you've gone too far. It's spacious and relaxed, with good comfortable rooms which have balconies looking straight out over the sea. You step out of the hotel onto the beach. There's a little grass in front if you feel like sunbathing without getting sandy. Good views from the bar upstairs. A good family hotel, with 128 rooms.

Double room 8,000–12,000 ptas

Terraza
(HR)M *Passeig Marítim, 16 (972) 25 61 54 Cl. Oct.–Easter*

Just next door. It's smart, spruce and professional with all mod. cons. including a small garden and pool on the roof. Most rooms have sea views, and there is grassy shade and a pool just by the beach. As before, you're right on the sand.

Double room 11,000–14,000 ptas

Flor de Lis
(R)M-L *C/ Cosconilles, 47 (972) 25 43 16 Open evenings only; Cl. Tues. (except Jul–Sept), Nov.–Easter (except Christmas)*

This charming restaurant is up at the back of the town – keep walking uphill and right and you'll get close. Then ask. It's in a pretty old cottage, with flower-filled balconies and stone-arched windows, and there is a splendid curled iron plaque announcing its name. Within, the cottage is intimate – stone walls with small windows, benches and wooden chairs, old paintings, and black iron lights. You can sit upstairs or downstairs. The sophistication starts with the table service, and continues with the superb French cuisine. One of their star dishes is the cocktail of lobster, but it's difficult for me to advise – it all depends on today's market. Excellent fish.

Menú degustació 6,250 ptas; carte 5,000–6,000 ptas

Can Ramon
(R)S-M *C/ Sant Elm, 8 (972) 25 69 18 Cl. Sun. eve., Mon., 15 Oct.–15 Nov.*

A simpler alternative, at the front of the town on one of the main pedestrian crossings, where you can eat fish from the day's market and any of the favourite regional dishes like *sarsuela* or *suquet*. A pleasant, informal ambience.

Allow 3,000 ptas

La Llar
(R)M-L *Ctra Figueras-Rosas, Km 40 (972) 25 53 68 Cl. Thurs. (except summer), 15 Dec.–15 Mar.*

Just before you get to Roses from Figueres, you pass this house on the right. Inside, it's elegantly romantic – wood beams in the ceiling, black and white checked floor, a couple of fine old pieces of furniture, and pink patterned tablecloths. Here you are served fine creative Catalan cuisine. The menus are entertaining in their seasonal setting – an entire menu of perhaps salmon, seabass, braised beef or roast lamb with the fragrance of different types of wild mushroom; or a menu, *el menú sorpresa*, that Sr. Joan Viñas keeps secret until the dishes arrive at your table. For a simpler meal, try the quail salad or chicken braised with little onions.

Menú degustació 4,750 ptas; menú *sorpresa* 5,900 ptas; carte approx. 5,000–6,000 ptas

On beyond Roses, along an atrocious road that carries you up behind the town and on down to a tiny cove some eight kilometres away, is a restaurant that has achieved an almost mythical standing here in Catalunya – El Bulli.

➧ **El Bulli**
(R)L *Cala Montjoi (973) 25 76 51 Cl. Mon., Tues. (except Jul.–Sept.), 15 Oct.–15 Mar.*

Really the best way to approach this paradise is by boat.

This is a place you come to and never forget. When you get close to the small cove of Montjoi, the restaurant suddenly announces itself on rusted iron plates. Drive down carefully through the pines and you'll arrive at a wonderfully peaceful bay, probably with a number of yachts moored in the deeper water and a similar number of little hulls pulled up on the beach. The restaurant itself is a splendid villa with a great terrace from where you can enjoy the tranquil vistas while tasting the works of art created by the chef, Fernando Adrià, who holds two Michelin stars. The dishes are most original and inventive – fascinating for the gastronome and a luxury to the taste buds. Here, I sincerely advise you to relax, take the *menú degustació*, and savour every moment of the experience.

Menú degustació 8,000 ptas; carte approx. 10,000 ptas

Arrowed for the wonderful setting, and the culinary excellence.

Driving back down towards **Girona**, you pass the pretty medieval town of **Castelló d'Empúries** with an attractive romanesque church and ruined walls. The important **Aiguamolls** bird reserve is just south.

Map 9C AIGUAMOLLS DE L'EMPORDÀ NATURAL PARK

This fertile area of marshland is part of the estuaries of the rivers Ter and Fluviá. Two centuries ago the whole region as far south as Pals was dotted with a series of lakes, and only in the last two centuries has the agricultural plain been reclaimed. The park itself is a watery haven for birds, and an enclave of peace and tranquillity among the urban holiday resorts of the coast. The hides are well-placed to see dozens of different species – you can rent binoculars from the main office if you've come ill-equipped. You can't fail to see moorhens, coots or mallards but you should also spot golden plovers, lapwings, and snipe wading in the water, as well as stone curlews, marsh harriers, purple herons, egrets, bitterns, and maybe a kingfisher or two. On your way along the paths from one hide to the next, keep your eyes skinned for the tiny painted frogs and the terrapins. It's best to wear dull-coloured clothing, and make sure you take something anti-mosquito with you if you're bird-watching at dusk in the summertime. The best time to visit is spring and early autumn.

Information Centre El Cortalet (972) 45 42 22

Just south of the park is the seaside town of **L'Escala**, which has risen beside the astonishing Greek and Roman settlement of **Empúries**, today one of the finest archaeological sites of the Iberian peninsular.

Girona and east to L'Escala, Medes Islands Marine Reserve, Palafrugell, Palamós, Sant Feliu de Guíxols

Map 8C GIRONA

There is plenty of parking under the raised railway crossing, on the modern side of town – the old walled city is really only for walking. The expansive medieval centre of this city clusters on the slope of a steep hill on the far side of the river, with a myriad of narrow cobbled and stepped streets navigating between the tall old buildings. Crossing the

Onyar river to the old quarter, you can enjoy the picturesque view of the ochre-coloured houses hanging over the water.

The cathedral is magnificent, a huge gothic temple which dominates the city, set on one of the highest points of the hill with a gigantic sweep of steps leading up to its monumental baroque façade. You can escape the strenuous ascent by walking round and approaching the cathedral from the Plaça at the side. Once inside, the sensation of size still persists, caused by the extraordinary width of the single nave. The cloisters are romanesque, and the **Museu Capitular** exhibits a number of priceless religious treasures which include an illuminated Beatus (comentary on the Apocalypse) dating from 975, and the famous eleventh-century Tapís de la Creació, a unique, wonderful romanesque tapestry which requires some moments of contemplation. In the Plaça by the cathedral is the **Museu d'Art**, with an extensive collection of medieval religious frescos, painting and sculptures. On beyond the cathedral you find the main body of the medieval town, particularly the attractive old Jewish quarter – an area you have to explore with comfortable shoes given the number of steps you go up and down. The tourist office will give you a map which marks out the **Call** clearly – it's one of the best preserved Jewish quarters of Catalunya.

Down towards the river you come to the Rambla de la Llibertat, a wide arcaded area of cafés and shops which brings you to the main road bridge over the river (the tourist office is here). Down behind the cathedral on the other side there are lovely gardens and another ancient curiosity – much restored twelfth-century baths, known as the **Banys Arabs** with three rooms, channels for the heating system, and a fragile central cupola set on elegant columns. Further on from here you come to the **Monestir de Sant Pere de Galligants**, which is built into the city wall and now houses the archaeological museum. Go in, if just to see the delightful romanesque church and the exceptional cloister.

Museu Capitular Open Jul.–Aug. 9.45 a.m.–8.00 p.m., Sept.–Jun. 10.00 a.m.–1.30 p.m. & 3.00 p.m.–5.00 p.m.; Cl. p.m. & Mon. Nov.–Mar.

Museu d'Art Open weekdays 10.00 a.m.–6.00 p.m. (10.00 a.m.–7.00 p.m. in summer), Sun. 10.00 a.m.–2.00 p.m.; Cl. Mon.

Banys Arabs Open weekdays 10.00 a.m.–7.00 p.m., Sun. 10.00 a.m.–2.00 p.m.; Cl. Mon.

Museu Arqueològic Open 10.00 a.m.–1.00 p.m. & 4.00 p.m.–7.00 p.m.; Cl. Sun. p.m., Mon.

Girona is poorly served with hotels for holiday-makers, while business travellers have plenty of choice – it shows, I'm afraid. There is quite a mixture of restaurants, ranging from the height of excellence to the popular classic.

Ultonia
(H)M *Avda Jaume I, 22 (972) 20 38 50 Open all year*

Not a family-run hotel, but spacious and convenient, with forty-five rooms fully equipped with travellers' comforts. It's close to the parking area on the modern side of town, only minutes away from the medieval heart of the city.

Double room 8,000 ptas

Fornells Park
(H)M *Ctr N11, Km 711, Fornells de la Selva (972) 47 61 25 Open all year*

About two kilometres south of the city, with fifty comfortable rooms, a good garden, swimming pool and plentiful parking. The hotel is well-run, with views of countryside. Better for a short stay for executives, or a place for conferences or receptions, but it could be a useful alternative.

Double room 9,000 ptas

Hostal Bellmirall
(H)S-M *C/ Bellmirall, 3 (972) 20 40 09 Open all year*

A very simple hostel, installed in one of the old mansions in the medieval quarter. The rooms are no great luxury, with straightforward furnishings and showers, but they look out towards the cathedral and you can really feel that you are in the heart of the old town. There's no lift, just splendid stone stairs. Breakfast is pleasant, in the cosy rooms beside the patio-entrance.

Double room with shower 6,000 ptas

→ El Celler de Can Roca
(R)M-L *Ctra Taialà, 40 (972) 22 21 57 Cl. Sat. midday, Sun.*

This is a bit difficult to get to, in the small northern suburb of Taialà, but ask anyone how to get there and they'll help you. It is definitely worth it. This is one of Catalunya's best restaurants, run by the two young Roca brothers. Joan is an aspiring chef, dedicated to the art and blessed with a creative streak with which he devises his seasonal menus. The dishes are highly sophisticated in elaboration, using the best of the regional produce to a startling effect. After a glass of *cava* and savoury biscuits, what a delicious surprise to be presented with an elegant carpaccio of *peu de porc* with light white beans and a vinaigrette of ceps; or a rich pumpkin mouse with dill, a sweet potato purée with warm foie gras, and then lobster sliced over a delectable parmentier accompanied by *trompetes de la mort* (blackest wild mushrooms). The magret of duck with muscatel grapes was sweet and succulent. After, the desserts: an exquisite banana pastry with crème anglaise, and more. Granted, we went for the full works – and I sincerely suggest you do the same. This is top-class cooking, very professional and at the same time welcoming. It is essential to book.

Seasonal menu 3,200 ptas; menú degustació 4,500 ptas; carte approx. 5,000–6,000 ptas

Arrowed for the energy, enthusiasm and talent of the chef.

Albereda
(R)M *C/ Albereda, 7 bis (972) 22 60 02 Cl. Sun., Aug.*

A very formal restaurant just off the Rambla de la Llibertat, on the far side of the river. Set in an elegant room with pristine white linen and impeccable service, the kitchen offers a carte of sophisticated cuisine based on the regional products. You can choose to take half portions if you wish. Up-market and very good, but tailored specifically to the executive market.

Seasonal menu 3,100 ptas; menú gastronòmic 4,100 ptas; carte approx. 4,000–5,500 ptas

L'Hostalet del Call
(R)S-M *C/ Batlle i Prats, 4 (972) 21 26 88 Cl. Sun. eve., Mon.*

Close to the cathedral and at the top of the Call, this is a good place to stop for lunch during your exploration of the old city. It's small and unpretentious, with handsome furniture and pretty tableware. The food is quite sophisticated, prepared with care, and attractively presented. A gratin of broccoli with pink béchamel, a terrine of fish with a crab sauce, bacallà with a honey mousseline, or a simpler dish of lamb *a la brasa*. The desserts are well-made.

Allow 2,500–3,000 ptas

Casa Marieta
(R)S *Plaça Independència, 5 (972) 20 10 16 Cl. Sun. eve., Mon., Jan.*

One of the old favourites of the city, and still bursting with life. It's very traditional, with loads of tables, old-fashioned decoration of pictures and mirrors on the walls, and a happy hum of people eating platefuls of canelones, rabbit with *allioli, truites, botifarra* with white beans, etc. No surprises, and good honest food.

Allow 2,000 ptas

Boira
(R)S-M *Plaça Independència, 17 (972) 20 30 96 Open all year*

Much patronised by large groups of French, but good if you can get here after them, before them (difficult!), or out of season. The main reason for coming is to sit upstairs by the river, with a fine view across to the colourful hanging houses. Good value, with an entertaining daily menu.

Menú del dia 1,850 ptas; carte approx. 3,000 ptas

A good road leads northwest of Girona to the volcanic region of the Garrotxa, going through **Banyoles** and then on to either to the pretty old town of **Besalú** or the medieval hamlet of **Santa Pau** (see Route B).

En route to **Banyoles** there are two restaurants, Can Xapes and Can Mìa, the one specialising in fish, and the other in fowl.

Map 8C **CORNELLÀ DEL TERRI**

Can Xapes
(R)M *C/ Cinto Verdaguer, 5 (972) 59 40 22 Cl. Sun., Mon.*

A small, quiet restaurant, which specialises in fish brought daily from the coast. The short carte has a selection of good meat dishes, and the fish and shellfish offered changes every day. The cooking is knowlegeable and steeped in tradition – the most famous dish here is *l'olla de peix de l'avia Fina*, a recipe which has come down from fishermen a couple of generations back in the family. It's a particularly rich white *suquet* of monkfish and *sépia* thickened with the liver of the fish – a dish that you need to have ordered the day before you go.

Menú del dia 2,500 ptas; menú *especial* 3,800 ptas; carte approx. 3,500–5,000 ptas

Map 8C **PALOL DE REVARDIT**

➔ **Can Mià**
(R)S *(972) 59 42 46 Cl. Sun. eve., Mon., Tues.*

An amazing place which you reach by watching out for the sign on the road to Palol de Revardit which takes you onto a track leading up the hill. At the end of the track, in the forest, you find yourself next to an old farmhouse, surrounded by chicken, duck, pheasant, guineafowl and pigeon runs. On the far side of the house is the vegetable patch. The restaurant is on the ground floor – stone walls, beams, check cloths, and a merry country feel. I don't think I need to tell you the menu – all that's in the garden. In winter, of course, it's extended to what's in the forest beyond – this is a very good place to eat game. You cannot eat here without booking, particuarly at weekends when the place is absolutely buzzing. Unmissable.

Allow 2,500 ptas

Arrowed for being a unique place, with first-rate farm produce and a great country kitchen.

Map 8C **BANYOLES**

Banyoles is a small old town with a dignified porticoed plaça major where a thoroughly animated market takes place on Wednesday mornings. The natural lake is rather lovely, and as you drive round it (or walk – it only takes a few hours), you can see where they elongated it just a few metres for the rowing events of the 1992 Olympic Games. On the way, take a breather in **Porqueres**, where they treasure a pretty romanesque church. For archaeologists, the Banyoles **Museu Arqueològic Comarcal** exhibits a pre-Neanderthal jawbone found near here, some 100,000 years old.

L'Ast
(H)M *Passeig Dalmau, 63 (972) 57 04 14 Open all year*

A simple family-run hotel overlooking the lake, with 27 fully-equipped comfortable rooms decorated in pale wood. There's a pleasant garden with a swimming pool, solarium, and a terrace just made for that early evening aperitif. No restaurant.
Double room 8,000 ptas

Quatre Estacions
(R)M *Passeig de la Farga, 5 (972) 57 33 00 Cl. Sun. eve., Mon.*

Coming from Girona the first contact with Banyoles is a roundabout with a strange sculpture in the middle. Take the very first exit to the right, with rough land on your right, and immediately on the left you will find a very elegant restaurant. It's an enterprise which involves two young couples, Amadeu Ferres and Montserrat Compte, the manager and maître d', and Joan Vilá and Dolores Morente, the chef and pâtissière. The diningroom is elegant with pink and white linen and smooth wooden panelling, and the standards are high and individual. Joan Vilá is dedicated to his art, self-taught, and inventive. There is an excellent *menú gastronòmic,* worth every peseta, which changes every month, and the carte is very selective. The house wine is a Raïmat which matches the required standards of the house. The meals here are memorable from the bonne bouchée, which may be a vol-au-vent, or a slice of foie gras, to the splendid pâtisserie. Specialities include *endívies amb salmó al roquefort,* served warm and gratinée rather than as a salad; fillet steak of veal with three sauces; a gratin of monkfish with *llagostins.* This is a must.
Allow 3,500–4,000 ptas

Crossing the river Ter towards the coast, the ancient ruins of **Empúries** are thirty minutes away from Girona, beside the coastal town of **L'Escala.**

Map 9C **L'ESCALA**

L'Escala has two reasons for fame throughout all Catalunya: the ancient Greek and Roman remains of the city of **Empúries** lie here; and some of the best salted anchovies in Spain come from this town. Given the Catalan predilection for anchovies, I'm not sure which takes priority! The two are in fact closely connected, the Greeks having begun the anchovy-salting industry in the sixth century BC. Today, you can go to any one of several salters to buy pots of anchovies direct. Remember that an hour or two before you plan to eat some, you need to desalt them thoroughly and then soak them in a generous quantitiy of good olive oil. Only then will they be totally delicious, especially if served on a thick slice of toast.

Apart from the legacy of the Greeks, L'Escala has some good restaurants to offer the holiday-maker.

Nieves Mar
(HR)M *Passeig Marítim 8 (972) 77 03 00 Cl. Dec.–Jan.*

Smart and up to date, this is a very comfortable hotel in the centre of the seafront in L'Escala. The eighty rooms are spacious and well-furnished, most with unsurpassed sea views, and there's the added pleasure of a garden, tennis court and swimming pool. Downstairs the restaurant is well-known for its fish and *suquet.*
Double room 5,000–8,500 ptas

Voramar
(HR)M *Passeig Lluís Albert, 2 (972) 77 01 08 Cl. 15 Dec.–Apr.*

A 36-room family hotel on the seafront, with loyal clientele, particularly French and Belgian, who return year after year. It seems a little sombre as you enter, but the rooms upstairs are bright and refreshing. Just across the road, built on the rock, is a big terrace which surrounds a bright blue pool filled daily by water pumped up from the sea. Around it are dozens of easy chairs and, more important, a good bar.
Double room 4,000–7,600 ptas

Ampurias
(H)S *Platja Portixol (972) 77 02 07 Open Jun.–Sept.*

This is an old hotel with thirty-nine rooms, which has been open since the 1920s, not recommended for anyone who revels in luxury accomodation. It is very simple, has a modest restaurant with unambitious menu, and fills with the same families year after year. I like it because of its position – it is a little apart from the town, with the gardens of the Greek ruins just behind, and a small beach just in front. Cars coming to the hotel park beside it and go no further, so that in effect the beach is private. You can walk to the town within a matter of minutes, and the ruins within seconds.
Double room 5,300 ptas

L'Avi Freu
(R)M *Passeig Lluís Albert, 7 (972) 77 12 41 Cl. Nov.*

The grandfather of the present chef was a fisherman, and the restaurant began as a humble place which cooked for the fishermen just in from the sea. The two professions are still working together here – although the restaurant is now a neat, cool room on the main sea front in the town. The *suquet* is excellent, and the fish dishes change according to the morning's market. At weekends, book before you go.

Menú del dia 1,200 ptas; carte approx. 2,500–3,500 ptas

El Roser 2
(R)M *Passeig Lluís Albert, 1 (972) 77 11 02 Cl. Wed., Feb.*

This has a marvellous view, with the restaurant perched on the curved rock edge overlooking the bay of the town. Again, a family business, again with very good fish. The *mariscada* is huge.

Allow 3,500 ptas

Bar Els Pescadors
(R)S *Port la Clota (972) 77 02 83 Open every day*

Just past the mainstream tourist area of the town is a turning into the La Clota port. The bar at the end, just by the fishing boats, serves excellent grilled fish and tapas simply and very reasonably. Unsophisticated and relaxed.

El Molí de l'Escala
(R)M *Camp dels Pilans, Camí de les Corts (972) 10 47 27 Cl. Wed.*

At night this 16th century building is spectacularly lit to show up the old stone arches of the mill. It's just outside the town, on the turning towards **Albons** on the main road in to L'Escala from the N-11. Come here for a romantic summer evening on the garden terrace beneath the arches, or sit in one of the various carefully restored stone-vaulted rooms of the old house, and enjoy the culinary expertise of Martí Boix and Josep García. Their restaurant is very new, but has met with immediate success here. The carte is selective but wide-ranging, offering regional cuisine: terrine of *escalivada* with anchovies, meat *a la brasa,* game in season, *marisc* of all types, and the classic fish dishes, as well as some delicious creations like their *pastís de porros* and fish terrine. Afterwards, they have a fine cheeseboard. Book before you go.

Menú del dia 1,200 ptas; carte approx. 3,500 ptas

Map 9C **EMPÚRIES**

This is the site of the first Greek settlement on the Iberian Peninsula. They came here in the sixth century BC, and from then until the second century AD the town thrived from its Mediterranean trading. With the landing of the Romans, set to fight the Carthaginians, a second bigger town grew behind the first, only withering as the Roman centres of power shifted to the growing cities of what are now Girona, Barcelona and Tarragona. It was still important in Visigothic times, when it was raised to an episcopal see, but its significance disappeared soon after. The site today is spectacular – a whole field of clearly labelled ruins, from which you can imagine the layout of the cities. Beyond is the strong deep blue of the Mediterranean.

Before exploring, go into the museum and try to catch one of the video-showings of the site: it graphically illustrates the nature of the city buildings in their heyday.

Going round the site, the monumental jetty of the port is furthest away, after which you can see the main body of the city including the family houses, the water amphorae, the anchovy-salting factory, and the splendid market square.

In the Roman city, there are a series of marvellous mosaic floors, as well as the layout of the forum – the main religious and political centres of the city.

Seventy-five per cent of the site still remains to be uncovered.

Open 10.00 a.m.–2.00 p.m., 3.00 p.m.–7.00 p.m. (5.00 p.m. in winter); Cl.Mon.

Map 9C **SANT MARTI D'EMPÚRIES**

This delightful walled hamlet, originally an island and the first landing place of the Greeks, is on the far side of the ruins at the end of a lovely stroll along the seafront from L'Escala. The terraces of several restaurants converge on its small central square, and are filled by a mixture of bathers just up from the beach, or well-dressed visitors who've arrived by car. This is a gentle place in the evening.

Mesón del Conde
(R)M *Plaça Major, 4 (972) 77 03 06 Cl. Tues.*

The Mesón serves good regional fish dishes to a Catalan clientele, in an old mansion decorated with paintings. The service is a bit slow, but the ambience has a nice hum to it, and a feeling of seaside leisure. You can also enjoy *calçots* in season (see specialities of Valls, Route G), if you are unable to get down to Valls.

Allow approx. 3,000 ptas

Map 9C **MONTGÓ**

Just down the coast from Empúries is Montgó – a lovely bay with a wide curved beach and clear sea. This is a favourite area for diving, but suffers from being a corner of awkward one-way traffic jams amongst relaxed bikini-clad campers. If you like the disorganised bustle, and the tranquil evenings after the visiting traffic has gone, then this might be a good place to stay.

Can Miquel
(HR)S-M *Platja Montgó (972) 77 14 52 Cl. Oct.–Easter*

It's family-run, catering for Catalans until high summer when the German and Swiss brigade takes over. There are no frills, but the swimming pool (fresh water) and gardens make a nice refuge from the midday beach, and in the evening there is the added pleasure of sitting in front of the quiet bay sipping a cool drink. If there is a choice of room, the view on the swimming pool side is pretty. The other side is not as good.

Double room 5,600–6700 ptas

There are lots of things on offer here in the way of excursions, from trips down the coast to sea-fishing or day and night views of the sea life in a glass-bottomed catamaran. But for a really fascinating exploration of marine life you should go to the **Illes Medes**. The best launching point is **L'Estartit**, just beyond the old hill-town of **Torroella de Montgrí** with its narrow streets and huge medieval castle.

Map 9C MEDES ISLANDS MARINE RESERVE

This is a group of small, abrupt limestone islands – two sizeable ones and five tiny others, rising out of the sea just over a mile off the coast. There are practically no trees here, and only plants adapted to salty, windy weather can survive.

The bird life is vibrant – huge colonies of yellow-legged gulls which feed off the fertile plains of the Empordà, and quantities of over-wintering cormorants, shags and swifts. Beneath the sea there's a fantastic variety of marine life here amongst the differing levels, tunnels, caves and cavities in the rock. Coral hunting used to be a lucrative occupation here – now strictly prohibited by the protective laws. So strict are these that the islands have been uninhabited by people since 1932, after having served as military outposts for several centuries. The old lighthouse you see from the coast no longer works, replaced now by one which uses solar power. No boats are allowed to drop anchor here, nor may you land.

The islands are at their prettiest in spring, with soft pink seaweed hugging the rocky waterline which turns dry and white in the summer.

Just under the surface, the water is coloured by the reds, greens and ochres of algae, while red and yellow sponges, sea urchins and starfish live below. The length of sunlight in the summer intensifies the colours. Neptune grass, complete with roots and flowers, lines the shallower sea bed.

This is also a paradise for lobsters of all sorts, crabs, octopus and all sorts of fish: scorpion fish, anglers, spotted dogfish, thornback and marbled electric rays, even conger eels.

For sub-aqua divers there is another world brimming with life some twenty metres down, amongst the coral.

You can visit the area by glass-bottomed boat from L'Estartit. *There are hourly outings Jun.–Sept., otherwise daily excursions when there is demand.* There are good diving centres with training teams and equipment for rent here.

L'Estartit tourist office (972) 75 89 10

The whole area between Girona and the sea, curving down the coast to Palamós and beyond, is rich with the pleasures of eating and living well. Attractive restaurants and pleasant hotels abound, and I can truly say that any visitor is spoilt for choice. There are two main towns here: **La Bisbal d'Empordà**, the main industrial centre, and **Palafrugell**, the hub of the coastal region in the practicalities of market life. Otherwise, the area is covered by a network of inland villages – mostly delightfully medieval – and a fan of pretty coves etched out of the mountainous, rocky coastline, around which have risen small, select holiday villages.

Map 8C **MONELLS**

While you are here, take a look at the pretty porticoed main square, and if you enjoy medieval towns, drop into Cruïlles afterwards to see the fine romanesque tower of the castle and, if you are lucky enough to get inside, the murals of the San Miquel monastery's eleventh-century church.

➔ **L'Hort del Rector**
(R)S-M *Davant l'Església (972) 63 03 96 Open Fri.–Sun. in winter, every day in summer; Cl. Oct.*

This is one of my favourite restaurants. It's the country house just opposite the church, surrounded by a flourishing cottage garden full of flowers, shrubs and trees. Beyond the garden on all sides are fields and woodland, so birdsong is everywhere – you could be in the Cotswolds. The carte is by the gate, and you walk down the garden path to the side entrance of the house. Sitting in the simply-dressed little restaurant, you look towards the bumpy back lawn and trees, perfect for Sunday lunch aperitifs or coffee.

L'Hort del Rector (literally the parson's vegetable garden) is famous for it's *bacallà*, indeed it's nigh impossible to eat anything else. There are more than seventy dishes of salt cod – and certain days are allocated for certain specialities. On the first weekend of the month you can partake of the crunchy-topped *arròs de bacallà*, or on the second a *fideuà*. And on Friday evenings, *al pil-pil*. It's difficult to choose from the vast range, so ask for advice – you are at home. There is a modest but interesting selection of other dishes, both first and second courses, if you feel that a whole meal of *bacallà* would be overdoing it. A lovely place.

Allow 3,000 ptas

Arrowed because it is a delightful place.

Map 9D **LA BISBAL D'EMPORDÀ**

The offering here is pottery – in bulk! If you're not sure what to take home for presents, you'll find it here – that is if you are decisive enough to choose from the dozens of pottery shops that line the main road through. Even on Sunday you'll find some open. The style is distinctive to the area with a deep green glaze.

Map 9D **VULPELLAC**

The restaurant here is easy to find, just outside **La Bisbal d'Empordà**, as you can see its façade easily from the main road towards **Pals**.

El Gall Blanc
(R)M *C/ Sis de Febrer, 7 (972) 64 02 31 Cl. Tues. in winter, 1–15 Feb.*

This is a tiny, intimate restaurant of only seven tables, more for evenings than daytime. The restaurant is within the vaults of a seventeenth-century *masia* which is like a collector's den of antique furniture, heavy red curtains and old brown oil paintings. Part of the delight is getting to your table – crossing through the old-fashioned bar furnished with country antiques and then passing a splendid long-tabled diningroom in another rib of the vaults, before you find yourself in the restaurant itself. The cooking is first rate – wonderful rice dishes of the region, peas stewed with mint, braised partridge (in season), and, if you order it beforehand, a house speciality – chicken with lobster. The vegetables and poultry come from the garden.
Allow 3,500–4,000 ptas

Map 9C **PERATALLADA**

This is a pretty medieval town, walled and well-preserved, with old noble houses and artfully overgrowing gardens. Leave your car outside the walls (it's practically impossible to drive inside) and stroll round the fine old cobbled streets. There is no new town attachment, and modern life has incorporated itself well, offering the visitor sustenance from the many restaurants. The food here is local rustic fare, and the Catalan families on their weekend outings love it.

Can Nau
(R)M *C/ d'en Bas, 12 (972) 63 40 35 Cl. Wed., Feb.*

The family of the proprietor/chef have lived here for generations, and the bunch of rooms downstairs, each with old pieces of furniture, makes a cosy restaurant. Andreu Castells has been in the trade since the 1950s, first on the coast where he tired of the seasonal nature of the business and, for the last twenty years, here in his old family house. His dishes are mainly traditional casseroles – snails, braised chicken with aubergine, or rabbit deliciously stewed with crushed almonds, (the name *conill al jaç* is impossible to translate: it's the local name for the indentation in the grass left after a rabbit gets up from his midday siesta!).

Allow 3,000 ptas

Bonay
(R)M *Plaça de les Voltes, 13 (972) 63 40 34 Cl. Mon., Nov.*

Run by two brothers who are carrying the business into the third generation, this is a famous Catalan restaurant on the first floor of another old house. In the light and simply decorated room, you can enjoy an excellent *oca amb naps* (goose with turnips), pigeon stewed with Catalan sausage, pig's trotters with snails, or fish baked in the oven. The family are famed for the quality of their traditional cooking. This is a place to sit and relax in – no views or outstanding scenery, but just a very comfortable sense of family. To give your hunger an edge, pop downstairs to the cellar – you are welcome to look around what is an impressive collection of bottles. Good value.

Carte approx. 3,000 ptas; menú degustació 4,300 ptas

Map 9C **ULLASTRET**

Just beyond the medieval village an abrupt turning off the road takes you to the ruins of a pre-Roman settlement. This is a lovely spot for a pre- or post-lunch stroll. The site, now a shady garden, is on a hill overlooking the colourful fields of the Baix Empordà, and dates from the seventh century BC. A small museum in the middle displays local findings (hellenic pottery, lead inscriptions, tools, contemporary trade).

Open Jul.–Aug. 10.30 a.m.–1.00 p.m., 4.00 p.m.–8.00 p.m. (museum and grounds); Sept.–Jun. 10.00 a.m.–2.00 p.m., 4.00 p.m.–6.00 p.m. (museum), all day (grounds); Cl. Mon.

The village itself is charming, enclosed by stone walls, with its streets recently relaid in the Italian San Gimignano style. It's utterly peaceful, animated only by one shop and a couple of bars. Few people enter.

L'Ibèric
(R)M *C/ Valls, 5 (972) 75 71 08 Cl. Thurs., Christmas*
*

I asked in the shop where this restaurant was: 'Carry on round the walls until you come to a house with a big snail on it. You can't miss it.' It's true, you can't. The restaurant is in a splendid old house, with tables in all three main rooms downstairs. The chef has been cooking here for fourteen years, and waxed lyrical about his art. He does his own bottling of tunny, mushrooms, and tomatoes. The *allioli* is powerful and excellent (nothing to do with garlic mayonnaise). The anchovies are the best you can try anywhere, home-salted only when their weight reaches the optimum twenty-eight to thirty fish per kilo. (He assured us candidly that no woman had been involved in the salting – strictly against the superstitions of the trade.) Specialities of the house? None: it depends on today's market. The emblem of the snail? Just that: great food comes from the simplest, best ingredients. Be sure to book before you go, and then enjoy whatever takes your fancy. He is a well-known personality in the local fish auctions – and it shows. His fish is superb.

Allow 3,500–4,000 ptas

Map 9C **PALAU-SATOR**

This is another tiny medieval hamlet, well worth a visit, which is well-known to local and foreign visitors for the splendid meals provided in the old *masia* just outside the walls.

Mas Pou
(R)S-M *C/ Extramurs, 8 (972) 63 41 25 Cl. Mon., Jan.*

Snails are a hot favourite here, along with the *pastís de truita, bacallà* and grilled meats. The family were farmers, following generations of tradition, until some eight years ago they decided to change to a more profitable business. Their old house has several ample downstairs rooms, laden with old furniture, and filled at the weekends with Catalan family celebrations. The foreign clientele flock in after sundown, the Catalans later. You must book if you are thinking of a weekend visit.

Allow 2,500–3,000 ptas

Map 9C **PALS**

Pals is an old, carefully restored, walled town within which remain some remarkable old mansions. Being pretty and much visited, it has developed an ample selection of modest restaurants.

El Pedró
(R)S-M *Placeta d'en Bou, 29 (972) 63 69 83 Cl. Thurs., Nov.*

If you are looking for good no-nonsense regional food, you can't go wrong here – it's just down the right-hand street behind the church. The family live opposite, where they originally started their restaurant business on the patio until the demand forced them to work the ruins of number 29 into two floors of chequered tablecloths. Even in winter the

family keeps the place open during the week in case a hungry visitor should wander in.
Allow 2,500 ptas

Sa Gatonera
(R)M *La Font, 30 (972) 66 75 82 Open Jun.–Sept., Easter.*

Here you can eat refined Catalan-French cuisine, in the pretty, carefully decorated surroundings of a seventeenth century mansion just outside the walls. There are four light rooms here, each decorated in a different style, and an attractive outside terrace in the courtyard. The carte is a trifle flamboyant, but the food is good and the ambience very pleasant. They serve an interesting *suquet de bacallà i llagostins.*
Allow 4,000 ptas

Near **Pals**, there are two exceptional places, one offering a wonderful hotel with very good food, and the other marvellous cuisine with a very good hotel. These are the beautiful mansion **Mas de Torrent** just south of Pals, and the highly acclaimed restaurant **Sa Punta**, on down towards the enticing beach coves near **Begur**. If both can't be included in a visit to the Baix Empordà, I would definitely suggest a drink in the former while it is light, and a menu in the latter. (Should you have the inclination, a round of golf is also highly recommended around here – there are several excellent courses to choose from.)

Map 9D **TORRENT**

➔ Mas de Torrent
(HR)L *Torrent (972) 30 32 92 Open all year*

Hidden in the countryside between Pals and Palafrugell, this *masia*, dating from 1751, has been most beautifully converted into a thirty-room hotel with a breathtaking extension of gardens. The peace and tranquillity here is profound and, needless to say, the quality of rooms and service is beyond reproach. If you are a lover of the Relais & Châteaux of France, you'll recognise that this is one of the same group. The rooms in the manor house are splendidly set with period furniture, and the quarry-tiled landings are arranged as open sitting rooms for admiring the country views. Running down beside the house are a series of individual rooms which lead straight out into the grassed front garden. The restaurant has a finesse which matches that of the hotel, and the grounds are a delight. If you're not staying, take a detour here even if it's only for a glass of white wine, and book for your next trip.
Menú 4,650 ptas; double rooms 20,000–24,000 ptas
Arrowed because it is superbly restored and utterly peaceful.

Torrent: Mas de Torrent

Map 9C **PLATJA DE PALS**

➔ **Sa Punta**
(RH)L *Platja de Pals (972) 63 64 10 Open all year*

Sa Punta first began in 1976 when the surrounding coastal area was just beginning to be populated with summer villas, and since then has been raised to its present heights by the brothers, Jaume and Josep Font (Jaume in the kitchen, Josep in the dining room). The hotel of sixteen rooms was only added four years ago and is finished to the ultimate degree of comfort. The philosophy here is to take the best ingredients and cherish them (fish from Roses and Palamós, vegetables from the Empordà markets) – the dishes are exquisite, not over elaborate, and the presentation is beautiful. This is Empordà cooking at its best. I can't promise that *flor de carbassó farcit de marisc* (courgette flower filled with shellfish) or the crudité with *gambes* bathed in a vinaigrette of *cava* will be on the menu when you go – the menu changes several times a year, and varies according to the market. You are in one of the very finest Catalan restaurants – prepare yourself beforehand, relax as you gaze over the delightful gardens and pool, soothe yourself with a glance at the splendid wine list, and let the day's menu bring you what it may. Recently awarded its second Michelin star.

Menú 3,900 ptas; carte approx. 5,000 ptas; double room 16,000 ptas
Arrowed for wonderful cooking in a beautiful setting.

Map 9D **BEGUR**

The sea around this curve of the Costa Brava is awkward to get to but stunning when you get there. The coast is made up of cove beaches and mountains, thus making it difficult to drive from one cove to another. You are in one of the most appreciated areas on the coast, where summer houses are prized by the upper echelons of Catalan society.

The central town is **Begur**, an old hill-town high above the sea with a spectacular ruined medieval castle just above, where the choice of hotels and restaurants is basic.

Plaja
(HR)S *Plaça Pella i Forgas (972) 62 21 97 Open all year*

A small hotel in the central square of the town, with sixteen rooms. It's family-run, very simple and welcoming, with a good restaurant below.

Double room 5,300 ptas

Esquiró
(R)M *Av. Onze de Setembre, 21 (972) 62 20 02 Cl. Mon. (except in summer) 15 Nov.–Easter*

A restaurant in the second street back, with a range of regional Catalan cuisine. They offer interesting fish dishes with wild mushrooms, light country stews and serve good oven-baked fish. The family work with the seasons, and adjust their culinary talents according to the local markets. After the coastal tourism dies down,
the restaurant closes and they go up to the Vall d'Aran to over-winter and cook the warming food of the mountains in their other restaurant.

Allow 4,000 ptas

Roads fanning out from the town lead to the pretty *coves* of Sa Riera, Sa Tuna and Fornells. To get close to the elevated character of this coastal region, make your way to **Aiguablava**, where there is a fabulous hotel to stay in, and a second with exceptional views.

Map 9D **AIGUABLAVA**

Aigua Blava
(HR)L *Platja de Fornells (972) 62 20 58 Cl. Nov.–Easter*

Nestling in the hills beside the sea is the smart summer village of Aiguablava, within which is one of the oldest and most famous hotels on the whole coast. It is held in such high esteem that it has become emblematic of the wonders of the Costa Brava. It merits its reputation. It's a huge place, spacious inside and out, extremely comfortable, overlooking one of the most beautiful rocky coves of the area. The gardens are lovely, with terraces and pine woods, and a stone's throw away is the crystal water of the beach. There are all the extras you could wish for in the eighty rooms, as well as tennis courts and a pool in the gardens. The restaurant is as it should be for a hotel of this standing, specialising in fish, of course.
Rest. allow 3,500 ptas; double room 9,000–15,000 ptas

Parador de Aiguablava
(HR)L *Platja de Aiguablava (972) 62 21 62 Open all year*

Perched on the top of a rocky outcrop, this is a must for the view. The hotel itself is modern and fairly impersonal, but if you park the car and walk to the edge at the right of the building, you will see thousands of gulls nesting on the dramatic cliff face to face with the deep blue clarity of the sea below. The best way to appreciate the view is by relaxing on the terrace, drink in hand – particularly if you've just negotiated the winding road to get here. Pathways lead off from here across the top of the cliffs towards the next coves.
Double room 16,500 ptas

Map 9D **PALAFRUGELL**

This is a busy market town, buzzing with activity at the weekends when there is a big local street market with most shops staying open on Sundays. Parking is difficult, as the centre is mostly pedestrianised, but you can usually find a place in the side streets just out of the centre. From here you can reach the tiny beach coves of the coast and the small summer villages which surround them.

La Xicra
(R)M *C/ Estret, 17 (972) 30 56 30 Cl. Tue. eve., Wed., Nov.*

This is an intimate little restaurant installed in the small rooms of an old town house just off the main square of the town. The carte changes every day, designed according to the morning's market, and presented in whatever language you prefer to read. The cuisine specialises in the

very Catalan art of mixing *mar i muntanya*. When we were there, they were serving baby octopus with onion, white beans with *gambes* from Palamós, a casserole of rabbit with snails and *escamarlans*, and *olla baquera* – a rice dish with fish and a rich stock. The cooking is done with style and finesse, and the presentation is pretty, in keeping with the tiny stone-walled rooms, the small collector's cabinets of glass, and the delicate decoration of the china. You must reserve.
Allow 4,500 ptas

La Casona
(R)S-M *C/ Paratge La Sauleda, 4 (972) 30 36 61 Cl. Sun. eve., Mon., Nov.–15 Dec.*

A popular place on the road entering Palafrugell from Palamós. The ambience is rustic with white walls, dark beams, flagstones, and a collection of country tools hung here and there. The food is traditional Catalan country fare: canelones, rice dishes, courgettes stuffed with tunny, and a delicious *rossejat de fideus* with *allioli*. A good place to eat artichokes and grilled meats. Reserve throughout the summer.
Allow 2,500–3,000 ptas

Map 9D **MONT-RAS**

Madame Zozó
(R)M *Av. de Catalunya, 6, C255 (972) 30 01 17 Open Easter–30 Sept.*

This is a great place for fish. You walk into a big enclosed patio filled with tables, beyond which is the restaurant itself. Beside you, in one corner of the patio, is a large table spread with the freshest fish, which swiftly reduces in quantity as the afternoon or evening goes by. Eating here in the patio among a contented party of tables enjoying the exceptional cooking is a lovely experience. The kitchen doesn't complicate the dishes – your fish is simply and beautifully cooked, following the traditions of the family: oven-baking, grilling and steaming. The house itself has a curious history, which you can best appreciate by popping through to the bar at the front. It's decorated in a 1920s Parisian style, complete with huge red awnings, posters, paintings and mirrors, and dates from the early 1960s when Madame Zozó was a popular dance hall serving cocktails, and pandering to the fun-loving holiday-makers of the coast.
Allow 3,000–4,500 ptas

Map 9D **LLAFRANC**

Llafranc is an old seaside village with a small beach half-filled with sardine fishing boats. I can recommend two small, family-run hotels here, both on the seafront, both offering good regional fish dishes. A cliff-top walk, or a short drive in the car will take you round to the charming bay and summer village of **Tamariu.**

Llevant
(HR)M *C/ Francesc de Blanes, 5 (972) 30 03 66 Open all year*

A hotel with twenty-four big spacious rooms, quite smart and bright, and it offers a quite inventive menu. The restaurant terrace leads straight onto the promenade of the beach. The family are charming, and well used to looking after British guests – fifty per cent of their rooms are filled by us. You are expected to take full board.
Full board 7,700–10,400 ptas

Llafranch
(HR)M *Passeig Cypsele, 16 (972) 30 02 08 Open all year*

On the seafront, only separated from the beach by a one-way street. The twenty-six rooms are spacious with an additional small 'sitting area' in each bedroom. Here there are more French guests. The family started this business in 1958, and their guest book boasts a long list of famous names from Spain and Hollywood. In summer you can choose the type of accommodation you wish, full or half-board, or only bedroom.
Full board 8,000–9,000 ptas

Map 9D CALELLA DE PALAFRUGELL

This is a bigger village than Llafranc, built round the tiny beach, with hotels and villas spread amongst the hillside *coves* beyond. With a car you can go through the centre of the village to the beach, but you can't park down there.

If you happen to be in Calella on the first Saturday of July, be prepared to find huge quantities of people imbibing *cremat* (a flamed rum concoction), sitting round fires on the beach or huddled in boats, listening to the singing of *havaneres* (fishermen's songs). For the locals it retains a strong sense of nostalgia, but as more and more visitors come, it is more an experience of the Catalan night-life.

Sant Roc
(HR)M *Plaça Atlàntic, 2 (972) 61 42 50 Open Easter–Oct., weekends Feb.–Easter*

A brisk walk from the centre of town, built on a rocky outcrop with lovely views of the bay of Calella. It's a traditional summer family hotel with lots of space, forty-eight big rooms all with balconies, and a garden full of trees. The terrace overlooks the delightful *coves* of the coastline. Just down below there are steps which lead down to the tiny beach enclosed by high walls of rock, from which you can bathe in the sparkling, clear waters.
Double room 8,000–10,500 ptas

Callela de Palafrugell – sea view

Can Pep
(R)S-M *C/ Lladó, 22 (972) 61 50 00 Cl. Tues. eve., Wed. (in winter), Nov.*

This is a very popular restaurant up at the back of the town – ask for directions to find it, but make sure you reserve first. The building is covered with bougainvillea, and is decorated in a simple rustic style within, with check tablecloths and old furniture. The kitchen produces traditional Catalan fish cooking, and is particularly well-known for its rice dishes, *rossejat de fideus, sípia* braised with peas, and fish stews. To start off, take the *poti-poti,* a selection of the tapas of the house, and for afters, a touch of fresh cheese with honey. A happy place, always busy.
Allow 2,500–3,000 ptas

Jardí Botànic de Cap Roig
Open daily 8.00 a.m.–8.00 p.m.

As an appetizer, or digestif, I strongly recommend a stroll around this beautiful botanic garden. It was created by a Russian colonel and his English wife, who arrived in 1927 and set to, building a splendid medieval-style mansion and bringing exotic plants from their world travels and from London's Kew Gardens. The best time to visit is spring and early summer. The views from these cliff-tops are breathtaking. Check – there are often concerts and exhibitions here in the summer.

Map 9D **PALAMOS**

➜ La Gamba
(R)M *Plaça Sant Pere, 1 (972) 31 46 33 Cl. Wed. (except Jun.–Sept.), Nov.*

La Gamba opened in 1967, in a building just above the old fish auctions (now a big car park). Since then, it has built up a tremendous reputation for its cooking of the famous local produce – *gambes* from Palamós and fish. The cuisine is traditional, but marked by some interesting new dishes that come straight from the creative talent of the kitchen. This is a true family business, founded and nurtured by the parents, and passing gradually to the sons who have specialised as chef and sommelier. The service is exemplary here – it's a pleasure to watch the deft filleting of a fish. The room is comfortably old-fashioned with fishing pictures hung at all heights, and in summer the restaurant moves outside to the huge terrace overlooking the fishing bay.
The stuffed and gratinéed sea urchins are delicately delicious, well-followed by a classic *suquet* of turbot with *gambes*, or a baked fish garnished with anemonies and algae. The bread is hand-made here, the pâtisserie is excellent, and the wine list extensive. You must reserve at weekends.

Menú 4,200 ptas; carte approx. 4,500 ptas

Arrowed for its fine culinary tradition and the wonderful *gambes.*

La Menta
(R)M *C/ Tauler i Servià, 1 (972) 31 47 09 Cl. Wed., Nov.*

Just up the diagonal street to the left off the big parking in the centre. La Menta is a rather special little place, with very few tables and a quiet, intimate ambience. The main specialities here are finely-worked traditional recipes of the fishing fraternity – *ranxo de peix*, a casserole of tasty fish, and a *fregida*, a fry-up of all sorts of little fish served with toast *amb tomàquet.* These balance very well with the very up-to-date dishes like the carpaccios of *gambes* with *cava* vinaigrette or of *bacallà* laid around a light lentil salad. The carte changes frequently.

Menú del dia 3,000 ptas; carte approx. 3,500–4,000 ptas

Map 9D SANT ANTONI DE CALONGE

Reimar
(HR)M *Torre Valentina (972) 65 22 11 Open Jun.–Sept.*

A simple hotel surrounded by pine trees just a couple of kilometres from Palamós at the edge of the wide bay. It has only forty-eight rooms, all with balconies, and has a lovely view across to Palamós. The feeling of smallness here is unusual in this part of the coast – there are only three floors, and the rooms look out to the small garden and swimming pool, and on to the wide beach just beyond. If you are keen on watersports, you can keep your equipment on the sand just in front.
Double room 7,000–9,000 ptas

Park Hotel San Jorge
(HR)L *Ctra de Palamós, s/n (972) 65 23 11 Cl. Nov.–Feb.*

As a luxury hotel with 104 rooms this is not in the 'small and family' class. In a very beautiful position looking out to sea, it is surrounded by gardens and perched between two pretty *coves* to which you have access via the steps leading down from the terrace. All the extras are there too – gymnasium, pool, tennis, etc., but the main thing is the peaceful place itself – with no holiday bustle to mar the experience.
Double room 10,000–12,500 ptas (17,000 ptas Aug.)

From Palamós onwards, the character of the coastline changes, becoming more urban, with bigger bays, broader beaches and more hotels. **Platja d'Aro** is a huge resort with numerous places to stay and eat, but as it's more suitable for package holidays than travellers, I've passed straight by. Just outside, however, there are a number of very fine restaurants.

Map 9D PLATJA D'ARO

Carles Camós – Big Rock
(RH)M-L *C/ Barri de Fanals, 5 (972) 81 80 12 Cl. Sun. eve., Mon., Jan.*

Up in the hills well behind the town, this is one of the very fine restaurants of the coast. The building dates from the seventeenth century, a beautifully kept *masia* with fine beams, stone walls and a multitude of little rooms. The restaurant occupies several – giving a select, serious and dignified ambience. The cooking here is exemplary, taking humble ingredients, working them with care and invention, and presenting them with contemporary panache: lentils cooked *a la marinera*, a warm salad of fresh pasta with *llagostins*, lamb's brains with a mustard vinaigrette, duckling with pears, or another speciality – *suquet* of monkfish and *llagostins* followed by *fideus*. Upstairs there are five very splendid suites, furnished with antiques in keeping with the character of the house. After coffee, take a stroll round the extensive gardens, from which you get a fabulous view.

Menú degustació 4,800 ptas; carte approx. 6,000 ptas; suites 20,000–24,000 ptas

Map 8D **CASTELL D'ARO**

Joan Piqué
(R)M *C/ Barri de Crota, 3 (972) 81 79 25 Cl. Mon., Tues., Nov.*

This is a young restaurant housed in a restored fortified mansion in the hillside village behind Platja d'Aro. It's a very attractive setting, with a multi-level floor of stone flags, old stone walls, vaulted ceilings and a general ambience of quiet elegance. In the summer the wood-framed terrace is a delightful place to eat, looking across towards the great expanse of blue. Joan Piqué is one of the young high-flyers of the gastronomic scene here in Catalunya. He works within the culinary traditions of the Empordà but with a very personal, refined touch. Some of the carte reads curiously: fried egg pastry puff, or pigs' trotters with oysters, salad of quail in *escabetx*; and other dishes sounding less strange: tartlet of *bacallà* with *samfaina*, sweetbreads with ceps and asparagus, or guineafowl with grapes. This is part of the fun – he works with the traditional products of the region, and creates new dishes that are a delight to the palate. You shouldn't miss the desserts.

Allow 4,000–5,000 ptas

Map 9D **S'AGARÓ**

S'Agaró is a very select residential area on the Costa Brava, the most elite of the coast.

➔ **Hostal de La Gavina**
(HR)L *S'Agaró (972) 32 11 00 Open Easter–Oct.*

This is *the* hotel of the Catalan Mediterranean coast. A Relais & Châteaux hotel of the highest order. It was built in 1932 on a rocky promontory and is like a small palace of luxury surrounded by wonderful gardens with vistas out to sea in all directions. Inside the house is steeped in elegance and dignity. The ground floor rooms vary from patterned marble floors to rich oakwood panelling, each with its own style of period antique furniture. There are fifty-six sumptuous bedrooms and a further sixteen suites which are really only accessible if you are blessed with blue blood. One of the diningrooms is splendidly lit from great conch shell lights sculpted into the arches of the ceiling, while the other is romantically set for dining amidst the flicker of candlelight. There is a sparkling seawater pool, beside which there is a summer terrace restaurant, perhaps the most relaxing of the restaurants, but choose whichever suits your mood, book early, and soak in the splendour.

Rest. approx. 6,000 ptas; double room 19,000–34,000 ptas

Map 8D SANTA CRISTINA D'ARO

Les Panolles
(R)M *Ctra Girona St. Feliu, Km 27 (972) 83 70 11 Cl. Wed. eve.*

What a pretty house! When it was a working *masia,* the corn used to be hung all over the façade to dry – hence the name Les Panolles (the corncobs). The house dates from 1671, and has been carefully restored to maintain the old character. You walk in through the splendid entrance, to be greeted with old furniture and stone archways leading off the hallway to select small dining rooms. The main rooms are beyond, the biggest one with beams in the roof and a great fireplace to heat it in winter, and the second one out in a new glassed section. In the summer, the terrace between the two opens up for even more tables. The carte is extensive, partly based on the seasonal change of local produce, partly true to the traditional regional dishes. When I was there, the autumn menu included a warm terrine of wild mushrooms, a salad of lentils with dried ham, stuffed *calamarsons,* and civet of hare with chestnuts. Or, I could have chosen any of several fish baked or grilled; or called for rabbit with *allioli.* This restaurant fills daily in the summer, and the atmosphere is congenial and very good humoured. Fun.

Menú del dia (Mon.–Fri.) 2,500 ptas; carte approx. 3,500 ptas

Mas Torrellas
(HR)M *Ctra Sta. Cristina Platja d'Aro, Km 1,7 (972) 83 75 26 Open all year*

This is an old *masia,* in a quiet area of fields and gardens some three kilometres from the Platja d'Aro. The rooms are very humble, but the sense of peace is welcome. There was an enormous wedding going on when I visited, and the hotel really is a perfect spot for big parties, so I recommend that you don't plan to stay on a weekend just in case.

Double room 7,000–10,000 ptas

Map 8D LLAGOSTERA

➔ Els Tinars
(R)M *Ctra Llagostera St. Cristina d'Aro, Km 25 (972) 83 06 26 Cl. Tues., Feb.*

Els Tinars is a famous restaurant a couple of km away from Llagostera heading towards Sant Feliu. There is a big parking space on both sides of the road, and you can't miss the big house. Their reputation is based on the excellent cooking of traditional dishes, extremely good value and a very pleasant, relaxed ambience. The carte is incredibly long – offering French cuisine to the travellers who prefer that style; regional dishes; a selection of refined fish dishes; meat and game. They are well prepared for visitors from everywhere – even Russians receive the menu in their own language. Whatever you choose, the *patates Tinars* are a must – thinly sliced and then baked with the rich juices of *carn de perol.* You should also try the delicate salad of partridge with a julienne of wild mushrooms. And after, the lobster casserole with white beans, or maybe the grilled turbot with rosemary. Remember that you can choose half portions here if you wish – the portions are generous. Amongst the highly professional team of chefs, there are two specialists in pâtisserie, so desserts are obligatory. The cellar is vast and comprehensive, with an impressive list to read through – should you become a regular client you can build up your own collection here. You must reserve at weekends.

Allow 3,000–3,500 ptas

An arrow for the good value of the excellent traditional Catalan dishes.

Map 8D **SANT FELIU DE GUÍXOLS**

This is a busy fishing town, hard-working in the back streets all year and full of holidaying Catalans on the shoreline in the summer.

Murlà Park

(H)M *Passeig del Guíxols, 22 (972) 32 04 50 Cl. Nov.–Dec.*

This is not very attractive from outside, but is comfortable, practical and in the centre. It's family-owned, and the Srs Murlà themselves look after you personally – so you feel thoroughly welcome. It's just across the promenade from the beach.

Double room 6,800–10,000 ptas

Eldorado Petit

(R)M *Rambla Vidal, 23 (972) 32 10 29 Cl. Mon.–Thurs. from 15 Oct.–Easter*

This is one of the prized restaurants of the Costa Brava, a quiet, elegant place decorated in pale green tones, where Lluís Cruañas offers a selection of exquisite fish dishes. It is right in the centre of the town, a stone's throw away from the main seafront promenade. The restaurant has nearly twenty-five years of history, and a very high reputation for l'Empordà traditional food. The carte is governed by the seasonal markets – enjoying wild mushrooms, sea urchins, mussels, oily fish etc. as they come. I had an excellent menu of *escamarlans* gratinéed with a light *allioli,* pike with clams and asparagus tips, and to finish, a sublime *tiramisú.* The canelones of *marisc* being eaten on the other side of the table were delicious. The set menu is inventive and very good value.

Menú gastronòmic 3,250 ptas; carte approx. 5,000–6,000 ptas

Can Toni
(R)M *C/ Garrofers, 54 (972) 32 10 26 Cl. Tues.*

This is rather difficult to find, in amongst the awkward one-way streets at the top of the hill before you start driving down towards the shore. There are signs on the main road into the town from Llagostera – follow them and keep your fingers crossed. Can Toni has two sides, the old tavern where the locals swig brandies and buy their barrel wine, and the tiny, intimate restaurant which is the preserve of gourmets. The decor is charming – ochre walls, beamed ceilings, rustic chairs, and pretty table settings each graced with a rose. The dishes sound traditional, and indeed they are, but done to a precision and delicacy that places them apart. The specialities of the house are the *suquet* of baby monkfish, and oven-baked fish from San Feliu. If you can, try the locally-fished anchovies stuffed with *escalivada.*

Menú del dia 1,500 ptas; menú degustació 3,500 ptas

Can Salvi
(R)M *Passeig del Mar, 23 (972) 32 10 13 Cl. Wed., 15 Nov.–15 Dec.*

On the sea promenade, with an elegant room decorated with pictures and a refreshing glass-fronted terrace out in the middle. This is a typical seaside restaurant, passing from generation to generation, with a long carte of fish dishes to choose from. The *pica-pica* is fun – a string of appetising *marisco* and fish tapas followed by oven-baked or salt-baked fish.

Menú del dia 1,875 ptas; Menú *pica-pica* 3,500 ptas; carte approx. 4,000 ptas

Girona south east to Tossa de Mar, Blanes, Hostalric

Map 8D **TOSSA DE MAR**

Apart from having a good wide beach, Tossa de Mar is one of the most attractive towns on the coast, with a very pretty old centre of narrow streets and small white houses still partly enclosed by a great medieval wall.

Diana
(H)M *Placa d'Espanya, 6 (972) 34 18 86 Cl. Nov.–Easter*

A delightful hotel on the sea front. The house was originally built towards the end of last century for a family newly returned from the Americas, and carries the Modernist stamp of the time – it was built by architects following Gaudí's style. You can spot it immediately, bright white with arched windows, standing back from the street with a tall palm tree growing from the patio. Inside it is stunning – attractive stained glass in the windows, stencil work decorating the curvy door and window frames, splendid tiled fireplaces with heraldic-scaled chimney pieces, statues, fine floors and wrought-iron balustrades. The sense of personality even reaches the bedrooms, with fine old furniture and, of course, wonderful views.

Double room 7,000–8,000 ptas

Mar Menuda
(HR)M *Platja Mar Menuda, s/n (972) 34 10 00 Cl. 7 Jan.–Easter*

This is at the northern end of the beach, an escape from the vivacious activity of the town, but only a brisk walk from the centre. It's surrounded by pine trees, with a garden and pool, and leads directly onto the quiet, uncrowded beach of the Mar Menuda cove. There are only 40 rooms in the three storeys of the hotel, and it retains a pleasant feeling of family welcome.

Double room 8,000–10,000 ptas

Castell Vell
(R)M *Plaça Roig i Soler, 2 (972) 34 10 30 Cl. Mon.; Oct.–Easter*

This is up inside the walled area, in the furthest corner just opposite the castle museum. The wall decorations are very intriguing, with quantities of paintings, souveniers, and collections of this and that. The rooms are low-ceilinged and beamed and the whole ambience is rustic and rather fun. There's also an ivy-hung terrace which is delightful at night. The food is regional and international, with a wide-ranging carte so there is something for all palates. Fish is particularly good.

Menú del dia 2,100 ptas; menú de degustació 4,500 ptas

Bahía
(R)S-M *Passeig del Mar, 19 (972) 34 83 22 Cl. Mon., Nov.–Feb.*

Bahía is a very popular restaurant on the seafront which has been going for the last forty years, serving good fish and a variety of meat dishes. The room is big, hung with big dark paintings and fronted by a great window from which you can enjoy the view of the beach. The *suquet* here is said to be the finest in town. There is also an interesting range of the classic *mar i muntanya* cuisine, like rabbit with *escamarlans* or meatballs with *sípia*. If they are on the menu, ask for the delicious *rogers* from the bay of Tossa.

Menú del dia 1,750 ptas; carte 3,500 ptas

Es Molí
(R)S-M *C/ Tarull, 3 (972) 34 14 14 Cl. Tues. (except in summer) Feb.*

This is an attractive place at the back of the town, installed in the patio garden and house of a old windmill dating from 1856. The garden is rather lovely, particularly in the evening, with pine trees and shrubs enclosed by an arcaded cloister within which tables are set. The main room is beneath more arches which surround the cupola formed by the second floor. A hint of southern Spain, with the green of the garden contrasting romantically with the warm ochre tones of the arches. Here you have a menu which gives you an ample choice of first and second courses as well as desserts – all good regional or traditional fare.

Menú del dia 2,000 ptas; menú *especial* 3,000 ptas

Map 8D LLORET DE MAR

Lloret is a huge summer tourist resort, mostly filled by European tour operators. As with Platja d'Aro, I've passed by without entering.

Santa Marta
(HR)L *Platja de Santa Cristina (972) 36 49 04 15 Dec.–1 Feb.*

This is a lovely hotel built on the coast between Lloret de Mar and Blanes, amidst a glorious fifteen-acre garden of pines, flowers, and lawns. It stands above a beautiful sweep of beach, completely out of sight of other buildings. The hotel itself is totally luxurious, with stunning views either out to sea or over the forests behind. The restaurant looks over the gardens and the beach. This is a blissfully peaceful place to stay. A Relais & Châteaux hotel.

Double room 14,500–25,000 ptas

El Trull
(R)M *Cala Canyelles (972) 36 49 28 Open all year*

This is a huge restaurant built like a many-levelled *masia*, catering for hundreds of covers a day in the high season. Out of season, it's very popular for big family celebrations and weddings, and the energy of the occasions is catching. Given the size of the place – there are several rooms as well as a terrace overlooking the swimming pool – the kitchen manages to produce a high standard of cooking, and the waiters are efficient. The carte offers fairly unsophisticated dishes like potato crêpes with mousseline of shrimps, *rossejat de fideus* or fish baked in salt, rabbit braised with green peppers.

Menú del dia 1,500 ptas; menú especial 3,750 ptas; carte 4,000–5,000 ptas

Map 8D BLANES

The best part of Blanes is the wide beach with its generous promenade and the marvellous gardens. There are two botanic gardens, one founded in 1924 (Mar i Murtra) occupying fifteen hillside hectares, and the other (Pinya de Rosa) dating from 1945 with African plants. Both are internationally famous for their vast collections of species. There's also an important aquarium at the end of the promenade with a large exhibition of Mediterranean marine life.

Can Patacano
(R)S *Passeig del Mar, 12 (972) 33 00 02 Cl. Mon. in winter, 7 Jan.–7 Feb.*

A restaurant that's been going since the beginning of the century, although the modern room doesn't show it. Grilled fish is the speciality, particuarly good as they use wood and charcoal as fuel. You really need to come here a couple of times to do justice to the menu – you shouldn't miss the rice *a la cassola*, a famous dish of the house, or the *suquet de peix amb sípia i calamar*, or, of course, the grilled fish, which you might combine with the delicious grilled artichokes. The desserts are home made – save at least a corner.

Menú 1,700 ptas; carte approx. 3,000–4,000 ptas

S'Auguer
(R)M *C/ S'Auguer, 2 (972) 35 14 05 Cl. Jan.*

Just to the right of the main road entrance to the seafront, in the beamed upper floor of an old building. They offer a simple carte of fish and shellfish here, mostly *a la planxa* or *a la graella*. A happy place, unsophisticated and with good food.

Allow 3,000 ptas

From Blanes you can cross over to the fast motorway entrance to **Barcelona**, or potter down the coastal road which takes you past the long beaches and summer villages of the Maresme. (See Chapter 2, Day excursions from Barcelona.)

Heading on down towards **Barcelona** from **Girona** there are a number of good traditional places to eat, and a spa hotel.

Map 8D **RIUDELLOTS DE LA SELVA**

La Roca 'Petita'
(R)S *Ctra de l'Aeroport (972) 47 71 32 Cl. Tues.*

Just outside Girona in a modern country house on the way to the airport; this is a simple, very popular restaurant that fills with families at the weekends. The food is all the most traditional Catalan home-cooking – partridge with cabbage, duck with pears, canelones, roast kid, etc. For a good filling meal without pretensions. Reserve at weekends.

Allow 2,500–3,500 ptas

Map 8D **CALDES DE MALAVELLA**

Balneario Vichy Catalán
(HR)M-L *Av. Dr Furest, 32 (972) 47 00 00 Open all year*

This is one of the most splendid spa hotels in Catalunya. It opened in

Caldes de Malavella – Hotel Vichy Catalán

1891, and is built and decorated in the romantic style of the modernist epoch, surrounded by expansive gardens. The waters here are famous – any restaurant you visit will have 'Vichy' in the fridge, as one of the preferred, slightly salty mineral waters. The hotel is fully equipped as a spa with modern installations and eighty-three bedrooms. A great feeling of spaciousness, and the sound of water everywhere. Immensely relaxing and very pleasant.

As usual, the Romans first discovered these waters, and you can find ruins of their buildings in the village.

Double room 8,700–15,000 ptas

Map 8D **SILS**

On the main N-11 near Sils there is a private car museum, the Salvador Claret collection, which was started in the 1950s and has accumulated some 150 cars. The earliest is a fine Merryweather dating from 1883.

Hostal de la Granota
(R)S-M *Ctra N-11, Km 695 (972) 85 32 44 Cl. Wed., Nov.*

Just by exit no. 9 of the motorway.

This is delightful in the summer – an old post-house complete with barn and outbuildings which has been a restaurant now for thirty years. You can either eat in the main barn (the restaurant proper) where there are bench tables and a splendid collection of farm tools and harness hung about the stone walls, or go on down to the tavern bar, or sit in the middle, under the roof of the open barn with quantities of garden flowers to one side. The food is the most traditional – country salads (particularly *del pastor* with a selection of *bacallà*, cured ham, white beans, tomatoes and more), omelettes, grilled meat, braised poultry, etc. On Fridays they serve *escudella i carn d'olla.* If you are a frog expert (granota in Catalan), take a look at the amazing collection at the back of the barn.

Allow 3,000–3,500 ptas

Map 8D **RIUDARENES**

La Brasa
(R)S *Ctra Santa Coloma, 21 (972) 85 60 17 Cl. Sun. eve., Mon. 15 Jan.–end Feb.*

One of the classic traditional restaurants of the region. The restaurant, built on a hillside, has spread into several diningrooms, the most attractive being in the cool *celler*, on the same level as the other rooms but effectively several metres below ground level, having been cut into the hill. The carte is exclusively regional, mostly meat – country chicken, rabbit, beef or lamb, and sausage of all sorts accompanied by the typical white beans or grilled vegetables. To start, there are plenty of salads, a whole range of omelettes, and a string of other simple dishes. Every table has its *pa amb tomàquet* and the portions come up plentiful and delicious. There's no choice when it comes to wine – they make it themselves and draw it in quantity from the barrels in the bodega. All rustic, check tablecloths and great fun.

Allow 2,000–3,000 ptas

Map 8D **HOSTALRIC**

This is a old walled town with a spectacular castle above, in the middle of the green agricultural hills of Girona. Compared with the medieval towns further north, however, it has almost nothing to offer except for the restored castle above, which you should aproach by road to appreciate the solid, many-layered feat of building. The castle has a long history, beginning in the twelfth century and making its herioc exit from the records in 1810 when it withstood a four-month seige against Napoleon's troops, after which it fell into ruins. Now restored, and a favourite choice for wedding banquets, the building houses a restaurant in the sombre vaults.

La Fortalesa
(R)S-M *Castell d'Hostalric (972) 86 41 22 Cl. Tues.*

Although it serves fairly mediocre Catalan food, it is quite fun and tends to be a meeting ground for families as well as, on Sundays, the local vicar and friends. The atmosphere is pleasant and unpretentious, and the menu is entertaining, with dishes named after battle terms. You should try one of the inventive salads, or the succulent but more filling *endivias en armadura* (chicory in armour – ham and béchamel), and the *pincho Fortalesa* (a meat kebab) makes a tender, though unsophisticated second dish. Enjoy the marvellous view from above.
Allow 3,000 ptas

From Hostalric, it takes a mere forty-five minutes to reach **Barcelona,** unless you plan to stop at possibly the very finest restaurant in Catalunya, the inimitable **El Racó de Can Fabes,** in **Sant Celoni** (see chapter 2, Day excursions from Barcelona).

ROUTE B FROM PERPIGNAN (INLAND)

* Camprodon and Ripoll south to Vic
* Olot and Garrotxa Natural Park

Camprodon and Ripoll south to Vic

This route takes Perpignan as a departure point, going south to Le Boulou and then south-west by the N115, passing Amélie-les-Bains and the old walled town of Prats de Molló to enter Spain over the pass of **Coll d'Ares.** This pass was only opened to traffic in 1965 and still doesn't carry a great deal of it. The customs frontier was formally withdrawn in 1992 so you have no need to stop except to admire the views. These are spectacular, with the great **Canigó** to the north of you and the ranges of peaks stretching away on all sides. The famous cellist, Pablo Casals, when he went into exile, chose a place from which he could see the **Canigó** every day to 'refresh his life'.

From here, you wind down through splendid scenery towards the important mountain town of **Camprodon** and then on, following the river Ter through woods and pastures, to the old monastery town of **Ripoll.** The river takes the road down to **Vic,** an attractive market town, where it diverts towards the sea via the reservoir of Sau. The wonderful forests of the mountain of **Montseny** are just south-east of here and Barcelona is an hour away.

For a different trip, turn off towards **Olot** after you leave **Camprodon**, from where you can enjoy the extraordinary volcanic beauty of La **Garrotxa**.

Map 7B **MOLLÓ**

Just about ten kilometres into Spain you come to the first Spanish village, the little pueblo of **Molló** and your first romanesque church. There's a fine example, eleventh century, with a spectacular tower just on your right as you approach.

Hostal Calitxó
(HR)S-M *Passatge El Serrat (972) 74 03 86 Cl. Mon except in summer*

This is a family business, with Josep Solè running the kitchen and his wife the 25-room hotel, while their two older children are studying the hotel and catering business. The rooms are simple and modern with excellent bathrooms, mostly with balconies, and all have wonderful mountain views. Breakfast is a splendid buffet to suit all tastes and appetites – they'll even produce eggs and bacon on request.

Sr. Solè changes the restaurant menu every month, sticking closely to the seasonal local produce, especially the river trout, and the cooking is of a high standard. Desserts are made on the premises.

Rest. allow 3,500 ptas; half-board 5,000 ptas; double room 5,200 ptas

The road descends through the mountains, winding as all mountain roads do, and in another eight kilometres it comes to the ancient mountain town of **Camprodon**.

Map 7B **CAMPRODON**

Rushing water dominates the townscape – there's a confluence of rivers, the Ter and the Ritort, right in the middle. This is a lovely old market town, with its tenth-century monastery of St. Pere, and its picturesque 'New' Bridge, which dates from the fourteenth century! The local produce is prepared here in abundance – superb *embotits* and charcuterie of all kinds, and just outside the town you can catch the delicious scent of two important biscuit factories.

The Plaça Espanya is the centre of town, round which you find the Hotel Güell, two good restaurants, and the little shop Alimentación Ramón Pairo which has hand-made charcuterie of an excellent quality. The main shopping street is C/ Valencia, where you can buy the local biscuits (called *Birba* and *Pujol*). The other hotel, the **Edelweiss**, is on the southern side of town, next to the tourist office.

Hotel Güell
(H)M *Plaça Espanya, 8 (972) 74 00 11 Cl. fortnight June, 15 days Nov.*

An old-established hotel built in 1935, with thirty-five comfortable rooms, owned and run by the Güell family. It's very welcoming, with rather fine traditional decor, and some much-polished dark wood furniture. If you reserve in time, ask for a room overlooking the attractive *Plaça Major*. Your car can be safely locked in here, so you don't need to take everything out of it. Highly recommended, and right in the heart of the town. No restaurant.

Double room 6,600 ptas

Hotel Edelweiss
(H)M *Ctra Sant Joan, 28 (972) 74 09 13 Cl. 25 Dec.*

Again a family business, headed by Sr. Joan Rous. It's just on the edge of town at the Barcelona entrance, so the twenty-one balconied bedrooms have fabulous views out over the valley. The building is handsome, and inside the decoration is elegant, well-finished

Camprodon – Hotel Edelweiss

in polished wood with parquet floors. Spacious and very comfortable.
Double room 10,000 ptas

La Plaça
(R)S-M *Plaça Espanya, 3 (972) 74 07 39 Cl. Tues.*

This little restaurant seats only twenty-six, so you should book at weekends. It's owned by Marcel Vinyeta and his American wife Karen, both of whom speak English, French, Spanish and Catalan, besides doing the cooking. Service is charming, handled by Nati Fernández. Specialties of the house are shoulder of lamb, entrecôte and canelones made by Karen. Ask about the dish of the day.
Allow 3,000–3,200 ptas

Núria
(R)S *Plaça Espanya, 11 (972) 74 00 04 Cl. Sun. eve. except in summer*

Don't be put off by the unprepossessing entrance to this restaurant. Again, it is a family business – aren't they all? – run by Sr. Luis Vilà with his brother Francisco in the kitchen. The restaurant proper is at the back, through the rather depressing bar and cafeteria section. The cooking is definitely good here, with specialties of game in season, and good grilled meats, snails, and roast lamb. There is a menu in English. Good value.
Menú del dia 900 ptas; carte 2,500 ptas

Camprodon is a major centre for mountain activities and excursions in this part of the Pyrenees. There's a pleasant drive from here, which takes the road towards France for three kilometres and turns off to the right towards **Rocabruna** and **Beget**, with the important added attraction that one of the finest restaurants in the valley, Can 'Po', is in Rocabruna. Going on towards Beget the road is single track and very twisty, so go carefully. My first visit to Beget was by bicycle – a great way to enjoy the marvellous wild countryside and the quantities of cows, which you may meet at any moment, balancing on the rocks to browse the herbiage. In the spring the roadside flowers are profuse and varied – keep the car windows open to enjoy the scented air. At the very end of the road is the tiny hamlet of Beget, so tucked away in a hidden valley that you only see it when you are almost there.

Map 7B **ROCABRUNA**

Can 'Po'
(R)S *Rocabruna (972) 74 10 45 Open 15 Jul.–15 Sept., rest of year open weekends only. No credit cards*

Owned by the Sala family, this little restaurant with only forty covers is immensely popular so it is essential to book. It's located in a charming old rustic house overlooking the valleys, with a traditional atmosphere but with top class linen and tableware, and sophisticated cuisine. Meats and fish, traditional dishes, entrecôte *a la llosa* and *a la crema de ceps*, rabbit *a la mostassa* and a fine *escudella*. The best way to enjoy the range of delicious offerings from the kitchen is to start with the apéritifs. A good range of wines. Can "Po" is reputed to be the finest restaurant in the entire region. You won't get in unless you book well in advance.

Allow 1,750 ptas

Map 7B **BEGET**

Park at the entrance to the village as there is no more road – here you are away from noise, traffic, shops, etc. The village itself is all stone-built and has been here for ever, an old stopping point on the walking tracks from Oix (just south) up over the Pyrenees to the French village of Lamanere. There's a pretty romanesque church here, which contains a fine eleventh-century crucifixion. You can spend time in and beyond Beget – there is good trout fishing and plenty of game, and of course the walks and rambles are innumerable. The addresses in Beget are really a joke, as the place itself is so tiny. Walk on past Can Joanic and over the bridge and you will come to the Plaça Major, then left up a narrow cobbled way and you come to the Bar El Forn at the very end.

Can Joanic
(R)S *C/ Vell Aire, 1 (972) 74 12 41 Open Jul., Aug., Sept., rest of the year open weekends only. Cl. Feb. No credit cards*

An inn at the world's end, simple and honest. You come here to rest from bustle and enjoy peace, the river, and the woods. The inn is an old farm house, the bar-restaurant-living room is low and cosy, with chequered tablecloths and a warm welcoming atmosphere. Antonio Martínez and his wife look after you and produce homely fare. Their specialties are the good mountain beef and lamb, and they'll cook your trout for you when you've caught it. There is local charcuterie of a high standard, and of course the fresh goat's cheese and honey are delectable. There are seven simple bedrooms here with a couple of bathrooms, in case you can't bear to leave.

Menú del dia 1,100 ptas; carte aprox. 2,000 ptas; double room 4,000 ptas

Bar-Restaurant El Forn
(R)S *C/ França,9 (972) 74 12 31 Cl. Mon. in winter*

Simple, small, with traditional Catalan country cooking, and a very resourceful kitchen – this is where we ate when I came to Beget by bicycle: 14 hungry people on a spring Sunday without any warning. We had to wait a bit, but Sra. Duñac managed to feed us all amply, with a beaming smile.

Allow 1,750 ptas

Also approached from Camprodon is the mountain village of **Setcases**. This is a popular place for walking, hiking, pony trekking and general mountain activities.

Map 7B SETCASES

This is quite a big village, built of stone and timber in the mountain style, although most houses are not that old. There are shops and general amenities, and plenty of bars and inns which cater for the mountain tourism.

Hostal Nueva Tiranda
(HR)S-M *Setcases (972) 13 60 52 Cl. Wed. in winter No credit cards*

There's a long, comfy bar with lots of sofas, a big dining room, and simple well-furnished bedrooms. The cooking is typical of the region, with casseroles of mixed meats, grilled kid, and wild river trout. There are only fifteen rooms, not all with bathrooms, and you either take full or half board.

Menú del dia 1,500 ptas; carte 2,000 ptas; half-board, 4,200 ptas; full-board 5,000 ptas

Hotel La Coma
(HR)M *Setcases (972) 13 60 73 Cl. 25 Dec.*

At the entrance to the village coming from Camprodon you come across this hotel. It's very comfortable for families with loads of leisure space indoors and out, a swimming pool, solarium, children's playground, ping-pong, etc. and also has ample enclosed parking. The bedrooms are big and bright, all with balconies and lovely mountain views. The cooking is typical mountain Catalan, casseroles and grilled and roasted meat.

Menú del dia 1,600 ptas; carte 2,500 ptas; half-board 4,800 ptas; double room 6,200 ptas

Onwards south from **Camprodon**, through gorgeous scenery opening out and softening with broad fields and vistas of far-off mountains, the next place to enjoy is **Sant Joan de les Abadesses**. The monastery here, after which the town is named, was founded in 887 by Wilfred the Hairy for his daughter Emma, the first of the abbesses. The cloisters are charming, and in the collegiate romanesque church you can see a wonderful wooden calvary from the mid-thirteenth century. I first saw this in its natural state, some 750 years old, woodwormed at the edges and with faint brown-tinged colouring, but it has now been restored to the bright polychrome of its earlier days and, to me at least, this has robbed it of much of its emotion. A remarkable work in any event, in the rather beautiful church where the alabaster windows shed a special quality of light.

From this town there is a fast route to **Olot** via the *tuneles de Capsa costa* which brings you to the wonders of the volcanic region of **La Garrotxa** in under half an hour.

Continuing south for some ten kilometres the road leads to **Ripoll**, a very important place, often referred to as the cradle of Catalunya.

Map 6C **RIPOLL**

Guifré el Pelòs was responsible for the cathedral here, one of the finest examples in existence of Catalan romanesque architecture. The main portal, protected by a glass-fronted porch, is a marvel of biblical and allegorical narrative carving, sculpted in six great horizontal tiers which clothe the complex decorated arch. The inside of the church is plain but formidable, and to the right is the very beautiful cloister. There's a museum next door with a fascinating section devoted to the way of life of the medieval shepherds, and their migrations over the mountain passes. Catalunya, and indeed much of Spain, depended on the wool trade in the middle ages. Today, although most flocks move about the peninsular by road and rail, you can still see the transhumance with flocks of hundreds of sheep and goats proceeding on their traditional paths from north to south, particularly in the mountains. Their routes are part of the national heritage and are theoretically preserved even where they cross motorways or railways, although in the more difficult urban areas this is now somewhat impractical, and is only undertaken symbolically.

Good food can be found just outside the town at El Racó del Francès, across the river, and there is a good hotel, Solana del Ter just along the road towards Barcelona.

El Racó del Francès
(R)S-M *'Can Nerol', Plà d'Ordina (972) 70 18 94 Cl. Mon.*

This takes a bit of finding, but it is well worth the effort. The French chef-patron, Jean Quevy, has been here for ages and runs an immaculate and slightly eccentric restaurant much loved by the people of Ripoll. He is a happy, humourous delight of a man whose cooking is sometimes French, sometimes Belgian, sometimes Catalan, and sometimes Chinese. It depends on what's in the market and on how he feels. The carte is changed every month. Specialties are fillet of veal à la Perigourdine, monkfish sauce Nantua, palourdes, *gambes* with beurre d'écrevisses, not to mention frogs' legs and snails. (How he laughed when he told me that.) There are only twenty-eight covers, so you *must* book.

Menú del dia 2,500 ptas; all inclusive; carte approx. 3,500 ptas

Solana del Ter
(HR)M *Ctra Barcelona-Puigcerdà (972) 70 10 62 Cl. Nov., rest. Cl. Sun. eve. in winter*

A big modern, traditional-style building on your left as you go towards

Barcelona, perhaps one kilometre from Ripoll. It's family-owned, with ample parking space, and a garage if you feel safer that way. The thirty-nine rooms are standard and comfortable, everything is light and airy, and the bar is huge, doubling as a leisure area. There's a swimming pool and toddlers' pool which is open in July and August, a gym, a sauna, hydromassage, tennis, and everything else you can think of. The specialties of the restaurant are the lamb from Ripoll, canelones, and fresh trout with walnuts.

Menú del dia 2,400 ptas; carte approx. 4,000 ptas; double room 9,000 ptas

From Ripoll, the road curves through spectacular hills, woodlands and green fields, following the Ter down into the agricultural plain of Osona with its central market town of **Vic**. For country pleasures, there are two extremely pretty (and winding) roads leading westwards. Either head just north of Ripoll and turn off towards **La Pobla de Lillet**, or continue south and turn off towards **Sant Agustí de Lluçanès** which will eventually deliver you to **Berga** (see Route C).

Map 6D VIC

This is a fine town, mostly pedestrian, treasuring some fine buildings and a superb museum of romanesque art, and for lovers of sausage, some of the finest *embotits* in Catalunya. As you drive into Vic the main road rings the town, and you will come to a wide *rambla,* in which you can park. If it's full, it's best to seek out somewhere on a street leading away from the centre. Whatever the weather, the big Plaça Major is a hive of activity on Saturdays, the town's market day, and fills with big stalls of local vegetables and fruit, rails of clothes, tables of pottery, and crates of baby chickens and ducks. Round the edge you'll find old magazines, books and stamps to browse through. On other days, the square is a quiet dignified expanse of space, with arcaded sides. In the far corner you can see a church tower, which leads you towards the historic town centre.

The cathedral is a rather sombre building with wall paintings by Josep Maria Sert, a celebrated Catalan artist who painted heavy dramatic biblical figures in tones of gold and silver. As your eyes adjust to the dark, remember that the original paintings were burnt in 1936, and he had to repaint everything again. The cloisters are attractive, the lower storey dating from the twelfth century, the same era as the crypt. Beside the romanesque bell tower you find the famous **Museu Episcopal** which treasures a wonderful collection of romanesque frescos, statuary, and painted objects, taken from the little churches sprinkled around the mountain regions. Ask at the reception desk for a guide folder, which will explain (in English) just what you're looking at. It's a quiet place with few visitors so you can stroll round uninhibited. Fascinating for anyone interested in medieval Catalan religion and imagery.

The Roman legacy to the town is the portico of a second-century Roman temple which stands proudly in the pedestrian part of town, close to the top of the Ramblas.

There are good restaurants in and about Vic. They've recently introduced a new 'traditional' dish here which you are bound to come across. It consists of a mixture of sautéed wild mushroom, *bacallà*, chopped almonds, parsley and garlic enclosed like a parcel in fine bacon, laid on a bed of chopped potato, onion and *botifarra*. It's called *l'almosta* – something that should fit into the cup of your hands, inspired from an ancient courtesy in this region of presenting an offering to the host on being invited to dine.

Hotels are thin on the ground here, most being of the executive type. The best place to stay is several kilometres out of town, in the Parador de Vic.

Ausa
(H)M *Plaça Major, 2 (93) 885 53 11 Open all year*

This is a simple hotel, with some twenty-six straightforward rooms half of which overlook the Plaça Major. It feels more like a hostel than a hotel, with the reception on the first floor, but the rooms are lighthearted and the view is fun. Beware, though, if you are staying on a Friday evening, as the market begins setting up early on Saturday. There are apartments here too, if you feel like staying a few days. No restaurant.

Double room 7,000–10,000 ptas

La Taula
(R)M *Plaça de Don Miquel Clariana, 4 (93) 886 32 29 Cl. Sun. eve. Mon. Feb, one week in Aug.*

The big old door of this eighteenth century building is close to the Roman portico in a quiet, pretty corner of Vic. Inside, the restaurant is long and thin, tastefully decorated with photographic portraits and paintings, and the windows at the end look on to the green trees of a garden. The food is excellent, Catalan with a touch of French sophistication. If you go on Wednesdays or Thursdays during the summer, there's a tremendous buffet here. Otherwise, the menu depends on the season – perhaps a warm salad with goat's cheese, a confit of duck with potato and garlic purée, and a fine tarte tatin to finish with. It gets very busy at weekends so you should book.

Menú del dia 1,300 ptas; weekend menu 2,500 ptas; carte approx. 3,500 ptas

Cal 'U'
(R)M *Plaça de Santa Teresa, 4–5 (93) 889 03 45 Cl. Sun. eve., Mon.*

One of the oldest restaurants of the region, which has served for generations as the meeting point of the town folk. It fills at weekends and you need to get there early for lunch. A happy, unsophisticated, family atmosphere, good regional food, and a reputation for serving excellent game in season. It's on the Rambla, so very easy to find.

Menú del dia 1,200–1,800 ptas; carte approx. 3,000 ptas

Parador de Vic
(HR)L *15 km from Vic (93) 812 23 23 Open all year*

Following the clear signs, you leave Vic and head eastwards past Tavernoles and find this lovely place at the end of the road. It's built overlooking the beautiful reservoir of Sau, with a great big terrace from which you can breathe in the views, surrounded by an exceptional feeling of peace. It's a new but handsome building, following the style of a Catalan *masia* with arched balconied bedrooms and plenty of space. Extremely comfortable.

Double room 12,000 ptas

From **Vic** you can drive on down to **Barcelona** within an hour. The road is very fast – you need to go with some caution as the traffic often moves at motorway speeds although the road itself isn't one, and has bends which warrant slower speeds. Alternatively, take a gastronomic excursion to **Olost**, a detour south over the hill to **Collsuspina**, or drive up to the delightful village of **Rupit**.

Map 7C OLOST

A quiet half-hour drive twisting through wooded hills, with views stretching up to the **Cadí** mountains, brings you to a quite superb restaurant in this hamlet.

Fonda Sala
(R)M *Plaça Major, 4 (93) 888 01 06 Cl. Sun. eve., 1–15 Sept., Christmas.*

This is a special place, in an unremarkable building just opposite the village church. It's an attractive mixture: the heart and soul of the village with its lively bar and card players downstairs, a humble travellers' *fonda* (inn) upstairs, and a marvellous, sophisticated restaurant just in behind. The room is modern, decorated simply with pictures, with the extensive *celler* visible through a glass wall at the back. The carte celebrates the local produce – a warm wild mushroom terrine; home-smoked salmon; salad of marinaded *bacallà* with white beans; partridge served pickled or with cabbage; *civet* of hare or wild boar (in season). And if you feel like tasting a succulent dish of sea bass, Antoni Sala brings the fish daily from the coast. Finish with a fragrant selection of sorbets, or one of the day's specialities. As a restaurant of distinction, it is renowned throughout Catalunya. If you come for dinner, you can pop upstairs to bed, and leave the winding roads 'til morning.

Allow 4,000–5,000 ptas; double room 4,500 ptas

Back in the plain of Vic, heading south on the last leg towards Barcelona, there is a pretty diversion which takes you up over the hill which dominates the west side of the valley, past **Collsuspina,** and carries you across towards Manresa, or down to Barcelona via the soft country route which goes through **Moià** and **Sant Feliu de Codines.**

Map 6D COLLSUSPINA

There are two traditional restaurants here – both good, but completely different in character.

Floriac
(R)M *Ctra Manresa – Vic, Km 39,5 (93) 887 09 91 Cl. Mon. eve., Tues., Feb.*

Half-way up the bends of the hill, you suddenly come across a huge sign – react immediately or you'll miss it. The track leads to a big country house, built in 1568, in which four rooms are used as a traditional restaurant. The site itself is splendid, with views across the plain of Vic to the mountain of Montseny, so it's a good place for big parties. It has its own vegetable garden and the house has a grand feeling of age. Regional country dishes.

Menú del dia 2,200 ptas; carte 3,000 ptas

Can Xarína
(R)M *Major, 10 (93) 830 05 77 Cl. Sun. eve., Mon. last week Jun.–first week July, Nov.*

This is in the village itself, a family-run restaurant in the *casa pairal*, the oldest house of the hamlet. Inside, stone-walled and vaulted with a great fireplace at the end, is the long diningroom, complete with checked tablecloths, *porrons* of wine and country bread, where you are served simple traditional fare: a board of dried sausage, wild mushrooms, duck with pears and prunes, meat *a la brasa*, and *crema catalana*.

Allow 3,000 ptas

Just twenty kilometres from **Vic** along a bendy road following the meanderings of the river Fluvía, through cereal fields, wild patches of forest and rocky outcrops, you come to the hamlet of **Rupit**, a sudden turn off the road which links Vic with **Olot**, the provincial capital of the volcanic region of La Garrotxa.

Map 7C RUPIT

As you approach, you'll be tempted to leave the main road early – the neighbouring village Pruit has a confusingly similar name! Rupit is a delightful place, definitely best in the early morning mist or out of season, still preserving a medieval ambience with cobbled streets, and a jumble of stone and slate-roofed houses. The Carrer Fossar is one of the most famous streets, stepped steeply up the hillside and lined with old village cottages, with an ironmongers' that was considered so typical that it was reproduced in Barcelona's *Poble Espanyol* (see Chapter 1). As you enter the hamlet, you'll see a long hanging bridge over the rocky expanse of the river, connecting the few houses on the other side with the main body of the village – it's a bit stomach-lurching but part of the experience. For a pretty walk, go down to the house at the end of the main street, through beneath the arch, and stroll along the paths through the vegetable gardens and woods to the beautiful waterfall of Sallent – spectacular when the river is flowing well.

For light refreshment, there is delicious *coca* produced here. Irresistible, and especially good as a late breakfast.

Hostal L'Estrella
(HR)S *Plaça Bisbe Font, 1 (93) 856 50 05 Open all year*

A simple old *hostal* which has been here for fifty years, with some thirty rooms and a big, popular restaurant which serves scores of covers at the weekends. Traditional food. Make sure you taste the *embotits* and the thick country bread of the village.

Carte approx. 2,500 ptas; double room 4,000–6,000 ptas

Continuing north from **Rupit** or driving east through tunnels and spectacular scenery from **Sant Joan de les Abadesses**, you can reach the dignified, proud provincial capital, **Olot**, which acts as a gateway to the lovely soothing countryside of the **Garrotxa Natural Park**.

Olot and Garrotxa Natural Park

Map 7C **OLOT**

Although it's ringed with mountains, and peppered with small volcanic mounds, Olot seems quite unsympathetic and modern as you enter. Stop, walk around and look up at the splendid modernist buildings in the *Eixample*, enjoy the wide avenues of plane trees, and you begin to appreciate the studied calm and prosperity which helped create the Olot school of landscape painting at the end of the last century, and which still nurtures a Fine Arts Academy today. You can see a good selection of these paintings, and the famous *La Càrrega* (the charge) by the celebrated Catalan painter Ramon Casas, in the local *Museu Comarcal* housed in a neo-classical hospice in the centre. Apart from the numerous art galleries in the town, there are also several workshops here specialising in the making of religious imagery.

Volcanic activity has played an integral part in the history of Olot – most of the old part of the town disappeared after the earthquakes of the 1427 and 1428. For a little quiet studying, there's the *Museu dels Volcans* which has a thoroughly educative exhibition.

Museu Comarcal Open 11.00 a.m.–2.00 p.m., 4.00 p.m.–7.00 p.m.; Cl. Tues., Sun. p.m.

Museu dels Volcans Open 10.00 a.m.–2.00 p.m. & 5.00 p.m.–7.00 p.m. Jul.–Sept., 10.00 a.m.–2.00 p.m. & 4.00 p.m.–6.00 p.m. Oct.–Jun; Cl. Tues., Sun. p.m.

There is an attractive hotel and a healthy scattering of restaurants around Olot.

Riu Olot
(H)M *Crta Santa Pau, s/n (972) 26 94 44 Always open*

On the way to Santa Pau, there is a purpose-built hotel on your right. Purpose-built, but not a barracks – this was designed with care and love. It is run entirely by ladies and it shows. The lounge is done in pale colours, with attractive mouldings on the ceiling, and is quiet and spacious. Every room has a balcony and there's a grand terrace which enjoys magnificent views. Breakfast is a self-service buffet, ample and satisfying. Lots of people make this hotel a centre for excursions into La Garrotxa. No restaurant.

Double room 9,540 ptas

Les Cols
(R)M *Mas Les Cols, Ctra de la Canya (972) 26 92 09 Cl. Mon., 1–15 Aug.*

An old *casa pairal* has been converted into a high class restaurant here, just north of Olot, with an imaginative carte based on the local produce. As befits a place called Les Cols (the cabbages), these figure among the specialities, in the form of leaves stuffed with a heavenly mixture of duck foie gras, *farcellets de col amb foie d'ànec.* Then there is excellent fish, home-prepared patisserie, and all is to be enjoyed in the terrace dining room, with fine views, or indoors if it's too hot.

Allow 3,000–3,500 ptas

Els Ossos
(R)S *Ctra de Santa Pau, Km 2,7 (972) 26 61 34 Cl. Thurs., Jul.*

The first place you come to on the way from Olot to Santa Pau, a restaurant which has been going for a century. They serve good *cuina casolana,* or typical country home-cooking, and are ready to feed large numbers at the weekends. A popular, jolly place.

Allow 1,500–2,000 ptas

Can Xel
(R)S *Ctra de Santa Pau, Km 5 (972) 68 02 11 Cl. Wed., 15–30 Jan.*

The next place you come to on the way from Olot to Santa Pau, just at the entrance to the district of Santa Pau. The owner is Joan Fábrega and he and his wife will welcome you. The dining rooms are upstairs – a series of small rooms, well-furnished, with chequered cloths and nicely laid out. They have huge rooms for weddings and so forth too, but don't let that put you off. There is a genuine family atmosphere, and people come from all around to eat here. Sr. Fabrega bases his cooking on local and typical fare: specialities include *ous a la caputxina*, (his own invention) a dish of hardboiled eggs stuffed and fried and served with a sauce, something along the lines of canelones; snails (much enjoyed in Catalunya); pigs' trotters (another favourite): and there is good fish too. Sweets include *crema catalana* and *maté* with honey.

Menú del dia approx. 950 ptas; carte approx. 1,500–2,000 ptas

Map 7C **SANTA PAU**

In the heart of the Garrotxa Natural Park, just beyond Olot, is this ancient barony with a castle founded in the eleventh century. It's a

Santa Pau – Village

delightful walled hamlet of fieldstone houses built round the big square castle, and although it was substantially altered in the fifteenth and sixteenth centuries the medieval feel still endures. The small *Plaça Major*, completely enclosed and surrounded by arcades, is also known as *Fira dels Bous* (Ox Market), having been used for this purpose in days gone by. You approach from Olot along a country road which winds among the volcanic hills of La Garrotxa. The town itself is entered only with great caution, the streets are so narrow and the turns so acute that there are usually mirrors to tell you if another car is coming – watch them well!

Not only a pretty place, but a unique area for the growing of beans and grain. *Fesols de Santa Pau* are famous – these beans are very special, of such quality that they even have a *denominació d'origen* to vouch for their excellence which is due to the volcanic soil and local microclimate. Only here, in this area, grows a grain called *fajola*, which looks something like rice but darker. You cannot buy the grain, there is so little, but the fields in flower are a superb sight. To taste the special sweets made from the grain, you should visit Cal Sastre.

➜ Cal Sastre

(HR)M *Carrer de les Cases Noves, 1 (972) 68 00 49 Cl. Mon. 1–15 Jan. 1–15 Jun.*

Once upon a time there was a couple who had a restaurant in Santa Pau. Business was good and they thought they would expand so they moved to Olot and opened a bigger place, helped by their daughter. One day a young man, a tailor from Santa Pau, came to dine in the restaurant and fell in love with the daughter, married her, and joined into the restaurant life. During the civil war, when all the men went away, the women thought it safer to return to the village, and so installed themselves in the old family house in the centre of Santa Pau. The badge of Cal Sastre, (the house of the tailor), is thus a felicitous needle-and-thread and a fork-and-plate.

Sra. Margarita Coll de Carrera, the daughter of the tailor and the present chef of Cal Sastre, has really spent her whole life here, and carries on the family's restaurant tradition with genuine flair while her son looks after the dining room. Her cooking is country and typical, but done in a refined manner, with emphasis on some very special salads – of salt-herring, of wild fungi in season. There is wild boar with a special conserve made by Sra. Margarita, excellent lamb, rabbit with little meatballs and fungi, and of course *botifarra* with the special beans.

Among the sweets is a real novelty unique to here, using the *fajola* grain – *farinetes de fajola amb mel.* The grain is made into a paste, fried in oil and served with honey or sugar. You have to try it.

Recently, the family has renovated another old building just outside the walls of the village, and installed 10 rooms and bathrooms. Green views, cowbells and fruit trees. Delightful.

There is a half-board menú at 1,200 ptas for the lucky people who are staying, otherwise allow 2,500–3,000 ptas; Double room 7,000 ptas

Arrowed for its uniqueness, good cooking and the wonderful peace of the village and surroundings.

Map 7C GARROTXA NATURAL PARK

This is a beautiful part of Girona, an area of volcanic cones, strange lava formations, beech and oak forests, green pastures and an abundance of water. You can still clearly see the craters either at the top of the cones or where they burst at the side to release the lava. You needn't fear an eruption though, the last one happened some 11,500 years ago, when El Croscat volcano blew. Earthquakes rocked the area in the fifteenth century but since then barely a murmur has been felt.

The cones are mainly dressed with deciduous or evergreen woodland, and all around are neat, pretty meadows and agricultural fields. There are forests of various types of oak, beech with box shrubs or scattered wood anemonies, river courses strung with alder trees – this is a lovely landscape for the walker.

The most visited cone is that of Santa Margarida, nearly 350m in diameter at its crater with a romanesque sanctuary within, which is a short walk from Santa Pau or a longer one via the wonderful beech forest of **La Fageda d'en Jordà**. There are dozens of others, so you need time, comfortable shoes and a tourist office map of the paths before you set out and explore the countryside.

In terms of wildlife, there are plenty of wild boar (although you're unlikely to see any), so many indeed that farmers regret the passing of the carbon burners of yore who looked after the forests, produced fuel for the city kitchens and kept the wild boar population down. If you're extremely lucky you might come across an otter. You should also see a goshawk or two, a peregrine falcon and perhaps a short-toed eagle.

It's all incredibly pretty here – old farm buildings built of volcanic stone, romanesque chapels, sudden sheer hillsides with blue-black and red-brown coloured lava rocks, hidden waterfalls and gorges, patches of early morning mist in summer and winter alike, and flowers and greenery everywhere.

Of the many picturesque villages in the area, apart from **Santa Pau**, you must pass by **Castellfollit de la Roca**, a medieval village perched above a sand-coloured cliff-face of jagged geometric basalt rock, set above the river Fluviá. It is spectacular, both at night when the basalt cliff is lit, and during the day, when you can appreciate the extraordinary formations. The romanesque houses and church of **Sant Joan les Fonts** are also worth a stop. By car you can journey gently on from Santa Pau along towards **Banyoles** and **Girona** (see Route A); or visit Castellfollit de la Roca and continue on to the charming town of **Besalú** which is some twenty minutes from **Figueres** (see Route A). Both roads are very beautiful.

Map 8C BESALÚ

This is a lovely town, with a historic medieval bridge stretching over the Fluviá, picturesque by day and romantic by night. It is a traditional market town, as it is the connecting point between **Olot** and the main towns of the highway which sweeps down from Perpignan to Barcelona: **Figueres** and **Girona** (see Route A). Spending time here is a real pleasure, especially out of season. The town is a delight of old streets and buildings where almost all the foundations date from the twelfth century. The original entrance was via the magnificent fortified bridge, now pedestrian, constructed with a sharp angle in the middle dictated by the rock foundations below. There is a good parking area at the foot of the bridge, so that you can still enter on foot, kindling your imagination as you go. The street leads to the main square, Plaça de la Llibertat which is surrounded by sixteenth-century arcades and presided over by the fine medieval building of the town hall (and tourist office). On the other side of the square is the Cúria Reial, the old justice court of the province, in which you can now enjoy a good Catalan plateful (see below). Beyond the Plaça you come to the Benedictine monastery of Sant Pere, which has left the town with a small but very solid romanesque church with some fine capitals inside. And across the square (you can park here too) you can visit the patio of the twelfth-century house, Casa Cornellà. Back near the bridge, on the far side of town, is the old Jewish quarter, where you can visit the only Jewish purifying baths that have been found in the peninsular, dating again from the twelfth-century.

Fonda Siqués
(HR)S *Av. President Lluís Campanys, 6–8 (972) 59 01 10 Cl. 23 Dec–23 Jan., Sun. eve. & Mon. during winter*

On the main road, this place you truly cannot miss. Nor should you. It's one of those stone-built ancient inns that you are always looking for, though usually they are not what they look. This one emphatically is. Six generations have kept a hostelry here since its foundation in 1864, when they bought the land and built the *fonda* on the line of the new road. But even before that the family had looked after travellers on the old road through the centre of this little town, in the days when all the traffic used the old bridge. The main dining room is the old *quadra* where the horses were stabled and their drivers slept, and gradually rooms were added above for carriage travellers and so on. There are now ten double and three single rooms, all with bath, fitted into the old building. A lift they couldn't manage, so it's inexpensive.

The restaurant 'Cal Parent' developed too, simplicity for the drivers and quality for the guests. Nowadays, the hotel is run by Carme Teixidor and her mother Rosa Teixidor is the chef. This is top quality *cuina catalana* (Catalan cooking), classic and ample, including *pomes farcides amb carn* (apples stuffed with mince), *botifarra* of several kinds, *platillos* or stews and braises of meat in a sauce, and they also have fresh fish brought in every day. The sweet trolley is all home-made.

Menú del dia 1,100 ptas; carte approx. 2,500–3,000 ptas; double room 3,600 ptas

Cúria Reial
(R)M *Plaça de la Llibertat 15 (972) 59 02 63 Cl. Feb. Tues.*

Another lovely old building with stone arches. Cool and inviting with a terrace overlooking the ancient bridge and the river. *Cuina catalana* (Catalan cooking), including duck with pears, monkfish with green garlic, and game in season.
Allow 2,300–4,000 ptas

Residència Marià
(H)S *Plaça de la Llibertat, 4 (972) 59 01 06*

This is practically next door to the Cúria Reial, an old palace now turned into a simple hotel. There's no lift, but all seven rooms have baths. It's run by Sra. Montserrat Juanola i Sala, a motherly and welcoming lady who takes endless trouble to look after her guests. Half-board is arranged with the Cúria Reial. You must reserve.
Double room 3,500 ptas; half-board 4,200 ptas

Pont Vell
(R)M *C/ Pont Vell, 28 (972) 59 10 27 Fully open in summer, lunch only in winter except at weekends; Cl. 2–17 Jan., Tues.*

Right beside the old bridge, of course, small, welcoming and pretty. *Cuina catalana* (Catalan cooking), with specialities of the local charcuterie, *conill agridolc*, river trout with almonds. Desserts are made on the premises.
Allow 3,000–3,500 ptas
From here Route A and the town of **Figueres** is only 20 minutes away.

4 THE CENTRAL PYRENEES AND LLEIDA

ROUTE C FROM FOIX (PUIGCERDÀ)

*Puigcerdà, Ripoll, Ribes de Freser, Vall de Núria
*Puigcerdà (Cadí Tunnel), Berga, Manresa
*La Cerdanya (Puigcerdà to La Seu d'Urgell), Cadí-Moixeró Natural Park

Puigcerdà, Ribes de Freser, Vall de Núria

Approaching Catalunya from Foix (via the tunnel Puymorens) or Prades, the main entrance town is Puigcerdà, guarding the frontier with the French town of Bourg-Madame. The route then follows the twisting, wooded mountain pass down to Ripoll from where you can speed on down to Barcelona via **Vic** (see Route B), or stay up in the high Pyrenean mountain enclave of **Núria**.

Map 5B PUIGCERDÀ

This is a well-to-do town, busy in winter with the ski season and full of people escaping the heat in summer. It lost its gothic church in the civil war but the tower still stands in the middle of the main square. There are plenty of restaurants to choose from.

Hotel del Lago
(H)M *Av. Dr Piguillem, 7 (972) 88 10 00 Open all year*

As its name suggests, the hotel is next to a small artifical lake which has been here since the sixteenth century, in the outskirts of the town. It has a lovely grassy garden planted with trees and shrubs, and an inviting swimming pool. An added space, particularly comfortable in the winter evenings, is the circular wooden lounge with its large windows and fireplace, which is set into the garden. Very peaceful in the summer heat, and beautiful in the winter.

No animals allowed. No restaurant.
Double room 8,500 ptas

→ La Vila
(R)M–L *C/ Alfons I, 34 (972) 14 08 04 Cl. Mon. (except Aug.)*

This elegant restaurant, only a few years old, is a pleasure to visit. Inside it is decorated with plants, and the tablecloths are flower-covered prints. The restaurant is quite big, having expanded through a bar on one side section, into a small middle and crossing over to another room beside. The cooking is Catalan with a distinctly modern touch. A plate of little toasts of *jabugo* ham or somesuch delicacy make a good aperitif. There is a good range of rice dishes here, or a lighter warm salad of wild mushrooms and duck liver. To follow, a little truffled pigeon, or perhaps monkfish (*rap*) with baby vegetables and a light saffron sauce. Main courses vary frequently – particularly the fish – as the chef never knows what the market will bring in. For afters, a liqueur-flavoured compôte of apple with a crème anglaise is delicious.

Menú degustació 3,900 ptas, carte 4,000 ptas

Arrowed for the fresh creative energy of the chef, Lluís Bertran, and the pretty room.

La Tauleta
(R)S-M *C/ Major, 54 (972) 88 17 19 Cl. Mon.*

A restaurant with two comfortable rooms, run by a young team full of aspiration. Little tapas keep you going as the kitchen prepares your first course. This is honest modern home-cooking – fresh pasta with prawns, lamb with herbs, magret de canard with little sweet onions, peach sorbet, prunes with armagnac. Good value, thoughtful presentation and a constantly changing menu.

Menú del dia 1,750 ptas; carte aprox. 2,500 ptas

El Galet
(R)S-M *Plaça Santa Maria, 8 (972) 88 22 66 Cl. Tues.*

A long, thin room with a bar where you can eat whatever you want – from toasts, cheeses, pâtes, omelettes, salads, to meats grilled on the fire at the end of the room. This is a great place to try an assortment of the excellent dried sausages of the region.

Allow 1,000–3,000 ptas

La Tieta
(R)M *C/ dels Ferrers, 20 (972) 88 01 56 Cl. 15 Jun.–15 Jul., Tues., Wed. in winter*

A pretty restaurant installed in a centuries-old house, preserving the old stone walls and dark interiors, with the addition of old-fashioned washing basins. Most people come here to eat grilled meat with one of several sauces on offer, accompanied by baked potatoes and vegetables. Steamed hake is a speciality. In winter they offer civet of hare, onion soup, *escudella* and other warming dishes. There's an informal summer terrace at the back.

Menú del dia 2,150 ptas, carte 3,500 ptas

Map 6B **LLIVIA**

This town is in fact in Catalunya, although it's on the French side of the frontier – the result of some rather careless wording when drawing the boundary in the seventeenth-century. The oldest apothecary in Europe can be visited here, dating from around 1420, where the museum displays a stunning collection of instruments, pottery and glass jars used in days of yore. It's in the municipal museum opposite the church, up in the centre of the village.

Open 10.00 a.m.–1.00 p.m., 3.00 p.m.–6.00 p.m.; Cl. Mon.

Can Ventura
(R)M *Plaça Major, 1 (972) 89 61 78 Cl. Oct., Mon. eve., Tues.*

The main reason for coming here is the splendid old house, built in 1791 and carefully restored to hold a small number of tables. The thick ceiling beams are magnificent. The restaurant rooms are on the middle floor, lined with antique furniture, but it's worth exploring top to bottom, where more not-very-good works of art, old furniture and junk bring the old building romantically alive.

The food is pretty straightforward – a selection of salads to start with, then meat or trout *a la brasa* or *a la pedra* (on a hot piece of slate at the table). The best pud is the moscatel sabayon. You must reserve beforehand.

Allow 3,000–4,000 ptas

Map 6B **VILALLOBENT**

The turning off to Vilallobent is just on the eastern outskirts of Puigcerdà.

El Recó
(R)S *(972) 88 11 46 Open all year Cl. Sun. eve.*

This is a great place for a rowdy weekend lunch. It's a small house converted into a two-storey restaurant with paper coverings on pink tablecloths and thick pottery plates. The food is as simple as could be – and abundant. You are limited to a set menu consisting of a platter of local dried sausage, a salad, and grilled meat with chips (you can choose lamb cutlets, pork, chicken or *botifarra*). *Pa amb tomàquet* comes without asking, and the grilled snails make a great tapa while you're waiting.

Menu 1,500–1,900 ptas

Map 6B **LA MOLINA**

This is the oldest ski station in Catalunya, and is still one of the most popular as the railway station brings you practically to the slopes themselves. Hiking country in the summer.

Roc Blanc
(HR)M *(972) 14 50 00 Open Dec.–Apr., Jul.–10 Sept.*

Just below the ski station.
In summer this is a family hotel, full of clients (many French) who come back year after year. It has a swimming pool at the back which is surrounded (like the hotel) by woods which encroach into the grounds. A jolly place. In the summer, the hotel organises lots of activities should you be staying for any length of time. 52 rooms – simple and comfortable, looking out to the mountains. Home cooking.
Half-board 6,490 ptas

Map 6B **RIBES DE FRESER**

This is a narrow town on the banks of the river Freser. It's the point of departure for the mountain train that climbs up to the Núria valley, depositing dozens of walkers and lovers of mountain fresh air. It's worth going up for the spectacular journey itself, and for the sight of the ring of mountains that surround the valley when you get there. The train makes the trip every hour, so you can pop up there easily (see below).

Caçadors
(R)S *Balandrau, 24 (972) 72 70 06 Cl. Nov.*

Caçadors is just by the station – so it's handy if you're thinking of visiting Núria. It's no beauty as a room, but the food is good. Rabbit roasted or braised, roast lamb or kid, pigs' trotters with turnips, and lots of wild mushrooms – this is a typical Catalan restaurant, where you should drink a good stout wine to accompany the sturdy platefuls. It's a great favourite here, and tends to get full of families, particularly at weekends. The restaurant of the hotel Fanet, which has twenty-seven simple rooms.
Allow 1,500–2,000 ptas

Just past Ribes de Freser, there's a turning off to the small old village of **Campelles**, up in the western hills some ten kilometres away, where you can eat very well. The countryside here is a mixture of soft meadow and woodland, with lovely views – a gentle place for walking.

Map 6B **CAMPELLES**

Cabana de Can Salomó
(R)M *Campelles (972) 72 91 24 Open all weekends, Easter, summer season*

The Cabana is a surprising place in the midst of the undisturbed rural village. It's in a 1707 barn, which has been converted into a very

attractive, high-ceilinged, country restaurant. A great fireplace dominates one wall, and there are several different floor levels, so that it feels spacious but intimate, particularly when the candles are lit at night. In season the game is excellent here – wild boar, chamoix, hare. The menu is short but full of Pilar's personal recipes – the rabbit with herbs and little onions is an old favourite, and her roast lamb is very popular. Or there are grilled meats, snails, the chicken with hazlenuts ... You can also enjoy cheese or meat fondues (ring in advance). If you are hungering after cheese, try the selection of soft (French) or dry (Spanish). Pottery plates, wooden spoons, and quiet classical music.
Allow 2,500 – 3,000 ptas

Terralta
(HR)M *El Baell (972) 72 73 50 Open Jul.–15 Sept.*

A few kilometres away from Campelles, reached by the same road. A hotel on its own, built in the chalet style, with marvellous views of the countryside. It's a pretty walk along a forest track from here to Campelles, and there are limitless walks in the surrounding countryside. The hotel offers comfortable accomodation with half-board. The parking is somewhat messy, with cars parking on the roadside, but this is no great worry as there isn't any traffic at all.
Half-board approx. 6,000 ptas

Map 6B **VALL DE NÚRIA**

If you have a day or half a day in hand, stop in Ribes de Freser, head for the railway station and take the little mountain train up to the spectacular Núria valley. You can only go by train – there is no road. The trip itself is delightful, following the river path up through the steep mountain side with amazing views across the valley. You arrive close to the hotel and the sanctuary of Núria, beside the lake which is fed by the streams of the surrounding horseshoe of mountains. The valley has been a focus of pilgrimage since the 12th century, and the madonna of Núria is the much revered patroness of the Pyrenean shepherds. Access only became easy when the railway track was built in 1931. It's very beautiful, but nowadays you need to pick non-weekend days out of season to appreciate the tranquility in full.

The maps of the valley which you can get in Ribes de Freser from the information centre are excellent. The paths are well signposted, and there are telelifts which work in winter and summer alike. If you're fit, and haven't left a car in Ribes, there's a very satisfying walk over to La Molina. In winter, the valley converts into a skiing area which is excellent for beginners, all perfectly within reach of the hotel.

The birdlife is, of course, Pyrenean, promising views of kestrels, ptarmigans, golden eagles and crag martins. The animal life is more difficult to see, given the popularity of the valley – chamois, ermine and hare. The plants also follow the norm – oak, ash and birch lower down, mountain pine, rhododendron and juniper up to 2,200 m, and rocky treeless areas thereafter, with gentians and alpine pansies peeping out of the scree.

The half-hour train journey starts in Ribes at 7.35 a.m. and then leaves hourly from 9.23 a.m. til 5.23 p.m. It comes down from Núria at quarter past the hour. Check before you plan: (972) 72 70 31. There are four refuges for hikers.

Vall de Núria
(HR)M *Núria (972) 73 03 26 Open all year*

There are sixty-five rooms here, and the hotel gives respite to skiers and walkers alike. It's at 2,000m, the air is clear and there are uninterrupted views of the lake and mountains. The building itself is solid and grey, but it's pleasantly rustic and comfortable inside. The sanctuary of Mare de Déu de Núria is next door, and the station is only a stone's throw away. An early morning rise here (out of season) is blissful.

Double room 5,000–9,000 ptas

Map 6B **QUERALBS**

This old village, surrounded by pastures, is one stop before Núria on the mountain railway, and is also accessible by car from Ribes de Freser. While you're here, take a look at the romanesque church.

La Plaça
(R)M Plaça de la Vila, 2 (972) 72 70 37 Open lunchtimes during the week; Sat. eve.; Cl. Tues.

This is a simple restaurant in the centre of the village, where they serve good traditional cooking. The typical mountain dishes here are appropriately heavy – *canamillana* (a stew of potatoes with cabbage and meat), roast lamb with quantities of garlic, and grilled meats. There are only nine tables, so book beforehand.

Allow 2,000–3,000 ptas

Puigcerdà (Cadí Tunnel), Berga, Manresa

A rapid route south from Puigcerdà passes **Alp** and then speeds through the Túnel del Cadí (Cadí Tunnel) to reach the southern side of the Cadí-Moixeró Natural Park, **Bagà** and **Berga**.

Map 5B **ALP**

A small modern-looking town dedicated to the ski slopes of La Masella and Tossa d'Alp.

Aereo Hotel, Celler Ca l'Eudald
(HR)M *Passeig Inès Fabra, 4 (972) 89 08 62 Open all year*

This is a very agreeable 36 room hotel with a good restaurant, installed in a large family house in the town. As a hotel it is quite simple, with straightforward rooms and its own restaurant. It's very busy in the summer months when it adopts the air of a rather disorganised numerous family – with people sitting and chatting in the stairway and round the reception. The chef-owner hovers too – a pleasant, fatherly man.

The restaurant **Celler Ca l'Eudald**, is downstairs in a stone-walled, beamed room. Here you eat well – delicious chunky pâtes, magret of duck, trout from the river, wild mushrooms, and warming food like civets and thick stews in winter.

Menú del dia 1,800 ptas; carta 3,500 ptas; Half board 5,500 ptas

Map 5C BAGÀ

A partly-walled town, with a pretty porticoed main square.

Cal Batista
(HR)S *Bagà (93) 824 41 26 Open all year except Christmas week*

You can plan for this one – either just after or just before the tunnel, depending on your direction! It's a big, popular restaurant close to the Barcelona side of the Cadí Tunnel. They serve unrefined traditional Catalan food – salads, lamb cutlets, grilled meats (from the region) and a speciality: *truita del Bastareny* (trout from the local river, cooked in the oven with garlic, parsley and ham). There are three bedrooms with bathroom.

Menú del dia 1,000 ptas; carte approx. 1,500–2,000 ptas

A detour to the east takes you through wooded countryside to **La Pobla de Lillet**, a small picturesque town with a pretty romanesque bridge over the Llobregat river. Further on, you can turn off to **Castellar de N'Hug**, up a long winding road. On the way up you pass an old abandoned cement works, which is given a curious dignity by its modernist buildings. Train spotters can enjoy the various old engines and coaches left rusting below.

Map 6B CASTELLAR DE N'HUG

This is a famously pretty mountain village in the middle of nowhere. The fame has helped it to be almost entirely rebuilt, maintaining the pretty stone style. Unfortunately the tourist industry, in its coachloads, has wrested the romance from the village, which now has several bakeries loudly selling the local *coca* and dried sausages, with absurdly big display windows, each competitively advertising itself as the only wood-fired bakery of the village. You need to arrive before the coaches start in order to appreciate the charm of the village.

If you come here on the last Sunday in August, you can enjoy the annual sheepdog trials.

Les Fonts
(HR)M *Castellar de N'Hug (93) 823 60 89 Cl. 6 Jan.–6 Feb.; rest. Cl. Tues.*

A hotel in the woods just below the village. It has a swimming pool, café, a restaurant serving regional food and twenty-seven simple bedrooms. The main offerings here are the woods and the trickling stream of the young Llobregat river which rises just a short walk away. This does tend to be a coach stop, though, and has a foreground of souvenir shops, which takes away some of the potential tranquility.

Double room 5,000 ptas

Back on the main road south, the central town of the region is Berga.

Map 5C **BERGA**

This is quite a big town, with not that much to offer the tourist, apart from the restaurant Sala where you can further your education in the appreciation of wild mushrooms. The countryside of Berga, sprinkled with old stone villages and humid woodland, makes many a mushroom hunter happy in season. The number of varieties reaches into the seventies.

The Corpus festival here is renowned throughout Catalunya – the *Patum*. It involves a wild, pagan dance of skeletons, dragons and horned devils bellowing great puffs of fiery sparks over the crowds as they twizzle and twist to the heady beating of drums. An unforgettable experience if you are lucky enough to be there, but make sure you wear old cloths that protect from flying sparks.

For a superb panoramic view, a favourite local excursion is the sanctuary of Queralt, just to the west of the town. A lift takes you up the hillside to the sanctuary.

➜ **Sala**
(R)M *Passeig de la Pau, 27 (93) 821 11 85 Cl. Sun., Mon.*

If your imagination has been caught by the cooking of wild mushrooms, this is a must. The chef here, Miquel Màrquez, is known as *el Rei dels Bolets* (king of the wild mushrooms), and for good reason. His expertise and knowledge in the use of mushrooms is profound. He uses local varieties, and when these are plentiful in the autumn, his mushroom set menu is an eye-opener to the range of delicacies that can be made. His art and curiousity know no bounds – there is even mushroom honey and mushroom ice-cream.

The restaurant is aesthetically unremarkable outside and quietly elegant inside. The cooking is Catalan and modern, with the technical perfection (and eye-catching presentation) of haute cuisine. The menu is varied, with a range of sophisticated dishes and good home-cooking – (the croquettes really make a delicious aperitif). Delicate warm salads of confit of duck with wild mushroom vinegar, or farm chicken in *escabetx*; pates; succulent sea bass with a cream of *rovellons* and *mucoses* (types of mushroom) with oil of *cava*; pigeon with a light wine sauce, cream of courgette perfumed with white *mucoses*... This you have to experience.

Menú del dia 1,750 ptas; carte 2,000–3,500 ptas

Arrowed for the passion of fr. Marques for wild fungi.

Driving down from Berga along the Llobregat river, you pass beautiful countryside. It's mostly agricultural here, although towards Sallent and Manresa there are signs of the important textile industry of the region.

Map 5D **SALLENT**

A curious piece of history – the first weaving machines in Catalunya were installed here in 1824.

La Sala

(R)M *Ctra del Túnel del Cadí, Km. 37,5 (93) 837 02 68*

A sophisticated restaurant in a converted old *masia*, with stone walls and beamed ceilings, and rustic country furniture. The food is Catalan, more haute cuisine than traditional, with presentation to match. The kitchen mostly works with fish – their speciality is sole with dried fruits. If you feel like meat, try the roast kid with pears.

Allow 4,000–5,000 ptas

Map 5D **MANRESA**

Manresa is an important industrial centre with an economy based on textile, metal and chemical manufacturing, so it's not very suitable for tourists. If you do stop here, you must visit the Collegiata de Santa Maria, which is Catalan gothic in style, with one of the biggest central naves in the country. There's also a splendid thirteenth-century bridge here, and a collection of fine civic buildings.

Aligué
(R)M *Ctra de Vic-Barriada El Guix 8 (93) 873 25 62 Cl. Sun. eve., Mon.*

A restaurant on the road in from Vic, where a young aspiring team produce very good food. The cooking is very individual, so the menu is varied and fun – fresh pastas, Basque dishes, house creations, and contemporary Catalan cuisine. Ask advice when you're choosing – they cook according to the day's market and change the carte daily. The family has been in the business for some thirty-five years, and in the front room you can still eat a good, straightforward menu for 1,000 ptas in the old style. Make sure you don't miss the desserts (particuarly the mocha crêpes).

Allow 3,500 ptas

Just south of Manresa are the peaks of Montserrat, and to the east the Sant Llorenç del Munt Natural Park (see Chapter 2).

La Cerdanya, (Puigcerdà to La Seu d'Urgell), Cadí-Moixeró Natural Park

This beautiful wide valley leads from the south of Puigcerdà to La Seu d'Urgell. Its villages have been expanding in the last few decades with the city dwellers seeking refuge from the humid heat of the Barcelona summer. The offer of accomodation and food is excellent.

Driving down from Puigcerdà you can either go via **Alp** (see above) or **Bolvir**.

Map 5B **BOLVIR**

→ **Torre de Remei**
(HR)L *Camí Reial (972) 14 01 82 Open all year*

This was a modernist country palace, built in 1910, and is now a sumptuous, very beautiful hotel with only four bedrooms and seven suites. It is the labour of love of Josep Maria Boix, whose wife continues to direct the long-established hotel Boix in Martinet, nearby. Leaving the main road, you are directed up to the splendid gates of the house, an elegant turreted château. Through a half gathered curtain – royal blue velvet on one side and ochre satin on the other, you enter the central hall which leads to the restaurant, and the period wrought-iron staircase which winds up to the first floor. All the floors are of dark polished wood, the walls decorated with colours carefully chosen according to the room and the level in the building, and the furniture of simple, contemporary line raising the splendour to a tasteful sophistication. The bedrooms are unique, each one a masterpiece of creative imagination. They take advantage of the eccentricities of the house. A princely bedroom overlooks the front drive, complete with a handsome wardrobe that is a catalogued collector's piece; a steepled

Bolvir – Torre de Remei

circular bathroom occupies a turret. Many rooms have their own fireplace, and the lighting has been designed with great care. There is a marvellous feeling of space and tranquility, also reflected outside in the beautiful expansive gardens of mature trees and lawns, beyond which are the mountains.

The restaurant is very formal and extremely elegant – the tables are dressed with the finest linen and silver in keeping with the noble style of the house. The cooking is sophisticated and individual to Sr Boix, who cooked for Queen Elizabeth on her visit to Catalunya. The menu included his famous gigot of lamb roasted with herbs for seven hours, a surprising and delicious dish. His first courses are delectable, and his desserts are works of art.

If you can't stay here, at least come to lunch. The visit is unforgettable – like an excursion into a fantasy of splendour, where every detail has been cherished.

The hotel is a member of the Relais & Châteaux

Menú clàssic 4,500 ptas; menú degustació 5,500 ptas; carte aprox 6,000 ptas; double room 22,000 ptas

Arrowed for incomparable elegance in a wonderful setting.

Chalet del Golf
(HR)L *Devesa del Golf, Ctra N260 (972) 88 09 62 Open all year*

A small, very peaceful hotel on the golf course, surrounded by acres of lawn and trees. It's decorated in a very "English gentleman" style with 'horse and hounds' motifs and wood panelling throughout. Dark red and green as predominant colours. There's a red velvet smoking room, a lounge with a splendid fireplace, and an elegant dining room where the cooking is international. The eight bedrooms are small and pretty, decorated with matching bedspread and curtains. If you don't feel like golf, you can also swim, or play tennis and squash.

Double room 11,000 ptas, half-board 11,000 ptas

Map 5B **MERANGES**

An old village high in the Pyrenees, with good walks to the glacial lakes beyond.

Can Borrell
(HR)M *C/Retorn, 3 (972) 88 00 33 Open Jan.–Feb. only Fri.–Sun., open throughout rest of year; rest. Cl. Mon., Tues.*

On the far edge of the village.

For a touch of quaintness, this is a carefully converted house where you can enjoy the low ceilings, odd floor levels, deep windows and thick walls of an old *masia*. The eight rooms are all different, tucked in wherever possible, often with lofts above which can serve as bedrooms for children, reached by wooden steps. Don't expect much in the way of modern comforts – the priority is the old-world atmosphere, not modern services.

A narrow stone-walled room serves as lounge in the winter and breakfast room in the summer, while, on the other side of the kitchen, there's a delightful terrace between the old outhouses. Look at the bar too – which was once the hayloft.

The restaurant is better known, again in true rustic style – stone walls and beamed ceilings decorated with old wooden pieces of furniture, period-piece wash basins, turn-of-the-century photographs, etc. Grilled wild mushrooms, stuffed pigs' trotters, chicken with prunes and pinenuts, meat *a al brasa* or roasted – the dishes and sauces are all from favourite old recipes.

Allow 3,500–4,000 ptas

Map 5B **PRATS I SANSOR**

Germans Bertran
(R)S *Prats i Sansor (972) 89 00 26 Open weekends Dec.–Sept., all week in summer*

When you enter the village, continue to the open square and park. Walk up the left side of the small field and it's on the left.

This is an important centre of horse-riding here, and the restaurant is the low-key centre of the stables. Half the people eating have something to do with the riding excursions, the other half come to eat very good value food in a very informal ambience. It gets full, so its a good idea to reserve a table. Meat *a la brasa, trinxat* (a cake of chopped vegetables), *carn d'olla* – the best of local home-cooking. If you want to go on a riding excursion, ask here.

Allow 1,500–2,000 ptas.

Map 5B **BELLVER DE CERDANYA**

The walled village has a fine twelfth-century church, Santa Maria de Talló, and an attractive Plaça Major. If you are interested in caving, the famous **Fou de Bor** caves are nearby.

Mas Martí
(R)M *Urbanització Bades (973) 51 00 22 Open Aug., Christmas–Easter weekends only*

Heading towards the Cadí Tunnel from Bellver, watch out for a small sign to Mas Martí which will take you on to a track running parallel to the main road. Follow the track (not asphalted) for about two kilometres.

The *masia* is some 400 years old, and you enter through the pretty courtyard to reach the restaurant, which is upstairs in a small beamed room. The cuisine is more French than Catalan, more sauces than *brasa*, with a small range of fish and meat dishes: quiche of aubergines, trout 'a la Grenobloise', blanquette de veau, grilled turbot. Sr. Martí takes care of the dining room while his French wife looks after the kitchen. The family have made this a rather unusual restaurant, intimate but informal with attention to detail.

Allow 2,500–3,000 ptas

Map 5B **PRULLANS**

On the north side of the valley.

Muntanya
(HR)S-M *C/ Del Puig, 3 (973) 51 02 60 Open Easter–Oct., 27 Dec.–end of winter*

In summer this is very much a Catalan family hotel, where people come year after year. It's a happy place – when I went, there was a *petanca* championship going on, meanwhile children were splashing in the pool, or playing ping-pong, and couples were taking drinks in the garden. The hotel is up in the hills on the north side of the valley, and looks over towards the Sierra del Cadí. It's spacious, the simple bedrooms have balconies, and there is good home-cooking in the restaurant. Close by, at the bottom of the hill, is a stables where you can go riding.

Double room 5,000–6,000 ptas

Map 5B **MARTINET DE CERDANYA**

→ Boix
(HR)M–L *Ctra N260, Km 204 (973) 51 50 50 Open all year*

On the main road, just outside the town.

This is one of the great classics of Catalunya. The extraordinary prestige of this hotel comes mostly from its restaurant – for which Josep Maria Boix has won strings of awards. His cooking is representative of the finest techniques of nouvelle cuisine applied to the best of traditional Catalan cooking – and still serves as a model example for Catalan chefs. The diningroom is elegant, decorated with splendid bouquets of flowers, and with an air of gentle sophistication. The chef merits his fame, the menu includes all the great catalan dishes – with an extra magic touch: *bacallà* on a bed of *escalivada* with tarragon vinegar; a *salpicon* of river crabs and wild mushrooms; canelones; *merlluç de palangre* (hake) with a green sauce and clams; pigs' trotters with thyme. The desserts are, of course, wonderful.

The 26-room hotel is well-run and solid as a rock, with a staff that has been with the business since it began, and the utter dedication of Sr Boix and his wife throughout the twenty years of the establishment. This is a place to come and stay a few days, enjoy the comfortable hotel, and eat like a king.

For the restaurant, you must reserve at weekends.

Menú degustació 4,800 ptas; carte approx. 5,000 ptas; double room 10,000 ptas; half-board 10,700 ptas

Arrowed for the quite superb Catalan dishes in a splendid restaurant, surrounded by the beauty of the Cerdanya.

Martinet de Cerdanya – Boix Hotel

Map 5B **EL PONT DE BAR**

La Taverna dels Noguers
(R)M *El Pont de Bar, Ctra N260, Km 210 (973) 38 40 20 Open lunchtimes, Sat. eve.; Cl. Thurs, Jan., 1–15 Jul.*

On the main road, 3 km from El Pont de Bar and six kilometres from Martinet, close to the D'Ardax campsite, on the upper side of the road. If you miss it, keep going and do a U-turn a little further on in either direction.

This is a large open room with red check tablecloths, pine beams, a fireplace and a terrace in front. The decoration is pretty – tiles on the walls and on the front of the bar. Over your sherry and olives, you can choose good regional food from the short menu. In summer the *pica-pica* includes *esqueixada, escalivada* and cold meats. In winter, the *escudella* or *trinxat* (a cake of chopped vegetables) is more warming. An excellent second is the poulet stuffed with with raisins, prunes and apple, (cooked in a bag) or the rabbit cooked with mustard. There are always extra dishes of the day – ask the maître. They produce unsophisticated but very good food here, in ample portions, using herbs from the hillside behind the house, and traditional cooking methods.

An added curiosity: the table furniture and the splendid piece behind the bar were all made by the now-retired owner, whose son runs the restaurant.

Allow 3,500–4,500 ptas

Map 5B **ARSÈGUEL**

This village is very small, with old buildings and cobbled streets, on the edge of the Sierra del Cadí.

Ca la Lluïsa
(R)S *Plaça de l'Ajuntament (973) 38 40 41 Lunch only; Cl. Fri., Jul.*

Park by the romanesque church and walk along the street into the village turning left at the end. Ca la Lluïsa is at the country side of the little square.

This is quite a find for a peasant country lunch – you need to book in summer. The offering is limited but very wholesome – *escudella*, stuffed artichokes, *bacallà* with *samfaina* (catalan ratatoulle), roasts, *conill de l'avia*, (grandma's rabbit dish), and duck.

The room looks over the village vegetable gardens to the woods of the Cadí and the ambience has a delicious feeling of holiday escape. It's in the middle of nowhere with pretty walks beyond the old church.

Menú del dia 1,200 ptas; carte 2,000 ptas

Map 4B **ALÀS I CERC**

Hostal Dolcet
(R)M *Av. J Zulueta, 1 (973) 35 20 16 Lunch 1.00 p.m.–4.15 p.m., dinner 9.00 p.m.–11.15 p.m.; Cl. Fri., 20 Jun.–8 Jul., 5 Nov.–6 Dec.*

You can't reserve to eat here, so it's better to come a little early. It fills up fast, and is so popular that they now have a waiting room so that you can be comfortable while you wait. The food is regional using oven and wood-grill; roast kid, fillet, rabbit with *allioli*, local trout, and plenty of wild boar and venison. The boar stewed with potatoes and carrots is superb. The salad is always the same, onion, tomato, pepper and olives – marinaded in its dressing for a day before serving.

There is a menu, but Sra. Pepita only hands it out if asked – she much prefers advising you on what's best in the kitchen today. Busy, noisy and very good.

Allow 3,500 ptas

Map 4B **LA SEU D'URGELL**

This is the major market town at the east end of the beautiful Cerdanya region. It is worth spending time to visit the cathedral and, if you have planned sufficiently to book, to eat a magnificent meal in one of the most respected restaurants of the Lleida province. (As La Seu d'Urgell is also at the foot of the principality of Andorra, I've described it all in Route D.)

To cross through the Sierra del Cadí and explore it from the south side, there is a good, but windy road leading to **Tuixén** from **Alàs i Cerc**, which then continues on down to **Sant Llorenç de Morunys**. The scenery here is spectacular and beautiful, particularly continuing down towards Solsona. If you take this route, there is an abrupt entrance to the Cadí-Moixeró Natural Park just south of Tuixén, and a couple of good hotels close to Sant Llorenç.

Map 5C **LA COMA**

The road from Sant Llorenç de Morunys is winding, up through dry, bush-covered mountainside, with views looking back towards the town. In winter, there's a wooded circuit for cross-country skiing nearby (called Tuixén), and down-hill skiing in **Port del Comte**.

Hostal Fonts del Cardener
(HR)M *Ctra de Tuixén, s/n (973) 49 23 77 Cl. 1–15 May, 8–30 Nov.*

A hotel perched on the roadside, with a good restaurant and well-decorated rooms finished in noble wood which have views looking down the valley. The restaurant has a modern wood-panelled vaulted ceiling and a big grill at the end, which is lit throughout the year. Here the meats are cooked and the *pa amb tomàquet* prepared. Roast kid is particularly good here, and the *bacallà* with *gambes*. The hotel has a small garden and tennis court, and a short walk takes you to the *Fonts del Cardener* – a pretty spring surrounded by lush greenery. The winter skiing activities are complemented in spring and summer by the walks in the Cadí-Moixeró Natural Park, which has its southern boundary just over the crest of the hill.

Menú del dia 2,500 ptas; double room 5,000 ptas

Map 5C **SANT LLORENÇ DE MORUNYS**

There is a fine eleventh-century church here, and quite a lot of the medieval walls still stand. If you are passing through on your way to a day of skiing, Bar Llohis (beside the petrol station) makes a good road stop for a mighty breakfast of grilled sausage (*botifarra*) with thick tomatoed toast.

Cas-Tor
(H)M *Ctra de la Coma, Km 1 (973) 49 21 02 Open mid–Jun.–end Sept., Fri.–Sun. in winter*

A small hotel with sixteen rooms, very close to the village of Sant Llorenç, with a swimming pool, tennis court and a generous garden. It's surrounded by a delightful wood of pine trees. The restaurant serves good traditional food.

Menú del dia 1,700 ptas; half-board 4,800 ptas; double room 6,000 ptas

Map 4B/5C **CADÍ-MOIXERÓ NATURAL PARK**

This is a marvellous area for walking, spectacular and immense, bringing the two neighbouring sierras of Cadí and Moixeró within the boundary of the park. Just a glance at the map illustrates the difficult mobility in the area – no towns and no roads decorating the thirty-kilometre mass, just a circle of routes outlining along the northern valley (La Cerdanya) and the less frequented southern valleys. The height ranges from 900 m to over 2,500 m – so there are all sorts of landscapes, from the gentle rolling pastures and thick woods to rugged treeless rocky areas and scree slopes. The rock faces are sheer and dramatic – sometimes with cliffs of 500 m on the northern side. One of the favourite sites for Catalan adventurers is the noble twin-peaked mountain of Pedraforca (2,497 m), close to the village of Gósol, on the southern side of the Sierra del Cadí.

The vegetation high in the mountains tends towards species you'd find in the north of Europe or in the Arctic – due, they explain, to the height of the mountains, the length of time the peaks are snowbound (usually from November to May), and the high humidity. You find gentians high up, and below the pine forest there are quantities of rhododendron and juniper. Beeches, maples, aspens, Scots pines also abound.

Chamois, red deer and and roe deer are steadily increasing their presence here, and you should definitely see some in the pasture areas of the park, or in the fields which coat the woodland along the southern side. Bird life is in abundance – the capercaillie, black woodpecker, partridge and occasional golden eagle gracing the skies.

For overnight stays there are eight refuges. If you prefer, you can rent a four-wheel drive from the main entrance villages on both sides, and stay more comfortably in a hotel. Be prepared for a turn in the weather if you're walking far. This is a popular area for walkers, with good reason – it is an awe-inspiring sweep of mountains.

The information centres have good maps which show all the main tracks very clearly.

Bellver de Cerdanya (973) 51 00 16; Tuixén (973) 37 00 30; Túnel del Cadí petrol station; La Molina ski station; La Seu d'Urgell town hall (the Ajuntament) (973) 35 00 10.

ROUTE D FROM FOIX (ANDORRA)

Principality of Andorra, La Seu d'Urgell, Solsona, Cardona

The small principality of Andorra, set in the high Catalan Pyrenees, acts as a major connection route between France and Spain. It tends to suffer from congestion at the weekends or in August, due to Andorra's extraordinary attraction as a shopping ground, and the fact that there is only one main route through. If you travel straight through, the traffic and unsightly towns can make it a fairly irritating task – you have to get off the beaten track to appreciate the beauty of the mountains in tranquility. La Seu d'Urgell is a good resting point, from where you can explore the great sweep of the Cerdanya valley up to Puigcerdà (see Route C), or follow the river Segre south towards the reservoir of Oliana. Heading for Barcelona, you pass the spectacular castle of Cardona, and acres of woodland and fruit groves.

For eating and sleeping, there are excellent places in La Seu d'Urgell and Peramola, and a small selection of restaurants which range from the most refined to the simple and rural.

ANDORRA

Legend has it that the principality was founded by Charlemagne, making it one of the oldest states in Europe, but it's first constitution was only approved in 1993, after centuries of shared sovereignty under the Bishop of Urgell and the Andorran noble family of Caboet. Historicaly, it's economy was based on agriculture and livestock, but some thirty years ago that all changed. Today its main attaction is commercial – an exceptionally low VAT rate allows Andorra to sell almost anything you can imagine at cheaper prices than its neighbours. The search for good deals forms one of the main reasons for going to Andorra, and the result is a narrow valley of traffic-bound roads and people-bound town centres with shops open 365 days a year. It does have other much more attractive offers too, although you have to battle through the spiritless shop-lined towns to reach them: in the winter there is excellent skiing in Ordino, Pals, Arinsal and Soldeu, and throughout the rest of the year there is mountain countryside to enjoy, speckled with villages and some marvellous romanesque churches. The most outstanding churches are Sant Climent in Pal, Santa Coloma in Andorra la Vella, Sant Miquel de Engolasters in Escaldes and Sant Cerni de Nagol (1055) in Sant Julià de Lòria.

As Catalan has always been the official language here, Andorra is a rather special place for the Catalan people – the protector of their precious language whenever it has been supressed in Catalunya. However, Andorra can be a rather disappointing place – wonderful mountains spoilt by charmless towns – but if you get away from the main towns (Andorra la Vella, Escaldes, Encamp) and explore the areas around Soldeu, Ordino, La Massana and Arinsal, you can still enjoy some of the beauty of the principality.

There are quantities of hotels and restaurants, but unlike the rest of Catalunya, I found it quite difficult to find stable, family-owned establishments here. There is a lot of mobility in the trade – chefs leaving, tenancies changing, etc. (great gossip for those in the know) so a name and its reputation are not always as closely linked as they should be.

Map 5B SOLDEU – EL TARTER

These places are just after Soldeu, heading towards Canillo. (The ski lifts in El Tarter connect the village with Soldeu.)

Hotel del Tarter
(HR)M *Ctra Nacional (9738) 51 1 65 Cl. 15 Oct.–1 Dec., May*

A 37-bedroom hotel owned by a Catalan couple, faced in stone and roofed in slate, with good straightforward balconied rooms looking onto the mountains and a good restaurant run by a French chef. The interior is finished in pine and stone – refreshing and welcoming. In the winter this is ideal for skiing, (a ski lift is next door) and hefty buffet breakfasts and good dinners are served when you get back. In summer a stream runs past at the back of the building, and the guests go off walking. The chef cooks his own foie gras and duck confits, makes hearty salads, and produces some excellent wild mushroom sauces.

Double room 6,000–6,800 ptas; half board 5000–7,000 ptas

Hostal Sant Pere
(R)M-L *El Tarter (9738) 51 0 87 Rest. open only in ski season grill open all year*

This is a delightful place, a 300-year-old house with metre-thick walls decorated inside with old mountain charm. Two dining rooms have been installed here, the famous haute cuisine Catalan restaurant upstairs and the open wood-grill downstairs. The former is only open in the ski season, and is a place to eat exquisite imaginative dishes, and the finest desserts all beautifully presented. The grill, open all year, is a different matter – good meat for the hungry sportsman. In addition, there are six delightful country bedrooms hidden amongst the various adjoining rooms on differing levels. The chef was proclaimed runner-up as young chef of the year in Catalunya. The only question is whether he will still be there next year!

Allow 2,500 ptas downstairs; 5,000 ptas upstairs; double room 10,000 ptas

Map 5B CANILLO

Amongst the romanesque churches of Andorra, there is an interesting contemporary church – the sanctuary of Meritxell, close to Canillo just off the main road. This was a modernist building over a romanesque chapel, burnt down twenty years ago and rebuilt by Ricardo Bofill in 1976. La Mare de Déu de Meritxell is the patron saint of Andorra (the festival day is 8 September).

Molí del Peano
(R)M *Ctra General (9738) 51 2 58 Open all year*

Luckily I was told about this excellent little French restaurant, or I'd have driven straight past the Molí thinking it was just a little tourist restaurant on the main road. The French couple here had a well-known restaurant in the capital of the principality for some twenty years, and have since moved down to Canillo where they have a constant, faithful clientele who love the French cuisine. Everything is made there, including the game pate, foie, and the fresh cheese (*mató*). They offer two menus depending on your apetite, concentrating on local trout, duck and steaks *à la crème* or *al pebre.* Good value.

Menú 1,500 ptas; carte 2,500 ptas

Map 5B ENCAMP

Surprisingly there is a car museum here, with some eighty-two cars from 1898 to 1950, motorbikes and bicycles.

Coray
(HR)M *C/ dels Caballers, 38 (9738) 31 5 13 Cl. Nov.*

This is a bustling 85-room hotel with all the character of a strong Catalan family business. It tends to cater for Catalan holidaymakers, and is already well on the list for British passers-by. No frills here, in rooms or restaurant, just the good honest basics. A garden terrace overlooking tobacco fields is refreshing, and the enclosed car park is an advantage.

Half-board 3,500 ptas; double room 5,200 ptas

From the next town, **Les Escaldes**, you can continue down towards **La Seu D'Urgell** via Andorra la Vella, or turn off to **La Massana** and the pretty northern valley of the principality.

Map 4B **LA MASSANA**

Rutllan
(HR)M *La Massana (9738) 35 0 00 Open all year*

This is a big chalet hotel at the final turn of the town heading up the valley. It feels more international than family, but is very spacious and comfortable, with a pretty garden, swimming pool and tennis court. All the rooms have generous flower-decorated balconies, and the food is good.

Half-board 7,000 ptas; double room 8,000 ptas

La Borda de l'Avi
(R)M *Ctra d'Arinsal (9738) 35 1 54 Open all year*

It's easy to find on the main road heading out towards Arinsal, with a huge forecort for parking.

Long-established, highly regarded, and very successful. The house is splendid – dark tree-trunk ceiling beams over three largish but cosy rooms, huge patchwork metal hood over the wood griddle; red check tablecloths and straw-seated chairs. Here it's essential to book before you go, as it bubbles with people at the weekends. It excells in *a la brasa* cooking, and the typical mountain dishes.

Allow 4,500 ptas

El Rusc
(R)M-L *Ctra d'Arinsal (9738) 38 2 00 Cl. Sun. eve., Mon.*

In a spacious, light and airy chalet, this is an elegant Basque restaurant, where the fish and desserts are excellent. There are two dining rooms, one upstairs with the fireplace of the wood grill, and the other downstairs beside the splendid, carefully air-conditioned cellar of French and Spanish wines. The kitchen produces everything, including at least two baking sessions for the bread daily. The fish comes up from San Sebastián, and the meat from Andorra itself. The menu makes tempting reading, from the little *piquillo* peppers stuffed with crab; the tagliatelli with wild mushrooms, clams and prawns; the rich fish and shellfish soup; the *Txangurro.* Apart from the elaborate dishes, the chef believes that the finest fish is best cooked simply. I'm inclined to agree – the grilled turbot was superb. Leave room for the desserts.

Allow 5,000–6,000 ptas

Xopluc
(R)M *Ctra General, s/n, Sispony (9738) 35 6 45 Cl. Sun. eve., Mon.*

This famous restaurant has been going since 1988. It is housed in a spacious two-storey *masia* dating from 1827 – wood-panelled and vaulted, with the wood grill in full view upstairs. You have to be alert to find it – up in a quiet street with views extending down to the Masanna valley. As it has just changed hands, (literally in the two weeks before I got there) I really can't comment on future stability, but its chef is promising – creative and enthusiastic. His flakes of cod with a mousse of *allioli*, and *ous remenats* (scrambled egg) with duck liver and wild mushrooms hold to that. A place to eat grills.

Menú 3,000 ptas; carte 3,500 ptas

Xalet Ritz
(HR)L *Prat dels Noguers, Sispony (9738) 37 8 77 Open all year*

This is not a family-owned hotel – but it does have gardens with a small pool, woodland just above, and views across the Anyós valley. The building is like an enormous, splendid chalet (built in 1990), complete with stone walls, slate roof and irregular design. The standard of luxury is as you'd expect of a Husa-owned four star hotel – comfortable, tastefully furnished bedrooms mostly with balconies, ample rooms including a big English-style lounge. For peace and quiet this is a good choice.

Double room 8,000–18,000 ptas

Ordino is a small, pretty town, and the gateway to a string of delightful hamlets like Sornás, Ansalonga, La Cortinada, and El Serrat. This is where you can really appreciate some of more traditional quiet beauty of Andorra – sweeping rough green mountains, high lakes and streams. There is lots of information given out here about walks in the mountains with views, lakes, etc., ranging from a couple of hours stroll to a hard eight-hour hike. Its well worth asking about when you arrive.

Back on the main route through Andorra you will come to Les Escaldes-Engordany.

Map 4B LES ESCALDES-ENGORDANY

This town runs into Andorra la Vella, and is similarly overrun with shoppers at weekends. The latest highlight is the luxurious new thermal centre, Caldea, cased in a spectacular set of chrystal pyramids. It offers a delicious luxury of lagoons, turkish and roman baths, perfumed waters, etc. for relief from travelling or shopping stress.

Valira
(HR)M *Av. Carlemany, 37 (9738) 20 5 65 Open all year*

As the hotels here tend to be new, vast and splendid, I have picked this one – rather old-fashioned in look and refreshing. It's right in the centre, on the high street, decorated in Andalusian style with pretty yellow tiles in the lounge, and blue in the diningroom. The bedrooms are comfortable, attic-like at the top and straightforward on the floors below, reached by a modernist-style wooden lift. And if you don't have time to go to Caldea, the thermal water reaches your hotel room.

Double room with breakfast 3,350–4,250 ptas; half-board 5,100–6,350 ptas

El Retro
(R)L *C/ de la Unió, 11 (9738) 26 7 16 Cl. Mon, Jul.*

This is a hidden treasure – just where Andorra la Vella and Les Escaldes join. The restaurant is very small and intimate with a most unusual decoration – blue-green like the bloom on a dark plum, with elegant matching floral art-nouveau upholstery and tablecloths and soft light. The eight tables are laid with pale yellow table-linen, fine china, silver and candles. The *degustació* menu will set you back a bit but the quality and attention to detail merit the cost. The chef and maître own the restaurant together and serve French haute cuisine. Marinated foie gras from Haute Landes; Scottish wild salmon smoked by the chef; sea bass with a sauce of fresh tomato; filet of beef cooked in a shell of salt (fabulous); superb desserts including a fine apple tart. Unless you choose the menu, do ask advice – with such a small restaurant the chef can enjoy the liberty of cooking unexpected things. (If you've heard of the restaurant 1900, this is it – same personnel, same food but a new name.)

Menú degustació 7,500 ptas

Don Denis
(R)M *C/ Isabel Sandy, 3 (9738) 20 6 92 Open all year*

Don Denis is an institution in Andorra, a very popular restaurant at the lower end of Escaldes, almost touching Andorra la Vella. It's always packed and often has queues, with the added entertainment, as you go downstairs to the restaurant, of seeing the owner arm in arm with every famous face you can imagine, from Barcelona football club stars to Hollywood specials. Its reputation is built, for the tourists, on copious portions and a good value set menu (changing daily) and, for the locals, the excellent ham served in the bar upstairs.

I must admit that we found the set menu – moules marinière/canelones followed by Aranese trout/roast lamb – less than inspiring, but in this restaurant you get what you pay for. A la carte is not cheap, and it's dishes are of a different class. If you feel like eating shellfish, there's an wide range of fresh produce brought straight up from the Atlantic and Mediterranean coasts. Fast service and bustle. Tourists are expected – the long menu is in all major languages.

Menú del dia 1,000 ptas; carte aprox. 4,000–5,000 ptas

Map 4B ANDORRA LA VELLA

The main town of the principality, Andorra la Vella is really a place to avoid, especially at weekends, unless you are a determined shopper.

Parking is not easy – best to look for the major supermarket half-way up the town (Avda Meritxell) and squeeze in there.

→ **Andorra Park Hotel**
(HR)L *Les Canals, 24 (9738) 20 9 79 Open all year*

This is a lovely hotel – highly privileged in having a vast and very beautiful garden which distances it from the heart of the town just a stone's throw away. It's cleverly linked to the centre by the lift at the back of the main Pyrenees supermarket, on the C Andorra, which takes you up to its garden entrance. The hotel itself is elegant and sophisticated, well-furnished, with only forty rooms, each individually decorated in one of four colours – rose, salmon, grey and green.

The grounds are landscaped – grass lawns, mature trees, a swimming pool sculpted round the mountain rock itself, a small four-hole golf course, a childrens playground, a tennis court and areas of wild flowers. Of a summer evening, it is extremely pleasant to have dinner outside on the grass beside the pool – a touch of magic. The food is, of course, as elegant as the hotel – international haute cuisine

Andorra La Vella – Andorra Park Hotel

of a high standard. It is well worth considering as a fine restaurant of its own account.

Clients tend to be mostly Catalan, Spanish, with a few French and, as yet, almost no English guests at all.

The price depends on where your room is; attic skylight, window towards the mountain or window over the garden. Dogs are not allowed.

Half-board 12,200–17,540 ptas; double room 13,000–23,000 ptas
Arrowed for its elegant luxury within a delightful garden.

Xalet Sasplugues, Restaurant Metropol
(HR)M *C/ La Creu Grossa, 15 (9738) 20 3 11 Hotel open all year; rest. Cl. 15–30 Jun., Sun. eve., Mon. (except in summer)*

A secluded little hotel, twenty-five years old, with only twenty-six rooms and an excellent restaurant (the Metropol). Brother Gerard is the chef, and his sister runs the hotel. It is up above the town of Andorra la Vella, high enough to give a feeling of peace and tranquility, and close enough to be within walking distance of the centre. It feels like a large house, with a small but pretty terrace garden where one can take aperitifs.

The bedrooms are generous, modern and comfortable, with balconies overlooking the town view. The garage is under the hotel, and locked at night.

The restaurant Metropol, despite its rather cold decoration – grey and modern (lightened by pale yellow table-linen), is a delight of unusual haute cuisine, and a firm local favourite. I thoroughly recommend the *poti-poti*, (4,900 ptas each) which consists of a *desgustació* of some fourteen different dishes selected by Gerard, the chef, according to the day's market. He is a fan of wild mushrooms and of fish, and a great enthusiast. Pretty desserts.

Menú 3,000 ptas; half-board 6,000 ptas; double room 8,500 ptas

Font del Marge
(H)M *Baixada del Molí, 49 (9738) 23 4 43 Open all year*

This is a modern, family-run hotel with forty-two rooms, comfortable and reasonably central. It is a fairly characterless alternative if you can't get into the others, but the service is good and the staff agreeable.

Double room 6,000–8,000 ptas

Borda Estevet
(R)M *Ctra de la Comella, 2 (9738) 64 0 26 Open all year*

This is not in the mainstream shopping area, but down below, close to the town bypass. It has a carefully designed ambience – a high-roofed stone barn with paintings, old tools, period statuary, and dried country flowers for decoration, quiet classical music, and stylish traditional mountain food. The *pica-pica* is a good choice – a selection of two cold and two hot starters (probably including the delicious b*acallà with a* *garlic mousseline* and *enciams de Tudela* (lettuce hearts) with anchovies and duck ham. Apart from the grilling, and wood-oven roasting, you can also cook for yourself *a la llosa* – where the hot roof slate is brought to your table to cook the meat or trout you wish. You'll notice that the stone imparts a special flavour. Enjoy the desserts – they are made on the premises, and don't forget the terrace which looks on to the open fields beyond for a quiet aperitif or coffee.

Better to reserve at weekends.

Allow 3500 ptas

Celler d'En Toni

(R)M *C/ Verge del Pilar, 4 (9738) 21 2 52 Open all year*

Another classic of the town, in a wide room with terracotta-tiled vaulted ceilings with the kitchen in full view at the back of the room. The restaurant has been going for thirty years now, and is a firm favourite at lunchtime. Apart from the delicious canelones and the trout *a la andorrana* served with a slice of *jabugo* ham, I recommend the fish here. The daily menu is a little dear, but it is good. Ask what other fish there is today. When we were there the menu of the day included a fish salad, trout, Salmon beurre blanc, grilled swordfish, turbot and a few portions of several other fish not on the list.

Menú 3,300 ptas

Versailles

(R)M *Cap de Carrer, 1 (9738) 21 3 31 Open all year*

For a curious French refuge, try Versailles. This is a little two-roomed restaurant, rather Bohemian in feel, with old wooden furniture, red velvet curtains, and a French owner who cooks good, thoroughly French food. It's tucked into the old quarter of the town, and has a faithful young clientèle. Good wine and fine selection of cognacs.

Allow 3,000 ptas

Map 4B SANT JULIÀ DE LÒRIA

This is the town nearest the Spanish border, overawed by traffic and without much interest. Some six kilometres away up in the mountains to the east there's a lovely hotel.

→ Coma-Bella

(HR)M *Ctra de la Rabassa, Km 6 (9738) 41 2 20 Open all year*

In a garden surrounded by pine woods, where you can really go for silence, fragrant breezes, and tranquility. I found it refreshing beyond words, a world away from the main sweep of Andorra. The twenty-eight bedrooms are simple, and the hotel is not interested in luxuries.

Sant Julià de Lòria – Coma-Bella Hotel

Since it began thirty years ago, its pride has been the countryside and its priority the well-being of its clients. The food is healthy, unfussy and good – tailored whenever necessary to the needs of the client. From the dining room and lounge you look across the valley to snowy mountain peaks. Fabulous. The owner told us proudly that there was nothing at all to do there but relax and enjoy the mountain air – the walks nearby are as varied as you can imagine. A further health plus is the water: ferruginous – which the hotel uses as part of its health programmes when the guests come for curative stays. There's also an important shooting club a few kilometres away at La Rabassa.

Half-board 3,700–5,300 ptas; double room 5,000–7,800 ptas

Arrowed for the exceptional surrounding countryside and the peacefulness of the hotel.

Having struggled through the congested frontier between Andorra and Catalunya (there are still limits on the electronic goods you can bring into Catalunya from here), the expansive peaceful views of La Seu d'Urgell come as a wonderful relief.

CATALUNYA

Map 4B LA SEU D'URGELL

This is a busy regional capital, important for its agricultural markets. If you walk along the C Major, the central street of the old part of town, you can still see a couple of big stone grain measures, dating from the sixteenth and nineteenth-centuries. The streets here are narrow and often porticoed, (rather uncomfortable for cars – better to wander about after having parked somewhere along the main *rambla*). While you're here, you should try to visit the cathedral – it's a splendid heavy romanesque stone building, mixing the Lombard, Rosellon and Catalan styles of decoration. *The morning opening hours are short, 10.00 a.m.–1.00 p.m. although, like the museums, it's also open in the afternoon.*

The Diocesian Museum is very well laid-out, with some stunning pieces of romanesque and gothic religous art (particularly a copy of the tenth century Beatus de Liébana). In the romanesque cloisters next door (same entrance ticket), leading off the tall eleventh-century church of Sant Miquel, there is a rather special theatre production every August, when scenes from the life of Sant Ermengol are played, set between the columns of the cloister as if they were animated scenes of a church retablo.

Museums open 10.00 a.m.–1.30 p.m., 4.00 p.m.–7.00 p.m.; Cl. Sun. p.m., Oct.–May p.m.

Since 1992 La Seu d'Urgell has been the proud owner of a superb wild water canal: the Parc del Segre, in which the canoe events of the Olympic Games of 1992 were held. The park now offers its canal (which can regulate its water speed according to requirement), to canoe enthusiasts who want to test themselves in the safety of a controlled environment, or for anyone who has a touch of curiosity and wants to have a go. The teaching here is excellent, and it's great fun.

You'll see *agredolç* on the menu in the Alt Urgell region here. It's an old dish, recently being promoted, which uses the inner meat of hams that hasn't been fully cured. A thick slice of semi-cured ham, fried in olive oil, and served with a sweet sauce of honey warmed with a touch of vinegar. You won't find it anywhere else.

➜ El Castell

(HR)L *Ctra N260 Lleida-Puigcerdà, Km 129 (Castellciutat) (973) 35 07 04 Cl. mid–Jan.–mid–Feb.*

A fabulous hotel on the crest of a hill just a couple of kilometres outside La Seu d'Urgell – the pride of the province of Lleida. The hotel is carefully designed to blend with the surroundings: only two storeys high, running horizontally along a ridge, it is tucked in just below the fort, leaving the splendid old building uninterrupted. Beautifully kept gardens and a swimming pool lead up to the castle. Jaume Tapies and his wife Ludi established El Castell in 1973, and it continues to thrive from the extraordinary dedication of the three generations of the whole family – their parents (on both sides), and their son Jaume with his wife Katja. The older generation look after the market shopping, the vegetable and fruit gardens, the hotel pleasantries and, while the flowers and gardens are under Ludi and Katja. The chefs and staff are all from the neighbourhood.

The hotel rooms are spacious and tastefully furnished, each with a view right across the valley to the Sierra del Cadí, and in the morning nothing is better than a tranquil breakfast of pastries and fresh orange juice on the terrace with a gentle breeze fluttering the tablecloths.

The restaurant is excellent too, again with wonderful views. As a whole table, you can take the fabulous *menú degustació*, of seven delicate but exquisite dishes. Or there's the carte, full of inventive dishes created from local produce: little *piquillo* peppers stuffed with a tartar of prawns; a rivercrab risotto with mushrooms and gooseliver; sea bass with scales of potato served with a Riesling sauce; truffle-stuffed quail drumsticks with a rosemary and wild mushroom sauce. You can enjoy an extensive cheeseboard, and the desserts are superb – elaborate fresh puff pastries or a choice from a totally irresistable trolley.

The selection of wine is magnificent – the cellar is well worth a visit.

Relais & Châteaux vouch for the singular comfort of the hotel.

Carte approx. 5,500–6,000 ptas; menú degustació 6,750 ptas; double room 14,500 ptas

La Seu d'Urgell – El Castell Hotel

Arrowed for the exceptional balance between excellence, formality, comfort and welcome.

Parador de La Seu d'Urgell
(HR)L *C/ Sant Domènech, 6 (973) 35 20 00 Open all year*

In the centre of the old town, by the cathedral. It is very comfortable, and has incorporated the old cloisters of the fourteenth-century monastery of Santo Domingo spectacularly in its huge spacious salon with a shuttered glass ceiling from which hang an abundance of green plants.
Double room 10,000 ptas

Avenida
(H)M *Av. Pau Claris, 24 (973) 35 01 04 Open all year*

You can't miss the building – at the top of the Rambla, occupying the triangular confluence of two roads, with a modernist top storey capping the façade. Although the hotel itself is simple, the forty-seven bedrooms are modern, well-furnished and comfortable, with good views over the roofs to the mountains. Guests can eat in the pretty first floor dining room. The family all work here, and know the surrounding area extremely well. If you are interested in winter sports in the Pyrenees, the director Miguel Angel Sánchez, who was an Olympic skier, can tell you all about it.
Double room 5,000 ptas
The Chinese restaurant beneath the hotel, Drac D'Or (973) 35 21 26, serves a sensational Pekin duck. You need to order it beforehand (7,000 ptas per duck).

Mesón Teo
(R)M *Av. Pau Claris, 38 (973) 35 10 29 Cl. Sun. eve., Mon., most of Jun.*

You can eat good traditional food here – a fine selection of hams and dried sausages, garlic soup, roasts and wood-grilled meats (including lamb and kid). The kitchen is open, running along the side of the small restaurant.
Allow 3,000 ptas

Nice
(HR)M *Avda Pau Claris, 4–6 (973) 35 21 00 Hotel open all year; rest. Cl. Sun. in winter*

The restaurant has an executive ambience, where the menu includes international and regional dishes – *agridolç*, terrine of wild mushrooms, chicken with *gambes*, etc.
Menú del dia 1,300 ptas, Carte 3,000 ptas

Cal Pacho
(R)S *La Font, 11 (973) 35 27 19 Cl. Sun.*

On the way from the centre to the Parc del Segre, by the steps. A good-value family place for rice dishes, grills, roasts and trout.
Menú del dia 900 ptas; carte 1,800 ptas

Taking the C1313 out of La Seu d'Urgell, you head southwards towards Lleida or Barcelona via **Adrall.**

Going east from La Seu d'Urgell towards Puigcerdà takes you along the beautiful wide valley of La Cerdanya, with the great Sierra del Cadí running parallel on the south side and the high Pyrenees to the north. (See Route C, **La Cerdanya**.)

Map 4B **ADRALL**

Bonmajor
(R)M *C/ Afores, s/n (973) 38 72 52 Open lunchtimes, Sat. & Sun. eve.; Cl. Nov. (2 weeks), Feb. (1 week), June (1 week)*

On the way in to Adrall from the south, look for a turning up the hill with a sign saying 'Restaurant', which will take you up an unasphalted road for about half a kilometre.

Run by a young couple, the restaurant is like a large barn, with a fireplace in the middle of the room and huge windows opening out to the plain below. The menu is short, changes frequently and has more than a hint of French influence. Fish is good here – a vichysoisse of clams; paupiettes de *nero* and salmon; turbot; or whatever the market offers today. For dessert the pear crêpe with a Poire William sabayon is a favourite.

Allow 3,500 ptas

Llar de Foc
(R)S *Ctra N260, Km 33,5 (973) 38 71 18 Open all year*

On the main road at the north end of the village.

A simple restaurant, with bar downstairs and diningroom upstairs. For good traditional roasts and stews – kid with herbs, shoulder of lamb (grandma's recipe), chicken with prunes.

Allow 2,500 ptas

The drive following the Segre river is spectacular, with red-orange rock faces jutting out crowned with holm oaks and dry vegetation.

Map 4C **ORGANYÀ**

The pride of this town, apart from the garden produce and the abundance of water, is the possession of the first written document in the Catalan language – the twelfth-century *Homilies d'Organyà*. The original sermons, discussing liturgical texts, are now in Barcelona, but you can see a copy in the square, beneath the squat, round, slate roof. A short ten-kilometre drive up towards Cabó will bring you to the impressive Bordonera spring. There are dolmens close to the roadside.

Cal Jesús
(R)M *C/ Carretera (973) 38 30 68 Cl.20 Jun.–20 Jul., Thur. except in Aug.*

This is a very ordinary-looking restaurant halfway along the main street, which has very good cooking. You can describe the food as typical and regional – *a la brasa* and roasts, snails, local sausages, local vegetables, wild mushrooms in season, etc. They have their own vegetable garden which serves the restaurant until it runs out. White beans from the mountain accompany the *botifarra*; wood-oven bread is rubbed with tomato and seasoned with their own oil; wine comes from up the road (la Conca de Tremp)... all that they serve, beef and lamb included, comes from the neighbourhood. The *brasa* is used a lot – nothing better, says the chef, than a plate of plain grilled mushrooms. Vegetables are grilled too – try the artichokes if they're around. And for a snack, the young garlic or wild mushroom omelettes are quite delicious. For afters, the confit of figs, the ice-creams, the *cremes* – all are home-made.
Allow 3,000 ptas

Continuing southwards, you pass **Coll de Nargó**, clinging to the crest of the hill above. It has a fine romanesque church (Sant Climent) with an ancient belltower.

Map 4C **PERAMOLA**

➜ **Can Boix**
(HR)M-L *Can Boix, s/n (973) 47 02 66 Cl. 15–30 Nov, 10–10 Feb.*

This is a peaceful place to stay, nestling beneath hills of honey-coloured rock, with the wide agricultural plain of the Segre in the foreground. There are no roads nearby and the village of Peramola is a couple of kilometres away. At night the stillness is wonderful – with only the purr of *cigales* (a sort of grasshopper) to be heard.

If you stay at home, there is a large pool, tennis court, small football pitch, and, for complete relaxation, a peaceful garden. But you are in the depths of the country here, and it is worth taking time to go walking in the herb-covered hills just at the back of the house, (up to Coll de Nargó if you feel energetic). Walks have been mapped for you, and there's expert help to arrange adventures if you feel like exploring the hidden mountains tracks. Joan Pallarès' family has lived in this house since 1763, so his knowledge of the area is profound.

Can Boix has a range of rooms. In the main house they go from the very simple (and inexpensive) to the comfortable. A building just past the little chapel houses a set of twenty spacious, elegantly furnished suites, each with a big terrace and fitted with every modern luxury you could imagine.

You also eat extremely well here. This is a famous restaurant in its own right, with a reputation built over twenty-five years. There are three menus for the visitor, regional, gastronomic and game. The food

Peramola – Can Boix Hotel

has a hint of French technique, but is based on the fine olive oil and products of the region. The presentation is artistic (but not over the top) and the dishes prepared with great care. I can vouch for the delicate potato crêpes stuffed with smoked salmon with a cream of salmon and sweet vermouth; the slivers of *bacallà* with *llagostins*; and the partridge in *escabetx*. All delicious and beautifully presented (each on its own china). If you want sturdier regional food, dishes like duck with white beans are strong and filling. The desserts are, of course, a pleasure – try the honey ice-cream.

Set menus 2,800–4,500 ptas; half-board 2,300 ptas; double room 4,500–15,000 ptas

Arrowed for the tranquil beauty of the area, the comfortable hotel and the skill in the kitchen.

On towards Lleida you pass through **Ponts**. Alternatively, heading towards Barcelona, you turn off along the C1410 towards **Solsona** and **Cardona**, winding along the side of a ridged wooded and agricultural valley.

Map 3D **PONTS**

Ventureta
(R)M *Ctra La Seu, 2 (973) 46 03 45 Open all year*

A very old restaurant, family-run, which has been going since 1854. It's on the central crossroads of the town, with a large bar in front and a plain dining room behind. You need to reserve – there are only ten tables. The food is traditional – *bacallà* in tomato sauce, grilled meats, a chickpeas stew, partridge, etc. For desserts, try the pears in wine.

Allow 2,500–3,000 ptas

Map 4C **SOLSONA**

The old part of Solsona is known as the **Clos Antic**, within a largely intact city wall. It is well worth a wander. Look up as you go through the streets and squares – a number of fine town houses support their roofs on huge thick wooden beams, which have some splendidly ugly heads carved into the ends. Behind the solemn cathedral, there is a very important Diocesian Museum which displays one of the finest collections of romanesque art in Catalunya. If you are curious about the workings of salt, there is also an interesting section about the history of salt mining in Cardona, including some salt sculpture.

La Cabana d'en Geli
(R)M *Ctra de Sant Llorenç, s/n (973) 48 29 57 Cl. Wed, Nov.*

On the outskirts of town on the left as you head towards Sant Llorenç – if you reach the fields you've gone too far. It's very easy to miss, standing back from the road, with an old wooden sign pointing towards the restaurant.

This is a delightful, intimate restaurant in an eighteenth-century house, with five small rooms upstairs and downstairs, each decorated differently. Only three rooms are ever in use at the same time. The clients get to know and specify not only the room but the table they wish – evening romantics go downstairs, lunchers tend to stay in the main room. Downstairs leads through the bar to a shady garden, ideal for aperitifs. The menu is very limited with only ten main dishes of meat or fish, which change frequently (and include civets and stews of game in winter). The starters are carefully chosen too – if it is on, try the vichyssoise de *rap* (monkfish). The desserts include some exquisite creations, like the fig ice-cream with hot chocolate, and the apple tart with a strawbery coulis. Reserve just in case.

Allow 3,500 ptas

Map 4D **TORA**

Rather off the route, but worth the detour for the food, and the countryside.

Torà is a small rural town in a valley of olive groves and holm oaks, between Cardona and Tàrrega. There is very little traffic here, and the surrounding countryside hides various intriguing buildings that are well worth an excursion. The twelfth-century romanesque-byzantine church of the monastery of Cellers is seven kilometres away; the geographical centre of Catalunya, on a hilltop with stunning views, is only ten minutes by car; and deep in the thick valley forests, just nine kilometres to the north (turn off to Masia Clavells, then a ten-minute walk), is the wonderful thirty-three metre high romanesque defence tower, the Torre de Vallferosa, so well-built that it still stands intact.

➧ Hostal Jaumet

(HR)S–M *Ctra Barcelona-Andorra C1412 (973) 47 30 77 Cl. 15–30 Jan., Sun. eve., Mon. lunch*

This is a must – a place of pilgrimage for lovers of the old traditional Catalan food.

In 1990 the family (now fourth generation) celebrated the centenary of the Hostal, which used to be an old post-house supplying sustenance and lodging on the route from Barcelona to Andorra. Its recipes are just as old – and people travel from miles around to eat the *perdiu a la vinagreta*. Jaume, the son, runs the business now, while his mother still governs the kitchen. When the time came to renovate the kitchen

Torà – Hostal Jaumet R

some thirty years ago, she refused to change over to gas, and so continues to use a huge coal-fired range – a slow, constantly cooling heat which is perfect for the stews she loves to make. A coal fire, earthenware cooking pots, lots of herbs and time – these are her secrets.

The food is all regional – another speciality is her *l'ofegat de la Segarra* – a rich pork stew of snout, trotters and ear. If that doesn't appeal, try the wholesome beef *a la jardinera* (with vegetables).

The restaurant is big, with green check tables separated by benches. Below is the big cellar – worth a visit. And next door is the large bar, a gathering place for the locals where dominos and cards are slammed into play with roars of defiance. You must reserve at weekends.

You can also stay here in simple rooms – there is lots to see nearby and Jaume, with his catching enthusiasm, will tell you all about it. He can also help organise excursions for you, to get a little closer to the less accessible beauties of the countryside.

Allow 2,300 ptas

Arrowed for the enthusiasm of the family, and the great tradition and character of the restaurant.

Map 5D **CARDONA**

The most striking feature of Cardona is its dominating castle, standing proud above the salt mines and plains of the region.

It is worth visiting the strange natural sculptures of the salt mountain here, pockmarked by holes left by rain-dissolved salt. Take the road towards El Miracle and then turning down to the left towards the salt deposits and the Muntanya de Sal. They are planning to open a museum, to take you down the now-disused salt mines, and display some of the extraordinary changing salt formations in the caves below.

Parador Ducs de Cardona
(HR)L *Castell de Cardona (93) 869 12 75 Open all year*

A romantic and magnificent hotel, installed in the fortress, within which the romanesque church of Sant Vicenç stands. The fifty-two bedrooms have fantastic views. The great beamed rooms of the fortress have been used for the bar and dining room, and the high old walls, stone steps and spartan period decoration give the place a strongly medieval feel.

This is one of the most spectacular hotels in Catalunya – as with all Paradors, you are completely free to wander round and take a look. If it doesn't suit you to stay, I recommend that you take lunch, or a drink, and visit the church, which is tall, elegant and beautiful – an extraordinary example of romanesque architecture given its soaring height of nineteen metres.

Church Open Tues.–Sat. 10.00 a.m.–1.00 p.m. & 3.00 p.m.–6.00 p.m., Sun. 10.00 p.m.–1.00 p.m. Cl. Sun. p.m., Mon.

Menú del dia 2,200 ptas; double room 9,000–11,000 ptas

From here, you can reach **Barcelona** via **Manresa.**

ROUTE E FROM MONTREJEAU (VALL D'ARAN)

* Vall d'Aran, Vielha, Tavascan, Sort, Tremp, Balaguer
* Vall de Boí, El Pont de Suert, Vall Fosca
* Aigües Tortes and Lake Sant Maurici National Park

A spectacular way to enter Catalunya is via the extreme north-west point of the Catalan Pyrenees. The routes lead southwards towards the city of Lleida circling the great Aigües Tortes and Lake Sant Maurici National Park. The scenery is stunning – green valleys carving through walls of high mountain, thick woodland and alpine vegetation, soft lush pastures rising to rugged wild rock, streams and rivers everywhere. For mountain lovers, this area of the Pyrenees is fabulous, not only for the scenery but also for the country restaurants.

The National Park, famous for its multitude of transparent lakes and mountain peaks, can be entered by car from the west (Vall de Boí) and from the east (Espot/Sort) and you can hike over the mountain from the north (Vall d'Aran) and from the south (Vall Fosca). If you have plenty of time, the valleys surrounding the National Park are very beautiful, each with its entirely different character and scenery.

Remember always to take something waterproof and warm with you when walking in the high mountains: the weather can turn extremely fast.

Vall d'Aran, Vielha, Tavascan, Sort, Tremp, Balaguer

Map A2 VALL D'ARAN

Vall d'Aran (or valley of valleys, as it translates) has the distinction of being the only region of Catalunya on the north side of the Pyrenees. The valley has its own language – Aranese – and the 5,800 people who live here happily switch to French, Catalan or Spanish whenever necessary. There is a lot of French influence here in the finer offerings of food, the pâtés, civets, magrets, and the crêpes, while the more traditional mountain food consists of grilled meats and a variation of the Catalan *escudella i carn d'olla* – the rich, warming *olla aranesa.*

The valley has witnessed extraordinary changes since the 1970s. Against all odds, it retained its Spanish dependence throughout the centuries, although for at least six months a year it was completely cut off from Spain by the snows. The rest of the year communication was via the tortuous pass of Port de la Bonaigua. It was only in 1948 that the Vielha Tunnel made access easier. The story goes that King Alfonso XIII, on realising the difficulties his Aranese chauffer faced in order to see his family, offered him a request – and was asked to build a tunnel, which he did. Until the last few years the five-kilometre tunnel was quite a frightening experience by car – narrow, full of foggy humidity, with black streaming rock jutting out at the sides. Shepherds in the valley tell of how they used to pass through the tunnel with the flocks in almost pitch darkness, with only a flame torch to light the way.

Great expanses of mountainscape, pretty slate-roofed villages, and fine romanesque chapels are in profusion here. The countryside is completely different from that of the mountain regions of Lleida and Girona. Snowbound in the winter, it is fresh and green in the summer. The main valley is not very high -roughly 1,000 m altitude, so the range of vegetation is enormous. You can clearly see the bands of tree varieties changing as the altitude increases.

The most colourful time to be here is in late September when the colours of the trees are turning and the whole valley becomes a mixture of greens, browns, reds and oranges. You need four-wheel drive vehicles or sturdy legs to reach high up the valleys, but much beauty can be appreciated from walks from the villages themselves. Inform yourself – there are excellent walkers' maps and the tourist offices are full of brochures.

Today, with the smart, well-lit tunnel, and the finest ski stations of Catalunya, the Vall d'Aran has transformed itself from the poorest region of the Catalan Pyrenees to the richest. The King and his family ski here in Baqueira-Beret every year, and the fashion has taken a firm hold. The rise in standard of living has not spoiled the valley – the ski stations are unobtrusive until you are close, the small villages have mostly remained small, and new buildings have followed the traditional stone-and-slate formula.

For visitors, some of the clearest evidence of change can be seen in the restaurant trade: time and time again I came across delightful restaurants born out of the old stables and barns of cows and goats. The cooking of good food is clearly more lucrative than the production of milk. Carles, one of only two vets working in the valley, laments that there are almost not enough animals left for the two of them.

Map 2A **BOSSÒST**

This is one of the first towns you meet on your way in from Bagnères de Luchon via the Portillon pass or along the main N125 road down from Lourdes and Tarbes. If you want a quick dose of 'Spain', you will find it here – in Bossóst the restaurants offer good old 'Spanish' food to the day visitors, the shops are full of souvenirs and the spirit is decidedly festive – the bars lively until late. But for the real Vall d'Aran, I suggest you move on.

Batalla
(HR)M *Urbanització 'Sol del Valle' (973) 64 81 99 Open all year*

A little out of the centre towards Les, this is a nice, young hotel – a stone-faced chalet with sixteen compact, pine-finished rooms with balcony and mountain views, and a good bright restaurant downstairs. The regional food is good, and there is, of course, the option to eat *paella*.

Double room 5,000–7,000 ptas

Hostería Catalana
(HR)M *C/ Pietat, 34 (973) 64 82 02 Cl. Nov.*

If you want to be more in the centre, this is spacious and traditional hotel, with a fire-warmed lounge and a games room for long winter evenings. The restaurant is favoured by the French, and the chef has embarked on a task of educative cooking – he offers not only *paella* but also a wider variety of traditional Catalan food including the *arròz negre* (rice cooked with fish stock and blackened with squid ink) and *escalivada*.

Allow 2,000 ptas, double room 5,500–7,500 ptas

Brasería Candido
(R)M *C/ Pietati Aigua, 33 (973) 64 70 77 Open all year*

For lunch or dinner, this is fun – with two big well-decorated rooms full of partying French, and a charcoal grill working away. It offers a series of six set menus which allow you to choose between the tipical *paella*, or *sarsuela* alternatives or more locally typical pâtés, *olla aranesa*, trout, civets or grills.

Set menus from 1,750 ptas

Map 2A **ES BÒRDES**

This is a delightful village, just off the main road. You are now in the true Vall d'Aran.

D'es Bordes
(R)M *C/ Reial, 1 (973) 64 17 59 Open all year – ring just in case*

The chef (and owner), Josep Fondevila, loves French food, and loves to cook for clients who recognise and appreciate the skills of a passionate cook. He admits to strong French influences in his cooking, although he uses practically no butter. His speciality is duck, which he produces in various ways, the making of his own sausages and pâtes, and the curing of wild-boar hams. He works in a very small kitchen for a restaurant of nine tables, more frequented by the adventurous French than the Catalans. His menu is select and imaginative, although you can always choose a grilled steak or magret done on the fire in the room. If you're lucky, you might have the opportunity to try his snail pâte, or wild mushroom pâte. To finish, he produces home-made *mató* (fresh cheese), a delicate rice pudding, or even pancakes filled with a compôte of quince or fig. Should you be there in late June, try the wild strawberries, which he picks himself.

Note that he is a family man and stops serving lunch at 3.00 p.m. and takes last dinner orders at 10.00 p.m. On weekdays out of season, ring in case he has taken a day off.

Allow 2,000 ptas

Map 2A **ARRÒS**

There is a spectacular excursion to make near here. Take the turning off the main road for Arròs, without going to the village itself, and follow the river Varradòs for fourteen kilometres up the valley past the Pla de l'Artiga and on to Pla de les Artiguetes. Five minutes' walk away is a beautiful waterfall, the famous Salt del Pitx.

El Raconet
(R)M *C/ Crestalhera, 3 (973) 64 17 30 Open evenings only (Aug. midday and evening). Cl. Nov.–27 Dec; Jun. Cl. Mon. and Tues. in winter.*

To reach the house, park in the square and walk up behind the turreted building.

The village is tiny and the restaurant very special. It is so small and other-worldly that my Aranese friend, Xavier, describes it as 'a restaurant in which to declare your love'. There are four tables. The restaurant was Esther Muñoz's sitting room in her old cottage in the village, and still retains that warmth and intimacy. A big inglenook dominates one end of the little room, and the walls are covered with pictures. Violin or piano concertos play quietly in the background. Needless to say, you feel like a personal guest, and are treated as one. The first courses might range from onion or courgette soup, cured duck, a rich lentil dish to a warm goat's cheese salad, or confit. For seconds, Esther's specialities are creamed sauces without milk. You could try *filet* with creamed almond, Iceland salt-cod with a sauce of hazelnut, trout, or chicken with creamed apple. If you don't feel like sauces, there is always grilled steak or lamb. The desserts are good too – the apple tart is a firm favourite, and there are clients who order the banana and rum desert before they come.

You must reserve beforehand, and note that only noble drinks or water are served (beer is forbidden).

Allow 3,000 ptas

Map 2A **VIELHA**

This is the main town of the valley, with plenty of hotels, restaurants and shops. Big for the valley, it is still very small on the scale of Catalan towns. A small river runs through the middle – look over the main bridge and you can see the sparkle of trout playing below. Walk upstream for two minutes and you are surrounded by the tranquility of the country-backed old houses. Out of season Vielha is peaceful, and during the winter weekends and summer holidays it fills with passing skiers and families.

The church of Sant Miquel contains a very beautiful twelfth-century romanesque sculpture, the Christ of Mijaran (remarkable for the detail of the workmanship), which is now exhibited in a glass case on the right. And if you have time to visit to the museum, **Tor Deth Generau Martinhon**, you can absorb some of the history of this wonderful valley through the religious artefacts, the array of old objects, and the evocative collection of photographs.

Tor Deth Generau Martinhon (973) 64 18 15 Open 10.00 a.m.–1.00 p.m., 5.00 p.m.–8.00 p.m. Tues.–Sat.; Cl. Sun. p.m., Mon. Ring out of season to check

Fonfreda
(H)M *Paseig de la Llibertat, 14 (973) 64 04 86 Open all year*

This is a small, central family-owned hotel on the *rambla* just downstream from the main street. It feels thoroughly friendly. The rooms are comfortable, finished in old pine, with simple but pretty furniture, and parquet. There is no restaurant, but the lounge and breakfast room are spacious, decorated with dried flowers and there are chinese-style rugs everywhere. The breakfast is good – a buffet libre which is light in summer and suitably hefty in winter.

Double room 8,500–11,500 ptas

Parador del Vall de Aran
(HR)L *Ctra Túnel (973) 64 01 00 Open all year*

This is a splendid hotel – extremely comfortable as all Paradors are. It is just outside the town, on the road which leads to the Vielha Tunnel. I recommend it not as a hotel, but as a place to take an aperitif at the bar. There is a good reason for this – the building has a circular glass-walled turret in which the bar is installed: from here you have a marvellous view of the three valleys below. Take a stroll, drink in hand, round the balcony of the turret – breath deeply and look up each valley – wonderful.

Double room 10,000 ptas

Hostal Turrull
(HR)M *C/ Riau, 11 (973) 64 00 58 Open all year*

An ideal, no-frills hotel, with easy parking just outside, on the edge of the town just a few minutes' walk to the centre. It was one of the first to be established in Vielha, and has good bedrooms, carpeted passages, a large diningroom, and a cosy sitting room complete with log fire.
Double room 4,500–5,000 ptas

→ **Era Mola (Gustavo-Mª José)**
(R)M *Marrec, 8 (973) 64 24 19 Open weekends in winter, 15 Jul.–15 Sept.*

The house is a little difficult to find – the street is upstream and on the right. Era Mola is at the end, tucked into a corner, with no name except Gustavo-Mª José engraved on the window.

This is my favourite restaurant here – a delightful little place where the wall and ceiling beams of the old stables give a special intimacy to the room. There are only eight tables, so it is essential to book in advance. Maria José is welcoming and charming. She cooks in a little kitchen open to view, while her daughters help serve. The food is exquisite – touched with French and Catalan influences. The menu is short but interesting with starters including an onion tart with the finest pastry, and canelones of pork and duck. She was one of the pioneers of French duck dishes in the region, and these remain her speciality. She serves a good magret and well prepared confit, and also offers rabbit with plums, *filet* of pork with calvados, etc. On Tuesdays, Fridays and Saturdays (I was there on a Thursday) she also serves fish, just in from the Basque Country, and I've heard she cooks a fine salmon *al estragó* (tarragon). The general consensus in the town is that her desserts are the finest in the area. Personally I recommend the mandarin pancake – layers of pancake filled with a citrus-scented cream – fantastic. The cheesecake was also delicious.

Allow 3,000–3,500 ptas

Arrowed for the charming family, their delightful house and their skill in the kitchen.

Et Hurat
(R)M *Paseig de la Llibertat, 14 (973) 64 02 10 Cl. Jun., Nov.*

This crêpery has a high reputation here, and tends to be full. It is small and narrow, with a large fireplace (roaring in winter) occupying half of one wall, green macramé decorating the kitchen door and lamps, and menus written on wood. Apart from the selections of pâtés and cheeses, Et Hurat serves all kinds of pancakes here – a variety of generous savoury dishes and some delicious sweet recipes. We both tried house specialities –the stuffed cabbage roll and the chicken and mushroom mixture. They were good, but we came across the pizza problem – however delicious they are, half of one flavour is enough. Choose different fillings and swap halfway. If you order in advance, you can also enjoy a fondu or a Spanish-style raclette (a cook-it-yourself grilled supper) and then finish off with a sweet pancake.

Allow 2,200 ptas

Map 2A BETREN

This village is practically touching Vielha. La Bòrda de Betren is opposite one of the most outstanding romanesque church portals in the valley – where there are five-arch rings supporting some sixty sculpted figures.

➔ La Bòrda de Betren
(R)M *(973) 64 00 32 Open all year*

The restaurant looks attractive, with ivy creeping up the old walls and a sunken entrance. Until fifteen years ago it was a cow shed, and the polished byres are still there. Inside it is carefully decorated with contemporary paintings and small classical sculptures, which go well with the great thick ceiling beams of the house. There are eight tables.

The chef produces excellent wholesome Aranese cooking, with some French influences – blue-cheese soup, home-made pâtés, home-smoked trout, blanquette of veal, lamb with honey, grills, civets in winter. The offer changes according to the market – clients who know ask the chef what he recommends today. Be sure to reserve at weekends.

Allow 3,000 ptas

Arrowed for thoroughly good food in a very attractive room.

Map 2A **ESCUNHAU**

A little village, cobbled streets, quiet with a pretty romanesque church.

Hostal Casa Estampa
(HR)M *C/Sortaus, 9 (973) 64 00 48 Open all year*

This is a delightful place to stay – my personal first choice in the whole valley. It began many years ago as an eating house and with the encouragement of the clients who supped in the evening and stayed in the family home, the hotel began to emerge. Today the hotel has twenty-six rooms, all simply furnished and comfortable. There is plenty of room inside to spend winter evenings – extra rooms for playing games or chatting. The breakfast room has a large inglenook and just beyond is the dining room with another huge fireplace on which the grilled meats are cooked. Red-check tablecloths covered with paper are the order of the day – good traditional food and home-made desserts to follow.

The kitchen door is always open. When I was there two generations of the family were at work there (and a third, some two years old, was getting used to the future workplace, racing around on a plastic trycicle).

One of the most delightful aspects of the hotel is outside: the small garden leads straight out to the meadows and woods of the Vall d'Aran – neither road nor house in between. Wandering up the garden you find the vegetable patch from where your supper vegetables might have come (there is another larger patch further away). The eggs are 'home-laid' too. This is a place to relax in for several days, with the advantage that it is right in the middle of the valley.

Double room 5,950 ptas; Rest. allow 2,500–3,000 ptas

Arrowed for the welcome of the people, the charm of the old house, the garden and its extension into the woods.

Casa Turnay
(R)M *Sant Sebastiá, s/n (973) 64 02 92 Open weekends only Oct–Nov. Cl. May–Jun.*

This cosy restaurant, with dark wood beams and a warming fire in

Escunhau – Casa Estampa

winter, serves the traditional food of the valley – usually well-tested old recipes. First courses of a good *olla aranesa* or hot leek and wild mushroom terrine (delicious); main courses of beef stews, or civets of wild boar or venison, or stuffed cabbage. While their own garden allows, they serve the tables with their own produce. Wine and a little toast with home-made pâté keeps you going here while you make your choice. The cheesecake is a popular dessert here, along with the chocolate truffles. The family lives upstairs, and the animals used to live where the restaurant is.

Allow 2,500 ptas

Map 3A **CASARILH**

La Torrada
(R)S *C/ Major (973) 64 11 50 Cl. Wed., 15 Jun–15 Jul.*

I've mentioned this because it is fun – a simple place little-known by tourists which is very popular locally. Here you can come and have a

hunk of toast (Catalan style, of course) with ham, cheese, *escalivada*, smoked salmon, etc –a really good snack. If you're in the Vall d'Aran for a few days, this may be just the ticket when you don't fancy a full-blown meal. It cater for all apetites, with a full menu of grilled meats or rabbit with *allioli* just in case.
Allow 1,500–2,000 ptas

Map 3A **GARÒS**

Et Restillé
(R)M *Plaça Carrera (973) 64 15 39 Open winter eves., Jul.–end Sept.; Cl. Sun.*

Ask anyone in the valley what to eat here and they'll shout in unison. This is the place to eat the *olla aranesa* – the warming mountain broth thickened with vegetables, pulses and various types of sausage. You find it on every menu in every restaurant, but here the chef has achieved a richness that is hard to beat. The menu is very short, mainly offering meats *a la brasa* on the open wood fireplace in the room. The trout *a fins herbs* is also good. Seventeen years ago the restaurant began, and maintains the hayracks and beams of the erstwhile cow sheds to good effect. You must book in winter.
Allow 2,500–3,500 ptas

Map 3A **ARTIES**

This little town has two claims to fame: for the locals it is one of the access points to a winding stony track up the valley (better in a four-wheel drive vehicle) leading up through the forests and meadows to fantastic mountain views; for the traveller it is also home to one of the most admired restaurants in the whole of Catalunya: Casa Irène.

➜ **Valarties**
(HR)M-L *C/ Major, 3 (973) 64 09 00 Open ski season and mid-Jun–mid-Oct. (Opening dates may be extended – ring to check)*

Next to the famous restaurant, and sharing the same kitchen, chefs, and family ownership, is the very pleasant hotel Valarties. The garden is a delight – it is the labour of love of Irène and her son Andreu, who have carefully chosen indigenous trees and a great variety of plants to border the lawns. It is a pleasure to relax here, where you can read a book, or sip something delicious while listening to the birdsong and the gurgling stream. The chefs often pop out of the kitchen to fetch the herbs from the shady side of the garden. The hotel looks out over the garden and over the small town. The twenty-nine rooms are compact, tastefully decorated with parquet floors, rugs and elegant bathrooms.

Arties – Hotel Valarties

Downstairs is the comfortable restaurant, looking out to the garden. The hotel menu – incredibly good value – offers the same choice as the classic menu in Casa Irène. We started with a delectable vichysiosse and a fresh salad with toasts of melting goat cheese, lightly dressed with walnut oil. This was followed by a surprise – a delicate warm mousse of *escalivada* with a vinaigrette of shallot. Then came the main course: saddle of rabbit stuffed with cabbage and wild mushrooms, covered with the finest lattice of potato and with a rich dark glaze; and fillets of trout on a bed of aubergine and corianda. The desserts were spectacular – an exquisite flat apple tart individually cooked with the lightest pastry, and bunyoles (little balls of fried batter) filled with cream of anise. What a wonderful meal.

In the low season everybody eats in the restaurant Casa Irène itself, while in the high season both rooms are open.

Pension menu 2,200 ptas; double room 7,000–8,500 ptas

Arrowed for the great welcome that Sra. Irène gives her guests, for the beautiful garden, and for the extraodinary good value of dining as a guest in the hotel.

➜ Casa Irène

(R)M-L *C/ Major, 3 (973) 64 09 00 Open as Valarties above*

For a restaurant of such fame, a firm favourite of King Juan Carlos and his family, the restaurant is surprisingly relaxed in atmosphere. The room is clad in pine, with family-style pine benches with tables, or round tables and chairs. It is comfortable, with a great spirit of welcome given by Sra. Irène and her daughter-in-law. The waiters are highly professional, but thoroughly friendly and particularly helpful when you are choosing from the menu. As you sip your kir cardinal, you have four set menus to choose from. You need only choose the main course and the dessert – the first course coming as a series of surprises which change daily. In the case of the *menú gourmande* you can relax completely. There are no choices to make at all.

Menus 3,800 ptas, 4,600 ptas, 5,700 ptas; menú gourmande 4,800 ptas

Arrowed for the superb cooking, the elegant informality of the room, and the excellent service.

Besiberri
(H)M *C/ Deth Fort, 4 (973) 64 08 29 Open all year*

This is a chalet overlooking the main river of the town, with its many balconies full of flowers, dressed in pale pine both inside and outside. It's seventeen bedrooms each lead out to the balconies, and are decorated with pretty flowery fabrics for both beds and curtains. Although it is young in the business, the hotel is already popular with British travellers, who delight in the freshness of the place, and are even offered eggs and bacon for breakfast to prepare them for the exertions of the day. There is no traffic in Arties, so you are sung to sleep by the sound of the water.

Double room and breakfast 7,500 ptas; no restaurant

Map 3A **SALARDÙ**

The high season for Salardú is winter, when thousands come to ski in Baqueira-Beret, three kilometres away. In spring there are wonderful walks up through the meadows and woods of Aiguamòg and up to the lakes of Colomers. There is another fine romanesque church here, with an important thirteenth-century sculpture of Christ.

Lacreu
(HR)M *Ctra Baqueira (973) 64 42 22 Cl. Oct–Nov., May–Jun.*

This is an old favourite, a very popular hotel which has been building its high reputation since the 1920s. The atmosphere is lively and the service is personal – as you walk in you are greeted attentively and looked after by any one of the many staff. The food is good, and the views from the hotel are just of the mountains and valley. It fills equally in winter and summer, and is extremely good value. It has thirty simple rooms, a spacious lounge, bar and games room, and a restaurant which feeds not only its own clientele but those from the hotel opposite – the more glamorous, younger Petit Lacreu, which was set up by the son of the owners. The Petit Lacreu has a pool and garden and is significantly larger (tel: 64 41 42).

Double room Lacreu; 5,000–6,000 ptas; double room Petit Lecreu; 8,000–9,000 ptas

Map 3A **BAGERGUE**

This little village is the highest in the valley, just a few kilometres away from Salardú along a winding mountain road. Take a glance at the unusual dimpled dome of the church in Unha as you go by.

Casa Peru
(R)M *C/ San Antonio, s/n (973) 64 54 37 Cl. Jun.*

Here you can eat whatever you feel like. During the summer most of the vegetables and all the eggs are home-produced. It is a welcoming place without refinement, with a menu of home-made food ranging from a very good *truita de patata*, pâtés, *olla aranesa*, or *trinxat* (a cake of chopped vegetables) to solid second courses of a rich civet of wild boar, braised rabbit or poulet with raisins and port. The portions are very generous – great after a healthy march in the mountains or a long day's skiing. If your hunger doesn't stretch that far, a selection of first courses makes a very comfortable supper. The desserts? – all made here – include refreshing apple and calvados sorbet, pears in wine, and *crema aranesa*. After trying to analyse the difference between *crema catalana* and *crema aranesa* from the taste, I had to ask the chef: the difference is in the eggs, he said with a twinkle – they're from the Vall d'Aran.

In the twenty years since the restaurant began, it's grown into three rooms which fill on winter evenings. Make sure you reserve for the weekends in high season.

Allow 2,500 ptas

Map 3A **BAQUEIRA BERET**

In winter this is the key ski resort of the valley, with some seventy-three kilometres of interconnecting slopes. The nearby villages are packed with skiers, and the pulse of the area is rapid. The rest of the year is very quiet here, but some of the ski-lifts work in the summer season to take walkers up and down – well worthwhile if you have time. If you drive up past Beret to the Pla de Beret you gain a double advantage: a fabulous sight of the Maladeta peak from the road as it curves above Beret (there is a *mirador* to stop at); and further on, the view at close quarters of thousands of horses and cattle grazing free on the extensive plain of Beret. Beware here, there is great temptation to walk amongst the peaceful animals and touch them – remember that they are volatile and can react suddenly. If you look closely, you'll notice that two streams are born here at an altitude of 1,800m, trickling in opposite directions out of the mossy grass: this is where the Garonne and the Noguera Pallaresa have their source.

Val de Ruda
(H)M *Baqueira-Beret (973) 64 58 11 Open all year*

Unlike the vast hotels here, this is a small, comfortable hotel with only thirty-four rooms. It's decorated in typical mountain style with dark wood finishes, beamed ceilings, wood floors and stairs, and carpets. It serves a good buffet breakfast (there is no restaurant service) and feels inviting. The ski-lift is very close, and there are good restaurants just across the road.

Double room 7,750–12,850 ptas

Ticolet
(R)M-L *Baqueira (973) 64 54 77 Open ski season., Aug.*

A multi-facetted restaurant, the best in the town, with a first-rate a la carte dining room and two separate rooms for Swiss raclettes and hot stone cooking. The family, a Catalan and French couple with their five sons, have built up the business little by little, and in winter fill all three rooms easily. The raclette room is decorated in Swiss cottage-style, relaxed and young. Don't expect the panache of the Swiss – the cheese is melted by a small, flat, purpose-built hotplate, but the garnishes are as near the original as possible. The *pierrade* (hot stone cooking) room is furnished with rough blue-green wooden tables. Again, modernity has replaced the old slate rooftile with a ceramic tile, but the fun of a carnivorous cook-it-yourself evening still remains.

The most important part of the restaurant is the elegant haute cuisine room – where the chef produces some truly fine dishes. The daily dishes include fresh fish from the País Basc, while the carte offers mainly duck (magret with shallots), beef (*filet a la mostassa antiga*), trout, etc. His starters are pretty and inventive – (try the *pastel* of leeks) and his desserts come up beautifully presented. He professes a love of pâtisserie – he was trained in France, and it shows. He makes a fine apple tart, a orange mousse crêpe which comes as a gathered pancake parcel full of deliciousness, and a speciality that I've never seen in Catalunya before: a mousseline of rhubarb. For a cooler dessert, his ice-creams are excellent.

Allow 3,500 ptas

La Borda Lobato
(R)M *Baqueira (973) 64 57 08 Open winter eves., Aug.*

This is a great place for after a day of skiing. Barn-shaped with almost windowless stone walls and a steep slate roof, it has a great fire grilling chops, steak and rabbit while the wood oven roasts baby lamb and piglet and bakes fish. In summer the ambience quietens considerably.

The restaurant is rustic, Aranese-style, in decoration, but quite smart in tableware, with pink table cloths and good china.
Allow 3,500 ptas

From here, the road takes you soaring up to the **Port de la Bonaigua** (there's a *brasa* restaurant here, Les Ares) from where, on all but foggy days, there are fabulous views stretching through both the Vall d'Aran and the valley of the Noguera Pallaresa river.

Map 3A VALÈNCIA D'ANEU

You've now left Vall d'Aran and are now on the south side of the Pyrenees, curving down to the east of the great Aigües Tortes and Lake Sant Maurici National Park, amongst thick woodland.

Els Avets
(HR)M *Port de la Bonaigua (973) 62 63 55 Open 24 Jun.–25 Sept.*

A lovely hotel in the valley within its own tranquil park, with forest-covered mountains on all sides. This is a place for a rest – with lawns, a swimming pool, a couple of golf greens, and mountain walks all round. Espot is only an hour away, from where you can enter the National Park. The rooms are comfortable, all with balconies, and the hotel is spacious and well-furnished. There's a pleasant restaurant with a limited carte of regional and international dishes, which concentrates mainly on a daily menu for the hotel guests.
Half-board 4,500–8,200 ptas

Map 3A ESPOT

Espot serves as the entrance to the east side of the Aigües Tortes and Lake Sant Maurici National Park. In under two hours' walk from here, you can reach the chrystaline lake. The ski slopes of Superspot are just a few kilometres away.

Saurat
(HR)M *Plaça Sant Martí, s/n (973) 62 41 62 Open all year*

The family running this old hotel started offering bed and board to nature watchers over a century ago – it doesn't take much to imagine the struggle to get up here in those days. The hotel has fifty-two rooms, mostly pretty simple, with white walls and little decoration. There's a small garden below, a little relief from the summer traffic of people that visit the lakes. The restaurant is good value and provides a straightforward set menu which feeds many throughout the summer and ski seasons.

There are two restaurants – one informal for the passers by, and the other below the hotel, where the dishes of the day are displayed at the restaurant entrance, and the 'carte' is available. Canelones, *olla pallaresa* (the local stew), *botifarra*, civet of wild boar, roast kid – a general selection of regional food designed to be filling and sustaining. There are some fine Riojas on the wine list.

Half-board 4,842–5,982 ptas; double room with breakfast 6,300–8,500 ptas

For another spectacular valley up into the high Pyrenees, turn off at **Llavorsí** and go towards **Tavascan**. This is a departure point for mountain excursions to some of the most beautiful Pyrenean lakes including the biggest one of the range, Certascan. The few villages are small, with stone and slate-roof houses, accompanied by either cold damp drizzle or brilliant blue clear skies. This is hiking country in the summer and a good area for cross-country skiing in winter.

Map 4B RIBERA DE CARDÓS

Hostal Sol i Neu
(HR)M *C/ Llimera, 1 (973) 62 31 37 Cl. Dec.–Feb.*

This is a simple hotel with 32 rooms, and a garden with swimming pool. It's a mountain-style hotel, rather dour-looking in winter but the staff are welcoming and very helpful to families with young children (there is a children's playground and pool). River sports are popular here, and they are well-prepared to help you set up excursions.

Double room 4,000–5,500 ptas

Map 4A TAVASCAN

Llacs de Cardós
(HR)M *Tavascan (973) 63 30 78 Cl. Nov.*

A stone-faced building, in the small village, surrounded by splendid mountains with a river rushing by. It is decorated in chalet style, with pine furniture and twenty-six compact, simple rooms. The diningroom is big, serving good regional food.

Double room 4,500 – 6,600 ptas

Back down on the C147, following the Noguera Pallaresa river southwards towards **Sort**, there is a curious lunchtime detour on offer. The road off to **Llessuí** is long and windy, up through dry, scruffy rolls of hill.

Map 3B LLESSUI

When I arrived eventually, I had definite pangs of hunger and the rather disturbing feeling (given that it would take at least twenty minutes to go back down again) that perhaps the restaurant didn't exist. I found it difficult to find, as it has no sign outside, and only the clatter of knives and forks led me there – in the long block of apartments just outside the old village.

El Pigal (Can Kiko)
(R)S-M *Llesuí (973) 62 17 15 Cl. Tues. eve., Wed.; Jul.–Aug. open every day*

If you want to eat typical food of the region of Pallars Sobirà, this is the only choice. It is quite a trek to get there, but you do eat well in the end. The room is a modern, fairly bare hall full of tables – not very attractive. The menu consists of dishes entirely from the region. I suggest you take the *entrants de la casa* – a hunk of excellent Basque sheeps cheese (carefully chosen because it closely resembles the cheese that used to be produced here), *allioli* with oil of quince (slightly sweet and pale orange in colour), an excellent dried sausage made by Kiko, and home-made pâté (similar to a rillette). The main courses include snails, *escudella*, grilled meats and some excellent fried sausage again made by the house: *girella* -rich black pork sausage, and *corder* – a lamb sausage of rice and raisins. Its easy to overdo the oil here, so a salad is a good extra. A word of warning – the house invention, called *Filiberto,* is a dessert made of home set yoghurt, with sweet ice-cream on top, doused in bright pink syrup and served in a cup dipped in lurid green sugar. Not for the sensitive. El Pigal is best at lunchtime.

Allow 1,500–2,000 ptas

Map 3B SORT

This is a good base for an active holiday, with loads of information and help available for river or mountain sports.

Pessets
(HR)M *Ctra de la Seu d'Urgell, s/n (973) 62 00 00 Cl. Nov.*

A traditional hotel with some eighty comfortable rooms which has a lovely garden with big swimming pool and tennis court. If you want to stay in an apartment here, the hotel runs a block of well-furnished apartments in the centre overlooking the river, with a modernist façade which reminds me of Brighton pier – mermaids with twisting tails and white decorated balconies.

Double room 5,000–7,000 ptas

From Sort you can continue down towards **Lleida**, or fork east towards the **Cerdanya** – another breathtaking region of mountain scenery which extends eastwards from **La Seu d'Urgell** (at the foot of Andorra) towards Puigcerdà. This whole area, starting with La Seu, is speckled with superb restaurants and a number of very memorable hotels. (See Route C).

Continuing south, you pass through the small village of **Gerri de la Sal** – where, as the name suggests, salt is the local product. It suffers terribly from the coaches and colossal lorries which thunder through but would, otherwise, be a delightful place to stop and enjoy the views across the valley. There is one eyecatching building here on the other side of the river which you can see as you pass through – Santa Maria, the romanesque church of a ruined Benedictine monastery. It's built of a lovely pale golden stone, and stands glowing proudly. It's opening time is so erratic that I've never been able to get in, but from peering through the keyhole, I can assure you that it'd be worth a short visit! *If you're there between midday and 1.00 p.m. on Tuesday, Wednesday, Friday or Saturday, you might be lucky.* The village itself, below the road, is pretty, porticoed and quiet with a pointed old footbridge to take you across the river to the church.

Map 3C **CELLERS**

A small village above the lake just south of **Tremp**. The village of **Castell de Mur**, with clusters of old stone houses, the silhouette of the romantic castle, and the beautiful romanesque cloister of an eleventh-century Augustine Collegiata, makes a lovely detour from here. It's a couple of kilometres north of Cellers, turning off towards Guardia de Tremp. Further on from Castell de Mur, you can head for **Sant Esteve de la Sarga**, where you can walk along the spectacular narrow gorge of Mont-Rebei, cut through by deep blue water.

Terradets
(HR)M *Ctra Balaguer-Tremp C147, Km 41 (973) 65 11 20 Open all year*

This hotel is on a quiet road, by the lakeside with rooms looking over to the hills beyond. It is finished in dark pine, with some pretty fresh rooms, and with a big swimming pool and terrace just above the lake. The food is honest and the people very welcoming. If you are thinking of staying for a while, you can take advantage of the windsurfers, optimists and canoes of their little school. They also have mountain bikes, and take small groups walking into the hills to look at the plants and trees.

Double room with a breakfast 7,000 ptas; in summer they only offer full or half-board (half-board 6,280 ptas)

Map 3C FONTLLONGA

This is a tiny, virtually uninhabited hamlet overlooking the **Embassaument de Camarasa**, half way between **Balaguer** and **Tremp** perched just above the C147. (Be prepared for the turn-off up the hillside.) There is nothing here except a rather lovely view, singing grasshoppers, and a Catalan restaurant.

Can Quel
(R)S *Crta del Doll (973) 45 50 27 Open all year, lunch only*

It's an unlikely place for a successful restaurant, but the owner was born here and came back home ten years ago to start up the business. Quite a risk, especially as you can't see Can Quel from the road, but word has got around – good value and good food. A big room, red check tables, wine in a jug or *porró* and good country bread.

The dishes are sung out to you in thick Catalan, but ask for a carte if you want one (they've got one in English). The snails *a la gormanta* are quite delicious, cooked with a *sofregit* of tomato and onion enriched with a splash of cognac. I'd also recommend the canelones, the rabbit with wild mushrooms (*fredolics*) and the hefty *escudella* although I admit I found the stuffed pigs trotters very heavy on the stomach. A lot of people come here for the *a la brasa* meat. The *crema catalana* got high marks.

Allow 1,500–2,000 ptas

Turning west off the road towards **Àger**, you can take a longer but very scenic route down to **Lleida** driving beneath the high red cliffs that host international tournaments of hang-gliding. The countryside is rough and dry but with splendid views.

Map 2D BALAGUER

This is a dignified market town, with a fine porticoed main square, on the far side of the bridge over the Segre river. If you go on up the hill, you'll come to the gothic Collegiata de Santa Maria – worth it for the fine architecture and superb views.

Cal Morell
(R)M-L *Passeig de l'Estació, 18 (973) 44 80 09 Cl. Mon., end of Sept.*

Josep Maria Morell is as passionate about the traditional cooking of his region, as he is about the creative possibilities of haute cuisine. He's an enthusiast – a writer of books and articles, a demonstrator of cuisine, a voice that publicises the fine cooking of Lleida throughout the province and far beyond. His restaurant is elegant and attractive, with thick wood cross-beams, flower decorations, paintings, and old dressers full of bottles and preserves. The cooking is Catalan, both regional and inventive, touched with French influences, with some wonderful sauces. Starters range from garden salads and traditional broth with vegetables (*olla barrejada*) to a delicious warm salad of marinaded fresh salmon or little red peppers stuffed with *esqueixada* (preparation of salt-cod). Amongst the meat dishes is the *cor de filet a las herbes* – a dish of filet steak with herbs created in 1986 for Prince Felipe of Asturias who holds the title Senyor de Balaguer. A copy of the recipe, presented in the finest caligraphy, is exhibited on the wall. Sr. Morell has a high reputation for his fish dishes – the fish arrives here within a matter of hours from both Mediterranean and Cantabrian coasts – check the suggestions to see what's in today.

Menú del dia 1,500 ptas; menú executin 3,000 ptas; carte 3,500 ptas.

You are now very close to the capital of the province, **Lleida** (see Route F).

Vall de Boí, El Pont de Suert, Vall Fosca, Tremp

If you are planning to go south fast instead of exploring the Vall d'Aran, the tunnel of Vielha is your answer – a seven kilometre tunnel drilled through the mountains to take you straight in to the southern side of the Pyrenees. From here, you can speed on down towards **El Pont de Suert** and continue on towards the provincial capital, Lleida. You join the longer Route E at Tremp/Cellers.

However, there are two very lovely valleys that you should visit on your way: **Vall de Boí** and **Vall Fosca**. If you have to choose between these two, and your interest is cultural, take Boí. From there you can also drive into the west side of the Aigües Tortes and Lake Sant Maurici National Park. But if you are looking for quiet natural beauty, visit Vall Fosca.

Map 3B **VALL DE BOÍ**

This is an utterly beautiful valley on the western frontier of Catalunya. It is a wide valley, with abrupt mountains on either side, and rising promontories graced with small, huddled, slate-roofed villages. The river Noguera de Tor waters the lush meadows and thick forest of the valley. This is a place to visit for several days, breathe deeply and go walking through the countryside. Through the village of Boí itself you can also enter the fabulous National Park of Aigües Tortes (*bearing in mind that you can only enter by car before 10.00 a.m. and exit by car after 6.00 p.m.*, although there are plenty of four-wheel drive taxis here to take you in throughout the day – see National Park below) You can also ski here on the fourteen slopes of the Boí-Taüll resort up above the village of Taüll.

For any fan of Catalan romanesque architecture, this valley is outstanding. The little churches of Erill la Vall, Coll, Durro, Cardet and

Boí are lovely examples – each different. The most famous is in Taüll – the wonderful twelfth-century church of Sant Climent, with its breathtaking six-tier belltower and the emblematic Christ in Majesty (1123) painted within. As with most of the churches, apart from a few remaining vestiges, the original paintings were removed to the Museu d'Art de Catalunya in the 1920s, and what you see are unexpectedly bright replicas. Lying against the walls inside the churches are colossal dusty seventeenth century alterpieces behind which the old paintings had hidden.

For tourist information, you need to go to the tourist office in Barruera, the central town of the valley, and you can get more specific information about the National Park in Boí, in the square by the church.

Map 2B **ERILL LA VALL**

This village at the foot of the Erill peak (2,627 m) has another fabulous romanesque church with portico and a tall bell tower almost matching the height of the Sant Climent in Taüll. Lots of people come here for lunch in August and at weekends, so the short main street tends to pile up with cars.

Pensió L'Aüt
(HR)S-M *C/ Unic (973) 69 60 48 Open all year*

This is a well-established simple hotel, very close to the church, with a busy diningroom where you can eat a good-value menu of traditional valley food.

Menú del dia 1,550 ptas; half-board 4,400 ptas

Map 3B **BOÍ**

The old part of the village is hidden behind the pretty church.

Hostal Fondevila
(HR)S-M *C/ Unic, s/n (973) 69 60 11 Open for winter season, 15 Jun.–15 Oct.*

Easy to find on the way in to the village, with parking opposite. One of the most straightforward in the book – with white walls, polished floors and white curtains. Some rooms have a balcony, and nearly all have clear mountain views. It also has a little front terrace where the hotel family or guests sit to take the mountain sun, although the peace is a little interrupted at winter weekends or in August when cars go on up to Taüll and the slopes. The food is simple. Ideal as a short–term base.

Double room 5,500 ptas

La Cabana
(R)S *Ctra de Taüll, s/n (973) 69 61 10 Open every day in ski season and summer*

Just on the last left-hand bend of the road as you leave Boí going towards Taüll.

This is a red-check tablecloth restaurant, with a big wood grill at the back of the room. Salads, warming soups, grills and *crema catalana* – good honest food with no frills.

Menú del dia 1,500 ptas

Map 3B TAÜLL

Taüll is, not surprisingly, firmly on the tourist map, so you need to get here early to enjoy the peaceful beauty of Sant Climent or you'll find the little church crawling with people. *By 10.30 a.m. it is too late to take photographs of the church alone in its rural surroundings. You can see inside from 10.30 a.m.–2.00 p.m. and 4.00 p.m.–8.00 p.m., and can climb the wooden steps up the belfry to see the workmanship of the tower at close quarters.* After a gentle wander around the older, picturesque parts of the village, there are several places to eat locally. An alternative is to go back to Boí to the popular restaurant, La Cabana, on the first corner on the way down.

Map 3B CALDES DE BOÍ

At the top of the valley there is a reservoir – a lovely wooded three-kilometre walk away from the famous spa.

El Manantial
(HR)L *Caldes de Boí (973) 69 62 20 Open 15 Jun.–30 Sept.*

Spoil yourself – soak in the beauty of the valley, relax from the stress of driving, and be totally pampered by the humid greenery of the thick forests and the healing powers of the hot medicinal springs. The hotel is big, finished in wood and painted a therapeutic dark green and red. It is spacious, with the most wonderful garden and parkland surrounding it. The feeling of peace is total – this is the top of the valley, and the only sights are tree-lined mountains and the only sound is rushing water. There are, of course, hundreds of people – this is a site of pilgrimage (complete with little souvenir shop) for those who come year after year to visit the sanctuary and take the waters. The clients come for an average of two weeks, and are practically all Catalan, and the place throbs with relaxed family well-being.

Two hotels stand side by side, under the same ownership, sharing the health facilities and swimming pools. El Manantial is the leader – more comfortable and more prestigious, while hotel Caldes, absorbing the pretty square patio of the original seventeenth-century hostel (tel: 69 62 30) offers a range of rooms from very comfortable to spartan, thus catering for all pockets. The splendid little sanctuary of Mare de Déu de Caldes is here too, with frequent masses.

There are mineral waters for almost every complaint, coming from no less than thirty-seven different hot springs (24°C–56°C), each one of which you can discover as you walk through woods around the hotels. If you stay, you can benefit from the myriad of treatments (the resident doctor advises every guest on personal needs), the sports facilities, and also from daily organised excursions around the valley.

If you also expect wonderful food, you will be sorely disappointed (unless you are on a specially prepared diet). The set menu offers plenty of choice, but the food is adequate, no more. If you drop by to take a look (and possibly sign up for the return journey?) I suggest you don't stop for lunch – just take a drink.

Half-board 3,750 ptas; double room 13,250–15,000 ptas

Map 2B EL PONT DE SUERT

Having passed the Vall de Boí, this is the next town on the N230. It's a small, quiet town, with arcaded squares in the older part and a river flowing past at the back. On the main road through you'll notice an unusual contemporary church – worth popping into if it is open.

Hostal Cotori
(HR)M *Plaça Mercadal, 8 (973) 69 00 96 Cl. Christmas*

At the back of the old town, one side looking onto the square, and the other over the river to fields and hills. Hostal Cotori is one of the oldest hostels in the region, although today it is bright, new and welcoming, without traces of its age. The rooms are newly refurbished, and the stairs are full of plants. It's family-owned, with a reputation of really good home-cooking (by mum). You'll find all the regional dishes here, *escudella*, rabbit with wild mushrooms, *ternasco*, etc. Ample portions, and lots of choice in the daily set menu.

Menu 1,600 ptas

Continuing down towards **Tremp**, there is a turning off northwards at **Senterada** – this is the **Vall Fosca**.

Map 3B VALL FOSCA

This is a narrow valley, lush, green and beautiful, which follows the waters of the river Flamicell from its birth amongst the Pyrenean lakes of Montseny down towards the town of Tremp. The valley is poorly represented on road maps – just a thin, straight line running northwards – and if you don't know about it, it is very tempting to miss it out all together. (This is, of course, a great bonus for those who visit.) It is narrow, to the extent that much is permanently in the shade (hence the name), and lined with pastures and thick woods. The villages are small, of stone and slate, with romanesque churches. The walking is lovely. If you go right up to the top, there is a fantastic bonus: the spectacular silvery lakes of the rocky high mountains.

There is some impressive history locked into this valley. In 1914 the first hydro-electric works of Catalunya were carried out here amongst the natural lakes high in the mountains. Given the state of the access at that time, and the lack of powerful machinery, it was quite a feat of engineering to interlink the many lakes (all at different levels) by underground channels, so as to coordinate and employ the movement of water from one to another for the making of electricity. You can still see some small railtracks and pulleys from those days. (Most of the Pyrenean lakes are now used for electric power.)

The road leading up the valley comes to an abrupt halt in a mountain basin, beside the small resevoir of Sallent. If you are really fit, you can then climb up to the right to reach the first of the many natural lakes above. Otherwise, park at the far side of the resevoir, and take the historic cable car up (it was used to take machinery and men up to the lakes). *It makes the short journey at 9.00 a.m. and again at 4.00 p.m., and comes down at 1.00 p.m. and 6.00 p.m.. It only works from 15 June to 15 October, but when there is the demand, does frequent trips. For information: (973) 66 30 01. There is a café which serves good lunches.*

Few people reach here, particularly once you have passed the first couple of lakes. The mountainscape to the east is rugged, with few trees and mossy alpine vegetation. It thickens with forest to the west, from where you can hike over to the Vall de Boí. Several lakes' hike further on to the north will take you into the National Park of Aigües Tortes.

You can stay up here overnight using the refuges or, of course, potter (and picnic) for a few hours before catching the cable car back down again.

Map 3B **LA TORRE DE CAPDELLA**

Vall Fosca
(HR)S *Ctra Los Molinos (973) 66 30 24 Open mid-Jun.–mid-Oct.*

A very pleasant, simple hotel, perched beside the rushing stream, with a small pool and garden, surrounded by woodland. It is halfway up the valley, with twenty-seven rooms, and a clientele that returns year after year. The restaurant produces the best of honest home-cooking – in generous portions. Fresh vegetables, salads, warming soups, delicious herby home-made beefburgers, good filling stews. The pears in wine came up very prettily with a hint of spice, and the *crema* (a real test of a kitchen) was excellent. All this, added to the fact that there are very few places to stay in the valley, means that you should book in advance. There are also apartments run by the hotel if you feel like staying with a little more independence. This is a good place to find out about the lakes above, the family here has been showing visitors around for generations. Ask for a pack lunch if you're going up – its worth spending the day there.

Double room 4,000 ptas

Aigües Tortes and Lake Sant Maurici National Park

This huge area in the high Pyrenees, was given the status of a National Park in 1955. From Vall de Boí you enter the western region, Aigües Tortes – a deep valley which extends up to the famous lakes Llong and Rodó. From the east you enter via the valley of Espot into the region known for the still lake of Sant Maurici, and the beautiful high twin peaks of **Els Encantats** (the enchanted peaks) which rise up to 2,749 m beyond. The park is ringed by high mountains to the north (with the Vall d'Aran beyond) and to the south (Vall Fosca) – with the high peaks of Bassiero, Gran Tuc de Colomers, Sarradé, Subenuix and Peguera. It is quite tough crossing over from west to east as the passes between are high.

The park is very popular in the summer season, but if you get off the main trail you can find yourself completely alone amongst the most spectacular mountain scenery. Extraodinary formations of granite and slate, and water everywhere: rivers, rushing streams, waterfalls and over fifty glacial lakes. High meadows, and thick forests of pine, fir and beech. You should see capercaillie and golden eagles (although I confess I didn't spot any), and there are strong chances of seeing Pyrenean chamois (which I did).

If you visit in the autumn or early summer, the changing of the leaf colours is fabulous. In winter it's snowbound.

A word of warning: no matter what time of year, always take something warm or waterproof to put on just in case: you are in the high Pyrenees here and the weather can surprise you very suddenly.

Remember that access is limited: from either Boí or Espot you can only drive in before 10.00 a.m. and leave after 6.00 p.m. Otherwise you have to walk the five-kilometre leg both ways. Only official four-wheel drive taxis can circulate during the day – they provide the most comfortable way of entering. From Boí, you drive 1.5 kilometres to a parking spot, after which there is 4.5 kilometres of unasphalted road which you can drive before 10.00 a.m. From Espot you enter by a 4.5 kilometres long road. There are four refuges with limited room if you want to stay overnight.

Use the information centres – they have good maps: *Boí (973) 69 61 89, Espot (973) 62 40 36 Open 9.00 a.m.–1.00 p.m., 3.30 p.m.–7.00 p.m.*

Park entrances Open 9.30 a.m.–2.00 p.m., 4.00 p.m.–6.30 p.m.

5 LLEIDA FROM THE WEST (SANTANDER FERRY)

ROUTE F FROM ZARAGOZA OR HUESCA

Lleida, Tàrrega, Igualada

From Santander, the most direct route to Catalunya passes through Zaragoza (Saragossa) and then on to Lleida – a distance of some 560 kilometres. The main road from Lleida to Barcelona is busy and rapid, cutting through huge cereal-growing areas, and hilly passes. If you wander a little off the main road, you'll come across the beautiful Cistercian monastery of Vallbona de les Monges just south of Tàrrega, plenty of old castles north of Cervera and, nearer Barcelona, the strange rocky peaks of Montserrat. Diverting southwards, you pass through the olive groves of Les Borges Blanques en route to the famous monastery of Poblet, and can then enjoy the mountainous interior of the province of Tarragona (see Route G).

Map 2E **LLEIDA**

As the capital of a province famous for its fruit groves, its fertile valleys and its fields of cattle, the city of Lleida is blessed with a large collection of select and excellent restaurants. It is a small but busy commercial city, which expects few tourists. Lleida is on one of the major link roads between the Cantabrian coast and the Catalan Mediterranean, and on an important route between the Andorran Pyrenees and the south. Heavy traffic thunders (or crawls) through the outskirts. As a result, the capital is not a great tourist attraction, and the splendid fortress and romanesque-gothic cathedral which stand proud above the city are little visited. The cathedral is monumental, with beautiful sculptural work on the portals (you need to walk round to the far side to appreciate some of the finer workmanship), a very dignified interior and a set of elegant early gothic cloisters. A walk up here through the fortress walls is an absolute must, particularly in the early morning light (*around 10.30 a.m., when it opens!*) or at dusk to watch the evening set in across the spread of the surrounding plain. The new cathedral is not so eyecatching – a solid neoclassical splendour in the centre of town, just off the Rambla de Ferran which you drive into after crossing the main bridge.

The hotels here are clearly equipped for the business traveller, so if you want to continue in holiday spirit, you might think about sleeping out of town. Half an hour away, just outside Tàrrega, there is a very pleasant hotel.

NH Pirineos
(H)M-L *Passeig de Ronda, 63 (973) 27 31 99 Open all year*

Not a small or family hotel, but I found the reception genuinely welcoming and it's comfortable, easy and central, in a city with few alternatives. It's finished in polished marble and wood with blue upholstery in true executive style, and is on the main traffic flow round the town – the same road as La Pèrgola and close to La Mercè.
Double room 11,000 ptas

Segrià
(H)M *Segon Passeig de Ronda, 23 (973) 23 89 89 Open all year*

For a cheaper second choice – looking over the railway. Modern, simple and central with a garage.
Double room 6,800 ptas

➔ **El Petit Català**
(R)M *C/ Alfred Perenya, 64 (973) 23 07 95 Cl. Sun. eve., Mon.*

This is a small restaurant bursting with personality and vigour. The chef, Salvador Alarí, is a very engaging man, who loves to indulge in discussions about the art of cooking – Catalan cooking, with local ingredients. We listened speechless as he waxed lyrical about olive oil – for some thirty minutes – the flavours, the *denominació d'origen*, the effect of one or another with certain vegetables, salads, fish... His magic touch shows most in the patisserie – his wife confirms that he is happiest of all creating exquisite sweet delicacies. (His *menú gastrònómic* includes three courses and two puds.) The presentation is that of an artist. The carte here is varied, inventive and mouthwatering – so many delicious-sounding combinations I've never seen before or since. But he much prefers it if you just ask him what's in the kitchen today – this is a man who thoroughly enjoys his profession, and likes to share it.
Arrowed for inventive excellence and personality.
Menú del dia 2,500 ptas; menú gastrònómic 3,500 ptas

La Pèrgola
(R)M *Gran Passeig de Ronda, 123 (973) 23 82 37 Cl. Sun.*

An elegant little restaurant in a small chalet, light with a mellow, pale yellow decor. The chef-owner produces sophisticated, refined dishes – creative haute cuisine: a cassoulet of foie gras; a salmon roll with *gambetes* (delicious little prawns); monkfish with a delicate cream of sea urchin. The strength of the house is the selection of home-made desserts, beautifully presented.
Menú del dia 2,750 ptas

La Mercè
(R)M *Av. Navarra, 1 (973) 24 84 41 Cl. Sun, 15–31 Nov.*

La Mercè was the first little restaurant amongst the town chalets here –

now there are several others, including La Pèrgola, just round the corner. Magnolia rooms with tables dressed with splendid crystal and pretty table-linen. Apart from the small main room, there is another room upstairs, an outside terrace, and the cellar – lined with wine and equipped with wooden tables for less formal meals. The kitchen is run by one brother while the other minds the rooms. The food is excellent, with all the sophistication of method and grace of presentation of a serious haute cuisine chef. Apart from a concise carte, La Mercè has provided no less than five different set menus to suit all pockets and appetites –the working lunch, the regional, the seasonal, the gourmet, and finally the terrace menu: hard work for the kitchen, but very comfortable for the client. The fish is excellent here, and the desserts are a pleasure. Set menus from 2,100–4,400 ptas

Forn del Nastasi
(R)M-L *C/ Salmerón, 10 (973) 23 45 10 Cl. 1–15 Aug.*

This fine restaurant, founded in 1977, is at the foot of the castle hill, with a distinguished seignorial portal as its entrance. The restaurant is at the back, past the narrow but smart bar, and the decorative display of fruit and vegetables. The room is attractive, with small vaulted shelves of wine round the walls. Pepito, the owner, suggests you follow his recommendations of the day when ordering – and also confirmed that his lobster and seafood salad, and the *escalivada* terrine were favourites of his repetitive clients. As in most restaurants here, the desserts are highly considered, well-made and carefully presented. I particularly recommend the sophisticated pineapple and *crème anglaise* dish.
Allow 4,000–4,500 ptas

The giant companion to the Forn is the Fonda del Nastasi, a very astutely designed and decorated restaurant business two and a half kilometres along the road towards Huesca (Osca), which accommodates hundreds of eaters in its terrace, in its banqueting rooms, picturesque cellers, etc. Very popular, but also rather contrived. (973) 24 92 22.

Xalet Suís
(R)M *C/ Alcalde Rovira Roure, 9 (973) 23 55 67 Cl. Christmas*

A pretty, Swiss-style chalet on the corner of a square in the newer part of town, with the unlikely combination of red-checked tablecloths for a cosy, countrified effect, and formal, efficient service. The cooking is good, with a menu offering an unusual variety of fine Catalan dishes (roast kid, *romescu* of fish with potatoes), French (magret of duck, confit), and Swiss (fondues of various kinds including fish and shellfish). Good quality and a nice atmosphere.
Menú del dia 2,300 ptas

Outside Lleida

There are also some very good places to eat just outside the city. Once off the main highways, faith in hand, it is quite an adventure to find these locally famous restaurants hidden among the apple and pear orchards.

La Dolceta
(R)M *Camí Montcada, 48 (973) 12 13 64 Cl. mid-July–mid-Aug.*

Difficult to find: leave the town heading for Huesca (Osca), and turn right almost immediately down a small road just after the hospital. Turn left at the end of the block and keep going as the road bends to the right, and follow it through fields for some two kilometres.

To experience unadulterated local character at first hand, this is great fun, but you mustn't be phased by brusque waiters, clatter of plates, roars of noisy talkers, and food flung on the table. When you get there the menu is hurriedly shouted out by the waiter – there is no leisure to consider a delectable-sounding list. Here you eat excellently cooked traditional food – meat *a la brasa* or snails (really superb). As you'll see, the kitchen is basic, equipped with the mandatory wood range and precious little else. It's rough and ready, but the priorities are clear – there's great skill in the cooking, which is very highly regarded. You must book.

Menu 2,500 ptas

Cal Nenet
(R)M *C/ Partida de Butsènit, 38 (973) 26 00 16 Cl. 1–15 Nov.*

Take the sudden turning off the main Zaragoza (Saragossa) road about two kilometres from Lleida towards Butsènit. Keep going for some five minutes through fruit groves.

For good seasonal food of the region, this is a big old-timer here, whose chef talked with great sincerity about loyalty to local produce and traditional recipes. The short, no-nonsense menu offers various meats *a la brasa* (wood-burning), snails, salt-cod dishes, *escalivada,* etc. Game from the mountains in season. Try the fruit salad too – a delicately prepared plateful of the best of surrounding produce. You can eat inside or in the permanent marquee outside and there's a garden terrace for evening drinks and occasional dances.

Allow 2,500 ptas

Carballeira
(R)M *Ctra de Zaragoza, Km 459 (973) 27 27 28 Cl. Mon., Aug.*

It looks like an unremarkable roadside café – with parking outside and a very ordinary bar offering sandwiches and coffees at the entrance. One look at the menu tells otherwise, as does the fridge display between the bar and the pale blue restaurant tables. This is a superb *marisqueria* – a place to eat nothing but fish and shellfish. The fish arrives here direct – via the lorries heading for the Catalan capital from the Galician coasts.

A good choice is the *pica-pica* – a variety of tapas, or the selection of seven different shellfish in the *degustació*. Galicia also dominates the cheese and dessert choice.

Allow 3,500 ptas

Map 3E BELLPUIG

On the way to Tàrrega, you pass very close to this old town. If you have an interest in renaissance architecture, stop and visit the church of Sant Nicolau, where you can admire the mausoleum of Ramòn Folc de Cardona-Anglesola, a splendid work sculptured from Carrara marble. While you're there, take a look at the convent of Sant Bertomeu, which has two fine cloisters, one with pointed arches, and the other with flying butresses, twisted columns and capitals carved with floral motifs.

Map 3E TÀRREGA

Tàrrega is attractive and worth a short visit. There's a fine collection of sixteenth- and seventeenth-century buildings which clothe the main pedestrian shopping streets. The town becomes very animated in September when it has a terrific street theatre festival.

Hostal del Carme
(HR)M *Ctra Madrid-Barcelona km 504, Vilagrassa (973) 31 10 00 Open all year restaurant; Cl. Sun. eve.*

Half an hour from Lleida and two kilometres from Tàrrega on the old road, just outside Vilagrassa. It used to be a roadside hotel, but thanks to the Tàrrega bypass, it's now a quiet, comfortable place to stay with extensive garden and pool. The whole family work here, and the career is taken seriously – with training in Switzerland to prove it. The Hostal del Carme is best known for its excellent restaurant. The family has been in the cooking profession for four generations – starting with the grandmother of the present chef, Anna Maria Calvet, who cooks with her daughter Marta. The cuisine is mostly Catalan, with fresh fish on Wednesdays and Thursdays (delivery days) – the local favourite is sole stuffed with prawns, garnished with spinach à la crème. There is a good selection of rice dishes, and plenty of choice among the grilled and roast meats. The restaurant is elegant, decorated with elaborate flower arrangements, but if you just feel like a simpler meal, you can sit at the elegant bar, where the grill glows, and take a set menu there.

Bar 1,200 ptas; restaurant set menu 2,500–3,800 ptas; double room 4,000–7,000 ptas

Map 4E CERVERA

Although I have no recommendations here, the walled town is full of history. It is long and thin, built along the crest of a hill, with narrow, cobbled streets leading to the main porticoed square behind which you find the towered gothic church of Santa Maria. Closer to where you enter the town by car, you find the splendid neo-classical building of the university, with its two cloisters, from which strains of violins can be heard of a summer evening during the music festival.

There are numerous medieval castles in the area between **Cervera** and **Ponts** to the north (Route D), mainly built in the eleventh-century during the reconquest. Some are hilltop fortresses, and others nestle within old villages. You can visit **Florejacs**, to the north of Cervera, and beyond **Agramunt** (which has a twelfth- to thirteenth-century romanesque church of Santa Maria with a monumental, magnificently decorated portal), the castles of **Montclar** and **Montsonís** are also refurbished for inside viewing. For general castle-spotting, pass by **Montcortès, l'Aranyó**, and **Les Oluges** – all just north of Cervera.

Map E5 IGUALADA

This is a busy town with an old medieval centre, based on the textile and leather industries – not an attractive stop if you're travelling in country spirit, although there's a museum dedicated to the working of leather and an excellent restaurant to recuperate your strength.

El Jardí de Granja Pla
(R)M *Rambla de Sant Isidre, 12 (93) 803 18 64 Cl. Sun. eve, Mon., end Jul.–mid-Aug.*

This is a small, elegant place, serving refined Catalan dishes much influenced by French cuisine. As you'd expect in a commercial town, its clients are businessmen rather than travellers, so the ambience tends to be executive except at weekends. Try the warm *carpaccio* of fish, turbot 'en papillote', or one of the house specialities – stuffed saddle of rabbit with tarragon, or baked scallops with *cava*. (Just behind, served by the same kitchen, is an Italian restaurant, in case you should feel like a touch of pasta.) Good value.

Allow 4,000 ptas

On towards Barcelona, you pass beneath the strangely beautiful mountain of **Montserrat** (see Chapter 2) only fifty kilometres from the city.

An alternative route from **Lleida** towards **Tarragona** and the Costa Daurada (or **Barcelona**, of course) takes you a little south along the N240, into olive country. The virgin oil from this area is of such quality that it is distinguished by it's own *denominació d'origen* – Les Borges Blanques.

Map 3E LES BORGES BLANQUES

The fame of this town lies in its production of olive oil. Les Borges Blanques is the centre of the finest *arbequino* olive oil, and throughout the region, in the summer, there is a faint slightly rancid waft of olives. You can visit the Museu de l'Oli here, and the presses of Les Borges Blanques on weekdays.

Masia Salat
(R)S-M *Ctra Tarragona-Lleida, Km 71 (973) 14 23 92. Open every day*

You come across this restaurant just north of the town heading towards Lleida. Only a couple of years ago this was a simple *masia* serving lunches. A change of hands and some serious thinking have turned it into a highly successful restaurant bursting with people. The huge roadside car park is packed with cars and lorries at mealtimes – a very good sign. The weekday *menú del dia* is nothing to write home about – but the exceptional value pulls the crowds. If you eat off the carte the food is much better – grills, roasts, casseroles, general regional dishes. The ambience is lively and very noisy – garlic and tomato on the table to rub on the bread, good oil, and loads of people all talking loudly. You don't need to book – the efficiency is impressive, and the turnround of tables is amazing. If you don't make it in time for lunch or supper, the bar is open twenty-four hours a day, and will cook you a snack on the spot. The restaurant is equipped to serve hundreds of covers a session, and does.

Menú del dia 800 ptas; carte aprox. 2,500 ptas

From here, the great fortress-like Cistercian monastry of Poblet is only a stone's throw away, some thirty kilometres towards the coast (see Route G) or you can visit its peer, Vallbona de les Monges, (if you are a good map-reader) by taking the L201 towards Belianes and following the good signposting.

Map 3E VALLBONA DE LES MONGES

The monastery of Vallbona de les Monges is very beautiful – and as it is a little off the beaten track it has many fewer visitors than the other two famous Cistercian monastries nearby, Poblet and Santes Creus.

The church, cloisters and chapter house are the most important parts to visit, a dignified mixture of romanesque and gothic styles, with some fine renaissance sculptures.

Tours begin from 10.30 a.m.–1.30 p.m. (on Sundays from midday) and again from 4.30 p.m.– 6.45 p.m. It takes about an hour for a good visit led by the cloistered nuns. If you are lucky, you will be there when the nuns sing oration – there is a service at 4.15 p.m. (They sing six times a day.)

Vallbona de Les Monges

La Closa
(R)S *C/ Fossar Vell, s/n (973) 33 11 06 Open every day*

This is in a small passageway leading from the car park up to the monastery – a good place for a quick, simple meal before or after your visit. The restaurant is run by a small team of women who provide a very good value set menu and a short carte. (The kitchen is on the right as you go in). True home-cooking.
Menú del dia 1,300 ptas

Just south along the road towards Solivella (where there's an excellent restaurant) is the Santuari del Tallat – a small set of ruins perched on the crest of the mountains with superb panoramic views of the whole region. Unfortunately, it suffers the same problem as most favourite picnic spots and is not always as pristine as it should be.

Map 3E SOLIVELLA

Again, this village is a little off the route – but the restaurant is worth the diversion, and usefully close to the monasteries of both **Poblet** and **Vallbona de les Monges**. (See Route G for the former)

→ **Cal Travé**
(R)M *Ctra d'Andorra, 56 (977) 89 21 65 Cl. Wed., 15–30 Sept.*

A restaurant where the whole family works – parents, daughters and grandparents. A wood oven in the corner of the room produces the bread daily, and then works on the braised rabbit with snails or the roast kid, while the grill beside does the meat and the duck magret. A speciality of the house is the rich rice cooked with rabbit, and if you like salt cod, the *bacalla* with *allioli* on a bed of *escalivada* is excellent. In winter *calçotadass* are on. Desserts are mostly made by the daughters – cream cakes, profiterols, icecreams, sorbets (the thyme sorbet is unusual, not too sweet, and makes a very good digestif after a big meal). The presentation is a pleasure to see. As you eat, look round at the old furniture and various collections of old tools, keys, guns on the wall.

The wine list is extremely limited, for good reason – white, red and *cava* all come from their vinyards, taking the two family names as its lable: Sanstravé. The wine business has been going for a century now, and the *cava* a decade. You are welcome to see the wineries – just ask.

Allow 2,500–3,000 ptas

Arrowed for the extrovert home production, and the good value.

Another possible lunch spot, before or after visiting the monastery is in Santa Coloma de Queralt. On the way here, you pass **Guimerà**, a spectacular old village sprawling down the hillside. If you have the energy, and it's not too hot, it is worth wandering round the narrow medieval streets and up to the ruined towers of the castle.

Map 4E SANTA COLOMA DE QUERALT

This market town was once part of the Templar order, and retains the refurbished shell of the old castle along with a fine thirteenth-century parish church and a couple of pretty porticoed squares.

Hostal Colomí (de Germanes Camps)
(R)S-M *C/ Raval de Jesús, 10 (977) 88 06 53 Cl. Sun. eve.*

The restaurant Hostal Colomí is next to the castle on the park side. If you need directions, ask for *les Germanes Camps* (the Camps sisters).

For some ten years Rosita and Nati ran a restaurant in the centre called El Colomí, which still exists there. They've now moved back to the old family *fonda* beside the castle, although confusingly they've kept the name Colomí. The room of Hostal Colomi is new, light and very white, with a big fireplace at one end, where most of the cooking happens. *Porrons* and country bread are on the tables. One sister cooks, the other looks after the dining room. This is a place to enjoy regional cooking of the most traditional kind – braised broad beans (*faves*), baked wild mushrooms, grilled artichokes, *escalivada*, and *escudella i carn d'olla*, grilled meats, snails, or pigs' trotters. There is fish, but only on a daily basis – ask. The local cheese is good too (particularly the artisonal goat's cheese from Albió).

Menú del dia 1,500 ptas; carte 3,000 ptas

To reach Barcelona from here, you pass **Igualada** (see above) and the mountains of **Montserrat** (see Chapter 2).

6 THE COSTA DAURADA AND INLAND TARRAGONA

ROUTE G FROM BARCELONA

* Coastal – Tarragona, Cambrils, Delta de l'Ebre Natural Park
* Inland – Poblet, Valls, Reus, Gandesa, Tortosa

Coastal – Tarragona, Cambrils, Delta de l'Ebre Natural Park

The coastal road leading south from Barcelona is at its most spectacular in the twenty kilometres before **Sitges** (see Chapter 2), where it hugs the windy mountainous coastline, giving you a cliff-top view out to sea. Thereafter it becomes less engaging, with surprisingly few clear views of the sea as it passes cluttered appartment-filled towns. The Costa Daurada is rightly famous for its beaches – great wide expanses of golden sand that stretch for kilometres at a time. The towns have mostly developed with seaside tourism in mind, and are mainly made up of a small old quarter, usually around the port, surrounded by hefty blocks of modern flats which also extend along the beaches. This makes for a happy holiday ambience during the warm season, and the peacefulness of almost deserted towns the rest of the year. The Catalans tend to spend weekends by the sea as soon as the sharp winter cold has softened into early spring, but the tranquility remains unimpinged. This quality along with the deep blue colour of the sea on a clear day (it seldom clouds over), make the coastal region, out of season, a tempting place to be.

There are multitudes of enormous hotels along the coast, so I've selected severely, keeping the idea of 'small and friendly' clearly in mind. There is also an abundance of restaurants – many pander to a fairly undiscriminating client base, but there are also a number of superb places. The gastronomic fame of this coast lies in **Cambrils**, where there is a collection of expert chefs.

Passing Sitges and Vilanova i la Geltrú (see Chapter 2), Cubelles is the next coastal town, some thirty kilometres from Barcelona. Just before the town there is a fabulous hotel.

Map 5F **CUBELLES**

➔ **Llicorella**
(HR)L *C/ San Antonio, 101 (93) 895 00 44 Cl. Jan.; Rest. Cl. Sun. eve., Mon. (except Jul.–Aug.)*

This is a wonderful place – a large family chalet with an expanse of lawned and wooded garden adorned by scultpures. Inside, almost every room is an art gallery in itself, and each of the spacious thirteen bedrooms (complete with antique painted wooden beds) is named after the artist whose works are hung within – maybe Guinovart, Clavé, Bartolozzi... Downstairs, the restaurant follows the same artistic impulse, serving refined Catalan cuisine worked with contemporary creativity and expertise. I suggest you relax, enjoy the pleasant garden view, and take the *menú degustació*. A blissful place.

The hotel is a member of Relais & Châteaux.

Menus 4,000–7,000 ptas; carte aprox 5,000 ptas; double room 13,000–20,000 ptas

Arrowed for the exhuberant garden, and superbly decorated house. The height of elegance.

Map 5F **CUNIT**

L'Avi Pau
(R)M *Avda Barcelona, 160 (977) 67 48 61 Cl. Mon. eve., Tues.*

This is on the main road – an unusual circular building which is full

Cubelles – Llicorella

of light, paintings and plants. The restaurant is highly professional, and the dishes offered are both traditional (*suquet*, grilled fish with *escalivada)* and contemporary (crêpes of *llagostins* and *gambes* with a sauce of crab, lobster glazed with Penedès brandy). Finesse and elegance both in the kitchen and in the dining room. It's well patronised at weekends so it's a good idea to book.

Seasonal menu 2,850 ptas; carte approx. 4,500 ptas

Map 5F **CALAFELL**

A splendidly wide beach, and a largely Catalan summer community. There's no road between the front-line houses and the beach, only an extensive promenade, so this is a good place for children.

Kursaal
(HR)M *Av. St Joan de Déu, 119 (977) 69 23 00 Open all year*

Don't let the rather uninspired reception put you off. The bedrooms are bright and very comfortable and nearly all thirty-five rooms have front-line balconies. An adequate restaurant (Emilio) and a bar.

Double room 7,500–9,500 ptas

Giorgio
(R)S-M *C/Angel Guimerá, 4 (977) 69 11 59 Open Fri. eve.–Sun. eve., every day in summer*

An Italian restaurant which, like the hot-blooded explosive Giorgio himself, packs a punch as soon as you walk in – extrovertly decorated with swoops of ruby red cloth, and the walls dripping with paintings and letters dedicated to Giorgio by those many famous artists and writers who have passed through the doors in the last twenty-five years. Splendidly Bohemian, refined with classic china and candlesticks – a magnificent setting for the enjoyment of a dish of the finest fresh pasta, accompanied by crunchy home-made bread. Italian and Mediterranean cooking at its very best. Extremely popular so you must book.

Allow 2,000 ptas; menú degustació 3,000 ptas

La Barca de Ca l'Ardet
(R)M *Av. St. Joan de Déu, 79 (977) 69 15 59 Open all year*

If you want to eat on the seafront, this is a good restaurant with a long tradition of some forty years. Its quite narrow so you get the best beach views if you're outside on the small terrace. Elegant decor and elegant service. You can eat good traditional Catalan marine dishes here with a selection of local specialities like the Calafell *úrossejat*. There are various different set menus to choose from.

Menus 2,500–4,500 ptas

Masia de la Platja
(R)M *C/ Vilamar 67 (977) 69 13 41 Cl. Dec., Tues. eve., Wed.*

A happy restaurant, run by a delightful family who've been cooking here for over thirty years. It's one street back from the beach, with a pretty arched façade of blue and white tiles. Inside it's decorated in an attractive nautical style, with a rough wooden ceiling, and large, carefully lit paintings lining the walls. Salad of smoked salmon and *gambes*, monkfish and clam soup, hake baked with young garlic – the carte is interesting and the food very good. For dessert I thoroughly recommend the *madüixetes gratinades*: wild strawberries in a delicious and surprising crème (I promised I wouldn't give the secret ingredient away).

Menú degustació 2,700 ptas; carte approx. 4,000 ptas

Map 4F EL VENDRELL

This is a few kilometres inland, the main town of the Baix Penedès region. The great 'cellist Pablo Casals (Pau Casals here) was born here in 1876, and his house, Via Palcuriana, 14, in the Sant Salvador area of the town, is now a rather charming museum of his musical instruments, photos, furniture, sculptures and paintings. In the modern 400-seat auditorium built in his memory, there is a music festival every summer.

El Molí de Cal Tof
(R)M *Ctra Santa Oliva, 2 (977) 66 26 51 Cl. Mon.*

The business started with the grandparents, but this restaurant has only been around for a decade. Very popular, with stone walls, beamed ceilings and a round fireplace with an iron chimney funnel in the centre of the room where your meat or *calçots* are grilled in winter. Very snug in winter, cosy in summer – altogether a strong contrast from the bright coastal restaurants. The emphasis here is on tradition and the resurrection of regional recipes, so it's a good place to come to eat typical local dishes. Don't eat too much *fuet* or tomatoed toast while you wait because the portions are generous. Try the delicious *xató* of El Vendrell (a salad of lettuce, salt-cod, tunny, anchovies, onion, etc. marinaded in a rich spicy vinaigrette of almonds, hazelnuts, garlic and tomato), or the unusual braised monkfish with *rovellons* (wild mushrooms). Ask what's on today.

Menú from 1,800 ptas; carte approx. 2,500–4,500 ptas

Map 4F **COMA-RUGA**

Joila
(R)M *Av. Generalitat 24 (977) 68 08 27 Cl. Tues. eve., Wed., Nov.*

Joila is some way back from the sea, on the entrance road to Comarruga at the southern end. Outside and inside it is no great shakes, more like a modern roadside café with an adequately furnished restaurant. But the fish is very good here, and in the summer months it is thoroughly animated and busy. The hake with baby eels and clams in a herb sauce was delicious, served simply in its cooking dish, and so was the simpler baked monkfish. The table next door were tucking into roast kid, which looked good too. Puds are home-made and tempting.

Menús del dia 1,500–2,500 ptas; carte 3,500–4,000 ptas

On towards Torredembarra along the N-11 you pass a splendid second century triumphal arch (Arc de Barà) which was built by the Romans astride the old Via Augusta.

Map 4F **TORREDEMBARRA**

The seaside here is lovely – wide beaches, buildings only two or three storeys high, relaxed and quiet. The old centre of the town is lively in the summer, with the square filled with café tables and evening market stalls. My best recommendations are down by the sea, a good few minutes' walk away from the centre.

Morros
(R)M-L *Barri de Pescadors, C/ del Mar (977) 64 00 61 Cl. Sun. eve., Mon. from Oct.–Apr.*

This is a fine fish restaurant in a very elegant room right next to the beach. It's quite small (although there's a big room upstairs for receptions) and offers some exquisite and highly inventive fish dishes. Menus change, but if the warm salad of sole and green beans dressed with a sea-urchin vinegrette is still on, try it. You must reserve.

You can also eat here amongst the yellow parasols of the pretty terrace in front, or much more cheaply and informally (in bathers if you want) at the sandy terrace just to the side of the restaurant (El Chiringuito) – where you can try excellent tapas or a fully-fledged meal of *xató*, black rice, sea bass, etc.

Restaurant menú del dia 4,000 ptas. El Chiringuito menú del dia 2,500 ptas

Morros

(H)M *C/ Pérez Galdós, 13 (977) 64 02 25 Open all year*

A good, welcoming hotel run by the same family, a stone's throw away from the restaurant, with the added advantage of half-board offered at the restaurant. The hotel is small, and the rooms well-furnished. As it's one street back from the beach, ask for a room from the third floor or higher, as these have an uninhibited view of the sea.

Double room 6,000–7,500 ptas

Le Brussels

(R)S-M *C/ Antoni Roig, 56 (977) 64 05 10 Open Easter–Oct.*

In the centre of the old quarter, a well-established restaurant, with a peaceful patio within. It's pretty, with a blue-tiled bar at the front, and curious red and green Belgian chairs in the patio. The cooking is selectly international (Spanish, French and Belgian) and the long multilingual menus and early opening hours cater for tourists who want to eat early. Go late for Catalan company.

Menú del dia 1,100 ptas (lunchtime) carte approx. 2,500 ptas

Map 4F **ALTAFULLA**

Faristol

(R)M *C/ Sant Martí, 5 (977) 65 00 77 Open weekends all year, every day 15 Jun.–end Sept.*

A little difficult to find – head for the centre, not for the castle, and ask.

This is an extraordinary place hidden within the pale pink walls of an eighteenth-century mansion. With great care and imagination, Agustí and his English wife Lynne have created a restaurant, bar and guest house that are quite unique. The first room downstairs is the bar, once the stables, and now heavily atmospheric with dark wood, thick peach tones on the walls, and brown-tinged paintings. If you play jazz, or just like it, there are frequent open jam or blues sessions here (Augustí plays sax). In summer the restaurant is in the very pleasant patio and in winter the tables move into the wide covered passage surrounding the patio. Cooking is done on a *brasa* and in a wood oven, under the skilled hand of Agustí, who offers various starters – a shellfish or *escalivada* mousse, followed mostly by meat dishes – beef, rabbit, lamb, duck and the odd curry. Lynne makes the irresistable chocolate mousse.

The stairs (lined with an adventurous mixture of old art and junk) lead to the original dining room which still preserves fine murals, and further up are five bedrooms. These have been furnished, in keeping with the style of the house, still decorated with the old stencilling, and with compact spartan bathrooms carefully added to leave the original rooms intact. The stuff of dream and fantasy.

Restaurant allow 2,500–3,500 ptas

Map 4F **TARRAGONA**

As the capital of a province in which the seaside tourist industry is paramount, Tarragona is surprisingly unexploited by tourism. Legend has it that the beauty of the city led Jupiter to leave his mortal wife Tiria. For the Romans (who installed themselves here from 214 BC onwards) it was of such strategic importance that it became the capital of the Roman Iberian empire. As a result, Tarragona has a magnificent offering of Roman remains from those days of eminence spread throughout the town.

Apart from the Roman amphitheatre (near the sea beyond the end of the Rambla Nova), the sites are mostly scattered around the old town, which is in the upper reaches of the small city. A visit around the walls, the cathedral, the Museu Arqueològic, the Museu Històric and the amphitheatre will take a day. (There's an entry system here whereby one ticket serves for all the central museums.)

You can stroll round part of the old walls which protected the military and civil quarters, the *Passeig Arqueològic* entering at the Roser gate off the Via de L'Imperia Romà and coming out through a one-way gate close to the cathedral. You can appreciate the great thickness of the walls from a couple of closed door arches here.

The fourteenth to fifteenth-century cathedral is in the centre of the medieval part of the city, with the heavy solidity of the romanesque style, and the size and light of the early gothic. You enter through the cloisters, off which there are a number of museum rooms showing cathedral and city treasures. Curiously, in one of the cloister walls there's an imprint of another historic visiting culture – an arabic mihrab. The diocesian museum is worth a visit for its gothic paintings by Jaume Huguet and for its collection of fifteenth- and sixteenth-century tapestries.

To bring together the sheer physical size and importance of the Roman citadel, I recommend a visit to the the *Museu Històric* (housed in the restored Praetorio). The detailed scale model of the Roman circus, and the architectural drawings of the town then and today, illustrate beautifully how the Roman bastions and vaults have been incorporated into the modern day city. The evocative passageway network running below is also being opened up to the public.

For lovers of Roman mosaic the *Museu Arqueològic Nacional* is a must. It has an excellent display of the evolution of Roman mosaics throughout the centuries of occupation. You have a second museum dedicated to Roman mosaic some five kilometres away from the city, in the satallite village of **Constantí**, where the *Mausoleu Romà de Centcelles* has a stunning collection of glass and mosaics depicting biblical and hunting scenes. Because it is a little away from the tourist route, this museum is often missed off the tourist's itinerary – it's rather a hidden treasure. (There is an olive oil mill here, to which you can go on a Saturday afternoon to buy the virgin oil direct. It's delicious – don't miss the opportunity.)

Tarragona Cathedral

The *amphitheatre* is an exciting place to explore, partly because so much of the fabric of the building remains. Beware, the strength of the summer midday heat can intensify within the circle – although there's plenty of shade in the surrounding gardens. Finally, there are Roman relics, sarcophagi and burial urns in the *Necròpolis i Museu Paleocristià* on the southern outskirts of the city.

For a change from Roman remains, try the attractive restored fifteenth-century mansion, the *Casa-Museu Castellarnau*, a few streets below the cathedral (*C/ Caballeros 14 open 10.00 a.m.–1.00 p.m., 4.00 p.m.–7.00 p.m.*). It's small, but almost complete with eighteenth-century furnishings and (fairly mediocre) paintings. Don't hope to see the kitchen too, apparently it was too far gone to restore.

The relatively small quantity of visitors who stay in Tarragona is reflected in the limited choice of food and hotels. In the old part of town there are few places, particularly near the cathedral.

Centre of Tarragona

Imperial Tarraco
(HR)L *Rambla Vella, s/n (977) 23 30 40 Open all year*

On the best site in the city, with a fantastic view over the Roman amphitheatre and bay of Tarragona, this is an all-comforts hotel that has been the main hotel of the city for many years. Although it really doesn't come in the 'family' category, (it has 170 rooms) it has a pleasant staff and is a long way from the big, smart, impersonal hotels of the 1990s. If you happen to be here for the 15 August, the spectacular firework display is projected from the bay below – you couldn't have a better view.
Double room 15,000 ptas

Lauria
(H)M *Rambla Nova, 20 (977) 23 67 12 Open all year*

A family-run hotel in the heart of the prosperous new town, a stone's throw from the monumental centre. The entrance from the Rambla is attractive – a wide passageway past a dignified stairway that leads up to the principal floor of another house – typical of the late eighteenth-centry carriage entrances. The rooms are quite spacious and the beds comfortable, and the patio encloses a small, refreshing swimming pool. The higher rooms have a good view across to the sea. There is no restaurant, but it's a short stroll down to the port.
Double room 9,000 ptas

Les Coques
(R)M *Baixada Nou del Patriarca, 2 (977) 22 83 00 Cl. Sun., Aug.*

This is a quality restaurant just down to the right of the cathedral façade, and serves a variety of good, straightforward food and more sophisticated regional fish dishes. It has a thoughtful, individual menu, but I also recommend it for its daily choice of *ous remenats* (egg scrambled with mushrooms or shrimps, etc.) that make a delicious light lunch in the middle of the monument trail. It's more an executive than a tourist restaurant.
Allow 2,000–3,000 ptas

Les Voltes
(R)M *C/ Trinquet Vell, 12 (977) 21 88 30 Cl. Sun. eve.*

If you fancy eating within the roman vaults, there is an impressive place downhill from the cathedral which has set up inside some of the colossal barrel vaults of the Roman circus; long tables, international menu, catering for big groups of people.It holds a reputation amongst the tourist fraternity, and certainly I found it awe-inspiring when I went in, but I found the smell of musty old brick put me off, and I didn't stay.
Menú del dia 2,100 ptas

THE FISHING PORT OF TARRAGONA (SERRALLO)

Tarragona is the second most important fishing port of Catalunya, and its is always animated here, so it's an entertaining place to eat. I was lucky enough to be there on the feast of Saint Carmen, the patron saint of the fishermen (16 July). As in all ports around Spain, the Virgin of the local church was carried reverently through the streets, and finally taken on board one of the fishing vessels. There, after a short prayer, she was gently chugged round the port at the head of a host of other boats crammed with people, until she arrived back home again to her chapel. The *barri* turned out in their fishing costume to do homage, and went on to a rave-up in the evening. All restaurants were packed out for the *festa*.

The area is called **Serrallo** and a string of restaurants line the front of the port. If you walk along from the fishing boat quay to the end nearest the railway station (the Tinglados), you can see an evolution of styles of seaside restaurant – look at the style of menú, tablecloth, waiter, etc. The dusty-brown, once-fashionable La Puda (an old-time favourite for a strong and faithful clientele); the unpretentious, straightforward Sorli, serving a similar menu to the other restaurants very reasonably; the smart Club Náutico, with its splendid view and huge, loudly-advertised *mariscada* of seafood; and the Estació Marítima, bright white, big, spacious, modern, and with a terrace onto a quieter side of the port.

For a flash tour of Palma de Mallorca, a ferry leaves from the Estació Marítima at 11.00 a.m. every day except Wednesday, and leaves Palma for the return trip at 4.30 p.m. It runs from 17 June to 15 September, and only costs 6,000 ptas there and back.

Náutico
(R)M-L *Edifici Club Náutic (977) 24 00 62 Cl. Mon. eve.*

This is up the stairs on the first floor, in a room with a glass front onto the port. You need to arrive here hungry, and be prepared to refrain from eating elsewhere for at least a day afterwards. The Mare Nostrum, their most popular offering, is a marathon of the best of crustaceans and fish dishes which arrive at your table, one dish after another, during the meal. It is not cheap – 7,000 ptas for the meal, but it's good – if you have the stamina.

Allow 4,000 ptas for the carte

Estació Marítima
(R)M *Tinglado, 4, Moll de Costa (977) 23 21 00 Cl. Jan., Mon. in winter*

This serves a reasonably priced menu of rice and simple fish dishes. It is a busy, young restaurant, airy and refreshing, with a buzz of well-dressed Catalan clientele in party spirit. The service is lively. A further plus is the wide terrace on the water's edge, overlooking the port (without suffering the fishy smells). The Tinglado (warehouse) is part of a big building mostly dedicated to travellers taking the new daily hydrofoil service to Mallorca (only three and a half hours away).

Allow 2,500 ptas

Sorli
(R)S-M *C/ Trafalgar, 3 (977) 21 10 16 Cl. Tues., Nov. for two weeks*

If you are looking for a rather simpler place, this is an unassuming restaurant, with a good-value offering of fish dishes and *marisco.*
Menú del dia 1,500 ptas; carte 3,000 ptas

Approaching Tarragona from Barcelona

Sol Ric
(R)M *Via Augusta, 227 (977) 23 20 32 Cl. Sun. eve., Mon., mid-Dec–mid-Jan.*

Quite difficult to reach if you approach from Reus or from the south. It's on the Barcelona side of town, on the sea side of the main road, just after the bypass forks off towards Reus.
This old *masia* restaurant, which has been going since the end of the 1950s, has a high reputation – a trusted favourite where you can savour the best of the regional recipes, particularly the *romescu.* It's air-conditioned inside, but there's also a big terrace outside where you can enjoy the breeze. It is clearly a fish restaurant, although it offers a good variety of meat and the steaks are generous and excellent. It gets full particularly at weekends, so you should book.
Allow 3,500 ptas; menú del dia 1,500 ptas

El Trull
(R)S-M *Ctra N340, Km 255, Las Palmeras (977) 20 79 12 Cl. Mon., Tues.*

Just on the turning off the road to the Las Palmeras campsite, a couple of kilometres north of Tarragona.
For a good, simple Catalan meal, come here. It's a rustic place for straightforward regional food – toasts with ham or *escalivada, escudella,* meat or poultry with beans or chips. Housed in an old *masia* with a big garden terrace.
Menú de dia 2,000 ptas; carte allow 1,500–3,000 ptas

Heading out from Tarragona towards Valls

Just outside Tarragona, only four kilometres along the road to **Valls**, is the magnificent *Roman aqueduct* – a little-visited and rather beautiful survivor of the Roman occupation. It dates from the second century, and if you follow the path sign, you can get close to the arches. A nice spot beside an overgrown valley.

Les Fonts de Can Sala
(R)M *Ctra de Valls, 62 (977) 22 85 75 Open all year*

If you are approaching from Tarragona city, be very careful turning off the dual carriageway to reach the restaurant. The underpass is very sudden and very tight.
This is a big business, surrounded by agricultural fields, many of which belong to it, with large halls inside and a pretty terrace outside.

Roman Aqueduct – Tarragona

The views stretch over the fields and the city to the sea. A place for big family get-togethers, noise and celebration, with lots of room for children to run about. Typical Catalan dishes, *calçots* in season, and *crema catalana.*

Allow 2,500–3,000 ptas.

Map 3G **SALOU**

This used to be a small but select seaside village for the residents of Zaragoza (inland Spain, beyond Lleida) and a few noble houses still remain near the marina. The fabulous expanse of beach here is what has made Salou, in the last twenty years, into such a huge seaside resort. Like Lloret de Mar, it has paid a high price for its commercial success: the short three-month season packs the town with hoards of holiday-makers, who cram onto the beaches and then dance the night away in any one of numerous discos. Fish'n'chips Brit-style, beer swilling, and lobster-coloured German, British and Italian tourists.

However, out of season, it really is beautiful, with a splendid promenade lined with mature palm-trees running along the seafront – a magnificent sight

Planas
(H)M *Plaça Bonet, 3 (977) 38 01 08 Open Easter-Oct.*

This no-frills hotel is just behind the yacht club, in the heart of the town, with the beach just across the road. The rooms are very simple, the restaurant adequate and there's a terrace beneath pine trees for quiet afternoons.

Double room 6,500 ptas

Albatros
(R)M *C/ Bruselas, 60 (977) 38 50 70 Cl. Sun. eve., Mon. Christmas, Jan.*

This is a small but excellent restaurant at the north end of the bay, just behind the small Capellans cove. Although it has no view, the summer terrace is bright and full of plants, and the decor inside is refined and welcoming, with walls hung with pictures and tables decorated with flowers. Sr. Fernando Lòpez has been here for fifteen years, during which he's accumulated several prestigious awards for his creative art. Not only are his fish dishes superb – sea bass '*en papillotte*'; hake with tarragon vinegar; *calamarsons* with fresh pasta; but he also prepares a fine fillet of beef *a la sal*. Ask his advice when you order, and don't miss the desserts. It tends to be busy at weekends so you should book.

Set menu 2,500 ptas; allow 4,500–5,000 ptas

Casa Font
(R)M *C/ Colón, 17 (977) 38 04 35 Cl. mon. eve., late Dec.–early Jan.*

On the rocky outcrop at the north end of Salou, not far from the Albatros. There are plenty of bars and small terraces here where you can enjoy typical tapas and the view.

This is a smart place to come for the marvellous views across the bay, though not for the gastronomic delights. It has a carte well-designed for the tourist with four different set menus ranging from a paella menu to a series of surprises.

Set menus from 2,000–5,000 ptas

Casa Soler
(R)M *C/ Verge del Carme, s/n, Ctra Salou-Cambrils (977) 38 04 63 Open all year*

At the Cambrils end of the town, with a spacious terrace and lots of parking space in front. They've constructed a complete set menu, with loads of choice for first and second courses and wine to accompany. A popular place.

Menú 2,500 ptas

Just between Salou and Vilaseca there is a giant theme park – **Port Aventura** – which covers some 15 hectares with a sensational offer of family entertainment. It is very recently opened, with four spectacular cultural parks presenting customs, buildings, restaurants, dances etc. of Mexico, China, Pòlynesia and the Far West. The biggest roller-coaster in Europe is here. Lots of activity, plenty of water and gardens, and enough to see to take up two full days. Loads of fun.

Map 3A **CAMBRILS**

The small town has grown with apartment blocks in the last few decades, but its economic base remains the very lively fishing port that fronts the town. You can see the boats come in during the early afternoon and watch the fish auction in the *llotja* (the fish market), although this is a commercial affair, not as picturesque as the open market place years back. It's a pleasant place to stay if you are looking for some seaside character without falling into serious mass tourism. Some of the finest restaurants of the Tarragona coast are here – serving superb fish straight off the boats. If you are not a fish-eater, you are in the wrong town – the devotion of these chefs is exclusive. Don't expect to eat cheaply here.

If you enjoy boating, there is a twice-daily chugger which goes along the coast to l'Ametlla de Mar or to Salou.

Port Eugeni
(H)M *Plaça Aragó, 49 (977) 36 52 61 Open all year*

It looks thoroughly modern, clearly a member of a chain, with mirror walls and a huge dining room. But the ambience of family, with toddlers and youngsters running around, make it a happy place to be. There is a pretty gardened patio inside (closed off so as to be admired rather than visited), and a big lively bar, which tends to be full and noisy in the evenings. There are about 100 rooms, most with views of the sea as the hotel is at the end of a short road leading from the Rambla Jaume I to the beach.

Double room 6,500–8,000 ptas

Princep
(H)M *Plaça de l'Església, 2 (977) 36 11 27 Open all year*

This is a friendly 27-room hotel, modern and bright, with views across to the sea from the third and fourth floors. It's a couple of blocks back from the harbour, just off the main market square. The family have been running the hotel for over ten years, and their clients tend to return. Simple, straightforward rooms all of which have balconies. They have an inviting restaurant, Can Pessic.

Double room 5,000–8,000 ptas; half-board 10,000 ptas

➜ Can Bosch
(R)M-L *Rambla Jaume I, 19 (977) 36 00 19 Cl. Sun. eve., Mon.*

Can Bosch is a first-rate restaurant some four streets back from the port. You come here to eat wonderful fish in a spacious room of quiet sophistication. The room is simply vaulted with terracota tiles, and the tables are elegantly laid. I suggest you either take the set menu or the *entremesos* of fish and shellfish, both of which include an ample selection of dishes, each beautifully presented. If you feel like a simpler meal, take a baked fish, or the *arròs negre* which is rich but utterly delicious. Keep a space for the desserts. Be sure to reserve.

Set menu 4,350–4,900 ptas.

Arrowed for the finesse and expertise of the chef.

➔ Joan Gatell-Casa Gatell

(R)M-L *Passeig Miramar, 26 (977) 36 00 57 Cl. Christmas, Jan.*

This is one of the most respected restaurants on the coast, and one of the oldest (founded in 1914). It is now well into its third generation, and under the distinguished hand of Joan Pedrell you can enjoy some of the finest traditional Catalan fish dishes. Casa Gatell was *the* restaurant south of Tarragona twenty years ago when I first ate here, and is still at the forefront. You can sit on the terrace downstairs, enjoying the street bustle and looking out to the sardine boats in the port, or on the terrace upstairs with sensational views out to sea (rather romantic at night with the port lights and dark stillness beyond). Indoors it is elegant and comfortable, with pretty pale green and patterned table-linen laid with white china and silver.

If you're only here once, take the *menú gastronòmic* or the *entremesos*, or take different dishes and swap. If you're ordering from the carte, ask – you never know what else might have come off the fishing boats today.

Set menu 5,000 ptas

Arrowed for the long tradition of cooking fish superbly.

Eugènia

(R)M-L *C/ Consolat de Mar, 80 (977) 36 01 68 Cl. Tues. eve., Wed., Nov.; in summer Wed., Thurs. mid-day*

This is a very attractive restaurant, with a lovely terrace of mature trees and shrubs through which you enter in the winter, and where the tables are put in the summertime. Very professional, both in terms of the running of the room and in terms of the cuisine. The chef Josep Pedrell, another of the Gatell dynasty, has been here for twenty-three years, and has a highly individual approach to traditional cooking, to which he applies a studied interest in contemporary French developments. Pretty tables inside, classic presentation, and excellent cooking. You can't go wrong with the *fideus* with lobster, and his sea bass with compôte of onion is superb. For dessert, try the *menjablanc* – a set almond mousse.

Seasonal menu 4,500 ptas; allow 5,000 ptas

La Roca d'en Manel

(R)M *Passeig Miramar, 38 (977) 36 30 24 Cl. Mon.*

If you are looking for a simpler, less formal restaurant, this is a good

choice. It's on the port front, and has a good display of fish inside from where you can select what you'd like. As elsewhere, the star dishes are the selections of shellfish or grilled fish.
Allow 4,500 ptas

Rincón de Diego
(R)M-L *C/ Drassanes, 7 (977) 36 13 07 Cl. Sun. eve., Mon.*

This is a small and curious restaurant – off the seafront, in a cosy but attractive room. Large contemporary paintings decorate the walls, and the tables are laid with imposing china. The menu is original – *carpaccio* of *gambes*, hot cream of shellfish, crab-filled little peppers, ravioli of *escamarlans*, and the baked fish and black *fideus* are certainly excellent. While you wait, a little tapa, presented on an enormous plate, keeps your hunger at bay. The dishes were good, but I found the presentation a little over the top, particularly frustrating with the exhuberant desserts when most of the temptingly delicious-looking decoration went back to the kitchen. Expect opulence of presentation, and enjoy it. It fills with well-dressed regular clients.
Menú degustació 3,300 ptas; carte 5,000 ptas

Mas Gallau
(R)M *Ctra Valencia-Barcelona N340, Km 236 (977) 36 05 88 Open every day; Cl. Jan.*

This is on the fast main road which passes behind the town, between Salou and Cambrils, on the side nearest the coast just on the turning off to **Vilafortuny**. If you miss it, don't attempt a U-turn as the traffic (and the police fine) is very heavy.

A big *masia*-style restaurant for family parties, which concentrates on the spectacular side of good cooking. The main room is big, rustic in style and decorated at the far end with catalan frescos. The busy wood grill and oven are by the entrance as you go in. The chefs are friendly and thoroughly proud of their cooking – both Catalan haute cuisine and traditional. The fish is good – leek and prawn mousse; salad of crêpes filled with crab in lemon vinaigrette; monkfish cooked with a burnt garlic bouillon, salmon tartare. As for meat, they will spit roast a leg of lamb, bake a rib of beef in salt, or prepare a steak tartare at your table. The hot desserts and sabayons are also prepared in front of you.
Allow 4,000 ptas

Map 3F MONTBRIO DEL CAMP

This town is just inland from the coastal road between Cambrils and Miami Platja. On the way here from the sea you come to the lovely gardens of **Parc Samá**, with plane tree avenues, lily ponds, beds of exotic plants, and strange sandcastle follies in the centre of which stands a small French-style château. *The gardens are open throughout the year from early morning to dusk.* If you lucky enough to get tickets, you can enjoy the delightful music festival held here, where recitals, opera, and ballet are performed in truly romantic surroundings. Perched on the top of a nearby hill is the fortified monastery of **Escornalbou.** Take the turning off to Riudecanyes (close to a usually half-full reservoir), and follow the signs. This was founded in the twelfth century and passed from being an Augustinian house to a fort and, in the seventeenth century a Franciscan monastery. By the beginning of this century it had fallen into ruin, and was bought and restored by an enthusiast. Purists may judge the result with disdain, but it makes a good excursion with its fantastic views from the romanesque cloisters, and from the small sanctuary some ten minutes up a woodland path at the peak. *Open 10.00 a.m.–1.30 p.m., 3.00 p.m.–6.30 p.m.; Cl. Sun. eve., Mon. and at 5.30 p.m. in autumn and winter.*

A few kilometres south of Montbrió del Camp is **Mont-roig del Camp,** the village where the famous Catalan artist Joan Miró lived from an early age. The *masias* here inspired some of his greatest works.

Torre dels Cavallers
(R)M *Ctra de Cambrils a Montbrió (977) 82 60 53 Cl. Tues.*

A splendid restaurant, well off the beaten track (which is a blessing here in the tourist season), quiet, surrounded by fruit groves, and very close to Parc Samá. It is housed in an old *masia,* although the emblematic tower itself is a comparatively recent addition. The two rooms are big and seignorial, with great fireplaces, high beams, and medieval-style decoration. In summer there is a big covered terrace which is used as a refreshing alternative. You can eat grilled beef and lamb, roast kid, game, and a fine *calçotada* in the winter. The place fills at weekends throughout the year, so book.
Allow 3,000 ptas

La Caseta del Rellotge
(R)M *Ctra N340, Km 1,139 (977) 83 78 44 Open all year, Cl. Mon., (summer Cl. Mon. midday only)*

It's on the main road south from Cambrils, in an old post-house which dates from 1614. There are three small diningrooms – each rustic in style with beamed ceilings, fine old furniture, and collectors' paintings on the walls. The old well, still in use, is in the far room. In summer you can eat out on the terrace, but the road can be a bit loud and it's more relaxing to be inside.

The cooking here is traditional Catalan with haute-cuisine finesse. Starters include a dish of stuffed little sweet peppers, *gambes* with calvados, scrambled egg with wild mushrooms and *llagostins.* For the main course, there's beef, lamb and kid *a la brasa* or roast (game too in winter), good sauces, fresh fish (the poached hake with young beans is excellent), and to finish, a selection of home-produced desserts. Country bread, garlic and tomato are at your table to accompany.

It is worth taking a look at the extensive cellar.

Allow 2,500–3,500 ptas

Map 3G **MIAMI PLATJA**

Pino Alto
(HR)L *Playa Cristal (977) 81 10 00 Open all year*

For families with young children this is a marvellous place close to the sea. It's a two-storey white building in the form of an extended horseshoe around a spacious terrace, swimming pools and pretty mediterranean gardens. The rooms are spacious with broad balconies, and look outside across the little garden villas and countryside to the sea, or inside over the animated terraces. The hotel organises lots of activities for the children and has a big games room, and the sports and watersports available are all you could wish for. The dining room serves a good daily menu, and the whole place feels happy, relaxed and totally free of anxiety.

Double room 15,000 ptas

La Borda d'en Manel
(R)M *Av. Barcelona, 172 (977) 81 04 22 Open all year*

On the main road which runs through the village.

This is a pleasant restaurant, stone-walled and carefully decorated in a rustic style. The cooking is modern Catalan and international, with more than a hint of French influence in the sauces. The presentation is impressive, particularly for the desserts (which are worth saving space for). Apart from a good value *menú del dia*, its carte has a wide selection of well-prepared meat and fish dishes, which you can choose while nibbling slices of dried sausage. A few suggestions: scrambled egg (*ous remenats*) with esparragos and *jabugo* ham; a shrimp salad on a bed of fresh tomato; chateaubriand; filet of pork with calvados; baked sea bass. The portions are generous, so it is wise to choose with care, although the *porró* of moscatel which appears after the coffee serves as a good digestif. You must book in the summer season and at weekends.

Menú del dia 1,000 ptas; carte 3,000–4,000 ptas

Map 2G **L'AMETLLA DE MAR**

This is a fishing village, not particularly picturesque in itself, but quiet and not overly built-up. It's served by a number of rocky coves, one of which provides the village with its very small beach. On weekday afternoons you can watch the fish auctions going on.

Bon Repós
(HR)S-M *Plaça Cataluña, 49 (977) 45 60 25 Cl. Oct.-Easter*

This is a simple hotel in what was, half a century ago, the family home of Jaume Ferrán i Clua, who invented the vaccine for cholera in Tortosa. That family feel, so difficult to find on the Costa Brava, still reigns here. The rooms are very simple, with old-fashioned tall doorways and a few pieces of passed-down furniture here and there. The garden is full of trees and plants, mostly pine with the occasional carob, or cyprus or prickly pear. After a morning on the beach, you can relax here to the accompaniment of birdsong, take an occasional dip in the pool, or knock a tennis ball around the court. Very relaxing for parents and great fun for children.

The restaurant is unpretentious and just right – everything from an omelette to a *suquet*.

Double room 7,000 ptas

L'Alguer
(R)M *C/ Trafalgar, 21 (977) 45 61 24 Cl. Christmas*

A pleasant restaurant with marvellous views looking out over the sea and a terrace on the palm tree-lined *passeig*. It's dedicated to fish cooking with an excellent first course selection of *marisc* – (*entremesos*), after which the renowned *suquet*, or baked turbot make a fine main course.

Allow 3,000–5,000 ptas

L'Alguer
(H)M *C/ del Mar, 20 (977) 49 33 72 Open all year*

Hotel L'Alguer is modern, looking over the sea with thirty-seven comfortable rooms. The views are unimpaired, and the hotel is only fifty metres from the restaurant.

Double room 7,500–8,000 ptas

Map 2G **L'AMPOLLA**

A small, pretty fishing port.

El Moli
(R)M *C/ Castaños, 4 (977) 46 02 07 Cl. Mon, Nov., Dec.*

This is in the centre, on the inland side of the railway line, just a short walk from the port.

It's an attractive homely place, decorated with dried flowers, with beamed ceilings, and the old oil mill equipment still in the corner. Specialising in fish –the prize dish is the *llenguado* (sole) cooked with a slightly spicy stock flavoured with burnt garlic. The *suquet* is also very good.

Allow 2,500–3,500 ptas

Map 2H AMPOSTA

If you haven't time to visit the delta, there's a museum here (Museu del Montsià) which has a good display of some of the flora and fauna of the area. For a longer visit, you can take a boat from here in the morning and be taken right up the delta to the sea, fed a good lunch, and be back mid-afternoon.

Barco Santa Susanna
(R)M El Moll *(977) 48 01 28 Sails only Sat., Sun.; Cl. Nov. Only by previous reservation via telephone or at the restaurant Casa Nuri in the Delta de l'Ebre Departs aprox. 11.30 a.m. and returns approx. 5.30 p.m.*

This is a floating restaurant – a boat which seats some seventy people, and takes you on a cruise from the port of Amposta up through the delta to the sea, where you can appreciate the gradual changes in water colour and the strange currents as the river meets the sea. There are three menus to choose from, which offer all varieties of rice (black, meat or mixed *paella* etc), typical dishes of the Ebro, and a range of fish dishes.
Menus 3,000, 4,000, 5,800 ptas (including trip)

L'Aspic
(R)M *Av. Catalunya-Brasil, 2 (977) 70 32 13 Cl. Sun. eve., Mon., Sept., (2 weeks), Jan. (2 weeks)*

A restaurant with simple elegance, which offers an interesting range of dishes based on the regional products and cuisine, but with a distinctly creative touch by the chef. The specialities of the house include a terrine of smoked eel, *llagostins* with a truffle sauce, rice cooked with *llagostins* and *gambes*, and stuffed monkfish with a cream of sea-urchin.
Allow 3,000–4,000 ptas

Map 2H SANT CARLOS DE LA RÀPITA

This is an important fishing port, famous for its *llagostins* (a type of prawn), and a tourist town for Catalans. It was promoted by Carlos III, who hoped that the port would provide a good centre of trade with the American colonies, and as a result you'll see some fine cosmopolitan buildings in the centre of town, particularly around the Plaça Carles III and the Glorieta. Today it's more important for its sweeping beaches and dunes.

The quality of the fish is high, and prices naturally follow suit. There are many restaurants here, some of which are of the luxury chain-owned variety which are run with a heavily commercial hand. Here are some escapees.

Miami Can Pons
(R)M-L *Av. de la Constitució, 37 (977) 74 05 51 Open all year*

This is a classic of fish cuisine in the region. It's a fine fish restaurant, in a very elegant, light room on the first floor of the building. The family Pons earned their reputation over the last forty years for their excellent *suquet*, their *arròs pelat* (a local speciality called peeled rice) and for the splendid *picadetes* – a selection of shellfish tapas beautifully presented and perfectly prepared.
Allow 4,000 ptas; menú degustació 5,500 ptas

Miami Park
(H)M *Av. de la Constitució, 31–37 (977) 74 03 51 Open Apr.–Oct.*

Owned by the same family as the restaurant Miami Can Pons, with the advantage of half-board linked to the same kitchen. The hotel is next door, downhill towards the sailing club. Fairly simple rooms, no great views but comfortable. It's quite big, with eighty rooms.
Half-board 4,925–5,425 ptas; double room 6,500 ptas

Casa Ramón Marinés
(R)M *C/ Arsenal, 16 (977) 74 23 58 Cl. Mon. (except summer), Jan. (2 weeks)*

A smallish restaurant close to the port. It's part of a chain, but has maintained a personal welcome and a modesty which appeals. It's on two floors, with the main room downstairs, and beside it is the bar where delicious tapas can be taken. A cold cabinet inside displays some of the shellfish on ice. The chef produces some interesting regional dishes, promoting them throughout the summer festivals – the daily menus can be fun.
Allow 3,000 ptas

Map 2H **LES CASES D'ALCANAR**

A delightful fishing village just beyond Sant Carles, with at least a dozen fish restaurants, all small and relaxed, scattered around the port area. It has a special feeling of tranquility the French know about it and come, as do many Catalans, but for many travellers it hardly registers on the map. There's practically no traffic, nor seaside shops, as the beaches are away from the village.

El Pescador-Casa Angelina
(R)M *C/ Cádiz, 4 (977) 73 70 93 Cl. 11 Dec.–3 Jan.*

The attraction here is not only the air-conditioned, glass-fronted terrace restaurant above the port front, but also the kitchen. If you feel like eating fish or shellfish and want to choose it, cross over from the terrace to the street block and go up the steps into what looks like an open passage. On one side is a spectacular long table full of the freshest fish and shellfish displayed on beds on ice – just like a mediterranean shop. Choose your fish, and one of the family of chefs will take it and cook it for you right there, just behind the fish display in the narrow, very simple kitchen. The restaurant terrace is a complete contrast – sophisticated and elegant, with very pretty china, and it is here that you enjoy the excellent cooking.

Allow 3,500 ptas

Racó del Port
(R)M *C/ Lepanto, 41 (977) 73 70 50 Cl. Mon., Nov.*

A lovely place to eat, with its terrace alone and tranquil in the corner of the port front looking out to sea. The restaurant itself is narrow and small. For all seafood specialities. On hot days there is nearly always a light breeze ruffling through the awning of the terrace.

Allow 3,000 ptas

Patorrat
(R)M *Plaça Sant Pere, 6 (977) 73 51 05 Open all year except Christmas*

A long-established restaurant (going, they say, since 1882) just back from the port front, but with an open view of the sea. It has a terrace in front of the restaurant, so nobody eats inside in the summer. It's decorated with fishing things and curiosities, and the maître has a sense of humour that can make your meal memorable. He came out, with a twinkle in his eye and a hand behind his back, to check our order of rice with *nécora*, a type of crab – (a flavoursome rich addition to the stock) and, with a sudden 'Will this one suit?', cast a very lively crustacean onto the table, which went scurrying across. Screams of shock all round. The rice, by the way, was delicious.

Allow 2,500 ptas

Map 2H DELTA DE L'EBRE NATURAL PARK

This is a vast triangular area jutting out to sea at the southern tip of the Tarragona province. Completely flat, with the fields permanently flooded and criss-crossed by dozens of water canals, it's more reminiscent of Holland than Catalunya. Rich green in the summer, waterlogged in the spring and a bleak brown in the winter, its colour is dictated by the local agriculture: rice. They grow rice here in huge quantities (over 300 square kilometres of water and paddies) so it's a fantastic place to eat the great Catalan rice dishes like *paella*, *arròs a banda*, or *seixat* (rice cooked with salt and fresh fish stock). As there is fresh water (or 'sweet water' as it translates from Catalan) and sea water, the fish and algae are particular to the area, so dishes of carp, eel, anemonies, seaweed, crawfish, etc. are on the menu.

The delta is an exceptional area, not so much for its gastronomic merits, but for the immense extension of watered flatness that attracts hundreds of thousands of migrating birds to rest in the area. Curiously, the landmass is always changing, being eroded constantly by the sea, but continually gaining silt deposits which the Ebro has carried down on its long course through northern Spain from its spring in the mountains of Cantabria. Where there isn't rice, there are large swamps and lagoons surrounded by reeds, where bird life is abundant. For a dip in the sea, the beaches here are fabulous – broad, very long and practically deserted.

If you are a bird watcher, or want to pass a few tranquil hours, there are excellent information centres strategically placed on both sides of the main river channel, and hides for you to watch from. (If you forget the binnocs, you can hire a pair from the centre.) The best time is, as always, the early autumn, when thousands and thousands of ducks and coots invade the harvested paddies and lagoons. Look out for shovelers, widgeon, shelducks, gadwalls, pochards and teals on the water, and you're likely to see marsh harriers, bitterns, oystercatchers, various types of heron, egret and grebe, and plenty of flamingos. The area boasts of some 300 species – so if you're skilled at bird-watching you can theoretically come across some sixty per cent of the species found in Europe.

The varieties of fish have changed over the years. The once famous sturgeon and lamprey have now become superseded by pike and black bullheads. And there are quantities of eel and mullet.

Unfortunately the insect life continues to be dominated by mosquitoes. If you're here at dusk, use anti-mosquito protection, otherwise you'll be bitten to bits.

There's a crossing point between Deltebre and Sant Jaume d'Enveja where a small ferry goes to and fro every fifteen minutes. It'll take both you and the car, normally with no queue. On the far side there are less people and many more birds.

For boat visits, there are frequent trips round Buda Island (from outside restaurant Casa Nuri beyond Deltebre) or tours leaving Amposta in the morning which go all the way up the delta to the sea, and serve lunch on the way. (see Amposta above.)

Information centre, Deltebre, C/ Ulldecona, 22 (977) 48 96 79 Open Mon.–Fri. 10.00 a.m.–2.00 p.m., 3.00 p.m.–6.00 p.m.; Sat. 10.00 a.m.–1.00 p.m., 3.30 p.m.–6.00 p.m.; Sun. 10.00 a.m.–1.00 p.m. Just beside there is a good exhibition of the delta plant and animal life in the Ecomuseu.

The delta is deceptively large, and you can easily find yourself seriously underestimating the mileage you have to cover here. I mention a few extra places to eat in the far reaches of the delta, in case time takes you by surprise.

DELTEBRE and beyond

El Buitre
(HR)S *Ctra Riumar, Deltebre-La Cava (977) 48 05 28 Open all year*

This is just beyond the village of Deltebre – an excellent place to stay if you are seriously interested in the birds of the Delta de l'Ebre. The bedrooms are plain but perfectly adequate, as is the rest of the hotel, and the view of the flats is unimpaired from all sides. The restaurant serves good home-cooking of regional dishes. El Buitre's speciality, though, is the expert advice, information and organisation it offers to visitors who really want to take advantage of a trip to the delta (even pack lunches). At the back of the building there is an aviary, where a pair of each species that you can see in the delta lives. Good news for frustrated photographers (who can go in for close-ups) and for anyone who is in need of a visual briefing on what to look for.

Half-board 3,200 ptas; double room 3,800 ptas

A few kilometres beyond the village of Deltebre, you come to a clear tourist corner on the banks of the river, with stalls of souvenirs, gift-packed rice and country goodies. There are two buildings here, one on each side of the road. Both restaurants offer traditional delta dishes.

Buda Parc
(R)M *Ctra de les Goles (977) 908 73 30 62 Open all year except Christmas*

A big modern circular building, not particularly inviting from outside but with fine views from within. It's a good restaurant, with a menu almost exclusive to the local specialities. A good bet here is to take the *entremeses*, which consist of eight or nine different tasters of the local cuisine, and follow that with eel (*anguila*) or a rich rice dish (*a banda* is particularly good).

Menú del dia 1,400 ptas; menú degustació 3,500–4,000 ptas

Casa Nuri
(R)M *Ctra de les Goles (977) 48 01 28 Open all year*

Just opposite, less formal and extremely popular, offering an extensive menu, but where most people eat rice. The paellas here are an institution. It runs a fleet of sightseeing boats just outside which take you to the tip of the delta.

Allow 2,000–4,000 ptas

If you go on a bit further, towards Riumar, you come at the end of the road to a very informal restaurant, the Galatxo (977) 48 01 41 with eels hanging out to dry at the back like washing on a line. For regional dishes – a tapa of local sun-dried eels (*xapadillo*), or eels cooked with tomato, frog's legs, or rice.

This is the closest you can get on foot to the mouth of the river Ebro.

Map 2H **SANT JAUME D'ENVEJA** and beyond

You and your car can cross the main river by Deltebro. There are good signs to the little flat boats, which cross every fifteen minutes. It is worth it to see the quieter side of the delta, less urbanised, even more thickly spread with rice paddies.

L'Estany
(R)S-M *C/ L'Encanyissada (977) 26 10 26 Open all year*

For traditions of the Delta, you couldn't visit a more conscientious restaurant. The owner is a passionate promoter of tradition, to the point of re-starting the festivals of rice planting, and celebratory Sundays with special gastronomic offerings accompanied by a group of traditional musicians who sing improvised *jotas* to the clients. Apart from the old favourites – the *paellas*, and shellfish – you can enjoy some very interesting dishes here, most of which are dependent on the seasons: sun-dried carp or eel, carp eggs, deep-fried seaweed and anemonies, wild duck, rice cooked with sea and fresh water fish (*seixat*), local crayfish, and more. A good option is to ask for the *entremesos* – thereby getting a bit of everything.

If you feel like just a tapa, there is a tree-shaded terrace in front for breezy refreshment. Afterwards, for a bit more cultural improvement, pop into the traditional thatched hut next door, in which there is a museum dedicated to the culture of the Delta de l'Ebre.

Entremesos 1,100 ptas; carte approx. 1,500 ptas

Inland – Poblet, Valls, Reus, Gandesa, Tortosa

Unlike the coast, there are few hotels and few travellers in the interior of the province of Tarragona – a general sense of tranquillity pervades the whole area. Going south from Barcelona, the countryside varies continuously: the expanse of vineyards around Vilafranca del Penedès; the dry hilly landscape on the northern approach to the monastery of Santes Creus; the flat *calçot* fields of Valls and the fruit groves of Reus; the valley of the monastery of Poblet; the winding mountain roads on past Prades towards the spectacular narrow-cut meander of the Ebro which flows down from Mora to Tortosa and on towards the sea.

For sight-seeing you have the great Cistercian monastries of Poblet and Santes Creus, the old towns of Montblanc and Prades; the medieval fortified villages of Miravet and Horta de Sant Joan; and the small cities of Reus and Tortosa. For accomodation you have a small but varied choice from simple and charming to splendid. And for memorable eating there is such an abundance of delightful country places that I've had to leave the selection up to you. To eat *calçots* (the grilled young onions eaten in winter and early spring, dipped into a toasted almond and tomato sauce) you should go near the heart of the tradition, Valls.

The Cistercian Monasteries and around

The Cistercian monasteries of **Poblet** and **Santes Creus** make a fine excursion from Barcelona, or impressive stopping points en route south. Along with **Vallbona de les Monges** just a little further north (see Route F), these are part of Catalunya's most prized cultural heritage. Unlike Vallbona de les Monges, which is in a small village, both Poblet and Santes Creus are in the middle of acres of fruit and olive groves. Close to Poblet there is a delightful hotel, and good restaurants abound. (See Chapter 2 for the monasteries of Poblet and Santes Creus).

Map 3F **LES MASIES DE POBLET**

➔ **Masia del Cadet**
(HR)M *Les Masies de Poblet (977) 87 08 69 Cl. 7–20 Nov., Rest. Cl. Sun. eve., Mon. (except Jun.–Sept.)*

In a tiny village a couple of kilometres from Poblet.

A very pretty family-run hotel, converted from a fifteenth-century *masia*, which stands only a kilometre away from Poblet. The twelve bedrooms are comfortable, with lovely views extending across the green plain of fruit and olive trees. Downstairs there is space to relax, read, take a drink on the terrace or eat in the elegant, fresh restaurant. It is worth coming here just to eat – good home-cooking, regional with a touch of haute cuisine sophistication. The carte is short, mostly meat. Good salads, snails in a hot rich tomato sauce, beef braised with flambéd prune and apple, pigs' trotters stuffed with wild mushrooms. Outside there is a small swimming pool.

Restaurant allow 2,500–3,000 ptas; double room 5,000–6,500 ptas

Arrowed for the welcome of the Corominas family, and the utter peacefulness of the *masia*.

Map 3F **L'ESPLUGA DE FRANCOLÍ**

This is the closest town to Poblet. In itself, it has a varied offering to the traveller – the museum of rural life, with displays of old tools and traditional farm equipment; a fine Modernist wine cooperative built by Lluís Domènech i Montaner; the cultural centre by the contemporary architect Lluís Bonet and the natural splendour of the caves of Font Major.

Les Masies de Poblet – Masia del Cadet

Hostal del Senglar
(HR)M *Plaça Montserrat Canals, 1 (977) 87 01 21 Cl. 1–15 Jan.*

As you leave l'Espluga de Francolí heading for Poblet, you will see it, very well signposted, next to the cultural centre. You can't miss it.

This is an amazing restaurant – a giant both commercially and in terms of covers. It serves hundreds at the weekends, and has earned its popularity from the fantastic old *masia* decoration. Surprisingly, the building was created only twenty-five years ago, complete with quaint differences in floor level, a little sunken room here, a narrow gallery of tables hidden there, a romantic old kitchen next door with a handful of tables, a great beamed hall with seignorial fireplace to serve dozens of tables. Old furniture, pots and pans, antique farm tools and Catalan rural frescoes animate it further. Explore round – it's great fun, with a tremendous weekend atmosphere. The gardens deserve a stroll too –

with an old wine press and tools for close inspection. Food is typically Catalan, *escalivada* kid, duck, meat *a la brasa*, civet of wild boar, etc. And in season, plenty of *calçots*.

Upstairs there are some forty bedrooms looking over the garden.

Menú del dia 2,300 ptas; double room 4,000–7,000 ptas

Map 3F **MONTBLANC**

The great walls of Montblanc are magnificent when approached from Poblet or Solivella, and enclose the town almost completely. It's worth stopping to wander inside – the town has a pretty porticoed *Plaça Major*, some fine old aristocratic houses, and narrow streets of shops. A walk up behind the huge parish church will take you to the crest of the town, from where there are views of the whole valley.

Leaving Montblanc for **Valls**, you drive up the spectacular **Coll de l'Illa**. It's not very high at all, but the views are splendid. On the way, you pass Les Espelmes, a simple restaurant with marvellous views over the valley.

Les Espelmes
(R)S *Ctra N240, Km 28, Coll de l'Illa (977) 60 10 42 Cl. Wed.*

Refresh yourself with a drink on the terrace, or go through to the red-check tablecloth room, which also enjoys the views. The menu is a simple as could be – grilled meats, rabbit with *allioli*, snails, etc., and *calçots* in season.

Allow 1,500 ptas

Map 4F **VALLS** and around

Although Valls is more famous for its *calçots* (pronounced calshot) and its *castellers*, don't forget to visit the church of Sant Joan Baptista, where there is a fine example of Catalan tile-painting in the chapel of Roser. It's famous for the seventeenth-century ceramic tiles that clothe its walls – painted with scenes of the battle of Lepanto.

Valls is the centre of the famous *calçot* region. In winter and early spring the *calçotada* is the typical party meal, great fun and extremely messy. The restaurants are invariably full of noisy, raucous parties – you get to your table, and set to with the toasted bread, tomato, garlic, oil and salt, and, of course, the *porró*. You are given a small dish of *romescu* – a delicious sauce of toasted almond, tomato, garlic, red pimentoes, hot peppers and olive oil. The thin tender onions, which have been grilled over vine trimmings, arrive on rooftiles looking thoroughly burnt. You strip the charred skin off, and then eat the hot onion with a good dipping of the sauce. Delicious, although a bit indigestible if you overdo the quantity. The mandatory bibs are provided. The meal continues, after the paper tablecloths have disappeared, with grilled meats, *botifarra* and white beans; then *crema catalana* and *cava*. It's a mighty meal, a once a year party that you simply must experience if you are here at the right time.

Valls is also the capital of the Catalan tradition of *castellers*, the building of human towers. This is a heroic feat, which you will certainly see on postcards if you aren't lucky enough to see it live. The key day to see the two rival teams of Valls is around the 21 October, Santa Ursula, when the *castellers* season ends and a grand competition is held with teams of other Catalan towns in the Plaça del Blat to build the best and highest towers. There are different patterns of tower according to the number of men who form the base, and the number of tiers formed above, the highest of which is made by *l'anxaneta*, a child who climbs up to the top of the tower, makes the sign of the cross, and then starts the process of dismounting.

Masia Bou
(R)M *Ctra de Lleida, Km 21,5 (977) 60 04 27 Cl. Christmas*

This now huge restaurant is the founding place of the popular *calçot* feast. It all began on the farms when the young onions were grilled on the vine trimmings. Popularised through Masia Bou, it is now a huge business in the area surrounding Valls. It's typical here to eat *calçots* as a party – family reunions, gatherings of friends, etc. Coachloads arrive from the cities for the fun.

Since the first *calçot* days, Masia Bou has grown into several big dining rooms; a smart, wood-finished room downstairs with the polished bar running beside, and a great hall upstairs. In season it's essential to book. Out of season, the food is good but undistinguished, serving traditional dishes. *Calçots* are served almost all year for visitors who can't make it in season, but they are not as tender, and the party atmosphere is missing.

Menú del dia 2,000 ptas; Calçotada 3,400 ptas (Oct.–Mar.)

Fèlix Hotel
(H)M *Ctra N240, Km 17 (977) 60 60 82 Open all year*

The Fèlix Hotel is new, built for executive travellers rather than touring families, but the service is very pleasant and the rooms excellent. There's a young garden (with lots of potential) and a pool behind the building. The road is quite busy, but the noise of traffic doesn't reach to the garden.

Double room 5,000–8,500 ptas

Casa Fèlix
(R)M *Ctra N240, Km 17 (977) 60 13 50 Open all year*

Another classic *calçot* restaurant, very popular indeed, which also serves *calçots* as a starter out of season. The room is simply furnished, with a separate hall for the numerous *calçot* influx. The menu apart from *calçots* is very complete, with traditional and international cuisine on the carte. The Fèlix Hotel is next door.

Menu 1,075 ptas; *calçotada* 3,000 ptas

Map 4F MASMOLETS

The only difficulty here is to go slowly enough along the Montblanc-Valls road (close to Valls) to spot the turn-off to the tiny, virtually uninhabited village.

Cal Ganxo
(R)S-M *C/ Eglésia, 13 (977) 60 59 60 Cl. 15 Jul.–early Sept.*

This is a tremendous place for *calçots* in winter, and later in the year for good Catalan home-cooking. Their other speciality is rabbit with snails. If you go out of *calçot* season, a good starter is their *entremesos*, after which they serve roasts and *brasa* meats. *Crema catalana* is the typical pud. The cellar of the old eighteenth-century house has been converted into the country restaurant, with old furniture, benches and a very congenial atmosphere of informality.

Allow 3,000–4,000 ptas

Map 4F MONTFERRI

On the top edge of a field just on the north side of the village there's a curious half-constructed temple. It's the unfinished work of the Catalan architect Josep Maria Jujol, a disciple of Gaudí, who designed it in 1926 as a sanctuary for the devotions of the village folk who couldn't travel to the mountains of Montserrat, just west of Barcelona city. You need to turn off up a narrow lane just after having passed through the village pointing towards Valls, and then follow your nose. Work is continuing true to the craftsman method, so you can see just how Gaudí used the wooden curved structures to support his own designs when in construction.

Castell de Rocamora
(R)M *Montferri (977) 62 01 20 Cl. Mon.–Thurs.*

You need a keen eye on the roadsigns to get here. Once in Montferri, turn off the main road downhill, and then follow the lane below the village. It bends round towards the castle on the crest of the facing hill.

The castle, once extremely powerful in terms of land ownership, has been in the same family for 400 years, and the present generation live upstairs. Quite a lot of reconstruction, and a great deal of dedication went in to the creation of the restaurant. There are some five different rooms separated by open doorways, one with a bay of windows looking over the lands once held by the castle, one several steps down in what was the cellar, another heavily beamed and vaulted nearer the entrance. Each is small, with its own atmosphere, decorated with old pictures. Framed castle documents hang in the *Saló Rosa.*

Lunch starts with slices of carrot, fuet and *sangría* while you read the menu. The food is regional but with originality, and well-presented. To start: little onions in a cream and thyme sauce, pâtés, *esqueixada*; the seconds are mostly meat – a rich dish of duck with orange, wood-grilled meat presented on a wooden board, roast lamb.

I'm told that in winter it is a splendid place to eat a *calçotada.*

Allow 2,500 ptas

Map 4F **PERAFORT**

A small village some ten kilometres from Tarragona just off the N240.

Ca Vidal
(R)S *Plaça de l'Església, 16 (977) 62 52 93 Cl. Mon. eve.*

It is well-hidden, and little known beyond the bounds of the locality, but it's popular in summer and in *calçot* season it fills to bursting and you need to book. The restaurant flows through the various downstairs rooms and cellar of an old *masia* that dates from 1777, and spills out into the pretty enclosed patio. The only places without tables are the old wine chambers. It's rustic, with old furniture and ceramics throughout. For meat *a la brasa* and typical local dishes.

Menú del dia 1,050; carte approx. 2,000 ptas

Map 3F **ALCOVER**

Mesón El Remei
(R)S-M *Ctra Reus-Montblanc (977) 84 61 87 Open Jul.–Aug., weekends Nov.–Jun.; Cl. Sept.*

Just before you reach the village.

The restaurant is run by two brothers and their wives, and has a gently sloping lawned garden in front, with a peaceful terrace overlooking the valley. It's well known for its selection of game (in season) – venison, mountain goat, hare, etc. and for its stews. The wild boar civet here is excellent, presented in an earthenware pot sealed with a bread lid. A good starter is the *entrants* – a selection of some eight to ten hot and cold tapas. To follow, the local lamb is particularly good, done *a la brasa* in the room, or roasted in the oven.

Downstairs they've converted the bare rock cellars into tiny dining rooms, a little musty at first, but then intimate with the candles and good food. Take a look.

Allow 2,500 ptas

Map 3F **REUS**

This is one of my favourite towns – dusty, busy, full of cars, difficult for parking but cosmopolitan and dignified once you escape the traffic. It's economy is based on dried fruits, and during the this century the textile trade and the making of eau-de-vie have bolstered its prosperity. Just by strolling around you can see the historical well-being of the town – particularly in the *eixample* (new town) where impresive baroque or neoclassical buildings line the streets. There are also a small number of fine modernist houses here. **Casa Navàs**, in Plaça del Mercadal, is an impressive example, recently opened to the public, and the local museum is in another, **Casa Rull**. Starting in the central Plaça Prim, stroll through the series of elegant squares, each leading on to another, linked by pedestrian shopping streets. The local shops are excellent too, particularly the delicatessens and *pastisseries.*

This is historically the commercial centre of the European hazelnut trade which brought the proud 'Reus, Paris, London' motto into being. The dried fruits market is still vital, and the olive oil from this area is held in the very highest esteem by all Catalans. You can visit the dried fruits and oil market (which has been held for the last 700 years) at the agricultural market on Monday mornings.

Hostal Simonet

(HR)S *C/ Raval Santa Anna, 18 (977) 34 59 74 Open all year; rest. Cl. Sun. eve.*

On the main road circling the old centre, easily reached by car. The hotel is still in the same family as it was 120 years ago. It is simple, up a flight of stairs and without views from its rooms, but as a one-nighter it's adequate and comfortable, with forty-five rooms. There's a welcoming terrace by the restaurant.

Double room 4,500–6,500 ptas

La Glorieta del Castell

(R)M *Plaça del Castell, 2 (977) 34 08 26 Cl. Sun., 15–30 Aug.*

A fine restaurant in one of the most tranquil squares. The room, both outside and in, is contemporary in style, with creative modern Catalan cuisine. It has a very good value *menú degustació*, and has specialities of marinaded prawns, a fragrant dish of foie-gras with moscatel grapes, and fish baked in salt.

Menú degustació 2,600 ptas; carte approx. 3,500 ptas

Casa Coder
(R)S *Plaça Mercadal, Open every day*

A bar and restaurant with an attractive etched-glass and varnished-wood front which boasts a history of over 200 years. Inside it maintains the same quietly Modernist style, and offers a good range of tapas, and general dishes.
Menú del dia 1,500 ptas

Cafè de Reus
(R)S *C/ Metge Fortuny, 3 (977) 75 27 67 Open all year*

This is a fashionable Parisian-style café up a side street just off the Plaça del Mercadal, where you can take a fine cocktail, a variety of hot *entrepans*, and a good *menú-del-dia* lunch in the next room. Marble tables, wood panelling, contemporary paintings, turn-of-the-century finishes and cabinets displaying pretty glass.
Menú del dia 1,200 ptas

Map 3F **CASTELLVELL**

El Pa Torrat
(R)S-M *Av. de Reus, 24 (977) 85 52 12 Cl. Tues., Sun. eve., 15–31 Aug., Christmas*

Inside an ordinary-looking house, with an entrance through a narrow bar to the hessian-lined diningroom. It's small, neat, intimate and well-run, with a first-rate kitchen. The clients are mostly Catalan, and the menu serves exclusively catalan dishes, well-prepared and beautifully presented. For a light supper just a plate of excellent dried ham with tomatoed toast is a treat. Or if you are still unconvinced about snails, try them here – the best I've eaten anywhere. The stuffed sweet peppers are delicious too. The delicate crêpes of salmon and cheese are out of the ordinary, and *a la brasa* or roasts are also on offer if you feel like a good plateful. Good value.
Allow 2,500 ptas

Map 3F **ALMOSTER**

Morrofi
(R)M *C/ Raval, 9 (977) 85 54 45 Cl. Tues., Sun. eve.*

At the back of the village, well-signposted and accessible by car through the narrow streets.

This is a young, aspiring Catalan restaurant that is moving up the ladder fast. It's in a converted *masia*, with an entrance from below up a flight of stairs. The main room is very pretty, beamed, white-walled,

and with rock jutting through in one corner. Above there is another room and a terrace on the roof for evening aperitifs or coffee, and for springtime lunches. (In summer it's far too hot at midday.) A good range of well-prepared Catalan dishes, meat *a la brasa* with fine sauces, roasted, or braised. Excellent service, and an ambience that breathes high quality. There's no fresh fish here. Reserve in July and August.
Allow 2,500 ptas.

The mountains inland

From **Poblet** you can take the climbing, winding road up to Prades, which launches you into the pretty mountain interior of the province of Tarragona.

Map 3F **PRADES**

It's worth walking round this mountain village, where the houses and church are built of red stone. The romanesque-gothic church stands on one side of the Plaça Major, in the middle of which is a splendid fountain. Take a drink from the fountain even if you're not thirsty – the water is delicious.

L'Estanc
(R)M *Plaça Major, 9 (977) 86 81 67 Cl. Wed., mid-Jan.–mid-Feb.*

A restaurant installed in an old house, with great wooden beams in the ceiling. It serves good home-cooking of the traditional kind – grilled meats and sausages of the region. You can't miss it – on the far side of the splendid water fountain in the square.
Allow 2,500–3,000 ptas

Some fifteen kilometres away on the dry olive slopes of the Montsant mountain close to **Poboleda** are the wonderful monastic ruins of the **Cartoixa d'Escaladei,** which has tumbled with a rather romantic dignity. It was the first Carthusian monastery to be built in the peninsular, and laid its foundation stone in 1167. The romanesque church still stands, although weed-ridden, and you can enter by the splendid neo-classical portal although the adjoining walls have fallen into ruins. You need to turn off to the right as you enter the small village (where there's a simple bar) and go up a stony track for a couple of kilometres.
Open 10.00 a.m.–1.30 p.m., 3.00 p.m.–5.30 p.m.

Map 3F **ARBOLÍ**

A small village which you reach at the end of a mountain road, down in a valley between Prades and Reus. The fountain here is renowned for its superb water, and people come here from far to queue and collect their weekly supply of drinking water.

➜ El Pigot d'Arbolí
(R)S-M *By the fountain (977) 81 60 63 Open lunches only, Sat. eve., eves. in Aug. Cl. Tues., Jun.*

You go upstairs to the room, which just fits in the mountain slope, with the bare rock jutting in at the far end. Its spacious, airy and simple, with white-washed walls and tables with benches. The carte is not only in all the European languages, but also in Gallego and Basque.

The dried sausage is made, the hams cured, the truffles bottled, the tongue pressed and potted, and the marron glacé preserved by the family. Here you eat traditional food, cooked as it always has been. The salads come from the vegetable garden, the truffles and wild mushrooms from the mountain woodland behind.

A good starter here is the *entremesos El Pigot* which gives you a taste of various dried meats, followed by the *carn d'olla*, civet of hare (in winter only) or a stew of partridge or mature beef, or plain meat *a la brasa*. To finish – a selection of cheeses, *mató* with mountain honey, or home made quince cheese with almonds.

If you are interested in preserves, ask – and you will be shown the cellar of old wines and drying sausages, and the hundreds of bottles of goodies.

Allow 2,000–3,000 ptas

Arrowed for the enthusiasm of the family, and their true culinary craftsmanship.

Map 3F **PRADELL**

Can Ciurana
(HR)S *Ctra N420, Km 190 (977) 82 80 15 Open all year*

This is a simple guest house with only twelve rooms, alone in the mountains just by a peak, with spectacular views across the dry shrub- and herb covered valley towards the castle of Escornalbou. No frills, but tranquility and fresh air.

Double room: 4,500 ptas

Map 2F **FALSET**

This is the capital of the wine region of Priorat. I didn't find anywhere interesting to stay or eat here, but you might notice the attractive Modernist building of the Celler Cooperatiu (the wine cooperative) as you go through.

Map 2G **MORA D'EBRE**

This is not a gourmets paradise, and there is a pretty limited choice of places to eat.

La Rana Verde
(R)M *Av. Comarques Catalanes, 73 (977) 40 05 33 Cl. Sun.*

A welcoming restaurant, on the main through-road of the town, with a pleasant wood-finished decoration where you can eat good fresh fish and shellfish.
Allow 3,000–5,000 ptas

Enric
(R)S-M *Av. Comarques Catalanes, s/n (977) 40 30 68 Open all year*

A restaurant which has been around for some twenty years, and has recently moved to this address, on the edge of the town. Go through the bar to the elegant room, which has an extensive 'carte' covering Catalan and international dishes. The marinaded salmon is a speciality here.
Menú del dia 1,500

Map 1G **GANDESA**

This town was founded in Moorish times, and although it isn't particularly attractive from outside, preserves quite a selection of architectural styles in its centre.

Piqué
(HR)S *Via Catalunya, 68 (977) 42 00 68 Open all year*

There is very little choice here. Piqué is just at the entrance to the town, with ample parking. It's simple but adequate hotel, with a popular restaurant. The menu is long, with numerous international, Catalan and local dishes, but best known for its regional dishes.
Menú del dia 1,100 ptas; carte approx. 2,500–3,500 ptas; double room 3,000 ptas

Batea and Horta de Sant Joan are two pretty mountain villages nearby.

Map 1G **BATEA**

Batea is surrounded by medieval walls, with narrow covered passages, arch-lined streets, and a pretty porticoed main square. You should look out for the baroque church of Sant Miquel and the Torre del Castellà, but the whole village is really one delightful monument.

Map 1G HORTA DE SANT JOAN

This old village has a very beautiful Franciscan convent – Mare de Déu dels Angels (or Sant Salvador, the other name dedicated to it in memory of the sixteenth-century saint of the village). The convent is a couple of kilometres outside the village, but is definitely worth a visit, particularly the romanesque church. The village itself is old and picturesque, with narrow winding streets which inspired Picasso to paint one of his first cubist pictures. This is a 'no through road' village, but if you've made it here, go a little further to the **Roques de Benet**, for exceptional views, beautiful mountain scenery and absolute peace.

On the way to **Tortosa** from **Mora**, you can take either the south or the north bank of the river Ebro. This is a spectacular route, curving with the river, with beautiful views of the water particuarly from the south side.

Map 2G MIRAVET

This is a medieval fortress and village on the far side some fifteen kilometres from Mora. A side-road slips down to the river from the main road, and from there a small boat takes cars across to the village. It's well worth the trip and makes a delightful visit. Miravet was a Templar fort, and has two walled areas and a jumble of very well-preserved buildings. If it's open, pop into the romanesque church of Sant Martí, which has rather lovely capitals with floral decoration.

Map 2G BENIFALLET

Another little village, famous not for its architecture but for its cooking, particularly it's *pastissets* which are of Arab origin. These are delicious moon-shaped pastries filled with a sweet marrow preserve called *cabell d'àngel* (literally angel hair). The preserve itself you find all over Catalunya as one of the most popular pastry fillings, but the crumbly pastry of the *pastisset* itself, with a hint of cinamon, is special to here.

El Chiringuito
(R)S-M *C/ Alfons XII (977) 46 20 02, Open all year*

This is close to the entrance of the village, so it's best to park and then walk. There's no sign on the door, but if you're there at lunchtime, you'll hear where it is. It looks like an ordinary café, but go on through to the simple dining room, which is invariably full, where you can enjoy the famously delicious lamb chops. Their colossal set menu draws people from far: salad, *entremesos*, grilled meats, *llagostins*, jugs of strong wine, and then pud and *cava* – you need a Herculean appetite to get through it. Reserve before you go.

Allow 2,500 ptas; menú especial 5,000–6,000 ptas

Map 2G **TORTOSA**

Tortosa is dominated by its hilltop fortress, present since Moorish times, which today forms the backdrop of the cathedral. The façade of the cathedral is baroque, while the inside and cloisters are gothic, with a splendid fourteenth-century retablo gracing the high altar. You can go through to the fine gothic cloisters via the baroque Olivera door.

In general, the town is best seen from the walls of the castle above.

Parador de la Zuda
(HR)L *Castell de la Zuda (977) 44 44 50 Open all year*

One of the loveliest Paradors – installed in the castle above the city, with views over the cathedral and beyond to the sharp hills on the other side of the river. The name comes from the Arabic for a water well *Zuda* which was built when the site was an Moorish fortress in medieval times. The gardens around the hotel are limited to the area within the walls, but are nevertheless spacious. There are several buildings joined to it, few of which are historic, but the overall efect is harmonious and splendid. Inside, the decoration and furniture reflects the castle style. There are eighty-two bedrooms, and grand dining and ball rooms. Worth a visit even if you don't stay.

Double room 11,000 ptas

El Parc
(R)M *C/ Av. Generalitat s/n (977) 44 48 66 Open all year*

A fairly formal restaurant in a lovely position – in the main flower-filled park of the small city. It has a very inviting terrace which spreads under the big plane trees by the rose gardens – there are always people there taking a drink or chatting. The restaurant serves Catalan and international cuisine, with a good offering of fresh fish and meat dishes. It's very comfortable, and air conditioned.

Allow 2,500 ptas

Rosa
(R)M *C/ Marqués de Bellet, 13 (977) 44 48 01 Cl. Mon., Tues. midday, 15–30 Aug., 12–20 Sept.*

This is an Italian restaurant with style and elegance, just off the park, serving the best of fine Italian cuisine as well as pizzas and pastas. It is small, decorated in pink with flowers on each table. Try a salad here, and enjoy the opportunity to choose your oil and vinegar from a trolley full of different kinds – not just flavoured with herbs but from different mills, different regions and different bases (olive, walnut, etc.). This is a special restaurant, very popular and always full. You must book.

Allow 2,500 ptas

Map 2H **FREGINALS**

This is very close to the motorway on the way south towards Castellón by the interior road, after Amposta.

Masia Creu del Coll

(R)M *Ctra Ulldecona-Tortosa, Km 11 (977) 57 28 27 Open weekends (ring just in case if you are passing out of high season)*

In a 200-year-old *masia*, which was used to produce tiles, with thick stone walls and thick ceiling beams. The restaurant occupies several rooms: in the summer the new diningroom is used (carefully constructed to follow the lines of the old building) because of its air-conditioning and large windows. In winter you eat in the little cosy rooms of the old house.

It's along a windy road in the middle of nowhere, surrounded by dry hills of herbs, shrubs and olive trees (although one hill of golden stone is being slowly cut away). You eat roast meats and grills here, and the specialities are *ternasco* of lamb and confit of duck. Try the *bacallà*-stuffed sweet peppers as a starter. In season, a place for the *calçotada*.

Allow 2,200 ptas

If you are interested in cave painting, there are some stunning treasures hidden just on the southern frontier of Catalunya. In the caves near **Ulldecona** you'll find some impressive images of energetic hunters (archers or hunters with spears) chasing herds of running deer. The caves are up by the Santuari de la Pietat, some three kilometres outside the town. A barred gate prohibits entry, but you can see the paintings well from outside.

Continuing down from here, you leave Catalunya and enter the province of **Castellón**, in the region of **Valencia**.

GENERAL INFORMATION

Festivals

If you come across a big Catalan *festa*, you might see *sardanes*, dancing giants, *castellers*, and even a *correfoc*. The *sardana* is Catalunya's national dance, in which any number of people join in a circle with arms outstretched and hands held. The steps are counted strictly, involving simple but quite tiring movements of toe-pointing, following the rhythms of the *cobla*, the reed band which accompanies them. *Gegants* feature in the province of Barcelona, where each town has its own pair of giants – three-metre-high figures whose splendid robes hide their carriers as they swirl and turn up the streets during *festas*. The human towers of the *castellers* are really very impressive, sometimes rising as high as eight or nine tiers. You will see these around Valls and Tarragona (see Chapter 6, Valls). The *correfoc* is a tremendous, explosive event, always held at night, where fire-snorting dragons and weird beasts twirl through the streets hounded by red devils with spark-throwing forks, accompanied by strong drumbeats and lots of noise. The crowds run with the dragons, whooping and rushing to avoid the fire – a thoroughly pagan affair.

January

1 New Year: a family affair, starting late after the night before, accompanied by *torró* and *cava*.

5 Eve of the Feast of the Kings: one of the most delightful fiestas of the year. Like Father Christmas, the kings are responsible for bringing the children presents, and it's traditional for families to leave out a saucer of water for the camels and a glass of brandy for the kings (miraculously replaced by presents in the morning). Melchior, Caspar and Balthazar appear in the evening, parading splendidly through the streets each with his own chariot (float), horsemen, lorry of presents and lorry of blackest coal (for the bad children). Sweets are hurled among the crowds, and in the small villages the very young children climb up and speak to the kings, to say whether they've been good enough to have a present – little suspecting that one might be their uncle or grandfather. In Barcelona, the kings arrive by boat, and parade in great grandeur up the Rambla.

6 The Kings: this is the real present-giving day in Catalunya, with a huge lunch followed by a piece of heavy sponge cake in which a broad bean or a little image of a king may be hidden. He who receives the bean has to pay for next year's cake.

17 Sant Antoni: animals, particularly horses and mules, are blessed in various villages.

February

Carnival A week-long festival before the start of Lent.

Thursday before Ash Wednesday: rather like Mardi gras, when everyone eats *truites* (omelettes), *coca de llardons* (a sweet lard pastry) and *botifarra* sausage.

Weekend: dancing processions famous in **Vilanova i la Geltrú**, **Solsona** and **Sitges**, with the public as dressed-up (or undressed) as the floats.

Sunday after Carnival: the vintage car rally is run annually from Barcelona to Sitges, taking the winding coastal Garraf road. The cars collect in Plaça de Sant Jaume early in the morning, with their splendidly dressed owners – Hispano-Suizas and Bugattis amongst them.

March

3 Sant Medir, patron saint of horses: everyone who has a horse rides round Barcelona's *barri* of Gràcia, throwing out sweets.

Easter Throughout Easter there are passion plays. These are of particular renown in Esparreguera, Olesa and Ulldecona (province of Tarragona).

Sunday before Palm Sunday: streets fill with markets selling decorations made of naturally bleached fresh palm leaves (like extravagantly worked corn-dollies). Simple tall leaves for the boys, worked decorations for the girls. The fair in Vic is famous.

Palm Sunday: the palms are blessed in church. Pretty family gatherings.

Maundy Thursday: near Pals, in the village of Verges, they stage the 'dance of death'.

Good Friday: processions in Girona and Tarragona.

Easter Monday: families celebrate, and each child receives a chocolate creation called a *mona*.

April

23 Sant Jordi, patron saint of Catalunya (St George): men give women red roses, and women give the men books. Montblanc celebrates a week of medieval festivities.

27 Mare de Déu de Montserrat: dancing of *sardanes*.

May

1 Day of the workers.

11 Sant Ponç: street markets of herbs, preserved fruits and honey. In Barcelona, it's held along C/ Hospital.

Start of the *festa major* in Lleida (Sant Anastasi) and Ripoll (Sant Eudald).

June

23 Eve of Sant Joan: tremendous firework festivities throughout the Catalan countries (*països catalans*). The flame used to light the bonfires is first gathered at a ceremony on the mountain of Canigó (French Pyrenees) and is distributed from city to town to village during the morning of the 23 June. In Isil (Pyrenees of Lleida) the men of the village carry burning trunks of wood down the hillside, creating a spectacle of rivers of fire.

24	Appropriately a day off work, given that few have slept. The *festa major* in Valls, when they display their skill at building *castellers.*
29	Sant Pere: *festa major* in Reus, where the giants and devils come out to parade in force.

Corpus Christi

A delightful festival in many towns, where the streets are decked with patterns of flowers over which the procession of the blessed sacrament passes. It's particularly famous in Sitges, Arbúcies, Argentona and Sallent. You'll also see eggs dancing in the water jets of fountains in the province of Barcelona.
Berga celebrates with the *Patum* – a symbolic battle of Christians against Moors, followed by a firey whirl of dancing devils, skeletons and dragons backed by the incessant thud of drums.

July

Saturday	Calella de Palafrugell celebrates with the singing of *havaneres* in its little port, (first Saturday).
Sunday	In La Pobla de Segur the traditional *raiers* (wood rafts) navigate the river, (first Sunday).
16	Mare de Déu del Carme, patron saint of fishermen: all along the coast there are boating processions.
Saturday	In Arsèguel the tradition of accordion playing is kept alive by a yearly gathering, (last Saturday).
Sunday	Castellar de N'Hug holds sheepdog trials, (last Sunday).

August

15	Santa Maria, *Mare de Déu: festa major* in many villages. Barcelona's *barri* of Gràcia decorates its streets in themes and begins a week of night-time festivity and dancing in the streets. Falset celebrates with a curious, energetic 'battle of flowers'.
30	Sant Fèlix: *festa major* in Vilafranca del Penedès, with the best *castellers,* dancing giants and traditional dancing.
Week	*Retaule de Sant Ermengol* in La Seu d'Urgell: a traditional staging of the life of the saint in the cloisters of the cathedral. (second week)

September

8	*Festa major* in Olot, Solsona and Montblanc.
11	National day of Catalunya, a holiday.
23	Santa Tecla: *festa major* in Tarragona, with *castellers* and processions of giants from all of Catalunya.
24	Mare de Déu de la Mercè: *festa major* in Barcelona, with processions up the Rambla, and a tremendous *correfoc.*
First week	Celebrations of the *jota* in Tortosa.
Second Friday	Start of Tàrrega's street theatre festival.
Second Sunday	Bull chasing in Cardona.

October

21	Santa Ursula: the day of the *castellers* in Valls.
29	*Festa major* in Girona.

November

1	All Saints Day: traditionally celebrated with roasted chestnuts, sweet potatoes and *panellets* (small rich almond cakes).

December

6	Festival of the Holy Conception.
8	Constitution Day.
13	Sant Llúcia: the traditional start of the Christmas decoration fairs, held around the cathedrals and main parish churches until Christmas.
24	Christmas Eve: Christmas dinner, Midnight mass.
25	Christmas day: family meal. There is a tradition whereby a log, called the *cagatió*, is hit with a stick by the children and pours out sweets and small presents. Nativity scenes acted in several villages.
26	Sant Esteve: family meal.
28	Sants Innocents: Catalunya's April Fools' Day.
31	New Year's Eve: you should eat a grape for each chime of the clock. Plenty of *cava* to cheer in the new year.

General advice
Telephones

International operator: 008 (Europe) or 005 (outside Europe).
From inside Spain: full code.
From inside the province: code unnecessary.
From abroad: country code (34) + provincial code without the 9.

Banking hours. 8.30 a.m.–2.00 p.m. Mon.–Sat. (In summer only Mon.–Fri.). Most savings banks, *caixas,* also open Thursday afternoons.

Shopping hours. Food markets only open in the mornings except on Fridays when they open all day. Shops open approx.9.00 a.m. or 10.00 a.m.– 2.00 p.m. and approx. 4.30 p.m.–8.00 p.m.

You can buy stamps in post offices (yellow sign with red horn emblem), or in tobacconists.

Electricity. 240 V.

Health. High-street pharmacies are extremely helpful for minor problems. In biggish towns there are 24-hour pharmacies.

If you need an ambulance, dial 300 20 00 or 061 for emergency assistance.

When to come and what to bring

Winter The weather tends to be bright, clear and quite chilly around Barcelona and Tarragona. In Lleida and Girona it gets much colder, and there is plenty of snow in the Pyrenees. Bring warm clothes.

Spring: beautiful everywhere – rushing streams in the mountains, flowers, warmth and greenness. There can be sudden bursts of rain, and days without a cloud. It's early for the tourist season, and the city dwellers begin to go out for the weekends. This is the best time to visit. Bring something warm for the cool evenings, and beware of spring sun-bathing – you can get burnt easily.

Summer The tremendous heat only arrives in late July and August, when the cities empty and the mountains and beaches fill. Barcelona city gets very humid, Lleida heats like an oven, but the mountain regions are usually refreshing breezy retreats. If mountain walking figures in your plans, have a windproof jacket to hand in case a sharp turn in the weather catches you out.

Autumn: the leaf turn is quite beautiful in the mountains. Late September signals a sudden change from the softening summer tones to strong north winds, violent storms, buckets of rain, and a fast drop in temperature. Short sleeves are over by October, and jumpers are in by December.

What to buy Regional produce is a must. Olive oil ranges from good to marvellous, depending on the grade of acidity you buy, and the *denominació d'origen* (particularly fine from just south of Lleida); wines and craftsman-made cavas of Catalunya are well worth their weight; dried sausage (*fuet, llonganissa*) and charcuterie varies from village to village in the mountains – if you eat one you like, buy more immediately. Dried fruits are also good, particularly fat raisins, almonds and hazelnuts from Reus. *Torró* – sweet blocks of praline, or honey and almond, can be found around Christmas-time, the honey variety most famously produced in Agramunt.

For local produce, remember:

Delta de l'Ebre: rice, mussels, *llangostins*
Pals: rice
Palamós: *gambes*
Vic: *fuet, llonganissa*
Empordà: fresh cheeses

Apart from the food on offer, you'll probably be thoroughly tempted by the leather-work here: shoes are well-designed and beautifully made, without overburdening the wallet, and if you like gloves there are some delightful small, old-fashioned shops where it is a real pleasure to buy. Old shops near the city cathedrals have fine plain and fancy candles of all sizes. Finally, you'll find plenty of tempting pottery.

Transport The roads in Catalunya are generally excellent, with good motorways (quite expensive) and well-made main roads.

In the cities most streets are one way only, particularly in Barcelona's *Eixample,* so you need to calculate your turn-offs with care – lots of going round the block, and use of side-roads. There are plenty of well-signposted underground car parks.

Public transport is good in all the main cities – a map in the tourist office is the answer. Barcelona has an Underground and extensive buses, paid with a flat-fare or a 10-journey card system. Bus no. 100 will take you round all the main sights in Barcelona from May to October (see Chapter 1).

Car hire: plenty of choice, both European and national companies.

Visitors with disabilities

Since the Paralympic Games in 1992, Catalunya is very concious of the difficulties in getting about encountered by disabled people. The pavements of the city of Barcelona are now almost all ramped; the pedestrian lights are fitted with sound signals; and most lifts have braile buttons. The newer hotels throughout Catalunya are obliged to have rooms specially designed for the needs of wheelchair visitors – although it will clearly take time for all hotels to offer these facilities. Public transport is still difficult to handle, but the metro has a speaker system which announces each stop, the number of public buses with built-in ramps for wheelchairs is growing month by month and taxis are very helpful. Some beaches, especially those around the Port Olímpic in Barcelona have wooden slatted paths down to the sea, built with wheelchairs in mind. If you plan to come to Catalunya on holiday, contact the Catalan Tourist Board who will give you excellent advice.

Fire Catalunya suffers terrible forest fires in the summer, many raging for several days. You will surely come across some blackened areas with sprouting greenery on your journey through Catalunya. Be very careful – never, never leave glass or anything else behind if you stop for a picnic. And please don't light a barbecue in the countryside – one little spark is all it takes.

Tap water Tap water is safe everywhere. It's always good in the mountains, but along the coasts it can taste rather chlorinated in summer – fine for teeth-cleaning, but perhaps not for the table.

Sports in Catalunya

Golf There are some twenty-five golf courses here, many of them very beautiful. A very good area is on the Costa Brava close to Pals – an area which is also favoured by some excellent restaurants and hotels.

Barcelona: Club de Golf Sant Cugat (93) 674 39 08
Club de Golf Osona-Montanyà-El Brull, El Brull (93) 884 01 70
Club de Golf Masia Bach, Ctra. Martorell-Capallades Km 19,5, San Esteve Sesrovires (93) 772 63 10

Girona: Real Club de Cerdanya, Puigcerdá (972) 88 13 38
Club de Golf de Pals (972) 63.60.06
Club de Golf Mas Nou, Platja d'Aro (972) 82 60 84
Empordà Golf Club, Ctra Palafrugell-Torroella, Gualta (972) 76 04 50
Club de Golf Girona, Ctra Girona-Banyoles, Km 4 (972) 17 16 41
Peralada Golf, Peralada (972) 53 83 06

Tarragona: Club Golf Bonmont Terres Noves, Mont-Roig del Camp (977) 81 81 00

Sailing The coastal area has a string of very attractive marinas up and down the coast and is well equipped for yachts of all sizes.
Federació Catalana de Vela, Passeig Manuel Girona, 2, Barcelona (93) 203 38 00
Port Olímpic, Escollera de Poblenou, Barcelona (93) 221 08 68

Skiing For alpine skiers, the quality of snow is always excellent in the Vall d'Aran (the only north-facing slopes of the Catalan Pyrenees), and usually very good in Andorra and the other mountain pistes of Lleida and Girona. Cross-country skiing is still in its infancy here, but the off-piste skiing is as expansive as the mountains themselves.

Lleida: Baqueira Beret, Vall d'Aran (973) 64 50 25
Boí-Taüll, Vall de Boí (93) 414 66 60
Super Espot, Espot (973) 48 09 50
Girona: La Molina, Cerdanya (972) 89 20 31
Andorra: Arinsal, La Massana Tela (9738) 35 8 22
Ordino-Arcalís (9738) 36 3 20
Pal, La Massana (9738) 36 2 36
Pas de la Casa (9738) 62 5 15
Soldeu-El Tarter (9738) 51 7 77

Summer mountain sports have surged into the fore recently, particularly in the upper regions of Lleida – not only trekking but rafting, caving, climbing, mountain-biking, paragliding, etc.

The Catalans and sport

You only have to drop into a bar on a Wednesday or Saturday night to find out what the favourite sport is here – football. The local team, FC Barcelona (*el Barça*) has a colossal following and the fervour is such that the important match nights traumatise the restaurant trade, and the bars either suffer a static crowd of TV gazers or are deserted. When the home team plays a big match, you can keep abreast of the score by listening for the car horns and rockets. A win brings the streets of the city to a standstill, with elated supporters in their thousands converging on the Rambla to celebrate.

Basketball is second in line, with a healthy following both for men and women. Cycling is more watched than done – although you'll come across groups of earnest grey-haired cyclists of a Sunday morning. Having cycled my way round Catalunya and over the Pyrenees, I can vouch for the pleasure of a heady, herb-fragrant mountain pass by bike.

There's loads of sailing and windsurfing up and down the coast, with plenty of good marinas, and on Sundays the sea is sprinkled with the white dots of racing dinghies. You can rent dinghies and catamarans on the beaches. There are also splendid yachts berthed in the harbours.

The Olympic Games of 1992 have left surprisingly little mark on Catalunya apart from some superb sports facilities. Athletics is of minor interest, and shares a similar popular following to tennis: top-class Catalan or Spanish competitors are popular stars, but the competitions themselves are not much followed.

Tour operators

There are plenty of agencies that run package tours to the sunspots here. But to get away from it all, you can do much better to go it alone, or contact a tour operator that really appreciates the finer offerings of Catalunya.

Vintage Spain Ltd
75 Rampton Road, Willingham, Cambridge, CB4 5JQ 0954 261431

A small company that is expert in searching for and finding beautiful villas in hidden corners of Catalunya. With their profound understanding of the region, they will also design and arrange holidays for you which savour the rich beauty and wealth of traditions of Catalunya.

Prospect Art and Music Tours Ltd
454–458 Chiswick High Road, London W4 5TT 081 995 2151

For cultural tours to the fine romanesque churches and medieval villages of Catalunya. They also run short weekend breaks to Barcelona to enjoy the art museums and the modernist architecture.

The Catholic Travel Service
Suite C43, 16 Paddington Green, London W2 1LG 071 724 8932

An operator that specialises in historic pilgrimage routes, and can design itineraries to introduce you to the beautiful religious monuments of Catalunya.

The Magic of Spain
081 748 7575

An agency that is sensitive to the best that Catalunya has to offer the discerning traveller.

TOURIST INFORMATION

The tourist offices are well-stocked with free leaflets and maps. The staff are patient, helpful, and usually speak English well.

Main tourist offices

Barcelona
Gran Via de les Corts Catalanes, 658 (93) 301 74 43
El Prat de Llobregat
Aeroport de Barcelona (93) 478 47 04
La Jonquera
Autopista A7, Area de la Porta Catalana (972) 55 43 54
Girona
Rambla de la Llibertat, 1 (972) 22 65 75
Lleida
Av. Blondel, 3, Edificio Pallas (973) 24 81 20
Tarragona
C/ Fortuny, 4 (977) 23 34 15

LOCAL TOURIST OFFICES

Barcelona:

Arenys de Mar
Passeig Xifré, 25 (93) 795 83 51
Barcelona
Plaça de Sant Jaume, Ajuntament (93) 010
Oficina de Turisme de l'Estació de Sants (93) 491 44 31
Berga
Carrer dels Angels, 7 (93) 821 01 00
Ctra. 1411, Km 75,2 (93) 822 15 00
Caldes de Montbui
Bellit, 3 (93) 865 41 40
Calella de Palafrugell
C/ Sant Jaume, 231 (93) 769 05 59
Canet de Mar
Ctra. N11, s/n (93) 794 08 98
Cardona
Av. Rastrillo, s/n (93) 869 27 98
Castelldefels
Pl. Rosa dels Vents, s/n (93) 664 23 01
Cubelles
Passeig Narcís Barjadi, 12 (93) 895 25 00
Malgrat de Mar
C/ Carme, 30 (93) 765 33 00
Manresa

	Pl. Major, 1, planta baixa	(93) 872 53 78
	Mataró	
	Parc Central, s/n	(93) 799 03 55
	Moià	
	Ctra. de Vic, 2	(93) 820 80 00
	Montserrat	
	Monestir	(93) 835 02 51
	Pineda de Mar	
	Pl. Sant Joan	(93) 767 15 60
	Sabadell	
	Pl. del Dr Robert, 1	(93) 727 00 10
	Sant Celoni	
	C/ Campins, 24	(93) 867 47 80
	Sant Cugat del Vallès	
	Plaça de Barcelona, 17	(93) 674 09 50
	Sant Sadurní d'Anoia	
	Pl. Ajuntament, 1 baixos	(93) 891 12 12
	Sitges	
	C/ Sínia Morera (Oasis)	(93) 811 76 30
	Terrassa	
	Raval de Montserrat, 14	(93) 733 21 61
	Vic	
	Pl. Major, 1	(93) 886 20 91
	Vilafranca del Penedès	
	C/ Cort, 14	(93) 890 34 24
	Vilanova i la Geltrú	
	Passeig Ribes Roges, s/n. Torre Ribes Roges	(93) 815 45 17
Girona:		
	Arbúcies	
	C/ Major, 6	(972) 16 24 77
	Banyoles	
	Passeig Indústria, 25	(972) 57 55 73
	Begur	
	Plaça de l'Esglesia, 8	(972) 62 40 20
	Besalú	
	C/ Prat de St. Pere, 2	(972) 59 12 40
	Blanes	
	Pl. Catalunya, s/n	(972) 33 03 48
	Cadaquès	
	C/ Cotxe 2A	(972) 25 83 15
	Calella de Palafrugell	
	C/ Les Voltes, 4	(972) 61 44 75
	Camprodon	
	Ctra. Comarcal 151, km 23,5	(972) 74 09 36
	Pl. Espanya, 1	(972) 74 00 10
	Castelló d'Empúries	
	Pl. dels Homes, 1	(972) 15 62 33
	(Empúriabrava) Puigmal, 1	(972) 45 08 02
	El Port de la Selva	
	C/ Mar, 1	(972) 38 70 25

Figueres	
Pl. del Sol, s/n	(972) 50 31 55
Pl. de l'Estació	(972) 50 31 55
Girona	
Estació RENFE	(972) 21 62 96
L'Escala	
Pl. de les Escoles, 1	(972) 77 06 03
L'Estartit	
Passeig Marítim, 47	(972) 75 89 10
La Bisbal d'Empordà	
Passeig Marimon Asprer, s/n	(972) 64 09 75
La Molina – Alp	
Av. Supermolina, s/n	(972) 89 20 31
Llafranc	
C/ Roger de Llúria, s/n	(972) 30 50 08
Llançà	
Av. Europa, 37	(972) 38 08 55
Llívia	
Forns, 4	(972) 89 63 13
Lloret de Mar	
Terminal autobusos, Ctra. de Blanes	(972) 36 57 88
Plaça de la Vila, 1	(972) 36 47 35
Mont-ras	
Pl. de la Font, 1	(972) 30 19 74
Olot	
Casa dels volcans, Av. Sta Coloma, s/n	(972) 26 62 02
C/ Bisbe Lorenzana, 15	(972) 26 01 41
Palafrugell	
C/ Carrilet, 2	(972) 30 02 28
Palamós	
Passeig de Mar, s/n	(972) 61 33 52
Pals	
C/ Aniceta Figueras, 11	(972) 66 78 57
Platja d'Aro	
C/ Verdaguer, 11	(972) 81 71 79
Portbou	
Passeig Lluís Companys, s/n	(972) 39 02 84
Puigcerdà	
C/ Querol, 1	(972) 88 05 42
C/ Espanya, 40	(972) 88 21 61
Ribes de freser	
Pl. Ajuntament, 3	(972) 72 77 28
C/ Pedrera, 1 baixos	(972) 72 90 25
Ripoll	
Pl. Abat Oliba	(972) 70 23 51
Roses	
Pl. de les Botxes, s/n	(972) 25 73 31
Sant Antoni de Calonge	
Av. de Catalunya, s/n	(972) 66 17 14
Sant Feliu de Guíxols	
Pl. Monestir, 54	(972) 82 00 51

	Sant Feliu de Pallerols	
	C/ del Rec	(972) 44 44 74
	Sant Hilari Sacalm	
	Ctra d'Arbúcies, s/n	(972) 86 88 28
	Sant Joan de les Abadesses	
	Rambla Comte Guifré, 5	(972) 72 05 99
	Sant Joan les Fonts	
	Ctra Olot, 32	(972) 29 05 07
	Sant Pere Pescador	
	Ctra de Castelló, s/n	(972) 55 03 90
	Santa Cristina d'Aro	
	Pl. Mossèn Baldiri Reixach, 1	(972) 83 70 10
	Santa Pau	
	Pl. Major, s/n	(972) 68 03 49
	Tamariu / Palafrugell	
	C/ Riera, s/n	(972) 30 50 07
	Torroella de Montgrí	
	Av. Lluís Companys	(972) 75 89 10
	Tossa de Mar	
	Av. Pelegrí, 25, Edifici Terminal	(972) 34 01 08
Tarragona:		
	Altafulla	
	Plaça dels Vents, s/n	(977) 65 07 52
	Amposta	
	Av. Sant Jaume, 1	(977) 70 34 53
	Bellmunt del Priorat	
	C/ Major, 49	(977) 83 03 79
	Calafell	
	C/ Sant Pere, 37–39	(977) 69 29 81
	Cambrils	
	Pl. Creu de la Missió, 1	(977) 36 11 59
	Coma-ruga	
	Pl. Germanas Trillas, s/n, El Vendrell	(977) 68 00 10
	Cornudella de Montsant	
	C/ Comte Rius, 8	(977) 82 13 13
	Creixell	
	C/ Església, 1	(977) 80 02 02
	Deltebre	
	C/ Ulldecona, 22	(977) 48 96 79
	El Perelló	
	C/ Lluís Companys, 2	(977) 49 00 07
	El Vendrell	
	C/ del Doctor Robert, 33	(977) 66 02 92
	Falset	
	Av. Catalunya, 6	(977) 83 10 23
	Gandesa	
	Av. Catalunya, s/n, Estació d'autobusos	(977) 42 06 14
	L'Ametlla de Mar	
	Av. Amistat hispano-italiana, s/n	(977) 45 63 29
	Sant Joan, 55	(977) 45 64 77

	L'Ampolla	
	Pl. González Isla, s/n	(977) 59 30 11
	L'Espluga de Francolí	
	C/ Torres Jordi, 16	(977) 87 04 56
	L'Hospitalet de l'Infant	
	Passeig Marítim, s/n	(977) 82 33 28
	La Pineda (Vila-seca)	
	Passeig Pau Casals, 118	(977) 37 17 12
	Les Cases d'Alcanar	
	C/ Lepanto, s/n	(977) 73 76 39
	Miravet	
	Pl. Major, 1	(977) 40 71 34
	Mont-roig	
	Ctra N340, Km 1139	(977) 83 79 68
	Montblanc	
	Pl. Major, 1	(977) 86 00 09
	Muralla de Santa Tecla, 18	(977) 86 12 32
	Mora d'Ebre	
	Pl. Baix	(977) 40 00 12
	Reus	
	Pl. de la Llibertat, s/n	(977) 34 59 43
	Salou	
	C/ Montblanc, 1	(977) 38 01 36
	Espigó del Moll, s/n	(977) 38 02 33
	Sant Carles de la Ràpita	
	Pl. Carles III, 13	(977) 74 01 00
	Santa Coloma de Queralt	
	C/ Pati d'Armes del Castell, s/n	(977) 88 00 88
	Segur de Calafell	
	Pl. del Mediterrani	(977) 16 15 11
	Tarragona	
	Rambla Nova, 46	(977) 23 21 43
	Major, 39	(977) 24 19 53
	Torredembarra	
	Passeig Marítim, 1	(977) 64 21 10
	Pl. de la Vila, 1	(977) 64 06 38
	Tortosa	
	Av. Generalitat	(977) 44 25 67
	Pl. Bimillenari	(977) 51 08 22
	Ulldemolins	
	Pl. de la Vila, s/n	(977) 82 10 38
	Valls	
	Pl. del Blat, 1	(977) 60 10 50
Lleida:		
	Balaguer	
	Pl. Mercadal, 1	(973) 44 66 06
	Baqueira Beret	
	Pistas	(973) 64 50 50
	Barruera	
	C/ Rius, s/n	(973) 69 40 00

Bellver de Cerdanya	
Area del Cadí	(973) 51 02 33
Pl. de Sant Roc, s/n	(973) 51 02 29
Boí/Barruera	
Centre d'Informació Parc Nacional d'Aigüestortes	
Pl. Treio, s/n	(973) 69 61 89
Bossòst	
C/ d'Eduard Aunós	(973) 64 72 79
Cervera	
Passeig Balmes, 12 baixos	(973) 53 13 03
El Pont de Suert	
Pl. Mercadal, 9	(973) 69 06 40
Espot	
Centre d'Informació Parc Nacional d'Aigües tortes	
C/ Prat del Guarda, 2	(973) 62 40 36
Esterri d'Aneu	
C/ Major, 6	(973) 62 60 05
La Pobla de Segur	
C/ Verdaguer, 35	(973) 68 02 57
La Seu d'Urgell	
Av. Valira, s/n	(973) 35 15 11
Les	
Pl. de l'Ajuntament, 1	(973) 64 73 03
Llavorsí	
Ctra Vall d'Aran, 31	(973) 63 00 08
Mollerussa	
Av. Prat de la Riba, 1, Edificio Can Nubió	(973) 71 13 13
Organyà	
Pl. Homilíes, s/n	(973) 38 20 02
Salardú	
C/ Balmes, 2	(973) 64 50 30
Sant Llorenç de Morunys	
Ctra Berga, s/n	(973) 48 21 81
Solsona	
Av. Pont, s/n, Edificio Piscis, baixos	(973) 48 23 10
Sort	
Av. Comtes de Pallars, 21	(973) 62 10 02
Tàrrega	
C/ Agoders, 16	(973) 50 08 83
Tavascan	
Esports d'Hivern, C/ Major, 5	(973) 62 30 79
Tremp	
Pl. Capdevila, s/n	(973) 65 13 80
Tuixén	
C/ Serra del Cadí	(973) 37 00 30
València d'Aneu	
Ctra del Port de la Bonaigua, s/n	(973) 62 60 38
Vallbona de les Monges	
Passeig Montesquiu, s/n	(973) 33 05 67
Vielha	
C/ Sarriulera, 6	(973) 64 01 10

Useful telephone numbers

TELEPHONE OPERATOR

General directory enquiries	003
International directory enquiries	008

Airports

Barcelona	(93) 401 32 82
Girona	(972) 47 43 43
Reus	(977) 75 75 15

Transport

RENFE (Railways)	(93) 490 02 02
Public transport information office	(93) 412 00 00
Road information (toll-free)	900 – 12 35 05

Police

Lost & found office	(93) 318 95 31
Municipal police	092
National police	091
Barcelona tourist assistance police	(93) 301 90 60

Medical information

Emergency assistance	061

Credit card cancellation

American Express	(93) 217 00 70
Diners Club	(93) 302 14 28
Visa, Access, Master Card	(93) 315 25 12

Barcelona

Barcelona city information	010
Generalitat of Catalunya	(93) 402 46 00
Barcelona city government	(93) 402 70 00

GLOSSARY

CATALAN	*ENGLISH*	*SPANISH*
Apats	**Meals**	**Comidas**
berenar	snack	merienda
dinar	lunch	comida/almuerzo
esmorzar/desdejuni	breakfast	desayuno
sopar	supper	cena
Verdura	**Vegetables**	**Verdura**
albergínia	aubergine	berenjena
all	garlic	ajo
api	celery	apio
arròs	rice	arroz
bolets	wild mushrooms	hongos/setas
carbassó	courgette	calabacín
carxofa	artichoke	alcachofa
cebes	onions	cebollas
cigrons	chickpeas	garbanzos
cogombre	cucumber	pepino
col	cabbage	col
col de cabdell	round cabagge	repollo
col llombarda	red cabagge	col lombarda
col-i-flor	cauliflower	coliflor
enciam	lettuce	lechuga
endívia	chicory	endibia
espàrrecs	asparagus	espárragos
faves	broad beans	habas
llenties	lentils	lentejas
mongetes	beans	judías
mongetes tendres	French beans	judías verdes
nap	turnip	nabo
olives	olives	aceitunas/olivas
pastanagues	carrots	zanahorias
patates	potatoes	patatas
patates fregides	chips	patatas fritas
pebrot	sweet pepper	pimiento
pèsols	peas	guisantes
porro	leek	puerro
remolatxa	beetroot	remolacha
tàpera	caper	alcaparra
tomàquet	tomato	tomate
tòfona	truffle	trufa
xampinyó	mushroom	champiñón

Ous	**Eggs**	**Huevos**
remenats	scrambled egg	revoltillo
truita	omelette	tortilla

Peix	**Fish**	**Pescado**
anxova	anchovy	anchoa/boquerón
anguila	eel	anguila
bacallà	cod	bacalao
emperador	swordfish	emperador
llenguado	sole	lenguado
llobarro	sea bass	lubina
lluç	hake	merluza
nero	groupe	mero
davroda	bream	dorada
rap	monkfish	rape
rèmol	turbot	rodaballo
roger/moll	red mullet	salmonete
salmó	salmon	salmón
sardina	sardine	sardina
truita	trout	trucha
tonyina	tunny	atún
xanguets	gobies	chanquetes

Marisc	**Shellfish**	**Marisco**
calamar	squid	calamar
cloïsses	clams	almejas
cranc	crab	cangrejo
dàtils de Mar	date-shells	dátiles de mar
eriçó/garota	sea urchin	erizo
escamarlà	Dublin Bay prawn	cigala
gamba	Mediterranean prawn	gamba
gambeta	small prawn	camarón
llagosta	crawfish	langosta
llagostí	Mediterranean prawn	langostino
llamantol	lobster	bogarante
musclo	mussel	mejillón
ostra	oyster	ostra
pop	octopus	pulpo
sípia	cuttlefish	sepia
calamarsó	small squid	chipirón

Carn	**Meat**	**Carne**
bou	beef (mature)	buey
cabrit	kid	cabrito
cansalada	salt pork/bacon	tocino
conill	rabbit	conejo
cua de bou	ox tail	rabo de buey
escalopa	escalope	escalopa
fetge	liver	hígado
llom	loin of pork	lomo
mandonguilles	meatballs	albóndigas

pernil	ham	jamón
pernil dolç	cooked ham	jamón york
pernil serrà	cured ham	jamón serrano
peus de porc	pigs' trotters	pies de cerdo
porc	pork	cerdo
salsitxa	sausage	salchicha
filet	sirloin steak	solomillo
ternasco	roast shoulder of lamb	ternasco
tripes	tripes	callos
toro	bullfight beef	toro
vedella	veal/beef	ternera
xai	lamb	cordero
costella	chop	chuleta
Aus i caça	**Poultry and game**	**Aves y caza**
ànec/tiró	duck	pato
cérvol	venizon	ciervo/venado
faisà	pheasant	faisán
gall	capon	gallo
gall dindi	turkey	pavo
guatlla	quail	cordoniz
llebre	hare	liebre
perdiu	partridge	perdiz
pollastre	chicken	pollo
senglar	wild boar	jabalí
Fruita	**Fruit**	**Fruta**
albercoc	apricot	albaricoque
ametlla	almond	almendra
avellana	hazelnut	avellana
banana/plàtan	banana	plátano
cacauet	peanut	cacahuete
castanya	chestnut	castaña
cirera	cherry	cereza
codony	quince	membrillo
figa	fig	higo
llimona	lemon	limón
maduixa	strawberry	fresa
meló	melon	melón
nou	walnut	nuez
pera	pear	pera
pinya	pineapple	piña
poma	apple	manzana
préssec	peach	melocotón
raïm	grapes	uvas
síndria	watermelon	sandía
taronja	orange	naranja
Postres	**Dessert/pudding**	**Postre**
crema	crème anglais	crema
flam	crème caramel	flan

fruta del temps	fresh fruit	fruta del tiempo
gelat	ice-cream	helado
iogurt	yoghurt	yogur
macedònia	fruit salad	macedonia
músic	nuts and dried fruits	músico
pastís	gateau	pastel
rebosteria	pastries/cakes	repostería
safata de formatges	selection of cheeses	surtido de quesos
Begudes	**Drinks**	**Bebidas**
aigua	water	agua
aigua amb gas	fizzy water	agua con gas
aigua sensgas	stillwater	agna singas
cafè	coffee	café
cafè amb llet	white coffee	café con leche
café tallat	coffee with a dash of milk	café cortado
café descafeïnat	decafinated coffee	café descafinado
cervesa	beer	cerveza
infusió	herb tea	infusión
llet	milk	leche
porró	porron (for wine)	porrón
refresc	cold non-alcoholic drink	refresco
suc	juice	zumo
te	tea	té
vi	wine	vino
vi negre	red wine	tinto vino
vi blanc	white wine	vino blanco
vi rosat	rosé	vino rosado
Altres	**Others**	**Otros**
brou	broth/stock	caldo
cargols	snails	caracoles
entrepà	sandwich	bocadillo
tideus	noodles	fideos
formatge	cheese	queso
julivert	parsley	perejil
llardons	crackling	chicharrones
maionesa	mayonnaise	mayonesa
mantega	butter	mantequilla
mató	fresh cheese	requesón
mel	honey	miel
melmelada	jam	mermelada
mostassa	mustard	mostaza
nata	cream	nata
oli	oil	aceite
pa	bread	pan
safrà	saffron	azafrán
pebre	pepper	pimienta
sal	salt	sal
sucre	sugar	azúcar
vinagre	vinegar	vinagre
xocolata	chocolate	chocolate

Al restaurant	**At the restaurant**	**En el restaurante**
ampolla	bottle	botella
cadira	chair	silla
cambrer	waiter	camarero
carte	menu	carte
(el) canvi	(the) change	(el) cambio
celler	wine cellar	bodega
(el) compte	(the) bill	(la) cuenta
cullera	spoon	cuchara
diners	money	dinero
forquilla	fork	tenedor
ganivet	knife	cuchillo
got	glass	vaso
menú	set menu	menú
obert	open	abierto
preu	price	precio
propina	tip	propina
quant?	how much?	¿cuánto?
s/m	price acc. to market	según mercado
setrilleres	oil and vinegar set	vinagreras
tancat	closed	cerrado
targeta de crèdit	credit card	tarjeta de crédito
taula	table	mesa
tovalló	napkin/serviette	servilleta
xec	cheque	cheque

Verbs	**Verbs**	**Verbos**
encomanar	to book a table	reservar una mesa
beure	to drink	beber
menjar	to eat, to dine	comer
demanar	to order	pedir
pagar	to pay	pagar
recomanar	to recommend	recomendar

Preparació	**Cooking**	**Preparación**
a la brasa	charcoal/wood-grilled	a la brasa
a la cassola	cooked in a claypot	a la cazuela
a la graella	barbecued	a la parrilla
a la llauna	baked in a tin	a la llauna
a la llosa	cooked on a hot slate	a la piedra
a la marineva	marinière	a la marineva
a la planxa	cooked on a griddle	a la plancha
a la sal	baked in salt	a la sal
al forn	baked	al horno
arrebossat	in batter	rebozado
en salse	in sauce	en salse
estofat	stew	estofado
farcit	stuffed	relleno
fregit	fried	frito
fumat	smoked	ahumado
pastís	terrine	pastel

picat	minced	picado
rostit	roast	asado
saltat	sautéed	salteado

Specialities

Agredolç: sweet and sour.
Amanida: salad.
Arròs a banda: rice cooked in fish broth.
Arròs negre: rice cooked with almost black fried onions and squid ink.
A l'all cremat: cooked in oil flavoured with burnt garlic.
Allioli: cold sauce made with crushed garlic and olive oil.
Bacalao al pil-pil: salt cod cooked with garlic, a typical dish from the Basque country
Bollabessa: a fish stew like the French *bouillabaisse.*
Botifarra: a typical Catalan pork sausage.
Botifarra de perol: botifarra made of cooked pork. Typical of the Empordà region.
Brandada: purée of salt-cod.
Bunyols: doughnuts, savoury or sweet.
Cabell d'àngel: preserve of pumpkin or squash, used for pastries.
Calçot: a tender leek-shaped onion grilled over vine trimmings or charcoal, served with a sauce similar to a *romesco.* Only available during winter. Typical of the region around Valls, Tarragona.
Cap i pota: head and foot of veal or lamb. Like brawn.
Carn d'olla: see *Escudella i carn d'olla*
Cava: sparkling white wine from the Penedès made using the 'method champagnoise'
Changurro: crab preparation from the Basque country.
Coca: a long flat fancy bread, sweet or savoury.
Cogote: the part of a fish just below the head – a delicacy
Crema catalana: typical dessert of custard with a caramel crust.
Embotits: salami-like sausages, eaten cold; include blood sausage.
Entremesos: a selection of hors-d'oeuvres.
Entrepà: a sandwich – often a roll rather than sliced bread.
Escabetx: a highly spiced sauce used for small fish and game.
Escalivada: typical cold dish of red pepper, aubergine and onion grilled until black, peeled, and served dressed with olive oil.
Escudella i carn d'olla: a typical Catalan boiled meat dish served in two courses: the broth usually with pasta; and the meat usually including chicken, *botifarra,* pork and a huge meatball (the pilota) with chickpeas and other vegetables.
Espardenyes: a rare and very expensive mollusc only found in Catalan cuisine
Esqueixada: a salad of shredded salt-cod with onion, olives, pimento dressed with lemon and olive oil.
Fideuà: a dish of noodles cooked in fish stock.
Fuet: long dried sausage from Vic, eaten cold in thin slices.
Jabugo: the very finest mature dried ham from the south-west of Spain. Very expensive.
Llonganissa: dried sausage of lean pork and spices.
Mar i montanya: dish of poultry, usually chicken, with shellfish.

Mel i mató: typical dessert of fresh cheese served with honey.
Olla aranesa: thick winter potato and vegetable stew with chicken, sausage, pork and beef. The Vall d'Aran equivalent to the *Escudella i carn d'olla.*
Pa amb tomàquet: crusty bread or toast rubbed with tomato (and sometimes garlic), sprinkled with olive oil and salt.
Pa torrat: crusty toasted bread, sometimes known as *llescas.*
Paella: rice cooked in fish broth with mussels, clams and prawns. There is often a choice between *marisco* or *montanya* which has rabbit, chicken and pork.
Panellet: small rich cake of marzipan, traditionally eaten at the feast of All Saints.
Parrillada: a selection of meats or fish grilled.
Pebrots del piquillo: small pointed red peppers, usually stuffed.
Peix a la romana: fish fried in batter.
Peix blau: oily fish like mackerel, anchovies, sardines, tuna, etc.
Pica-pica: a selection of tapa portions as a starter.
Plat combinat: first and second course all on one plate.
Romesco: red sauce of tomato, crushed almond, garlic and hot red pepper (*nyoras*), served with fish. Also a dish of various fish cooked in this sauce.
Rossejat: noodles or rice cooked to a golden colour before adding the cooking liquid.
Samfaina: vegetable mixture of onion, green peppers, aubergine, tomatoes and courgette. Rather like a French *ratatouille.*
Sangría: a refreshing fruity wine cup.
Sarsuela: a variety of fish cooked in a fish bouillon with a sauce of almonds.
Salpicón: a salad of shellfish – pepper, tomato and onion sprinkled with mussels, clams and prawns.
Sofregit: a lightly-fried base of tomato, onion and garlic.
Suquet de peix: a variety of fish braised together with potatoes, tomatoes and onions.
Torró: a sweet bar made mainly of ground or whole almond, typically eaten around Christmas. There are several varieties.
Txangurro: see *changurro* above.
Xató: salad of lettuce, tomato and onion with cod, tuna, anchovies and olives, bathed in a strong *romesco* sauce.
Xixarrons: pork scratchings, often used in sweet pastries (also called *llardons*).

There are lots of varieties of wild mushrooms. You might see *camagrocs, ciureny (ceps), fredolics, gírgolas, llèmena, llenega, moixernons, mucosas, murgolas, rossinyol, rovellons, trompetes dels morts.*

INDEX OF PLACES

L'Ibeic

Snails

Anchovies

Asparague

Wild boar

HAKE

Vino et formaggio near St. Felix (St. Felicio)

next to fiesta - more or less

Posh restaurant when lost recommended

Barcelona - Hostal Olivia

Barcelonetta - fishing village

sausage sandwiches + pink champagne.